Debates in Stuart History

Debates in Stuart History

Ronald Hutton

palgrave
macmillan

First published 2004 by
PALGRAVE MACMILLAN
Houndmills, Basingstoke, Hampshire RG21 6XS and
175 Fifth Avenue, New York, N.Y. 10010
Companies and representatives throughout the world

PALGRAVE MACMILLAN is the global academic imprint of the Palgrave Macmillan division of St. Martin's Press, LLC and of Palgrave Macmillan Ltd. Macmillan® is a registered trademark in the United States, United Kingdom and other countries. Palgrave is a registered trademark in the European Union and other countries.

ISBN 1–4039–3588–2 hardback
ISBN 1–4039–3589–0 paperback

This book is printed on paper suitable for recycling and made from fully managed and sustained forest sources.

A catalogue record for this book is available from the British Library.

A catalog record for this title is available from the Library of Congress.

10 9 8 7 6 5 4 3 2 1
13 12 11 10 09 08 07 06 05 04

Printed in China

To
Sophia Elisabeth Sanford Hutton,
as a final proof that her father writes books

Contents

Acknowledgements   viii

Introduction   1

1   Revisionism   6

2   The Great Civil War   32

3   The New Framework for Early Stuart Studies   59

4   Oliver Cromwell   93

5   Charles II   132

6   The Glorious Revolution   171

7   Conclusion   194

Notes   199

Index   229

Acknowledgements

Earlier versions of Chapters 1 and 6 were published, respectively, as 'Revisionism', in Michael Bentley (ed.), *Companion to Historiography* (Routledge, 1998), and as *The Glory of 1688* (The Royal Stuart Society Occasional Papers, 1995). Both have been extensively revised for this book: as the first, despite its actual date of publication, was written in 1991, and the other in 1994, such transformation would be inevitable on historiographical grounds alone, but the intent of the present work is also very different. None the less, I am grateful to both Routledge and the Royal Stuart Society for permission to reuse some of the material. All the other chapters were composed from scratch, though there is some slight overlap between the second and the introduction that I provided for the second edition of my book *The Royalist War Effort*, also published by Routledge, in 2000.

Drafts of Chapter 4 were read by Austin Woolrych and Martyn Bennett and of Chapter 5 by Austin Woolrych and Kevin Sharpe. All made very helpful comments of very different kinds, for which I am extremely grateful.

Introduction

This is a textbook with a difference. It is designed for students of history at university and sixth-form level, for those who teach them, and for people with a general interest in seventeenth-century Britain, though it should have some significance for experts in the period as well. It treats major episodes in the politics of that century, with the assumption that those who read it will already have a rough idea of them: of which people ruled, and when, and the order in which major changes occurred. Ideally, it should be read immediately after any basic and conventional narrative history of the time, for it sets out to explain why scholars have put together that narrative, and why they have thought about parts of it in the ways in which they have done.

What it sets out to do is to accomplish two different results. One is to enable students to make sense of some of the key recent debates over the history of the Stuart period. It aims to introduce them to the issues that have been debated, and to the main participants and positions, in such a way as to help them to set their reading into context. The other aim is a complementary one to this, and to me more important: to introduce to the study of the this a strong element of what social scientists call reflexivity: the consciousness of why we write about things as we do. In theory, this has long been around in the historiography of this period, which has constantly been the subject of major differences of expert opinion, often clearly loaded by the political and social ideologies of those engaged in them. From the moment that I first entered the university system, I heard the phrase 'If you want to understand the history, first understand the historian.' Furthermore, there are books devoted to mapping out the course of research and disputation in particular areas of early modern British history, such as the Reformation and the English Revolution of the 1640s. None the less, it may be suggested that none of these add up to proper reflexivity in the modern academic sense. The historiographical surveys tend to explain what scholars write and when, rather than why they hold particular views at particular times. At no point has there been much genuine inclination to 'understand the historian' at all: instead virtually all effort is devoted to understanding the data used by historians and the manner in which they interpret it.

This pattern is bound up with the professionalisation of the writing of history in the nineteenth century, and its increasing concentration in an expanding academic system. It is built on the assumption that systematic training in the discipline inculcates certain skills in the location, reading and interpretation of source material, which are shared by all experts in a given field. These people are then equipped to compare and debate the conclusions that they draw from that material, in such a manner as to achieve a corporate and cumulative growth in understanding of the past. This is, more or less, what actually happens in the academic study of history. From time to time it is challenged by thinkers who draw attention to the inadequate nature of the surviving data and ask – to varying degrees – whether any accurate picture of past individuals, societies or economies can be retrieved from it. Practitioners react to these challenges in different ways, mostly to take account of them and to develop strategies to meet their criticisms. The basic format of historical enquiry, however, has not altered, mainly because it produces results that are, on the whole, interesting enough to sustain the faith of students, other disciplines, governments and the general public in the whole enterprise.

That enterprise was at its most powerful, confident and unreflective in the English-speaking world during the mid-twentieth century, as a result of the twin forces of a major expansion of properly funded higher education and of a euphoric celebration of the world-transforming potential of science and technology. Both swept up the study of history, into a sense that an unprecedented number of properly trained specialists, working full-time with generous financial support, really could deliver a huge amount of objectively tested new knowledge about the past at novel speed. This mission produced its own strains, for with expectations now set so high, and so much money and labour invested in the process of realising them, arguments between both individual scholars and schools of thought became more intense than before. These divisions, bitter though they often were, should not be allowed to disguise the fact that they occurred between practitioners united by the professional structure and culture within which they worked and the ideals that they served.

Since then, the structure has remained much the same, but the culture has altered, at least in the United Kingdom. It has done so in part under the impact of funding cuts, job losses and the replacement of the carrots of academic acclaim and book sales by the stick of the national Research Assessment Exercise as the driving force of publication. The change has also, however, been due to the practical consequences of having so many people engaged in full-time research, revealing as never before the difficulties and limitations, as well as the positive potential, of historical investigation. Both developments may be set in the wider national context of the disintegration of the former class system and its replacement by a more informal, diverse and mobile society of white-collar workers. One simple demonstration of changing attitudes – and a splendid first example of the sort of symptom of academic culture that is hardly ever recognised or discussed – is found in prevailing conventions for the form of names used for authors of history books. For much of the Victorian and Edwardian period, the latter presented themselves as fully formed individuals whose personalities were at one with their products, and who therefore gave all their names in full blast. Thus, in Stuart studies, we think of

Thomas Babington Macaulay, Samuel Rawson Gardiner and George Macaulay Trevelyan. By the mid-twentieth century, it had somehow become considered to be undignified and unprofessional to publish first names on a title page. By the 1970s, the giants of the discipline were usually called things like H.R. Trevor-Roper, G.R. Elton, J.H. Plumb or A.J.P. Taylor. The rising generation was published as J.S. Morrill or K.V. Sharpe. To be able to call historians by their first names – or indeed even to know them – was a sign of privilege and intimacy, like being admitted to their homes.

When I decided to be a Ronald on the cover of my first book, in 1980, rather than R.E. Hutton, it was therefore a highly charged gesture. I was reacting self-consciously, like many people who had come of age in the 1970s, against the perceived stuffiness and restriction of much of British society. Much to my surprise and relief, I found myself part of a trend, for by the end of the 1980s it was considered conservative and eccentric to retain the habit of confining names to initials; though it would have been deemed pompous and eccentric to use all names in full after the Victorian manner. Instead full use of the normal first name plus surname had become the rule, the young lions of the 1970s transformed into (to use the same examples) John Morrill and Kevin Sharpe. By the end of the 1990s some scholars were going further, to print first names shortened to their preferred familiar form (thus, Tim Harris, Tony Claydon); the literary equivalent of turning up to the office in an open-necked shirt as opposed merely to abandoning a three-piece suit.

Such symbolic changes as these are, of course, of vital importance to social anthropologists, and they have a clear significance in academic culture. The restriction to initials that was customary in the mid-century was associated with a much greater formality, hierarchy and restraint among university-based scholars than obtained subsequently, but also – like the white coats of scientists in the same period – signalled their professional detachment and objectivity. They distanced them from the general public and their source material alike, and gave an impression of a depersonalised expertise. The willingness to admit to a greater humanity in scholars in subsequent decades indicated not merely a greater informality and collectivity within the profession, but a recognition of a more intimate and personal relationship between historians and the way in which they went about their work.

This book is dedicated to exploring that relationship further, in the case of some of the most celebrated individuals and episodes of the Stuart period. Having set the scene by an analysis of the phenomenon of revisionism in early modern English history, it goes on to look at the recent historiography of the Civil War, early Stuart constitutional struggles, Oliver Cromwell, Charles II and the Glorious Revolution. In each case it seeks to inform general and student readers of what that historiography actually is, and in the process to convey also a sense of what new knowledge has been embodied in it. It also embodies my own opinions on the issues where these are significant. It attempts, however, to go further, by asking why it is that scholars adopt particular approaches at particular times, what their relationship is with popular views of history, and how they actually go about their work. Such an approach has recently become well established in studies of Victorian attitudes to the English past. It is applied here to those of the late twentieth and early twenty-first centuries.

In doing so, it is consciously following an agenda set by the Victorians themselves, to whom the political events of the seventeenth century were the most important in the whole of English history, and the most to be treated by writers of history and of fiction, and artists, alike. This was because, beyond doubt, they transformed a state with chronic structural and social weaknesses into a political entity of considerable stability, dynamism and strength. They were accompanied by other developments that were of equal importance to that achievement and considerably more interesting to many historians: the conquest of famine in England and Wales, the disappearance of bubonic plague, the installation of the best system of poor relief in Europe, the end of the fear of magic and the foundation of what became the first British Empire. None the less, the form of the emerging British state, and its practical success, were determined primarily by the political and religious affairs of England during this period. A lot of eggs got broken but a bumper omelette got made in the end, and the Victorians were still tucking into it. The problem by the opening of the twenty-first century was that the omelette had been eaten: the spoils system developed to reward adherents of the new superpower by 1700 had almost all disappeared. In that respect, we continue to benefit more from those other developments listed above than from the domestic political and religious achievements of the Stuart period. None the less, the model of political action established during that period is still substantially functioning, and we still gain from the solutions found to the problems that existed in 1600 and that produced a catastrophic breakdown in 1642. If many of the opportunities and rewards provided by those solutions are indeed now gone, then it is worth taking stock of what might be left, and how the records, memories and reconstructions of the key events are, and may be, employed.

To take up the perspective outlined above is, however, in itself to embody a number of political and social attitudes, in a manner present in the work of all or virtually all historians but rarely admitted. As much of what follows in this book is going to be concerned with that process, I am going to put some of my own instinctual presuppositions, ideological beliefs and cultural context up front, so that my reasons for taking certain stances may be more apparent, in a way that I wish occurred more often in my profession. My political attitudes are those of a liberal socialist, who has usually voted for the Labour Party. I was never brought up as a Christian, and have never had any close relationships with devout Christians, while I have read carefully through the basic literature of that faith and have closely studied aspects of its history. As a result, my attitude towards it is in general one of entirely benevolent neutrality, though it is possible that I am prejudiced against manifestations of it that are more militantly and intolerantly evangelical than others. In social and cultural heritage, I am an Anglo-Russian born in India and brought up in Essex. The English side of my family is the paternal one, and all of its male members for three generations, including myself, have Edmund as our first or second name. This was because of an antiquarian great-grandfather; it seems that the first of our line recorded in history was an Edmund de Hoton who received land from Henry I. In my adolescence, however, my own favourite members of this (objectively unconfirmed) ancestry were Sir Richard Hutton, the Cavalier, who died fighting for Charles I in the Civil War, and his father Sir Richard, the judge who defied the same king over the issue of Ship Money, in the name of the nation's liberties. What impressed me most then, and still does, is that there was no contradiction in the stances of the father and the son. Both were defending the same ideal of constitutional monarchy, with great courage, against dangers at opposite ends of the contemporary political spectrum.

Anybody trained in the subtleties of source analysis should notice at once the silences in the above account, amounting to ambiguity and perhaps to evasion. Which were the other parties for which I have voted when not supporting Labour: the Conservatives, or groups more radical than mainstream socialists? The distinction is going to place me at very different points in national politics. When I say that I was not brought up as a Christian, does this mean that my background was atheist or agnostic, or associated with a different sort of religion? Again, the answer is likely to have important implications for my religious attitudes. My characterisation of my social and cultural background did nothing to situate me in the class system or educational processes of Britain at the time of my youth, and both have a critical bearing on the formation of relationships with the national past and present. In saying what I have done already, however, I have gone much further than virtually all of my professional colleagues have ever done. The prevailing belief is still that academic training obliterates most personal prejudices to produce a common way of working. This book suggests that such a belief is not wholly wrong, but only in the sense that universities foster a sub-culture with its own assumptions, traditions and symbols, that react in turn with those of the parent society.

1 Revisionism

As scholarship almost invariably proceeds by amending previous assumptions, the writing of history is, by definition, very often an exercise in revisionism. Nevertheless, the expression came to be applied to particular developments in historiography in British and American universities during the 1970s. There was a widespread impression that these represented challenges to established views of a scale and force unusual by the normal standards of the profession. The purpose of this first chapter is to determine whether that impression was correct, and if so why the challenges were mounted at that time and to what, in the end, they amounted.

To a great extent the excitement created by the debates concerned was an artificial, parochial and misleading phenomenon. After all, nothing in the whole realm of historiography compared to the changes of perception taking place among British prehistorians during the same decade. Experts in the Neolithic shifted its basic chronology by up to two thousand years, and completely jettisoned prevailing orthodoxies concerning the cultural phases through which it progressed, the nature of its principal deity, the significance of its monuments and the existence of the race of people which had been supposed to have brought it to an end. All these alterations were achieved largely by consensus and without fuss. The national history which was most extensively reworked after 1960 was that of the Republic of Ireland, the most recently created state in the western world and one unusually dependent on a particular notion of its past. Yet the concept of 'revisionism' emerged within universities in the United States, Canada and Britain, and was concerned primarily with British history between about 1500 and about 1800.

The reason for that at least is clear: that Anglo-American culture was dominant in the west during the late twentieth century, and in that culture the early modern period was regarded as crucial to the formation of its common political and religious traditions. It had been served by able historians who had presented a detailed and long-lasting account of how those traditions were formed. The challenge which was to be mounted to this account was aimed not at its weakest points but at its strongest, supplied by the person whom one of the participants in the subsequent controversy was to describe as the 'favourite son' of the Muse of History.[1] This was the Englishman Samuel Rawson Gardiner, who between 1856 and 1901 had published successive volumes of a narrative history of the British Isles from 1603 to 1656, based on an unprecedented amount of archival research. His aim was to discover the origin of three characteristics of his England, of which its inhabitants were fiercely proud: English dominance of the archipelago, a monarchy limited by parliamentary democracy, and a national Church limited by freedom of worship for dissenters. He located them in an accelerating struggle between the first Stuart monarchs and what he sometimes termed 'the spirit of the nation', embodied most effectively in Parliament. During the early twentieth century his portrait of events remained the standard one upon both sides of the Atlantic, although almost everybody lost interest in its Scottish and Irish dimensions when the independence of Ireland destroyed that aspect of the English achievement. The results, however, differed markedly on opposite shores of the ocean. In America from 1924 onwards Wallace Notestein reinforced Gardiner's picture of an increasingly powerful House of Commons, responding to popular wishes and pitting itself against royal claims. In England during the 1950s Sir John Neale did provide an account of parliamentary affairs under Elizabeth I, which detected the origins of the growth of the Commons described by Gardiner and Notestein. In general, however, English historians of the early Stuart period were content to accept Gardiner's narrative and redirected their efforts to discovering presumed socio-economic causes for the political changes which that story portrayed. The contrast mirrored a divergence between American and English intellectuals during the century, both concerned with social justice but the former more preoccupied with issues of liberty and the latter with those of class. For the English, the influence of Gardiner had been reinforced by that of Marx. Around 1970 this quest for socio-economic underpinnings was still in full progress, represented most prominently in England by Christopher Hill and in America by the Englishman Lawrence Stone. It effectively represented a socialist modernisation of the Victorian historiographical achievement, much as the Welfare State represented a socialist modernisation of Victorian parliamentary democracy.

To group together those historians who sought the origins of the war in political, religious and constitutional developments, and those who attached greater importance to economic and social factors, is to do some violence to the manner in which many specialists in the period have regarded it, and in which some still do. After all, they could be represented as fundamentally different ways of writing history, one stressing the primacy of individual human agency and of contingency, and the other denying it, and a clash between them could legitimately be viewed as one of the major dialectics of twentieth-century historiography.[2] From another standpoint, however, they were merely different aspects of a single liberal-socialist interpretation of the war, both descending from Gardiner. The great Victorian had himself declared both that factors of personality and chance were of critical importance to the particular form that the conflict took and that the conflict itself was inevitable because of social, economic and cultural developments.[3] All that divided the experts of the mid-twentieth century was the relative emphasis that they placed on the respective parts of this analysis.

In the period since 1996 three historians have looked back upon the assault that had been mounted upon this dual tradition twenty years before, and provided explanations for it. It is perhaps significant that all were English scholars who had (at some point) taken up posts in the USA, and so straddled the continental division. It is certainly so that all were critical of several aspects of the attack concerned. One was Peter Lake, who summed up the appeal of the traditional historiography as lying in its apparent identification of the origins of the central aspects of modernity: capitalism, individualism, the modern state, representative democracy, and the modern scientific world-picture. It showed how the early modern period could be regarded as the midwife to the modern one, and provided a coherent and comforting story which justified as well as explained the nature of mid-twentieth-century western culture. It taught that modernity was good, that historical processes were controllable, and that state intervention was benign. To Lake, this consensus was naturally doomed when faith in those teachings crumbled in the 1970s, and the Welfare State and the middle ground in British politics began to erode with them. He saw revisionism as a product of the same politico-ideological conjuncture that produced Thatcherism.[4] The second analysis, by J.P. Sommerville, followed similar lines. To him the revisionists were one expression of the loss of British confidence during the 1970s and 1980s produced by economic decline and new social and ideological divisions. They were 'public-spirited citizens, anxious to avert the decline' of their country by rejecting a version of Stuart politics which had emphasised division and confrontation, and had celebrated the progress of the nation through a clash of conflicting principles.[5] The third, by David Cannadine, echoed the message of the first two: 'there was a definite tinge of Thatcherism in revisionism', both ideologies agreeing that high politics and religion mattered more than sociological concerns.[6]

Lake's characterisation of the instincts and emotions which underpinned the old historiography appears to me to be thoroughly accurate, but all three writers seem equally adrift in identifying the reasons for its dissolution. For one thing, the latter was not a peculiarly British phenomenon; it started across the Atlantic. For another, the historians who brought it about shared no one view of politics, even within their respective countries. For a third, both interpretations tend to credit historians with an understanding of contemporary social, political and economic trends, and an anticipation of the future, which most people do not possess. The launch pad for revisionism lay not in the later 1970s but in the earlier part of the decade. It may well have become part of the process whereby the consensus politics of the mid-century intellectual establishment were destroyed, but unlike Thatcherism it was not reacting against the radical libertarian movements of the 1960s but was one of its products. My memory of the events and personalities of those years suggests a very different story for them than that proposed by Lake, Sommerville and Cannadine, and one much more narrowly concerned with the particular culture of academic life. I would ascribe the revisionist outburst to particular features of that culture in the years between 1960 and 1975.

The first was the expansion of higher education which took place in Western Europe and North America during the 1950s and 1960s, resulting in a much greater number of professional historians than ever before. Not only did this make more likely a multiplicity of differing viewpoints, but also reduced the hitherto marked influence of a number of distinguished scholars over the disposal of posts, and thus arguably encouraged independence amongst their juniors. One consequence of a larger profession, and in part the price to be paid to governments for it, was a much greater formality and standardisation of the procedures by which the academic career was entered into and climbed. Between 1960 and 1975 the doctoral thesis became generally accepted as the essential first step, with a book or journal articles based upon its material supplying the proof that the author was capable of producing work fit for publication. This automatically pushed young historians into early and concentrated research projects, with a rapid airing and discussion of their views. As such, it increased the pace and intensity of scholarship to an unprecedented degree, a phenomenon glanced at in the previous chapter; arguably, it also tended to enhance a disposition to establish new work by questioning received views. By the 1970s the expansion of the university system had ceased, and a hiatus suddenly appeared in the availability of posts. As the decade progressed rumours set in of an impending contraction of academic jobs as funding of higher education was reduced, and this came to pass in the ice age of the 1980s. These harder times only reinforced the tendency of young academics to publish rapidly and to attempt to make as big an impression on their profession as possible, to secure first employment and then promotion. The impact on academic culture was obvious in the changing nature of its demonology. During the 1970s the favourite villain of those with senior positions and established reputations was the 'young man in a hurry', the rising scholar who cut corners in research and inflated the importance of his (sic) particular project in order to win preferment, violating the ideal of slow accumulation of professional expertise which had been developed in earlier and sleepier decades. By the late 1980s this figure had been replaced as the usual object of execration with the drone, who made perfectionism an excuse never to produce long-promised publications.

A second new feature of academic culture was the dramatic growth in the collections held by county record offices across Britain during the postwar period. In many respects this could be termed an archival revolution, affording historians a much larger and more accessible body of unpublished source material than ever before, inviting a reworking of existing ideas which had been based on more limited evidence. Like the expansion of higher education, this tended to have both a stimulant effect on productivity and a solvent effect on orthodoxy, and these two functional developments combined powerfully and explosively with a third, much less tangible one. This was the general distrust of established values which developed in Western Europe and North America during the 1960s. The dissolution of the European colonial empires and the spread of militarism and Marxist revolution in their former possessions, the discovery of reliable contraception, the marked growth of secularism in formerly Christian cultures, the unprecedented increases in economic production and social affluence in industrialised nations, and the consequent threat to the world ecosystem, represented perhaps the principal reasons for this change of attitudes. In many respects the nineteenth century lasted until about 1965, by which time the structures, beliefs and ambitions which it had instituted were finally completed, dismantled or made redundant. In this sense it was natural that its historiography should undergo wholesale revision as a result.

The results of these factors, in unison, were certainly remarkable. Around 1970 it was still known for a high-ranking historian, criticised by a junior one in a different university, to write to the latter's head of department demanding that the critic be rebuked. In 1975, as an undergraduate in Cambridge, I heard one of my tutors praise the first book of a young colleague for having presented research which questioned existing interpretations in such a way as to understate the destructive potential of his discoveries and so make them more acceptable to those in powerful positions. By the end of the decade such attitudes had become almost unthinkable. The erosion of long traditions of deference and caution was both rapid and dramatic, and for some individuals could achieve the intensity of an epiphany. The historian who came to be regarded by many as the greatest of all the 'revisionists' told me how, in about 1970, he realised that he could trust virtually nothing that he had been taught about early Stuart history; 'I decided that I could believe that James I and Charles I had existed, but everything else I had to discover for myself.' This attitude of wholesale rejection of received wisdom and complete reconstruction of world pictures was typical of the excitement, anger and optimism of the years around that date. I achieved a parallel moment of personal emancipation in January 1977, on a snowy day at the opening of my second term of research as a postgraduate student working upon the English Civil War. I was familiar with the generally accepted account of the war in the Severn valley, first narrated in detail by a classic Victorian study[7] and repeated by historians ever since. This laid great emphasis on two large battles in late 1642, in which the local parliamentarian general, the earl of Stamford, destroyed two successive royalist armies pushing out of Wales and so gravely weakened the king's military capacity in the region. That afternoon I read the despatches sent by Stamford to Parliament during the weeks concerned, which were not hidden in some hitherto unexplored archive but printed in such a prominent and well-thumbed source as the published journals of the House of Lords. They revealed that the battles concerned had never occurred; they were complete fictions invented by pamphleteers in London who were seeking to give an impression of continuing success for their cause when it was retreating or stalemated in most theatres of action. Just a few months after starting research into one of the most popular and populous fields of historiography, I had discovered that two of the basic facts repeated by its experts were lies.

Before the 1970s such experts had been respectful of authority in two quite different senses. Alongside the more obvious, of the deference paid by younger academics to the more senior and celebrated, ran a tendency to give the same respect to source material. In particular, there was a common reluctance to question or disparage those famous authors of great historical narratives who were regarded both as the principal witnesses to the events of their time and as mighty predecessors in the lineage of scholarship. At the head of this lineage stood the Greek, Herodotus. In 1974 I attended my first undergraduate lecture on ancient history. The speaker, one of Cambridge's foremost scholars in the field, beamed at his audience confidently and told us that Herodotus wrote so much better than many subsequent historians that his own instinct was to trust him wherever there was no clear reason for not doing so. His tone was very much that of somebody speaking not of the author of a piece of source material, to be contextualised in a long-vanished society, but of an old friend. I encountered much the same attitude when I came to carry out my own research on the Civil War, directed in this case towards the equivalent author in that field, Edward, earl of Clarendon. For the two and a half centuries since its publication, his *History of the Rebellion* had been regarded as the greatest single text for the study of the war, admired for the beauty of its literary style, the apparent wisdom and compassion of its character portraits, and the detail of its account of events. His part as a leading actor in many of the latter gave his analysis of them an additional importance, and his work was quarried uncritically for example and quoted by conservative narrative historians and hard-boiled Marxists alike. Like that of the other writers in this canon, it was part of the general inheritance of a cultured modern person, as familiar and beloved as a major public building. When I commenced my own research, it was commended to me by one of the most celebrated experts in Stuart history at that time, with a chuckle and the words that I would find Clarendon more perceptive and useful than many who had written upon the period since. So, indeed, I seemed to do as the successive volumes of his *History* provided me with what seemed to be the most detailed and considered account of the Civil War that I had ever read. My feelings about it gradually became tainted with suspicion as my work progressed, which rose to a climax in 1979 when I systematically worked through Clarendon's own collection of papers, which represented between them the basic sources upon which he himself had relied for the writing of his narrative. Again and again they proved to me how seriously, and how skilfully, he had misrepresented the truth of affairs, to gain revenge on old enemies and to vindicate his own career, his party, and his particular friends. My sagacious, magnanimous and perceptive guide had turned into a brilliant and ruthless deceiver. I wrote an article to express this view, which was published in 1982,[8] and it was accepted without argument by the other specialists in the field, once they had checked my evidence; including the one who had recommended Clarendon so warmly to me less than seven years before. At the age of twenty-five, which is how old I was when I wrote the piece, I had performed what seemed to my nervous eyes to be the equivalent in source analysis of giant-slaying. Moreover, I had done so with perfect ease, encountering only objectivity and generosity from those who might have been thought to have a vested interest in the orthodoxy which I had denounced. By the early 1980s, iconoclasm seemed both to be functionally necessary and professionally safe. A great traditional narrative was ceasing to be an authority and becoming a text.

I have related these personal anecdotes because, as they were my own experiences, I can share them at will; but I believe that they reflected a common pattern, and a common mood, among my generation of young historians. To understand what happened when that mood encountered the established leaders of our profession, it is important to understand a paradox in the nature of that leadership during the period around 1970. On the one hand, academic historians on both sides of the Atlantic were drawn overwhelmingly from the middle and upper ranks of society. Many of them had been privately educated and had patrician accents and manners, and almost all dressed conventionally and shared conservative cultural tastes. On the other, very few were political conservatives. In Britain in particular, the majority were liberal or socialist in their loyalties, on a spectrum ranging from mainstream postwar socialism to full-blown Marxism. The upsurge of Marxist ideology in the radical youth culture of the late 1960s underpinned and encouraged this tendency in universities, and at particular times and places in the early 1970s it verged upon dominance. One of the few right-wingers prominent in British academe was the Cambridge professor Geoffrey Elton, for decades the leading figure in Tudor historiography. He opened a lecture in January 1974 by declaring to his young audience that 'I suppose this is a historical moment, the last at which a man can stand up and say that Marx wrote rubbish.' I would have dismissed that as an isolated and preposterous outburst, propelled by Elton's feelings of isolation in an unsympathetic intellectual climate, were it not for the fact that during that period various Marxist friends and tutors were suggesting the same thing with less concision and more delight. In retrospect we all know that the Marxist influence on western culture was already at its high-water mark then, and was to undergo a near-complete collapse in the next decade; but to emphasise that nobody seemed to expect this at the time is to reinforce the point that revisionism among early modern historians looked backwards to the decade before the mid-1970s rather than forward to the next one. The revisionists were propelled by a radical distrust of received wisdom, but the wisdom against which they were reacting was that of figures who themselves represented political liberalism and socialism. It is easy to see how it could later be confused with movements such as Thatcherism which assaulted the same targets with fundamentally different instincts and aims. To readers outside the academy, Christopher Hill was the author of books which celebrated revolution and libertarianism; a determinedly anti-establishment figure. To those within it, he was the master of Balliol College, Oxford, one of the oldest, most prestigious and most powerful components of the nation's most richly endowed university. On the American shore Lawrence Stone occupied a chair amid the dignified opulence of Princeton and carried himself in a style which won him the (affectionate) nickname of 'Lorenzo the Magnificent'. It was difficult for new-comers to the recently transformed academic world of the early 1970s to see histo-rians such as these other than as wholly traditional figures, holding pivotal positions in the richest and most conservative institutions and representing a historiography which was itself developed generations before.

* * *

Such a perception was, of course, partly caricature, and it is plain in retrospect that elements of the revisionist challenge had been developing in the previous decade, and from within that traditional historiography. Research generated by the prevailing belief in the socio-economic underpinnings of political events had proved that in the House of Commons itself, the royalists and parliamentarians of the Civil War had been remarkably similar in social background and economic fortune. That discovery both called the original belief into question and propelled scholars into an examina-tion of provincial society during the period, to see whether something that was true of MPs also obtained for local elites. This quest was greatly assisted by the new trove of records available in county archives, and it revealed a local political world both fragmented and conservative, reacting to events at the political centre rather than imposing its will upon them, in which the Civil War partisans were small minorities struggling against confusion, apathy and local self-interest. Alan Everitt widely publi-cised this picture in the 1960s, and in 1976 John Morrill drew upon what was by then a fairly large body of work to argue for a prevalent provincial mentality which was intensely localised and essentially passive in national affairs. He did not deny the importance of ideology to the few partisans, and left open the possibility that Parliament's cause might have had a greater appeal to commoners. It was, however, his characterisation of the majority which made the most impact on his readers.[9]

Among those readers were scholars in North American universities who had been continuing the Notestein tradition of a concentration upon Parliaments and begun in the process to fault the master's views. They had been encouraged in this by an essay published in 1965 by Geoffrey Elton, which represented an excursion beyond his stronghold of early Tudor studies and drew very clearly on his own political ide-ology.[10] As said, he represented a rare case of a passionate and vocal Conservative among the leaders of the profession, and this essay launched an attack on the tri-umphalist account of early Stuart history traditionally presented by socialist (including Marxist) and liberal authors. To the former, he pointed out that the political nation had apparently been as united against Charles I in 1640 as it was divided by him when the Civil War began two years later, suggesting strongly that the war was the result of short-term political developments and not of long-term social movements. His reply to the latter consisted of a direct questioning of both

Notestein and Neale, arguing that Tudor Parliaments had been characterised chiefly by consensus and by skilful royal management, and that this had broken down subsequently because of the ineptitude of the Stuart kings, not because of any wish on the part of the Common. Over ten years after it appeared, Elton's essay was taken up by scholars based mainly in America, who by no means all shared his political attitudes[11] but felt that his historiographical criticisms had actually been too cautious.

In 1976 two of them, the Canadian Paul Christianson and the Englishman Conrad Russell, published essays calling for a new framework of early Stuart history.[12] The former made Stone his main target, arguing that parliamentary sovereignty and a decline in the power of the Crown and nobility were consequences of the Civil War instead of preconditions. He emphasised the vital importance of the peerage in the preceding four decades. Russell took issue most strongly with Notestein, inspired by the comparative work upon seventeenth-century regimes lately undertaken by historians of Europe as a whole. He claimed that English Parliaments of the age were typical of it, in being weak institutions with no common body of people or beliefs opposed to the Crown. In December 1977 a Chicago-based periodical, *The Journal of Modern History*, devoted a whole issue to five essays by different contributors from North American universities, one of them being Christianson.[13] Their collective import was to reinforce the assertions made in the previous year, especially those of the superior importance of the peerage and of the existence of a prevailing language of co-operation in the English political nation until the Civil War broke out. They also proved that the demands for a fundamental change of views first heard in 1976 were shared by a relatively large and determined body of academics. Countenance was given to them by Morrill's work on the provinces and Elton's contemporary addresses to the Royal Historical Society describing the spirit of political consensus prevalent in Tudor England.[14] It was with this clutch of articles in a single journal, arriving as one deliberate and concerted blow against historiographical orthodoxy, that revisionism first impressed itself as a movement upon the consciousness of western scholars.

In 1978 the English equivalent to this blow was delivered, in the shape of a collection of essays upon the same period from seven more writers, gathered by Kevin Sharpe into a book.[15] They were not directly encouraged by the previous seven pieces, but represented parallel work which had reached broadly similar conclusions. The tone of many was less overtly polemical than that of the *JMH* articles, but the introduction by Sharpe tied them firmly into the same process of a fundamental questioning of the familiar perspective; significantly, he was and remains an English scholar more sensitive than most to developments in American academic culture. The essays stressed that quarrels between Crown and Commons were often produced by divisions among royal councillors, that the peerage was important to the political process, and that the seventeenth-century expressions 'Court' and 'Country' referred not to opposed groupings but to overlapping and complementary spheres. In the next year Conrad Russell, who was himself on the point of moving to the United States, brought out a careful narrative and analytical study of the Parliaments of the 1620s which surpassed Gardiner's account and demonstrated all the assertions made in his pioneering essay.[16] This work established that the call for a major reinterpretation amounted to more than a volley of polemics. It commanded respect not merely for the depth of its scholarship but for the courtesy of its tone: indeed, it was largely because of Russell's natural gentility that the controversy which he had helped to provoke never achieved the bitterness of many others within the academy. The book was followed by two others by English scholars in 1981 which shared its qualities as well as its attitudes, Roger Lockyer's biography of Buckingham and Anthony Fletcher's study of the outbreak of the Civil War.[17] Both emphasised the complexity of early Stuart politics and the importance of accident and of practical problems in them.

Any attempt to set these publications in a cultural context must take account of the time-lag involved. Most of the writers concerned had developed their ideas in the first half of the 1970s. They were absorbed by the academy in general during the last two years of the decade, and reactions to them became widespread only in the early part of the following one. There were therefore about ten years between the formulation of the attack on the traditional historiography and the debate over it, during which time western cultural and political patterns were shifting significantly; if the former belonged to the libertarian, iconoclastic and optimistic atmosphere which was flourishing in 1970, the latter was a feature of the more polarized political societies and harsher academic climate which were forming by 1980. By that date, three sorts of reaction to the new, early Stuart historiography were becoming clear. One, very common among non-specialists, was expressed by a Tudor historian in that year, who told me that the early Stuart period now seemed so confusing that she no longer knew how to teach it. Another was trumpeted by Paul Christianson in 1981, that only the 'old' and the 'obstinate' now failed to accept the new ideas.[18]

The third reaction was represented by historians who expressed reservations about the latter, and between 1978 and 1982 a total of eight did so in print.[19] Six of them were based in the United States. All agreed that the model of Notestein and Gardiner had been found wanting, and some felt that its critics were closer to the truth. Stone, who had been the principal living target of the criticisms, made no rapid reply to them.[20] Instead, over half the published pieces which took issue with the new ideas were the work of two men, colleagues at Washington University, St Louis. They were also the first to respond, and at first sight they were not obvious opponents for the new critique. The more entertaining was J.H. Hexter, who was well known as a scourge of Marxist historians in general, and of Hill in particular. What emerged now was that this stance had been inspired by an old-fashioned American love of the traditional constitutional history as an epic story of a successful struggle for liberty, which was one of the targets of the new historiography. The more substantial was Derek Hirst, who like Russell and Stone was an Englishman currently working in America. He had published a first book upon parliamentary elections which had undermined Notestein's picture of them, and contributed the essay on the nature of Court and Country to *Faction and Parliament*. His belief was that the old and the new models were both wrong in important respects. He and Hexter demonstrated convincingly that the Lords, though important, were not the manipulators of the Commons and that ideological factors did play a consistent part in the problems experienced by the first Stuart kings in working with Parliaments.

The two of them also employed the word 'revisionism' to characterise the views which they were contesting. They used it immediately, in 1978, and Hirst did so consistently thereafter; within two years it had become standard. It was not he, however, who had first applied it to this context. In the winter of 1977–78, at a seminar in London, Russell himself had been asked for a term to define those who shared his approach, and settled upon 'revisionists' as the best that he could find. Before printing it, Hirst had applied to him and been given permission to use it.[21] Nor was Russell himself the person who had first made the application; he represents, rather, the earliest instance which I have been able to identify of the acceptance of the term by one of the proponents of the new historiography. It was already being used of them by their opponents, and was in familiar currency in that context by November 1977.[22] Its origin is perfectly clear, for it had commonly been employed during the early 1970s by Marxists across the world to describe those who adulterated and betrayed true doctrine. It was in this milieu that it was first applied, naturally enough, to those who challenged Marxist orthodoxy concerning the seventeenth century, although probably with some irony and reflexivity: but nobody seems to know who first did so. In view of its unflattering connotations, it is not surprising that those to whom it was applied in this debate adopted it with some reluctance, and in default of a better term. Only Christianson, who came close to being their ideologue, employed it readily of himself and his allies in print.

During the 1980s the debate lost pace. Morrill and Sharpe, who had both contracted for large books to match Russell's, grew cautious and postponed them in order to prepare the ground with a series of more closely defined projects.[23] Hexter ceased to write upon the subject and Christianson concentrated on a study of a single individual, John Selden, which was not ready until the late 1990s.[24] It was left to Derek Hirst, in 1986, to produce a textbook on the whole period 1603–58 which attempted, with much success, to rationalise the achievements of the controversy and to present a new narrative based on them.[25] The Civil War was now viewed firmly as the product of short-term political problems, but in a state afflicted by functional breakdown in the fiscal system and disagreements over the form of the Church, both issues with long-term antecedents. Parliaments were extremely important to the process of government, but were becoming neither stronger nor more innovatory. The monarchy was more of an innovator, responding to practical problems which needed to be viewed with sympathy, although Charles I was still a disastrous ruler.

If acceptance was developing for this picture, its details remained controversial, and during the 1980s another group of scholars proposed that major elements of the revisionist case had been faulty. They came from different generations and traditions. Johann Sommerville was a historian of political thought, while L.J. Reeve, Richard Cust and Thomas Cogswell were interested in the making of royal policies and in reactions to them. David Underdown, Stephen Roberts and Ann Hughes were all concerned with provincial society, and more impressed than previous workers in the genre with the lack of clearly defined county communities and distinctive local mentalities. They stressed instead the existence of ideological and cultural divisions in the localities and the importance of social factors as determinants of Civil War allegiance. Despite this heterogenous complexion, they were united in their determination to present counter-arguments to the revisionists, and certain broad patterns seem obvious among them. The first is the shift of the geographical focus of the debate across the Atlantic. In the 1970s, as shown, it was primarily a North American concern. Of the new wave of combatants, all but Cogswell (a pupil of Hirst) were English, and although Underdown was based in the USA and Sommerville later moved there, this made little difference to the overall tendency for the controversy over revisionism to become increasingly a phenomenon focused on English universities and served by English presses. This related to the second significant pattern, which was political. The narrative of politics presented by Hirst was sufficiently balanced to satisfy much of the traditional American preoccupation with constitutional history and high politics, but not the English interest in the relationship between social and political developments. As said, the revisionists were not a right-wing coalition; the most influential was proud to be the son of Bertrand Russell and himself later became a notable Liberal Democrat politician. None the less, they did not represent the spectrum of political attitudes, for by definition they included no Marxists or radical socialists. Conversely, those who appeared to oppose them in the 1980s were not a left-wing group, but they still included a strong element of people who had been touched by Marxist or other socialist ideas and had an instinctual sympathy with commoners and revolutionaries. Here the third factor came into play: that the mix of generations among them was largely illusory. It disappeared if one subtracted Underdown, who was older than most of the revisionists and belonged to the academic leadership of the years around 1970; his work in the 1980s partly consisted of an attempt to reassert an economic determinism for the Civil War, based now on cultural and ecological factors. If he was removed from the group, then it was composed of young academics who had first started to emerge in the years after 1980. Again, the issue of time-lag may be significant here. Most of them had been undergraduates during the 1970s, and their work was in several respects a more subtle restatement of the vision of Stuart politics which had prevailed until the last years of that decade. By the time that they came of age as authors, however, the revisionists had effectively interposed themselves as a new senior generation within the academy, leaving the newcomers a further incentive to question them, because by doing so they could make an immediate and dramatic contribution to debate. In a further uprising of youth against received wisdom, the revisionists themselves were turning into the authority-figures.

The new wave of critics established themselves in a set of monographs published during the second half of the 1980s.[26] By the last year of the decade their challenge to revisionism was sufficiently mature for Cust and Hughes to imitate the tactic of pooled contribution which had launched the revisionist attack. They edited a volume of essays by seven English historians, including themselves, which they presented as a 'post-revisionist' collection. One of the contributors had given an essay (like Hirst) to Sharpe's compilation, illustrating again the difficulty of consigning individuals firmly to historiographical groupings; but as in the case of Sharpe's volume, the editorial line was very much a polemical one. What the joint effort proved was the importance of ideology and the existence of a complex series of religious, fiscal, political and constitutional disputes at all levels of a functionally defective early Stuart system, some long-lasting and all inclined to simplify and polarise drastically at moments of crisis.[27] In 1991 Hughes published a textbook on the causes of the Civil War, which provided her own model of how those disputes had interacted with social and cultural changes to produce the conflict.[28]

At times in the late 1980s it seemed as if the rising tide of 'post-revisionist' writing would overtake and submerge revisionism itself, but the latter was about to make its second great surge as some of its leaders completed long research projects undertaken to substantiate their original suggestions. Geoffrey Elton, that giant from an older generation who had first paved the way for their work, closed a chronological gap with them by developing his attack upon the Neale view of Elizabethan Parliaments, culminating in a book in 1986 which asserted that they exhibited all the features detected by Russell in those of the early Stuarts. Quarrels within them reflected divisions within the government, no organised opposition to the Crown existed in either House, and no shift of power occurred within the institution.[29] This was underpinned in the same year by one of the American revisionists of 1977, Mark Kishlansky, who took a neat revenge on Hirst by challenging him on the ground of his original research, parliamentary elections. Kishlansky argued powerfully that before 1640 such events were expressions of conflict and co-operation within the landed elite, rarely motivated by ideology or subject to popular will.[30] In 1989 Kevin Sharpe brought out a collection of essays which articulated his own model for the breakdown of early Stuart politics, and John Morrill did the same in 1993. Both argued for functional and religious factors, and the role of political decision and expedient, and played down social developments and constitutional theory.[31]

Framed between them were four books which were to represent some of the most substantial monuments of the whole revisionist tradition. Two were the work of Conrad Russell, who had by now returned to England and was ready to produce his own account of the causes of the Civil War. In 1990 he published a thematic history of the subject, and in 1991 a narrative one.[32] Between them they postulated a set of long-term origins for the conflict, in the structural decay of the fiscal system, the tensions left in the Church by the Elizabethan Reformation, and those created by the formation of a multiple kingdom under the Stuart dynasty, and a set of short-term factors of circumstance and personality which inflamed them to the point of complete political breakdown. With them, Russell became the first historian of the period since Gardiner to work with so many issues at once and upon all three kingdoms, and in this fashion the achievement of the great Victorian was finally supplanted. They were followed in 1992 by another work which had taken more than ten years to mature, Kevin Sharpe's enormous history of the Personal Rule of Charles I.[33] It filled the chronological gap between Russell's accounts of the 1620s and the years around 1640, and provided a backdrop to the Civil War which emphasised the viability of royal government in those years and the role of contingency in its eventual failure. In the same year there appeared a fourth work which made less impact than the other three, but was still a significant addition to the revisionist canon. It was a study of early Stuart political thought by Glenn Burgess, which answered Sommerville by arguing that conflicts resulted from a complex breakdown of a traditional language of politics, to match the breakdown in the fiscal system, rather than a hardening opposition of two ideological positions.[34]

With the appearance of these titles, the debate solidified. It continued through the 1990s, as the familiar contributors made further suggestions or rejoinders, and a few newcomers reinforced both their coalitions.[35] None the less, a tired and static air was starting to creep over these exchanges. Many took the form of review articles or second editions of earlier works, and they were becoming routine discussions within a particular field of history rather than a clash of ideas which caught the attention of the profession and raised serious questions of historiography. In 2002 Kevin Sharpe formally drew his own line under the debate, declaring that 'the Civil War is over'.[36] Four main reasons may be suggested for these developments. One was the major shift in American culture during the 1980s. Until that decade, the United States had defined its history largely in terms of its English inheritance, so that the struggles of seventeenth-century England appeared crucial to the formation of its self-image and sense of historic destiny. During those years, this self-image was systematically challenged as divisive, limiting and elitist, and pressure was mounted to recast the American identity as a multicultural one which would enable the USA to function as a global microcosm dependent on the ideal of a unity of many national traditions. With the English one shrinking to one of these, interest in it diminished rapidly. Furthermore, the apparent collapse of Marxist historiography in the same period was actually a reformulation. Scholars who instinctively sought for an economic determinism in historical events had been faced by a frequent lack of hard evidence for one and an altering world economy which left a class-based view of society less relevant. They responded with a swift redefinition of terms, by making cultural forces the new motor for general change and for the struggle between oppressors and oppressed. The traditional preoccupation with 'high' political history, and the complementary interest in its socio-economic underpinnings, were coming to seem not merely old-fashioned but largely irrelevant. The subtraction of American interest removed the force which had first made the revisionist challenge into an international sensation, while the new pre-occupation with cultural studies, crossing to England, reshaped and marginalised the debate even in a land which could still locate it firmly in national history.

The second factor was the neutralisation of the generational conflict embedded in the controversy. By the mid-1990s, most of the academic leadership of the years around 1970 was either dead or in retirement, and the post-revisionists were as well promoted and honoured as their opponents. The historiographical establishment therefore spoke with different voices, even more than previously, and there was little competitive edge for newcomers in challenging one part of it rather than another, while the protagonists of the original debates were equally comfortably off. The third factor was that by the 1990s it was clear to many observers that revisionists and post-revisionists, rather than representing irreconcilable visions of the truth, had become a spectrum of different emphases. The revisionists had demonstrated, conclusively, that the English Civil War was not an inevitable event; that the central conflict between kings and some members of their Parliaments was the most important cause of its outbreak; and that historians of the early Stuart period had to study the court and the House of Lords as well as the House of Commons, and the British Isles as a whole instead of concentrating on England. Each of these new beliefs overthrew others which had been universally accepted for at least fifty years and some of which had been standard for over a century. In the process they had grounded the history of those years much more firmly in documentary evidence than ever before, and reversed the Marxist model for the causes of the Civil War. Whereas the latter had depended on the concept that changes in society had burst upward to shatter the central political system, revisionism had substituted the picture of a breakdown at the centre which had burst outward to shatter a formerly relatively stable and cohesive society. Nevertheless, that society would have had, logically, to shatter along pre-existing lines of tension and weakness, and the post-revisionists had come into their own by drawing attention to those fault-lines in early Stuart England.

The fourth reason for the decline of the debate, however, was that collectively the scholars concerned had done their work too well for comfort. By discarding the idea of the inevitability of the war, and its propulsion by mighty social and economic forces, they had also removed the sense of manifest destiny which connected it organically to the present day. By showing that the issues concerned were more complex than had been thought, they had also made them less readily comprehensible (as my colleague had complained in 1980), and by drawing attention to their detail they had engendered a sense of the period as more alien, more distant and less relevant to the present than it had appeared to be before. Source material was repeatedly revealed as patchy, opaque, or downright inadequate. Political ideas and instincts appeared to be far more fluid, inarticulate, and confused than had been thought, and the motivation behind Civil War allegiance to be something which in most cases could be studied only from the outside, in the rare cases in which the evidence survived to make any study possible at all. The same could be said of the processes by which royal policy was made and parliamentary debates conducted. It had become obvious that it was a far easier task to find shortcomings in the work of scholarly predecessors and colleagues than to produce an alternative which was decisively more convincing.

* * *

As the term 'revisionism' became big news in early modern historiography at the end of the 1970s, it was swiftly appropriated for other topics within the field. The first of these was the English Reformation, which had been regarded as the Tudor equivalent to the Civil War as a formative event for the ideas and institutions of the English-speaking world. From the mid-sixteenth to the mid-twentieth century that world had been predominantly a Protestant one, and the story of the Reformation was accordingly portrayed within it as both inevitable and triumphant. This was a continuing and dynamic portrayal. Whereas in 1970 the basic narrative of the early Stuart age was still Gardiner's, about a hundred years old, that for the Reformation had been published only six years before. It was the textbook by A.G. Dickens, who summed up not only a great deal of his own research but centuries of English Protestant tradition.[37] The latter depended on assertions that the late medieval Church had been decayed and unpopular, that the reformed faith made proportionately rapid progress at all levels of society, and that by the death of Edward VI in 1553, England was predominantly a Protestant nation. Thus the reign of Catholic Mary was seen as a futile attempt to revive a dying religion, and her brutality was believed to have reinforced the attachment of her subjects to the new one. As a result, the Protestant religion was swiftly and permanently re-established as soon as Elizabeth succeeded.

Dickens was the finest scholar in the field, as well as a devout Protestant. Understandably, his portrait was copied by virtually all the other textbooks on Tudor England until the end of the 1970s, including those of Elton which were the most widely read; but by that decade three factors were working against it. One was the flow of diocesan and parochial records into the new record offices, telling a much more complex tale. The second was the school of research students which Elton had built up at Cambridge. They, and others, uncovered a succession of factional conflicts in which final choices of religious policy were determined largely by accidents of mortality and personality. The third was the general decline of

Christianity in the English-speaking world. To agnostics and atheists the attraction of the Reformation was very hard to see, for it involved a mass destruction of tangible objects of beauty (carvings, stained glass, paintings and metalwork), and a substitution of printed words which had very little appeal to those not imbued with faith.

A challenge to the accepted view developed out of the sort of detailed county studies which had already made such an impact upon the historiography of the Civil War. From 1965 a small but growing number were devoted to the Reformation, and most emphasised the slow and uneven nature of the process at a local level. The most significant was Christopher Haigh's monograph on Lancashire, published in 1975.[38] Having commenced work on it to discover why that county remained more Catholic than any other, he completed it with the suspicion that for most of the Tudor period Lancashire had been more typical than exceptional in its very limited acceptance of religious change. Before the end of the decade Haigh had combined the import of the new studies of the provinces and of central politics to provide a comprehensive new view of the English Reformation. It portrayed a popular and flourishing late medieval Church, destroyed slowly by an alliance between a tiny number of local Protestants, concentrated in the southeast, and successive sets of court politicians, often opportunists. What secured an ultimate Protestant victory was only the early death of Mary without an heir and the exceptionally long life of Elizabeth. The reformed faith did not command the allegiance of most of the English until the middle of Elizabeth's reign, and never enjoyed the degree of popularity which had been accorded to the old Church, especially in rural areas. By arguing for all this, Haigh (himself an agnostic) gave obvious offence to Protestants, but by suggesting, explicitly, that English Catholicism had lost the struggle partly because of its own tactical blunders, he gave only slightly less irritation to the adherents of Rome.

In 1979 Haigh was appointed to a fellowship at Oxford and there, in the heart of English academe, he was in a position to give the maximum publicity to his ideas. He aired them all to packed lecture halls and seminars and founded a notably iconoclastic postgraduate discussion group. The result was to display to a greater than usual degree a phenomenon also very apparent in the debate over the early seventeenth century: that actual printed publications represented only the end product of a long and important process of verbal dissemination of views. In both cases the issues were discussed far more avidly in formal and informal academic gatherings than they were in print, and many more people expressed adherence or opposition to them in such situations than addressed them in their own writings. It was widely expected around 1980 that Haigh would soon publish his lectures in a textbook which would generate a set of replies. Instead, like most of the Stuart revisionists, he proceeded far more cautiously, preferring to print papers individually in the course of the early 1980s.[39] The books which supported his case were produced by others, a detailed study of the diocese of Lincoln by Margaret Bowker which came out in 1981 and a fiery series of lectures from Jack Scarisbrick published in 1984.[40] Scarisbrick, the much-respected biographer of Henry VIII, surveyed the whole period up till 1570 and thoroughly endorsed Haigh's opinions regarding the popularity of the old Church and the slow and reluctant acceptance of the new one. His entry into the debate marked the appearance of a phenomenon which revisionism was bringing in its wake: the new sympathy for pre-Reformation religion had allowed the escape of Catholic historiography from the ghetto in which it had been confined for centuries. Scarisbrick himself was a devout follower of Rome, and his book amounted to a brilliant polemic against the Protestant view of the Tudor period. In the same year, however, a young scholar who was a confirmed evangelical Protestant, Robert Whiting, deposited a doctoral thesis on Devon and Cornwall which provided a novel quantity of solid local evidence for the thriving condition of traditional English religion upon the eve of the Reformation. Extracts from it were soon published in essay form.[41]

In 1987 Haigh at last published a book devoted to the subject, boldly entitled *The English Reformation Revised*, but adopted for it the format which had featured so prominently in the controversy over the early Stuart age, of a set of essays by different contributors.[42] In this case, however, the pieces were not produced for the occasion. All but one had already been published, up to fifteen years before, and they represented between them the growth of the new view of the Reformation. Haigh's preface linked it to the simultaneous challenge made to the former orthodoxy concerning the early seventeenth century, cheerfully claiming for both the label of revisionism which most of the Stuart historians concerned had avoided. As a result, some hostile critics henceforth applied it to all the contributors to the volume, whether they identified themselves with it or not. At the same time the term 'post-revisionist', which was appearing in Stuart studies, also surfaced in the context of the Reformation (used of himself by the young historian Glyn Redworth[43]). In both areas of research it had the same rough connotation, of people who found the revisionists more persuasive than the traditional authorities, but both defective. Those most frequently assigned by others to this category, were Patrick Collinson, Diarmaid MacCulloch, John Guy and that same Robert Whiting already mentioned, whose later work more strongly pointed up the differences between his view of the issues and those of Haigh, Scarisbrick and Bowker.[44] There was a confessional divide latent in this division, for whereas the Reformation revisionists consisted (once Whiting was subtracted) of agnostics and Catholics, those labelled post-revisionists all had a background in Anglican or dissenting Protestantism, although not all remained believers. Unlike their Stuart equivalents, however, they never once operated as a group, nor regarded themselves as one. In the mid-to-late 1980s, also, both parts of the traditional historiography produced champions who struck back at the revisionists, Patrick McGrath speaking for Catholics against some of Haigh's arguments and Geoffrey Dickens defending the old mainstream view of which he had been the last great exponent.[45]

As in the case of early Stuart historiography, the debate peaked in the early 1990s. The revisionist tradition now produced its two greatest works. One was the long-awaited book by Haigh, which comprehensively restated all his arguments, now honed by more than a decade of debate.[46] The other was the most impressive product of the Catholic wing of revisionism, Eamon Duffy's huge study of late medieval English religion which included an account of its destruction during the Reformation that yielded nothing in polemical force to Haigh or Scarisbrick and supported most of the suggestions of both.[47] When these were placed alongside the publications of the various critics of revisionism, a proper sense of the agreements and differences between the two approaches could now be achieved. The critics recognised, to varying degrees, that the pre-Reformation Church was both a dynamic and well-loved institution and the object of fierce criticism by lay and clerical writers: attachment to a religion did not preclude dissatisfaction with the way in which it was run. They stressed that government policy was formed by personal religious commitment, often providing a coherent programme, as well as by squalid manoeuvres for power. MacCulloch argued that pre-Reformation native heresy did have considerable influence on the form of English Protestantism and that in some communities the latter made progress as rapidly as Dickens had thought. Whiting insisted that the collapse of the old religion was extremely fast once the Reformation began, and other research did at least support his assertion that certain aspects of it (pilgrimages, shrines, guilds, obits and cults of saints) went into swift and permanent decline once challenged.

Just as in the case of early Stuart historiography, the arguments lost pace rapidly in the middle of the decade. Even more than in that case, the run-down was the result of a sense that the contributors were now disputing aspects of a picture rather than the whole thing. It was now almost universally accepted that the old Church had flourished until the moment that the Crown had embraced reform, that the religious struggle was protracted and determined by royal whim and dynastic accident, and that England had become an unmistakably Protestant nation by the 1580s, rather than by the 1550s. This new story at once gave a greater dignity and credit to Catholicism and made the Protestant victory all the less predictable and more heroic. With some justification, Christopher Haigh could declare in the year 2000 that 'we are (almost) all post-revisionists now'.[48] A young American scholar, Ethan Shagan, suggested two years later that 'few historians' would now deny that in a simple contest between Dickens and Haigh or Duffy, the latter 'win hands down'.[49]

As in the case of early Stuart historiography, the new intensity of research had induced a novel sense of the difficulty of the material. It was now appreciated that there was an immense variation of duration and controversy in the process of reform between localities, that the government could compel external conformity with its wishes faster than changes of personal belief, and that a long interval could exist between a loss of faith in Catholicism and an enthusiastic acceptance of

Protestantism. It was also now understood that different categories of source material, such as printed tracts, churchwardens' accounts, church court records and wills, could furnish sharply contrasting impressions of the nature of religious change. Where evidence was good enough to support arguments at all, it was a common experience to find complex and contradictory reactions to it within the same communities, or even the same individuals. By the end of the 1990s attention was moving from the Reformation itself to the nature of the society which it had created, encouraged by the new interest in cultural studies; in the words of one of the new generation of specialists who had appeared in the decade, Alexandra Walsham, 'from why and when to how England became a Protestant country'.[50] Ethan Shagan put the same point in a way that suggested that the debate between revisionists and their critics was now beside the point: he declared that the fissures that recent research had revealed in traditional religion did not tell a story of 'success' or 'failure' of Protestantism but a complex process of cultural accommodation not easily mapped onto a straightforward polarity between the two sorts of faith.[51]

* * *

It was not until the mid-1980s that another, and much larger, sphere of interest was claimed for the label of revisionism, and this development was wholly the work of one individual, J.C.D. Clark. His early career at Cambridge had not been prosperous: despite obvious intelligence he did not secure a first-class degree and his research, upon mid-eighteenth-century party politics, did not lead to academic preferment. He left the profession for the business world. A less highly motivated person would simply have forgotten academe, while a political radical might have found reason for losing faith in the whole system of higher education. Jonathan Clark was, however, a political and religious reactionary, deeply in love with the past, and having secured a research fellowship at his old university he returned, literally, with a vengeance. His attack upon the existing historiography opened with a review article in 1984, followed by a pair of books during the next two years[52]: all three proceeding from Cambridge presses. Between them these suggested that the seventeenth and eighteenth centuries in England formed a continuous whole in which hierarchy, deference and authority were the key concepts of politics, and religion the most emotive factor. This *'ancien regime'* was said to have lasted until the years 1829–32, when it began to alter as a result of political circumstance. Clark denied that the period which he had defined ever underwent any class conflict or dramatic economic change, and claimed that Parliament remained for the whole of it a relatively weak and hesitant body in which parties had difficulty in preserving their identity if dynastic and religious conflicts were absent. Its most powerful and aggressive component remained the Crown, which was only challenged if the current monarch happened to be of a religion or a dynasty to which other members of the institution objected. Each of these proposals violated part of the existing notion of the age concerned, and would by themselves have generated considerable debate. This was supercharged by the fact that whereas the revisionists of other parts of the early modern period had tended to address issues rather than historians (at least in print), Clark's arguments were ferociously personalised. He believed that most scholars of his chosen epoch had distorted the truth about it because of their own left-wing political prejudices, and so betrayed their duty and the people about whom they wrote. Thus, they had inflated the importance of any elements within it which would win the approval of modern liberals or socialists, and consistently disparaged or neglected what Clark took to be the dominant culture of monarchy, aristocracy and Church. Those whom he accused included a great many of the most prestigious figures in modern academe, including Hexter, Hill and the man whom many regarded as the leading figure in early-eighteenth-century studies (and who certainly led them at Cambridge), Sir John Plumb. Clark applied to himself the name of revisionist, and claimed to be part of the same movement as those to whom this term had been applied in Stuart studies, sharing the same opponents. He also explicitly linked the challengers of the traditional historiography to the challenge to traditional British politics represented by Thatcherism; a linkage which most of the historians who had first mounted that challenge would vehemently have disavowed.

The result was a furore. On the one hand, Clark became an instant celebrity, awarded a post at All Souls College, Oxford, and hailed in a national newspaper as 'The Don Who is Rewriting History'.[53] On the other, he became one of the most hated of living historians. Mark Kishlansky, the leading Stuart revisionist, commented in 1988 that 'Clark-bashing has already become a popular blood sport.'[54] Professors who had grown up in an era in which it was considered disgraceful for a scholar to feature in a newspaper at all, now found the aforesaid Dr Clark denouncing them to the press. A letter-defending Plumb against his attack was duly published in reply, signed by all the Cambridge history professors except Sir John himself and (significantly) Elton. The latter's abstention, and its implied support for Clark, was typical of the rifts opened by the latter's assertions. Essays were rushed into print to pass judgement upon them.[55] Clark's treatment of opponents received no public commendation but caused much private glee. His conception of English history was endorsed by nobody in its entirety, but by several writers in part. The specialists in early Stuart history whom he had claimed as allies responded rather coolly to the suggestion, while recognising that they had some ideas and opponents in common. Historians of the late Stuarts tended to be gratified by the interest which Clark drew to their relatively neglected period, and hostile to his assumption that its political changes were essentially minor. Scholars of the Georgian age rather relished the attention which he had drawn to it. A spectrum of 'post-revisionist' opinion materialised almost immediately, united by a belief that Clark had performed a valuable service in drawing attention to important features of eighteenth-century society, particularly the religious element, which had hitherto been neglected. It was also accepted by the same writers that he had exaggerated the religious element, at the expense of others, of radicalism, dissent, commercial culture and social change, which had also been present.[56] Having come last upon the scene, this 'revisionist' controversy died down at the same time as all the others. It had been fuelled by a single remarkable personality, and by the 1990s he was moving on to fresh interests and a new country. His rereading of historiography had given a special emphasis to the contrast between the English and American traditions which put both into a new perspective, and he duly moved to the United States. In 1997 he could refer to 'that empty category, revisionist'.[57]

* * *

These, then, were the developments in English historiography to which the term 'revisionism' was most commonly and consistently applied. This account has inevitably made crude simplifications of the ideas involved and omitted mention of some lesser works relevant to the discussions concerned. It has also failed to include important scholarship to which some have applied the same label. Thus, from 1978 onward the Cambridge historian Alan Macfarlane published a series of major books concerning the development of English society, which challenged all previous thought on the matter and Marxist thought in particular, holding that the English had always possessed much the same social structures and attitudes.[58] He linked himself to the same mood which produced the Stuart revisionists, and shared some of their targets (such as Stone) and some of their allies (such as Elton). He was, however, not directly associated with the debates above, was not part of a body of thinkers, and the main emphasis of his argument lay upon the Middle Ages. He was certainly a part of the same tendency in academe which had produced early modern revisionism, but better viewed in the context of all the changes sweeping away old views of the British past, from that of the New Stone Age to that of the present. Also excluded from this chapter have been dramatic new assertions regarding relatively small issues. The most celebrated of these would probably be J.C. Davis's attack on the Marxist historians of the Civil War, such as Christopher Hill, for their alleged misrepresentation of the radical thinkers identified by their contemporary enemies as the 'Ranters'.[59]

Something that must be stressed now, which was only implicit before, is that the debates outlined above directly involved only some of the specialists at work in each field. It was perfectly possible for the others to produce important research which did not engage directly in those controversies.[60] Admittedly it was less easy for them to avoid being assigned to either of the opposed camps and sometimes to both, successively or even simultaneously.[61] At times this process was manifestly unjust, but it often reflected a complex reality, in which individuals could indeed be both for and against the presumed groupings. The most prominent case is that of Geoffrey Elton, whose career as the pre-eminent historian of the Tudor period was sustained throughout the 1980s, leading him to the tenure of the regius chair in history at Cambridge, and eventually to a knighthood. He was, as has been shown, the forefather or prophet of early Stuart revisionism and one of the few senior historians to show sympathy for Jonathan Clark. To revisionists in Reformation studies, however, he was associated with the old order. His position was further complicated when, in 1986 his own revision of Neale's theories appeared alongside a book edited by two of his former pupils and intended to re-evaluate the work which had first established Elton's reputation in the 1950s, *The Tudor Revolution in Government*. Many of the pieces openly challenged his findings.[62] The title, *Revolution Reassessed*, resembled that of Haigh's collection on the Reformation, the format of each was identical, and the two were understandably often referred to together as exercises in revisionism. Yet when one of the editors reviewed a book on Cardinal Wolsey in 1990, which explicitly declared itself to be a revisionist work and made Elton one of its main targets, he coldly disassociated himself from the term. Indeed, he recalled, quite correctly, that it had originated as a piece of Marxist jargon.[63]

Similar difficulties surround the use of the opposed term 'Whig', which featured prominently in the debates. It originated, of course, in seventeenth-century Scotland as a name for Presbyterian rebels, and was applied as an insult to one of the two opposed political parties which appeared in England around 1680. It was soon adopted by that party and retained until the latter metamorphosed into the Liberals in the mid-nineteenth century. In 1941 the Cambridge scholar Sir Herbert Butterfield applied it to historians who had overemphasised and glorified developments in the past which had created the institutions and attitudes of the modern age. It was thus, once again, an expression of opprobrium, and the more effective in that Butterfield himself never named the guilty parties. Instead it became a means to castigate individuals who were presumed to commit the fault concerned, selected according to the whim of the person employing it, and was cheerfully taken up by most of those called revisionists in the 1970s and 1980s. They used it to characterise Gardiner, Notestein, Dickens, Plumb and other exponents of the old orthodoxies who could not be grouped under the label of Marxist. Of all the participants in the debates concerned, only Hexter was prepared to apply it to himself, and then only in the sense that he celebrated past developments which produced aspects of modernity which most people valued. Among everybody else it was the most common term of criticism, increasingly applied to writers who had themselves issued challenges to former ideas. It was, in fact, the academic equivalent to the term revisionist, as originally used among Marxists: the word of abuse for an opponent within the same broad ideological camp as oneself. Thus, Derek Hirst used it in 1978 to asperse the ideas associated with Gardiner and Notestein, declaring that they had produced a view of history 'more ill-fitting than one of Ollie Hardy's suits'.[64] Mark Kishlansky used it in 1986 as a weapon in his feud with Hirst, stating confidently that the latter belonged to 'the Whig canon' of scholars.[65] Kishlansky himself then received the same label from a younger historian, John Adamson, whom he had provoked to a much more celebrated quarrel in 1991. Adamson announced that his opponent 'remains an unreconstructed Whig: one for whom revisionism is a matter of rearranging the deck-chairs on Gardiner's unsinkable *Titanic*'.[66] In part this apostolic succession of disdain did reflect a genuine progression of ideas, and in part the simple truth that nothing galls antagonists more than to employ their favourite weapon of disdain against them. However, the ubiquity, and almost universal iniquity, of the term also draws further attention to the identity of revisionism as part of a general rejection of Victorian historiography.

All this might be taken to indicate that the controversies engendered by the so-called revisionists were highly artificial creations produced by accidents of personality among historians. Certainly specialists in the late Stuart period sometimes looked on in amazement at the fuss going on around them. After all, the years 1660–1714 had long been regarded as crucial to the development of the English Church and state and had been the preserve of the historians most clearly to be characterised as Whigs (and most literally, as they had supported that party). As will be considered later, research into them continued steadily through the 1970s and 1980s, producing some differences of opinion but never disturbing a wider sense of community and co-operation among experts. The same tranquillity was found in the study of the fifteenth century. Obviously, what distinguished these quieter areas of scholarship was that they had not attracted the attention of a figure like Gardiner, capable of fastening a structure of interpretation about them which was accepted and elaborated by generations of successors. The air of unreality which sometimes appeared to cling to the debates between revisionists and their opponents was reinforced by the nebulous nature of the groupings concerned. After all, despite the efforts of Christianson, Haigh and Clark to perceive unified aims, revisionism never achieved the status of a school of academic thought. It had no journal, no conferences and no keynote addresses. Those associated with it often had little personal contact and often disagreed with each other.

All this makes more remarkable the size and permanence of the shift which they produced in the historiography of early modern England. It ceased to be a eulogy of the characteristics of the realm of Victoria, and a quest for their origins. Protestantism, representative democracy and a powerful middle class were no longer seen as organic and irresistible growths from early modern English society. In the changed circumstances of the late twentieth century, these things had come to seem much more fragile a set of creations, and (to some) much less worthy of respect. In an ironic sense the new view of the past came close to that of the most celebrated of all genuine Whig historians, Lord Macaulay, who had regarded his world as the product of human effort aided by providential good luck. What sharply separated the two visions was that Macaulay and his kind had treated the ultimate victors of early modern England as heroic progenitors, whereas in large part revisionism consisted of a novel sympathy with the vanquished. It could be suggested that Tudor Catholics, Stuart monarchs, Georgian aristocrats and Native Americans were all beneficiaries of the same recoil of opinion which occurred in the western world in the 1960s. As traditional institutions and values came to be questioned, it was easier to pity the victims of the processes which had created them. The achievement also extended to methodological and more narrowly professional concerns. The arguments provoked by revisionism set new standards of research, involving a more careful inspection of a much larger quantity and wider range of documents. They established, apparently forever, that the causes of the political events of early modern England were themselves, in the main, political, and that chance and short-term planning by individuals could produce immense change. They proved the supreme importance of central politics in national affairs and showed much more clearly how these related to social, cultural and economic contexts. They provided a much greater variety and richness of experience to the study of early modern England.

Such a confident and triumphant conclusion seems to be justified by the results, and yet it is only one perspective on them; it accords strangely with the concerns expressed at times in this chapter about the newly perceived complexity and difficulty of writing early modern political history. Like most revolutions, the revisionist one belonged to two worlds and faced in two directions. In a major respect it represented not the dismantling of Victorian historiography but its final great achievement. It had the same preoccupations, with the particular events which apparently created the modern world, and concerned itself with the same relationships, of Crown and Parliament, centre and localities, and Church and dissenters. It had the same faith in the ability of sustained professional research, concentrated above all on archival materials, to produce an ever clearer and more consensual knowledge of the past. It did not aim at multivocality and polyvalency, a past perceived in different ways by different people, but at a unified picture which would satisfy all groups. In many respects it was just a more ambitious way of writing nineteenth-century history, and as such it failed. With a tremendous underlying irony, it reproduced the experience of the two main phenomena which it set out to understand, the Reformation and the Civil War. Both of those had been propelled by critics who perceived serious faults in the existing status of affairs, and wished to produce a reunited nation based upon a better system of government and belief. Both shattered the considerable amount of common ground which the English had shared hitherto, to create a nation permanently divided, to an extent and with a depth never known before. Those divisions have never been closed, and the state has survived and prospered by learning to accept them. So it has been with historiographical revisionism. The inherited orthodoxy has been destroyed, and replaced not merely with a more complex spectrum of opinion but with a new sense of the intractability of much of the evidence and many of the issues.

The early modern world suddenly seems much further away, more alien and more mysterious. It has ceased to provide easy answers to big questions concerning how the British of the present came to be. By deconstructing a traditional story which privileged the victors, the revisionist historians had set out to reveal a past which, much more than before, belonged to all of the dead and all of living. Instead they revealed one which belonged to nobody.

2 The Great Civil War

The Great Civil War of 1642–46 was arguably the most traumatic experience that the English, Welsh and Cornish peoples have ever had; and it has accordingly been replayed in their minds every time that British society has been perceived to be under stress. There is no doubt that it was a tame event compared with the contemporary wars on the continent of Europe, or in Ireland, and that natural disasters regularly killed far more people in much less time. The best current estimate of those who died in action during its four years is around 60 000, almost all of them soldiers.[1] When a Catholic army stormed the Protestant city of Magdeburg in 1631, about 25 000 of its inhabitants were killed within forty-eight hours, almost all civilians. In this period as in all until the twentieth century, war despatched more people by the disease and exposure that were its almost inescapable side effects than those who fell in battle. It has been calculated that at least 100 000 – combatants and civilians – died from war-related illness during the fighting of 1642–46 and the two shorter civil conflicts (the Second Civil War of 1648 and the Third Civil War of 1651) that followed it.[2] About the same number, however, perished in just three months in London alone during the bubonic plague epidemic of 1665, and this was not the most destructive plague of the Tudor and Stuart age, proportionate to the size of the population. All epidemics in recorded European history pale beside the Black Death of the fourteenth century, which picked off between a third and a half of the human beings of each region in which it appeared, within a few months. When all this is said, the loss of life consequent upon the Great Civil War was still significant; it has been estimated that between 1643 and 1645, its effects increased the normal death toll of the county of Devon by over 50 per cent.[3] Relative to population, it was almost certainly the bloodiest war in English history.

What makes it 'great', however, is that it was also the most sustained and bitter period of internal conflict that the English state has ever suffered. It directly affected most parts of the country, and its demands and effects were felt in all. It polarised political and religious opinion, producing division in most counties and cities. Those that were apparently unanimous in their loyalties at the opening of the conflict often came to re-evaluate them towards the end: for example, the instinctual royalism of much of Wales turned into a realisation that the preservation of one's own community could be a higher cause than the preservation of the monarch. The war reaffirmed many traditional amities and alliances, but it also split parent from child, sibling from sibling, wife from husband, soldier from civilian, landlord from tenant, minister from congregation, sovereign from subjects and central from local government. It called into question the fundamental political, social and religious assumptions with which most people had grown up, and wrecked the mental landmarks that mapped out their view of the world. It also did a tremendous amount of physical damage – only exceeded by the bombing of the Second World War – and militarised the societies of southern Britain in a way never known before or since.

In many ways the nation never recovered from it. In 1640 it had a Church which, though riven with tensions, commanded the loyalty of at least 95 per cent of the population, in the manner of those in Scandinavian countries until the twentieth century. The war set Protestant against Protestant in a manner unknown in any of Europe's other religious conflicts, and left a new phenomenon – again unique in Europe upon that scale – of people who were not Catholics and yet were either unwilling or unable to be full members of the religion prescribed by a Protestant state. Likewise a political nation which, although again prone to differences of opinion, had always operated according to a model of co-operation and consensus, was left with an enduring tendency to polarise issues between two political blocs. There were decided long-term advantages to both developments, ultimately creating an unusually tolerant, pluralist and flexible sort of state, and for this the Civil War can effectively be thanked. These good results were, however, bought at the price of a further century of instability and insecurity. The first blood of the Great Civil War can be said to have flowed from the severed neck of the chief minister of Charles I, the earl of Strafford, when he knelt at the headsman's block on Tower Hill in May 1641. Not until the last of the executions that followed the failure of the rebellion of Bonnie Prince Charlie, in 1753, could the cycle of vengeance and counter-vengeance that began in that moment truly be said to have come to an end.

For two hundred years the writing of the history of the war was essentially a continuation of the hostilities themselves. As the last generation to have lived through it began to die out at the end of the seventeenth century, so the work of editing texts and memoirs of it began, to serve the purposes of rival groups of politicians and ideologues. This partisan purpose characterised the work of historians until the second half of the reign of Victoria, when distance at last put the conflict firmly into the past. Although less immediate, it did not seem less relevant to authors, who now saw the combatants as heroic ancestors rather than comrades in a continuing struggle. The pattern was set for the following hundred years, whereby the majority of those who wrote history, led by Samuel Rawson Gardiner, eulogised the parliamentarians as the progenitors of modern British liberties, while the majority of artists, and writers of romantic fiction, preferred the royalists, as exemplars of loyalty, chivalry and gentility, sharing in the glow of martyrdom that still clung around their king.

This situation still obtained at the opening of the 1970s, when the war achieved a new peak of importance in the national imagination. The United Kingdom was caught up in another process of painful, divisive and exciting self-definition, in the wake of the loss of empire and great power status, and in the face of the techno-logical and cultural changes sweeping through western societies as a whole. For the English, the war represented the last point at which their state had been seriously dysfunctional, and as such was used as a source of images, figures and concepts with which to confront contemporary hopes and worries. Inside the recently expanded university system, historians still viewed it as the crucible within which modern Britain had been made, and as such it was one of the most important, heavily populated and contentious areas of research. Radicals who were challeng-ing the norms of twentieth-century British society identified with the most extreme or adventurous of the thinkers and agitators who had emerged from the parliamentarian party in the hour of its victory. For those who read history as entertainment, the war represented one of the most exciting episodes in the nation's past. In 1958 Veronica Wedgwood had published a scholarly but colourful narrative history of it, which went into paperback eight years later to become a bestseller, the standard work for the informed general reader.[4] Lighter popular his-tories abounded, bridging the gap between history and the fictional works on the period that were also plentiful in the 1960s.[5] The film industry responded to pub-lic interest with two products in 1970, one a technicolour Hollywood blockbuster starring Richard Harris as Cromwell and Sir Alec Guiness as Charles I, and the other a low-budget black and white creation by a maverick producer, dedicated to the protocommunist thinker Gerrard Winstanley. In 1968 those who wanted to act out their enthusiasm for the period were provided with the perfect vehicle, with the foundation of Britain's first historical recreation society, the Sealed Knot. Dedicated to staging reconstructions of the war's actions, it rapidly grew into the largest such society in Europe, and retains that status despite the subsequent burgeoning of re-enactment groups for virtually every period of history. With three decades of the twentieth century yet to run, the war seemed to be established as the most inter-esting single event in the English past, at every level of society and both inside and outside the academy. It remains now to determine what were the particular char-acteristics of that interest and what happened to it during the period since.

* * *

One feature of the popularity of the subject around 1970 was the continuation of the division between 'high' and 'low' culture already visible under Victoria. The novels and many of the popular histories overwhelmingly took the king's adher-ents as their heroes or heroines. When the Sealed Knot was founded, it was initially difficult to recruit a parliamentarian army for it at all, and ever since then the roy-alist division of the society has generally been larger. Although film-makers tended (at least by 1970) to favour Parliament, when a British television series on the war was made at the opening of the 1980s, it followed, sympathetically, the fortunes of a family that supported Charles I. The pattern obtained which had been remorse-lessly and accurately satirised, along with so much else, in Sellar and Yeatman's *1066 and All That*, (a work of 1930 that resonated again with another iconoloclas-tic generation in the 1960s, being reprinted seven times in the first half of that decade alone). The war was 'the Central Period of English History', consisting of the 'utterly memorable struggle between the Cavaliers (Wrong but Wromantic) and the Roundheads (Right and Repulsive)'.[6] This picture fitted precisely (of course) with that taught, earnestly, in my own schoolbooks: the parliamentarians had the right principles, and were the natural moral ancestors of all decent, sober, responsible and right-thinking people. The royalists were politically in the wrong, but better looking, better dressed and more fun, and wrote better poetry.

Conversely, virtually all academic historians – being decent, sober (at least in print), responsible and right thinking – were natural parliamentarians. There were sound historical reasons, recently well analysed by John Adamson, Raphael Samuel, Timothy Lang and Blair Worden, why the Victorians should have devel-oped a cult of Puritans, Ironsides and the party that was exemplified (at least in the historical imagination) by both. The forces of dissent, imperialism, liberal consti-tutionalism, the empowerment of the middle class and of bourgeois values, and the new admiration for a narrowly defined 'manliness', all drove them towards such a response.[7] Given the suggestion already made, that the nineteenth century effec-tively lasted until the 1960s, it is not hard to find reasons for why this bias among academic scholars should have persisted until then. It is much more difficult, and delicate, to account for the undoubted fact that it has never disappeared, nor even lessened. The roll-call of professional historians of the period who have concentrated upon the parliamentarian party to the entire or partial exclusion of the royalists includes Christopher Hill, Austin Woolrych, Willie Lamont, Gerald Aylmer, Ivan Roots, Donald Pennington, John Morrill, Blair Worden, Clive Holmes, Anthony Fletcher, Robert Ashton, Ann Hughes, Ian Gentles, Stephen Roberts, Mark Kishlansky and John Adamson. This list contains most of the leading figures in the field to have published since 1970. In its 'hard' form, this tendency has consisted of an open antipathy towards the king's adherents and sympathy towards their opponents; more commonly it has taken a 'soft' form, of paying far more attention to the parliamentarians and treating them as more normative for the history of the war. Like all true intellectual hegemonies, this has been the more effective for having passed almost wholly without comment, or indeed any sign of being noticed. Breaches of that rule have been recent and rare, one of the most public being that made by Blair Worden in 1999, when he noted in the course of a review published in the *Times Literary Supplement* that for over a century historians of the Civil War 'have been writing about, and mainly for, the winning side'.[8]

It is by no means clear why this should be so. One frequently heard assertion, that history tends to be written by and about winning sides, fails completely in the face of the large academic industries devoted to studying the Jacobites, the Catholic Confederacy that ruled most of Ireland in the 1640s, or the Confederate States of America, not to mention the Nazis. It is obvious in those other cases that constituencies exist to create and sustain interest: Scottish nationalism lies behind the first, and the identity of the modern Republic of Eire behind the second, while the former American Confederate states survive with a robust local patriotism, and the Nazis are the favourite enemy against which modern liberal democracy can define itself. All this makes it the more striking that the royalists of the Great Civil War have failed to find any such natural constituency of interest in the recent past. Furthermore, it is by no means obvious that, ultimately, they *were* the losers; after all, the Restoration of 1660–62 bore some hallmarks of a royalist victory, and England is still part of a monarchy in which many of its subjects continue to manifest strong feelings of affection for the person and office of the sovereign. A second superficial answer to the problem would be to suggest that there is simply not much information about them; and this has certainly been done at times during the past. It is, however, itself an aspect of the prejudice against royalist studies, rather than a statement of fact. In the 1970s I was myself assured by two leading experts in the period that the history of royalist wartime administration could never be written, because the sources for it had perished, and then proceeded to find plenty of records of it. A third solution was proposed by me in a review published in 1993: that the neglect of royalism was simply a consequence of the generally liberal and socialist hue of academic historians, one aspect of that love affair of the British intelligentsia with socialism that kept domestic politics so consensual between 1945 and 1975.[9] The remark has, I believe, some truth to it, but is not a complete answer, for the neglect continued during the breakdown of consensus after 1975, and the list of historians who have concentrated more on Parliament's cause, made above, is not wholly one of liberals and socialists. Even more to the point, it transcends British preoccupations, for it includes an American, a Canadian and an Australian.

Some better insight may be provided into the problem by considering the identity of those few scholars working since 1970 who made a study of the king's adherents their starting point for research. Three did so during the 1970s and 1980s – Peter Newman, Martyn Bennett and myself – and all of us were united by a particular trait. To differing extents, we represented that radical counter-culture of the period which broke decisively with the norms of our parent society, without also identifying itself with particular parties or political programmes. It sought social and cultural transformation at the grassroots of the nation rather than a replacement of one group of leaders with another. There is no doubt that I was attracted to study the royalists simply because the dominant intellectual tendency under which I was educated either neglected or disparaged them, and that was sufficient to recommend them to my attention. Such an impulse was to produce a small but significant body of new work between the three of us.[10] It was not, however, enough to sustain the process. Peter left the academic profession, I moved out of the period, and although Martyn continued to specialise in it, he broadened his focus to include all aspects of it, and gradually began to shift his emphasis to the parliamentarians.[11] Likewise, in the 1990s a younger historian, David Smith, published a valuable monograph on the more moderate wing of royalist politicians during the war, but then went on to write generally about Stuart Parliaments.[12]

What has consistently been missing in the modern academic network is somebody willing to write about the king's party who instinctually shares their view of the world; which after all, has been both a widespread and powerful one in English politics. It is the spirit that was also to inform the Anglican-royalists of the 1660s and 1680s, the Tories to whom they gave birth and much of the Conservative party that in turn grew out of the Tory, and persisted as a major force until the mid-twentieth century. It is based on a view of society as hierarchically arranged and yet mutually reciprocal, united in an organic relationship with land and ancestors and a fundamental loyalty to Crown and Church as the focal points of community from the national to the parish level. Such a viewpoint has certainly been well represented during the past hundred years by writers of history books who have operated outside the university system, such as Sir Arthur Bryant and Sir Winston Churchill. In the microcosm of Civil War studies it inspired several military historians, most of all Brigadier Peter Young, founder of the Sealed Knot.[13] Embodied in the person and writings of the greatest royalist author, the earl of Clarendon, it won sympathy even as late as the 1980s, from non-academic authors such as Richard Ollard and Ronald Harris.[14] In national life it has only undergone a notable decline with the major social and political transformations of the period since 1975, including the Thatcherite revolution in Conservatism. Among academic historians of the Civil War, however, it has always been rare, and after 1970 disappeared altogether. On both sides of the Atlantic it has been the parliamentarians, and their partial descendants, the Whigs, who have scooped the attention, and the political and religious authors who are most intensively studied are from that tradition: Prynne, Baxter, Ludlow, Vane, Locke, Milton, Sidney, Bunyan, Winstanley and the Levellers. Where royalist, Tory or Anglican writers are noticed at all, it is usually as foils for their opponents, with the occasional exception of two unrepresentative extremists among the monarchists, Sir Robert Filmer and Thomas Hobbes. This pattern has persisted, without fluctuation or mitigation, right up till the present.[15] It is a tremendous irony that throughout three decades in which 'Whig' has been the greatest term of opprobrium employed against each other by historians of the Stuart period, they have collectively represented Whiggishness in the purest and most straightforward sense. The history of the Civil War, in particular, is unbalanced as a result.

For a time it did seem as if this bias would be shifted, but in a very different direction than that of an equality of interest between the parties: by concentration on, and sympathy for, people who were neither royalist nor parliamentarian. It began with a development already mentioned, of a turn to local evidence for the war, propelled by the need to test the Marxist assertion that it was a class struggle and supplied by the growth of county record offices. Led most obviously by Alan Everitt, it revealed a provincial world that was not, as had been expected, a miniature of the national struggle between the warring parties. Instead, the activists on either side appeared as small and unrepresentative minorities, struggling against the inclinations of the mass of their neighbours. That mass was concerned, above all, to preserve the peace and prosperity of their own communities, and their instinctual attitude to the conflict was one of neutralism. This had manifested in two different forms. One was of a passive kind, characterised by a tendency to lend as little support to either party as possible, in contributions of money or recruits, and to switch that minimal support to whichever one seemed to be stronger and to have the better prospect of winning, and so ending, the war as swiftly as possible. The other form was militant, and consisted of formal pacts made by local leaders to declare a cease-fire between the partisans in their particular county or region, or else to stop the fighting from breaking out there at all. In its most extreme form it produced groups of armed local vigilantes committed to preserving the peace in their own districts. At the opening of hostilities they were led by the county elite of greater gentry and their mission was to prevent the conflict from entering their shire. Towards the end, they took the form of Clubman associations, comprised mainly of lesser gentry and commoners, and designed to prevent the soldiers of either party from plundering their neighbourhoods. In this view, to the great majority of the English, Welsh and Cornish, the main enemy in the Great Civil War was the war itself.

The result was that there were three basic conceptual tools to the study of the war during the 1970s. One was that the obvious unit for research was a county, extended at times into a region consisting of a natural cluster of shires. The second was that the most common attitude of people to the conflict was one of aversion and resistance, pitting them against the small number of committed partisans. The third was that this attitude was associated with an ubiquitous mentality of localism, in which the county effectively represented the country for most of its inhabitants, and the latter had an automatic resentment of being governed by strangers to their community and having its resources harnessed for operations outside it. This mentality automatically set them in opposition to those who took a nationwide view of the war and of its priorities and logistics. In the first half of the 1970s, these concepts were built into a number of influential and much admired studies, by John Morrill, Anthony Fletcher, Clive Holmes and David Underdown.[16] There was one obvious professional reason why the model that they represented should have achieved popularity so swiftly: that the 'county community', or (when asking slightly different questions) a regional collection of counties, was virtually a perfect unit for a self-contained historical research project. Such a project appeared to offer ultimate solutions to the remaining puzzles concerning the causes, nature and course of the Civil War by showing what had happened 'on the ground' of the localities. It rested on a large, varied and accessible body of data, represented by the collections newly gathered and made easily available in the local record offices. It was on a scale that could be accomplished within a few years of steady work. These characteristics made it, in particular, a perfect subject for a doctoral thesis in the period at which the PhD was becoming established as the basic training degree and qualification for entry to the academic profession. There has, perhaps, never been a time before or since when the work of graduate students was so closely watched and anticipated by senior specialists in the Stuart age as it was in the 1970s and early 1980s. With so much untouched material now lying ready in the archives, completed theses represented so many laden trucks trundling back from the coal-face of research. For much of the former decade there was a widespread feeling that the future of Civil War historiography lay mainly in a succession of county studies, gradually increasing in sophistication until the whole nation was covered and the traditional questions about the war all answered.

This technical motivation did not, however, explain the preoccupation with localism, neutralism and resistance to the war. After all, the county study of the Civil War was a tradition that had commenced in the reign of Victoria, produced by local antiquarians, and continued to flourish until the 1930s.[17] The fact that no other episode in English history attracted equivalent attention from writers concerned with local experience and local pride testifies to the grip that the war had secured upon the national imagination; but it is noteworthy also that these earlier authors saw the local dimension as a microcosm of the nationwide one. They were concerned with the identity and fortunes of the partisans in their respective areas, and showed nothing of that attention to non-combatants and emphasis on weariness with war and aversion to it that characterised the books of the late 1960s and early 1970s. This was despite the fact that they were, essentially, using the same kinds of source. It is hard to escape the conclusion that the mood of that later period owed much to the two simultaneous developments. One was the outbreak of sustained sectarian violence in the United Kingdom, focused on its detached province of Northern Ireland. The other and more important was the controversial, protracted, squalid and apparently futile nature of the war in Vietnam, and the growing opposition to it in the western world. That opposition-focused attention on people who challenged or evaded the summons to fight in western nations engaged in the war, and invested them with heroic associations. Some of those associations apparently rubbed off onto the earlier conflict.

If correct, this interpretation of events would also explain what occurred subsequently. The vision of a succession of sophisticated county and regional studies, slowly covering the whole nation, always failed to take into account the dynamics of recent academic life. With posts in short supply from the middle of the 1970s, and promotion uncertain, research has most often tended to be expressed in competitive form; to show why one's own particular study surpasses those that have appeared in a field before and outclasses those of colleagues currently working in it. Freshness and novelty are two qualities that have a strong appeal in such a scholarly culture. This did not render impossible the essentially corporate and collegiate nature of the vision of a quiltwork of local monographs, but it made it somewhat unlikely. By the end of the 1970s it was already common to hear experts in the period starting to grumble about 'yet another county study'. This pattern almost certainly combined with the effects of the fall of Saigon, and the appearance of more divisive and bitterly partisan politics in the United Kingdom and United States towards the end of the same decade, to encourage a further decisive shift in Civil War historiography. Attention was returning to the warring parties, and those who had resisted or avoided the conflict were coming to be regarded once more as dull, and largely irrelevant. Historians who had concentrated on them were mocked for explaining 'why the Civil War did not happen'.[18]

By the 1980s localism and neutralism were definitely out of fashion. Clive Holmes and Ann Hughes opened the decade with attacks on both the model of the county as a natural unit of research and the concept of a distinctively localist mentality that had accompanied it. They pointed out that a shire was both too large and too small a space for the horizons of most people of the Stuart age. Economic, political and social networks overlapped its borders or were confined to particular zones within it, so that it represented more of an administrative invention than an organic community. Both historians suggested that the main group to whom the county represented a genuinely meaningful unit were the greater gentry, producing a neglect of the views and activities of the rest of society. Neither in the war itself nor in the seventeenth century in general did they find any neat division, in personnel or concerns, between central and local government, or between the politics and religion of the nation and those of the district. Where localist sentiments were blatantly articulated, Hughes characterised them as often temporary and opportunist postures, adopted as one feature of factional competition. Both she and Holmes considered that common ideologies, and ideological rivalries, transfused and linked together the whole nation.[19] When Hughes came to publish her own study of a county in the Civil War, in 1987, it was virtually a deconstruction of the principles and approaches on which the genre had been based at the opening of the 1970s: her county was definitively not a community.[20]

Since then books on the local history of the war have largely reverted to being the products of authors outside the community of academic historians and concerned with the experiences of their local areas; though these have retained the high standards of research, and many of the preoccupations, of the academics of the 1970s.[21] The outstanding professional exception, Mark Stoyle's book on Devon which appeared in 1996, could not have made a greater contrast with those preoccupations. It virtually wrote out localism and neutrality as potent forces, finding concealed partisan identity even in the Clubmen and arguing for the universal paramountcy of the division between royalist and parliamentarian. In this sense the writing of county histories had swung round a complete circle in half a century.[22] The same pattern was obvious in the most impressive case study of popular allegiance to be published in the same decade, John Walter's monograph on the Stour valley riots of August 1642.[23] It showed how the cloth-workers of the Colchester area had developed a local culture of fiercely evangelical Protestantism which made them natural and effective adherents of the parliamentarian cause as soon as hostilities commenced. This was popular partisanship with (literally) a vengeance.

What was lost in these more recent academic studies, fine and persuasive though they were within their own terms, was a clear sense of the distinction between the existence of ideological divisions and the willingness to translate that into physical violence. It is a distinction that, after all, lies at the heart of a civilised society, and its collapse in the English state in the 1640s was the factor that has made the Great Civil War so fascinating and so terrible. In my own book on the royalist war effort I characterised the conflict as 'an artificial insemination of violence into the local community'.[24] During the ten years after 1986, Ann Hughes, Peter Newman and Mark Stoyle were all to challenge me over this interpretation, holding that local partisans mobilised rapidly and eagerly, and over the same issues that produced the parties at a national level. The first and last also pointed out that certain towns, counties and regions had shown a marked partiality for one of the contending causes, associated with particular social and economic characteristics.[25] The distinction between our views turns on our interpretation of a single noun: that which I chose was not 'division' or 'ideology', but 'violence'. It is undeniable that differing opinions existed in the local communities of southern Britain in 1642, which matched those over which the war was to be fought and were sometimes passionately held. It is equally true that in many of those communities the supporters of one of the contending parties soon proved to be more numerous and effective than those of the other, or even (in examples as diverse as the overwhelming royalism of most of Wales and the parliamentarianism of Birmingham or Barnstaple) that one party never emerged at all.

What divides the historians of partisan enthusiasm from those who have also accorded importance to neutralism and localism is the recognition by the latter that in most areas the people who were initially prepared to commit their communities to a war effort were relatively few. The eruption of violence was the product of sustained and urgent pressure exerted on local populations by the two rival centres of command, working through the minority of local zealots and the handful of communities in which militant support for either party was early and vociferous. The historiography of the Civil War until the 1970s tended to regard it as a regrettable and tragic, but still noble and worthwhile, expression of important ideals and social tensions. Since 1980 there has been a tendency to return to that tone. It is obvious for historians who have concentrated more on the social and economic underpinnings of the conflict to view the latter more easily as a 'natural' development (though not an inevitable one). It is equally easy for scholars who study the passions and beliefs that inspired it to absorb from the latter an implicit attitude towards the fighting itself of indifference, acceptance or even approval. Only in that brief period between 1965 and 1980 did academic authors commonly manifest an acute consciousness of the intrinsic horror of civil bloodshed and question seriously whether the main English experience of it was either popular or worthwhile. Some of them have continued to articulate these reactions even though they have become less fashionable in general: when John Morrill's 1976 classic, *The Revolt of the Provinces*, went into a second edition in 1998, he gave it the subtitle *The People of England and the Tragedies of War*. In general, however, historians working since 1980 – in the period of the Falklands, Gulf and Afghan conflicts – have tended to be much less sensitive to, or interested in, the element of violence and suffering.[26]

* * *

The county and regional studies that appeared after 1965 did much to enhance understanding of the nature and course of the war itself, and of the logistics that underpinned it. For one thing, they established, more or less, what was its real history and what consisted of the inventions of parliamentarian pamphleteers. As has been said earlier, until the mid-1970s, historians still accepted as genuine major battles, and even campaigns, that had been invented wholly by the authors of cheap tracts issued in London. This process represented something of a minor publishing industry in late 1642, as the king advanced on the capital and Parliament's propagandists struggled to reassure the citizens that its adherents were still winning great victories somewhere in his rear.[27] Such fantasies were apparently the work of individual hacks working on their own initiative, anxious both to serve a political cause and to sell pamphlets, rather than a concerted official effort. They were ended by the establishment of a royalist newspaper, *Mercurius Aulicus*, in January 1643, which set new standards of reporting of military events and ruthlessly exposed the lies of hostile journalists. Until then, however, they were operating in a market in which they had no fear of contradiction and exposure, and had a small but significant impact in distorting knowledge of the early phases of the war.[28]

What the local studies also demonstrated was the unusual complexity of the conflict. It had about fifteen different theatres, within an overall area measuring no more than about five hundred by three hundred miles. By the first half of 1644, both the king and Parliament had eight different armies operating at once, and this figure does not take into account the commanders of large garrisons, who could mount their own local expeditions, or static bodies of soldiers such as the royalists permanently blockading the parliamentarian garrison of Plymouth. This pattern makes the local story of the war so important and engrossing, and its national history so excruciatingly difficult to write, unless by processes of drastic simplification and selection. Since 1970 important progress has been made in two different aspects of the subject, although they have not been integrated because of this overall difficulty of achieving a holistic view. The first consists of the basic logistics of recruiting and supplying soldiers. Here the county and regional studies really came into their own, and revealed a dual pattern. In the first six months, large and mobile forces were raised with great speed, partly because of partisan enthusiasm and partly because of the large sums that the military leaders offered in pay, in most cases drawing on their private resources and contributions made by local enthusiasts. Thereafter both money and manpower had to be obtained by duress, and armies tended to wax and wane drastically in size according to the hardships of service and the regularity and size of the payments made to members. In general, they held up well in numbers, or increased, if they were taking the offensive and winning actions. That process enabled them to live off the country even if they were not actually receiving money from their paymasters, and the profits of looting, taken after battle or after storming a town, could be considerable. Shrinkage or disintegration set in among forces that were put to long and hard marches to no obvious result, or had to remain stationary for long periods, or retired to home territory after a defeat.

The second area is that of the technicalities of warfare, and research here has been the most individual and unsystematic. It has always been the aspect of the subject that most academic historians have understood least, being left to specialists in military affairs; and in the case of the Civil War even the latter have not always been helpful. To state this is not to undervalue the considerable achievements of authors such as Peter Young, but to note that they tended to concentrate more on regimental histories and the reconstruction of particular campaigns and actions than the technical aspects of the fighting. As recently as the mid-1990s, I could not find either an academic or a popular book on the war which explained the practical difference between a culverin and a demi-cannon. The formal distinction was very clear, and often made so in the books: the former was a type of field gun that fired shot weighing fifteen to twenty pounds each and the latter was one that fired shot weighing twenty-four to thirty-eight pounds each.[29] The real significance of this, however, lay in the ballistic consequences: that the former could not by itself knock down a town or castle wall, and the latter could. Likewise, I found no secondary work that could explain why it was that medieval fortresses that were supposedly rendered obsolete by the invention of siege guns could hold out for months of constant bombardment in the Civil War. The answer provided by the primary sources was a dual one: an aspect of attack and one of defence. The former lay in the fact that some of the local forces operating in more remote areas did not have demi-cannon or whole cannon, the only artillery that could breach walls. Only Parliament's New Model Army, after June 1645, disposed of a siege train which included more than three guns firing shot over twenty pounds in weight and so could break through stone defences at more than one point within a few hours. The factor of defence was that even a medieval stone wall could hold out indefinitely against siege artillery if it had soil packed behind it, from its base to its parapet and more than fifteen feet in width. Castles or towns without this precaution would fall to a demi-cannon within a day; those who had invested in it could often only be starved out or else taken by undermining the defences. These basic facts matter because the siege was the basic military action of the war: it commenced with one (at Hull) and ended with one (at Harlech), and in the course of it over 300 strong points came under attack.

None of this sort of fundamental data were available even in specialist textbooks such as that on Civil War sieges by Peter Young and Wilfrid Emberton, which tended to narrate the course of the actions concerned rather than consider their logistics.[30] What has altered the picture is the development since 1980 of an entirely new sub-discipline, of Civil War archaeology. The systematic excavation of defences has been combined with written records to provide a much better sense of what was going on upon (and sometimes underneath) the ground.[31] This has explained, for example, why the king's forces could take one of the three biggest cities in the realm, Bristol, in one night, and immediately afterwards besiege the much smaller one of Gloucester, and fail to reduce it after a month. Historians have tended, following civilian royalist writers such as Clarendon, to blame mismanagement of the second siege, but excavation has revealed the reason for this pattern of events. Bristol had 1500 defenders stretched around a perimeter five miles in length, half of which consisted of nothing better than a shallow ditch in front of piled limestone blocks; the rock was just too hard for those digging into it to do better. Gloucester contained the same size of garrison, to defend only two miles of defences, most of which consisted of cannon-proof earthworks with projecting bastions and a flooded ditch 30-feet wide and 12 deep in front. The only sector that the royalists could reach was a high medieval stone wall packed behind with earth and with a 15-foot deep ditch before it. Under these circumstances they made probably the swiftest possible work of battering and undermining the wall, and would probably have taken the city within another week. What prevented them was that Parliament mobilised and despatched a large army for its relief, with a rapidity unique in the entire war. A knowledge of logistics also makes plain why the royalist city of York could hold out for two months against a combination of three enemy armies, even though it had a perimeter of almost four miles, defences consisting mainly of medieval walls, and a river dividing it: none of the besieging forces had guns any larger than culverins. After the city surrendered, one of those armies, led by the earl of Manchester, acquired a demi-cannon; and then the royalist fortresses of Yorkshire and Derbyshire fell to it like ninepins. The castles of Pontefract and Scarborough, however, had walls packed inside with earth, and resisted for almost another year.[32]

Knowledge of what goes on below the soil of battlefields can also transform or enhance impressions of what happened on its surface. Here archaeology has been much less systematic, but significant discoveries have still been made. The largest battle of the entire Civil War, and perhaps the biggest ever fought on English soil, was Marston Moor, in July 1644. By living next to the moor, and befriending the farmers who worked it, Peter Newman learned of the finds that they had made and were still making that indicated the pattern of the land at the time of the battle and of the fighting upon it. It had already been recognised that the royalists lost this pivotal action because they were outnumbered, and taken by surprise when an attack was launched on their lines in early evening. What the concentration of battlefield relics strongly indicated was that the standard plan of their disposition on the moor was not in fact how they were actually drawn up, but how they were intended to have been deployed. Twenty years later, Peter was able to deploy his knowledge of the terrain in conjunction with the more systematic plotting of buried artefacts by an expert in metal detecting, P.R. Roberts. They proved conclusively both that the surviving plan of the royalist dispositions did not correspond to their actual arrangement during the fighting, and that the King's men were taken so completely by surprise that the issue was essentially decided in a few minutes. That this could happen reflected heavily on the reputations of the two most celebrated soldiers on both sides: on the royalist Prince Rupert for failing so fatally to read his opponents' intentions, and on Oliver Cromwell for conducting the decisive assault with maximum efficiency.[33]

By the time of Peter Newman's second study, the same combination of techniques had been applied by Glenn Foard in his study of the other decisive battle of the war, Naseby. Once again the plans of the action drawn up by contemporary observers proved to have misled historians. This time they showed the initial dispositions of the rival armies accurately enough unit by unit, but gave a badly erroneous impression of how they corresponded to the ground itself, and therefore what happened when they clashed. The accounts of the action left by eyewitnesses, moreover, often telescoped important episodes in it. It was a combination of a close survey of the topography with a knowledge of the location of the military debris which had been dug up during the centuries since the battle that enabled Foard to reconstruct the latter in a manner that had never been possible before. He confirmed that the royalists had again lost because they were significantly outnumbered, but also that they had developed a plan of attack that was intended to compensate for their shortage of men. It was foiled only by the exceptional cohesion and discipline that had already been achieved by Parliament's freshly formed New Model Army, and the excellence of the latter's leadership.[34]

These advances in understanding of the practicalities of the war do, again, emphasise its homely scale. When Oliver Cromwell was sent to mop up the remaining royalist strongholds of Wiltshire and Hampshire in the last autumn of fighting, he towed with him a siege train of a strength hitherto unprecedented in the conflict, consisting of six guns, firing shot that between them weighed fifteen to sixty pounds. These enabled him to breach fortifications that had previously held out against all bombardments, and he swept the two counties clean in a few weeks.[35] To put these six pieces of siege artillery into perspective, it is worth bearing in mind that when the French king Charles VIII had invaded Italy one and a half centuries before, when the art of gunmaking was considerably less developed, he had taken a siege train of forty pieces. The Dutch had mounted 116 against the Spanish fortress of 's Hertogenbosch in 1629, and a deployment of 80 heavy guns would be routine for a siege in the Netherlands by this period.[36] In political terms, the English Civil War was a colossal affair; in military terms, it was a collection of miniature conflicts, and that is, of course, why it is so engrossing.

For much of the twentieth century, there was a tendency, especially in scholarly but non-academic writing, both to highlight the drama of the war and to downplay its impact on the life of the nation. This was a part of the nostalgic tendency, that set in towards the end of the Victorian period and intensified between the world wars, to construct a sense of enduring, organic and essentially imperturbable rural Englishness. This manifested in two successive mythical incidents. One, repeated as fact by no less a national representative than the Prime Minister, Stanley Baldwin, concerned a squire who galloped after his hounds near the two armies closing in to fight the battle of Edgehill, unaware that a civil war had broken out.[37] The populist, and subsequently more widely circulated, equivalent, was of a ploughman working at Marston Moor, who found himself surrounded by the rival armies and, on hearing that they represented King and Parliament, replied 'What, has they two fallen out again?'[38] Both stories were apocryphal, preposterous and deeply misleading, and have now vanished.

Some recent research has reinforced the point that, as seventeenth-century wars went, this one was relatively mild and decent. The American historian Barbara Donagan has consistently emphasised the manner in which the lack of clear geographical and religious boundaries between the two sides, and their derivation from the same society, limited the potential for hatred between them. Both tried to operate a military code that ultimately subordinated soldiers to the civil government, and invested heavily in treatment for sick and wounded soldiers and was intended to prevent barbarities and maintain order.[39] Stephen Porter has estimated that England's social and economic life sustained no lasting injury from the fighting. The latter produced no significant change in the social character of urban districts, and only served to enhance the difficulties of local trades that were already in decline, such as the Banbury shoemakers and the Lichfield cappers.[40]

The continuing work on local studies has, however, also deepened understanding of the other side of the picture. In the course of the whole struggle at least 150 towns and 50 villages sustained significant damage, and the second figure might plausibly be doubled.[41] The nation must indeed have had its quota of people who did well out of the hostilities by supplying equipment or expert services, but nobody was noted as making a fortune out of this work, and it never seems to have been of net benefit to any community. Stephen Porter has also estimated that it brought in a minimum of £500 000 worth of extra orders to London tradesmen,

but concluded that the drain of labour to the armies, the loss of the market represented by the royal court, and the disruption of commerce produced by the fighting, cost the capital a greater quantity of business; and London did better out of
the conflict than any other city except Norwich.[42] The research into local material
has confirmed that the murder or starvation of prisoners of war, the killing of civilians and the raping of women were all very rare, though each did occur. What it
has revealed instead is a tremendous amount of looting and bullying. For every
civilian who died at the hands of soldiers, there were thousands who got beaten up
and had their property pilfered. This war produced few examples of the sort of
behaviour that results from the complete collapse of social norms, and multitudes
of the sort of misdeeds that petty criminals and hooligans will routinely commit
given the opportunity.

* * *

None of these considerations have, however, been of central concern to most
historians of the period during the past twenty years. It is not the nature of the war
that has preoccupied most of them, but the reasons for the choice of allegiance by
partisans. This issue has produced the publications that have attracted general
attention, provoked most debate and engendered most of the essay titles and
examination questions set for school and university students. It reflects that concentration on the causation of major political events was a hallmark of mid-
twentieth-century history. For much of the 1970s there was an expectation that it
might be solved by the close attention to local experience that characterised the
interest in neutralism and the belief in the importance of the county community
as a conceptual tool. The prevalent hope was that if enough scholars read enough
documents dating from the early 1640s, recently arranged in brand new cardboard
boxes in county record offices, then the reasons why people took sides in the war,
or did not, would become obvious. This did not happen. By the 1980s it was clear
that very few people had left statements of any sort which made explicit their reasons for engaging in the conflict, or for trying to keep out of it. In default of these,
work had to be switched instead to the reconstruction of the contexts from which
civil strife had arisen. Historians began to x-ray English society in the early Stuart
period to detect reasons for the division into parties and to reassemble the complex
of mentalities from which internal strife arose.

Two historians above all devoted themselves to this task, having established
themselves as leaders of the genre of local studies in the 1970s and become determined to transcend its limitations. They were David Underdown and John Morrill.
Underdown's career had been a microhistory of the changes in interest and
emphasis among experts in the period. He had made his name with two books on
its central politics; one of them on conspiracies by the defeated and exiled royalists
during the 1950s, and the other – a blockbuster – on the partisan manoeuvres that

had produced the establishment of the English republic in 1649.[43] During the early 1970s he produced a county study of the Civil War and Interregnum in Somerset, but it stood out from the others in its much greater attention to traditional issues of class and party politics, its tendency to schematise local events much more strictly according to them, and its comparative lack of interest in neutralism as an independent force.[44] Instinctually, he seemed to be reaching for some explanatory model for the war, based on social and economic factors, to replace the traditional Marxist one that the work of the 1950s and 1960s had undermined. He was not alone in this quest, and two other attempts to achieve it had reached completion before his did. One was undertaken by Brian Manning, and represented an attempt to reassert the traditional Marxist interpretation in defiance of the recent refutations of it and with a disregard of the local sources on which they had been based. By using texts which in the main amounted to parliamentarian propaganda or the complaints of aristocratic royalist leaders, he asserted that Parliament had effectively led the party of the people, and the king that of ruling elites. It was an interpretation that begged the question of how Parliament had managed to attract the support of so many landowners and Charles I managed to recruit so many commoners to his armies.[45] An opposite model was constructed by an American, William Hunt, who made a case study of the county of Essex, drawing on the insights provided by a new wave of social historians such as Keith Wrightson. Themselves based heavily on the excellent Essex records, they had portrayed a polarisation of rich and poor in English parishes during the years between 1560 and 1640, produced by population pressure and a largely consequent rise in prices. In their vision, radical Protestantism, commonly known as puritanism, represented a useful ideology for the new local elites being produced by these changes, for it gave them a concept of themselves as an elect minority of godly, with a divine mandate to care for and to discipline their social and economic inferiors. As puritanism was very strongly associated with Parliament's party in the Civil War, this was effectively the story of the construction of the Essex parliamentarians.[46] As a county study it worked relatively well, but on a national level it begged the question of why the majority of the nation's landowners had not become puritans, and why most of those who had taken a side at the opening of the war had been royalist. Both Manning and Hunt, using very different sources, had produced diametrically opposed analyses that left the major problems of Civil War allegiance completely unsolved.

David Underdown believed that he had found the solution to this conundrum in a suggestion made by two other colleagues back in the 1960s. First, Joan Thirsk had pointed out that early modern industry had developed more easily in areas of forest and pasture than in those of arable farming, because of weaker social restraints and land divisions in the former. She suggested that the former districts also produced a greater independence of spirit and tendency to riot, and wondered whether this pattern might have some bearing on political rebellions in the Tudor and Stuart period.[47] Alan Everitt echoed this suggestion and extended it to religion, proposing that radical ideas had prospered better in the greater freedom of the wood-and-pasture communities.[48] By 1972, in Christopher Hill's bestseller *The World Turned Upside Down*, this speculation had already been accorded something of the status of truth. The areas of forest and wasteland were places of freedom and mobility, largely beyond the control of established clergy or gentry and nurseries of independent religious sects or even of witchcraft. It was an idea that seemed rooted in scientific fact, wedding the old Marxist economic determinism with the new concern for ecology. It also, however, drew on traditional images with powerful emotional resonance, of shepherds as exemplars of careless joy and of the greenwood as the home of the merry outlaw band. Around the borders of Hill's picture stalked the figure of Robin Hood.[49]

During the 1970s Underdown picked up this concept and ran with it, working his way carefully through the local records of Gloucestershire, Somerset and Dorset. These were ample for the investigative task that he had set himself, but also represented a personal homecoming for him, as a historian based in New England who had grown up at Wells. By the end of the decade he was publishing essays to support it, and his research was fully laid on the table in 1985, with the appearance of *Revel, Riot and Rebellion*.[50] This was a full-length study of the interrelation of politics, religion, economics and culture in the West Country between 1600 and 1660 which represented a powerhouse of ideas and a treasure-house of information. Its most celebrated contention – which was discussed to the point of eclipsing the other glories of such a rich book – was that land use had determined much of the pattern of allegiance in the Civil War. Forest, pasture and cloth-making areas tended naturally to puritanism in religion and parliamentarianism in politics, while, arable and downland regions were as naturally prone to conservative Anglicanism and to royalism.

This argument made an immediate appeal, and won great plaudits, from historians who were predisposed to take a schematic view of social relationships, as rooted primarily in economic patterns; it could be taken, as said, for a more sophisticated and timely reworking of the old Marxist model. It was disputed by others who were not so predisposed. The first heavyweight challenger was John Morrill, who faulted both Underdown's use of sources and his sense of ecology. In Morrill's scheme of things, wood, pasture and arable settlements were not clearly distinct social entities, and puritanism was found in both, especially in counties such as Essex that lay outside Underdown's chosen region.[51] One placed directly alongside it is Wiltshire, and that had been the subject of a monograph by Martin Ingram that directly considered the cultural history of people living in both sorts of terrain in the early Stuart period. He concluded that there was no significant distinction between them.[52] In 1991 Ann Hughes's textbook, *The Causes of the English Civil War*, reviewed the whole debate and pronounced that what had become known as 'the Underdown thesis' was seriously flawed. She concluded that it was impossible to draw straightforward conclusions about economic and social change or harmony simply from an examination of farming practices, let alone religious and cultural characteristics and Civil War allegiances. Coming from a leading historian of the war, who had initially been inclined to accept the thesis, this was fairly decisive.[53]

At the same time, almost every critic of the thesis had accepted that it had valuable aspects, and the work of the 1990s served more sharply to distinguish them. Ecological determinism was finally thrown out of the picture. The most devastating attack on it was by Buchanan Sharp, who demonstrated that most of the wood–pasture areas of Somerset, one of the counties studied by Underdown himself, were neither puritan nor parliamentarian: if they tended to any characteristic political stance, it was neutralism and independence.[54] I went over the records of his three counties in turn, and suggested that they were not sufficient to underpin the conclusions that they had drawn from them.[55] Mark Stoyle studied another neighbouring shire, Devon, and again found that distinctions between farming districts did not correspond, overall, to local patterns of wartime allegiance, and Simon Osborne reached the same conclusion for the midlands.[56] When the bathwater of determinism had been thrown away, however, there were not one but two healthy babies whom the Underdown thesis could leave to posterity. One was the demonstration that common people in the provinces could take a keen interest in national politics and make their own decisions as to how to react to them and upon them. The other was the proof that significant patterns of local allegiance did exist, more conservative Anglican areas with robust traditions of communal festivity being notably more royalist and those of obvious evangelical Protestantism being more parliamentarian. Furthermore, those patterns were linked to economic factors, some trades (such as mariner and clothier) being much more inclined to the support of Parliament and others (such as miner) to the king, although communities could always be found to buck these overall trends. Local ecological considerations did not seem to determine wartime loyalties, but local cultural traditions did, and it had been David Underdown, more than anybody else, who had drawn attention to these. For this reason, *Revel, Riot and Rebellion* remains one of the greatest history books of the 1980s.

Simultaneously, John Morrill was making his own attempt to explain partisan loyalties. He heralded his hypothesis in a series of essays between 1982 and 1985, which were summed up in his ringing statement that 'The English Civil War was not the first European revolution: it was the last of the Wars of Religion.'[57] He promised his readers a book, *England's Wars of Religion*, in which this argument would be fully developed. In part it was an attempt to counter the tendency, obvious for most of the twentieth century, to assimilate the Civil War and its consequences to 'classic' modern revolutions such as the French and Russian, and to relate it instead more clearly to the context of its own age. It was also, however, a natural extension of Morrill's own work on local records, which showed that religion was often the force which pushed activists forward. He had stated this clearly in 1976, even when he was concentrating more closely on neutralism and localism; 'Quite simply, in most counties the active royalists are the defenders of episcopacy who saw in puritanism a fundamental challenge to all society and order, and the parliamentarians are those determined to introduce a godly reformation which might, for a few of them, leave room for bishops, but in most cases did not.'[58] Towards the end of the 1970s, galled by the jibes that historians such as he had proved why the war could not have happened, he set out to concentrate on activism, and developed the argument for the primacy of religion. He never suggested that it was the sole reason for choices of allegiance, but proposed, powerfully, that it was the one that had the power to push people forward to commence a civil war. There was a lot of obvious truth in this argument, and like the Underdown thesis it stood in a long tradition. If that behind David Underdown's ideas led ultimately back to Marx, then the argument for the division of royalist and parliamentarian being essentially along religious lines had been made by that other mighty progenitor of twentieth-century historians of the Stuarts, Gardiner. The latter had stated quite firmly that constitutional questions alone would never have brought England to war in 1642, and that what propelled people to fight were incompatible views of the Church.[59]

This being so, it is remarkable how much criticism the trailers for Morrill's projected book actually received; the more effective for the fact that it tended to be expressed verbally rather than in print.[60] His greatest methodological weakness derived from his instinctual continuation of the prevailing tendency to concentrate on the parliamentarians and regard them as normative. There is certainly a lot of evidence for personal religious commitment on the part of parliamentarians, and the language with which Parliament promoted and defended its cause is soaked in evangelical Protestantism. It is also true that, as a body rebelling against the highest traditional human authority in the land, the monarch, Parliament *had* to cite the cause of God as its own, in order to appeal to the only greater authority in the cosmos, but the extent of religiosity among its supporters outran the demands of purely tactical considerations. The real problem was that the royalists exhibited nothing like an equivalent concern with religion, as the few historians who studied them in this context – Peter Newman, David Smith and Gerald Aylmer – pointed out.[61] They attached far more importance to social issues and those of loyalty and honour, so that in this respect the two parties were asymmetrical. It was a situation very unlike that of the classic, early modern Wars of Religion, as fought out between Protestant and Catholic on the Continent, and the part played by religious issues was significantly less straightforward than it was in the preceding rebellion of the Scottish Covenanters against Charles I, or the contemporary struggle between the Catholic Confederacy and its opponents in Ireland.

The main conceptual weakness of John Morrill's model was that religion was not a watertight phenomenon in early Stuart culture: it interwove with political, social and economic attitudes. This was highlighted in Ann Hughes's textbook on the causes of the war, published in 1991,[62] and was given particular point by a series of studies of individual cities, culminating in a set published in 1992.[63] They showed that the classic division within a large urban centre was between a dominant oligarchy of wealthy merchants, conservative Anglican in religion and royalist in allegiance, and an outer group of lesser merchants and retailers, puritan in religion and parliamentarian in politics, and determined to use the war as a means of breaking into the privileges of the former group. The test case of this pattern was David Scott's study of York, where for once it was reversed and accidents of local circumstance produced a dominant pre-war clique who were puritan and favoured Parliament at the outbreak of hostilities. The obvious question to be asked here is whether the disadvantaged merchants and retailers of York tended to be conservative Anglicans and royalists in response, and indeed they did.

It must be restated, however, that none of these considerations robbed John Morrill's model of most of its strength. The Underdown thesis had been flawed in fundamentals even while it was tremendously fruitful in drawing attention to particular issues and perspectives of study. The Morrill thesis was overstated, but it had a solid foundation in truth. Furthermore it prefigured the trend of historiography in the 1990s, which was to give prominence to ideology as a force in its own right, and religion as one of its most powerful and transformative manifestations. By contrast, David Underdown's work now seems to have represented a late and gallant rearguard action to save a place for economic determinism in human affairs, at a time when scholarly opinion was starting to move against it.

All this being so, it is significant that the criticisms made their mark, and *England's Wars of Religion* was never published. Had it appeared alongside *Revel, Riot and Rebellion* in the mid-1980s, then it would have been a book of the same kind; faulty in major respects and yet still unmistakably great. Instead John Morrill republished the most important of the earlier essays in 1993, with a retrospective overview that expressed an awareness of both their strengths and their limitations.[64] He acknowledged the force of the arguments against them outlined above, but restated his belief that religious factors were the most important single element of the whole complex which formed Civil War allegiances, and the one most effective in propelling people to take up arms, especially against the king. There is no doubt of the truth of this, and Morrill's work played a major part in bringing about a recognition of it. The loss of *England's Wars of Religion* testifies to the honourable and sensitive nature of the would-be author, but also to the treatment which his ideas were initially accorded. Unlike the Underdown thesis, they appealed to no pre-existing and established set of prejudices, and so found no immediate and enthusiastic group of supporters.

* * *

Towards the end of the century, views of the problem of why people chose sides in the war – or did not – had come to take four different forms. Collectively, they had disturbing implications for the grand project of the 1970s and 1980s, of solving the problem by use of local records, first by examining those for the outbreak of war itself and then by employing them to build up a picture of the strains in pre-war society that might have determined how people behaved. One of the four viewpoints was represented most obviously by Ann Hughes and Norah Carlin, both of them authors characterised by a particular interest in the social underpinnings of the conflict and in radical religious and political ideas which was (ultimately) a legacy of Marxist historiography. Towards the end of the 1990s they produced or reissued textbooks which confidently reasserted the utility of an approach that related social changes both to central politics and to local patterns of partisan loyalty.[65] It is important to note the differences between their interpretations and those made by writers more directly and explicitly influenced by Marxism in the middle decades of the century. They did not attempt to argue that the war itself had been caused by specific developments in society that had made conflict either likely or inevitable, and shattered the traditional framework of political and religious life. They had absorbed all the lessons of 1970s revisionism, and reshaped them to argue that the Civil War was the product of many different factors, and that particular contingencies of personality and events had combined with long-term structural problems to produce a breakdown in central politics. What they insisted on was that alterations in society still represented one of the factors that had led to war. Carlin was most explicit in adapting the Marxist model that conflict had been produced by the emergence of a new middle class which had seized power as a result of it. In her formulation, a newly enlarged and self-confident 'middling sort' of society had acted as a catalyst to political quarrels within the traditional ruling elite of landowners, polarising divisions over religion, politics and government in 1640–42 and especially supporting the idea that power in the state ultimately derived from the mass of its people. Hughes postulated a more diffuse pattern by which social change produced anxieties at all levels of the nation which fed into cultural conflicts and abetted political breakdown. She emphasised in particular that similar ideologies and mentalities, often conflicting, were found in most parts of the country and among all social groups. This meant that national leaders were often profoundly influenced by what they took to be the expectations and opinions of common people, both in the capital and the provinces. Such a process suggested that the best model for the play of forces that caused the war was neither one of an explosion of tension within society as a whole, which blew away central politics, nor of a collapse of relationships between politicians at the centre which ruptured local communities. It was a complex interplay of fears, hopes, pressures and needs between the political leaders concentrated in the capital, and the constituent parts of the nation.

These suggestions carry a great deal of weight, and in general the picture that they present can be regarded as acceptable to most experts currently working in the field. There are, however, two major problems with it. The first is that it demonstrates effectively that southern Britain in 1640–42 contained an identifiable mixture of social, ideological and political tensions, which bore some relation to the way in which civil conflict broke out and to the form which that conflict took. It provides a context for the war, and so goes far towards providing an understanding of its nature. What it does not do is show exactly how those component tensions interacted to produce the conflict.

Those who might argue that this is hardly necessary, because an understanding of the context of the war is essentially the same thing as an understanding of its causes, have to reckon with the second major difficulty in the Hughes–Carlin model. This is that it relies too much on a view of English, Welsh and Cornish society in the pre-war period as being like a rock fissured with faults. Whether the rock explodes from within, or is broken by a blow from the top, it is going to break along those lines of pre-existing weakness. To a great extent, this is actually what seems to have happened at the outbreak of war, but there are frequent cases that contradict the pattern. In Herefordshire and Somerset, the county in the 1630s had been divided between rival networks of gentry families, who sometimes incorporated national issues into their quarrels.[66] It would be expected that with the coming of war, those opposed blocs would automatically metamorphose into the local royalist and parliamentarian leadership, but the reverse occurred. Confronted with the new issues and emotions of 1642, the groups shattered and reformed, old enemies becoming allies and friendships turning to enmities. All over the north of England in the pre-war period, Anglican gentry had been accustomed, in their capacity as justices and deputy lieutenants, to watching, disarming and fining their Roman Catholic neighbours, a process that reached a new pitch of suspicion and activity in the winter of 1641–42, with the outbreak of a major Catholic uprising in Ireland. Soon after the coming of civil war, however, many of those same gentry armed and recruited the same Catholics to reinforce the royalist army and garrisons, and fought alongside them as comrades until the end of hostilities. The earl of Derby was a notably just and generous landlord, and a popular local magnate, but when war came some of his tenants fought against him, for Parliament, and embittered relations between them permanently.[67] It is now generally recognised that the explosion of radical ideas that marked the mid- and late 1640s was a result of the transformative impact of war on the imaginations of many of the English, and not a cause of the fighting itself. What must be acknowledged is that the traumatic and unprecedented events of 1640–42 already possessed the capacity to reconfigure and disrupt traditional patterns of thought and instinct, rather than simply to reproduce them.

This raises the possibility that in many cases Civil War allegiances were not pre-determined at all, and that it is necessary to restore mobility and dynamism to a picture that has too often been rendered static by the work of historians concerned with the origins of the conflict. There has been a tendency to reduce to parties, models and constructs phenomena that in reality consisted more of currents, moments and reactive outbursts. It may be wise to think more in terms of rhetorical positions, cathartic experiences, flows of information and changes of mind and of language. Such an approach represents a second viewpoint manifested in the historiography of the subject during the late 1990s, and has borne most obvious fruit in the work of Andy Wood on the Derbyshire miners, an indication of the pitch of sophistication to which local studies of the war have been raised, and the riches that might yet be garnered from them.[68] He explicitly criticised the lingering elements of socio-economic determinism in the thought of historians such as Underdown and Hughes, as a hangover from Marxist theory. The mining communities whom he studied formed a self-assertive and independent local society of commoners, occupying a landscape of wilderness and pasture: a classic breeding ground for parliamentarianism in the determinist models. They had not, however, manifested any general tendency to puritanism or hostility to the royal policies of the 1630s. Nor was their wartime allegiance determined by relations with the local gentry with whom they had frequently clashed over rights and dues, and who attempted to remain neutral as the national parties formed. Instead they divided in their responses to the war. The king bought the active support of many by offering direct economic concessions, while others turned to Parliament apparently because of personal links to local parliamentarian leaders or the misbehaviour of royalist soldiers crossing their district. Their loyalties proved to be both multifaceted and determined by short-term experience and opportunism.

The problem here is that even such a detailed study as this, based on unusually good local sources, relies ultimately on conjecture to account for some of the behaviour of the people concerned. There is a real danger that the number of variables involved in the responses made by most communities to the events of 1640–46, and by the individuals in them, were too great and too mutable, and the evidence too patchy, for safe conclusions to be drawn. A third scholarly position possible by the end of the century was, therefore, one of despair. This was invited most clearly by a textbook by Malcolm Smuts, who noted the lack of consensus among experts over why the war occurred, and commented that 'the problem may be that we are dealing with historical processes so complex that simple models of causation cannot adequately describe them. What is needed is more nuanced and closely textured analysis. Perhaps the most important example is the challenge of explaining relationships between religion, social change and politics.'[69] No expert in the subject would disagree with him; but many might be tempted to point out that this challenge had been attempted repeatedly for thirty years, in studies that had attempted to be as 'nuanced and closely textured' as possible. The records only survive to permit such an analysis in a few areas, and any case studies based on those must face the question of how representative they are. When looking at the related question of the nature and course of the war, Smuts added that 'we cannot filter out all the myths and polemical distortions from the story ... since many of these are integral to it. Knowing what actually happened can sometimes be less important than appreciating what contemporaries believed.'[70] Here he may be credited with a certain amount of vested interest, as a scholar whose own speciality lies in the study of literary texts, but the point that he makes can be given a more disturbing spin: that knowing what actually happened is generally much more difficult than appreciating what contemporaries believed. Indeed, the former may not be possible, whereas the latter is. Smuts acknowledged this himself, hesitantly and obliquely, by drawing attention to the undoubted tremendous increase in the printed discussion of politics and religion within the English state from 1641. He commented that 'the impact of this material on the country is not easily assessed'.[71]

Pessimism regarding the practicalities of making such assessments is increased by the diminishing number of scholars willing to undertake the work. During the 1990s those already immersed in the period continued, for the most part, to make contributions to it, but the supply of young reinforcements notably slackened. This was no doubt partly because of shifts of academic fashion. In practical terms, a subject already so heavily worked over, and in which the difficulties of evidence and interpretation had now been so abundantly displayed, was no longer a very inviting one. Ideological factors also played a part, as the new boom in cultural studies lured budding historians away from the continued struggle to explain major political events. Underpinning this last development, however, was a more profound and significant alteration. The Civil War had been central to the preoccupations of mid-twentieth century British society: with class, occupation and local community. It had also played a lesser, although still important, part in the American struggle to define a much more racially and culturally heterogenous nation-state in terms of a common set of political and social values achieved by a particular history. With the 1980s, economic forces propelled both nations into a world in which the traditional traits of class were fractured and geographical and occupational mobility dissolved accepted notions of community. The USA began to lose its sense of a common history that could accommodate all its citizens. Identity was increasingly defined throughout the western world in terms of gender, sexuality, transferable talents and ethnicity, and although the political and military events in England in the 1640s could be incorporated into such historical perspectives, in books or university seminar topics with titles like 'Women in the English Civil War', they were essentially peripheral to them. In this context it is significant that the young historian to write about them with most consistency and passion was Mark Stoyle, who discovered the one point at which they intersected with the new preoccupations: by treating them as examples of Welsh and Cornish separatist identity and its relationship with the English.[72] This was the fourth approach visible to the subject by the end of the twentieth century, and an important one although not capable of accommodating more than a few specialists.

It may be questioned whether these changes in the preoccupations of professional intellectuals will be reproduced straightforwardly in those of the English,
Welsh and Cornish public. In the year 2001 a powerful commissioning editor for
one of the five British public television channels declared that 'when it comes to
history, what we want is good stories – told *again*'. Even given the vagaries of policy in the broadcasting world, there was sound sense in this. History began its life
as tale-telling, the more alluring in that the tales concerned were supposed to be
representations of actual events, and that by listening to them, people might
understand how they came to be as they are, and perhaps how they might be
something different. The Civil War is a very engrossing story, or rather a whole
bundle of them, and can bear a lot of retelling.

This became very apparent in 1992, with the 350th anniversary of the outbreak
of the fighting. Academic exhaustion with the subject was manifest in the comparative absence of professional reaction to the date. The 300th anniversary of the
revolution of 1688, just four years before, had been celebrated with a cluster of
major conferences and publications involving leading historians of the period. The
year 1992, by contrast, elicited a major survey of the nature of the fighting and an
important collection of essays on the war's local dimension, but little else.
Furthermore, the survey was the work of a scholar based in the United States, and
the collection inspired and edited by one whose own publications had hitherto
consisted mainly of bibliographical surveys.[73] This comparative neglect was made
the more striking by the celebrations of the date held outside the academic system.
Town councils, local and national newspapers, amateur historians, museums and
societies united to produce a series of commemorative events that represented key
moments in regional festive calendars and tourist seasons. The Tower of London
Armouries mounted an exhibition that travelled between local capitals to considerable publicity and attracted a proportionately large number of visitors. The gap
left by the relative lack of academic participation was to some extent filled by the
Sealed Knot Society and its offspring the English Civil War Society, which provided
enthusiastic support for many of the civic commemorations and won much grati-
tude for doing so.[74] Since the mid-1990s, authors working outside the university
system have continued to pour out books on aspects of the war, without any sign
of the slackening of interest and output so manifest inside the academy.[75]

The Great Civil War remains, therefore, a major event in the public memory and
imagination. The contrast between its survival as one and the relative decline of its
status among academic historians may be simply a matter of time-lag, as the people who organised the commemorations of the 1990s were all or mostly educated
at least twenty years before, when excitement over the subject was at its peak in the
universities. It may, however, prove to be one of the points at which academics part
company with society about them. There is every sign at present as if the war
has become an integral part of modern popular history, rooted in landscapes,

monuments, literature and summer entertainment: at once a national epic and a patchwork of kitchen sink dramas. To the important new industry of 'heritage' that burgeoned in the last three decades of the twentieth century, it is a feature of the past with exceptional utility. Today's public has made the war its own, and it seems likely that anything that academic specialists think of it in the future must be tangential, supportive or irrelevant to that development.

3 The New Framework for Early Stuart Studies

In Chapter 1 of this book, it was suggested that the process of revisionism, and its critics, had between them contributed to a genuine increase in both the depth and the sophistication of modern knowledge of early Stuart history. It was also argued that the debates had achieved a large measure of consensus on many important points, producing a new model for interpretation of the period. Chapter 2 implied a very different set of conclusions: that the data is probably not sufficient to permit the resolution of major questions concerning the Great Civil War, that experts adopt different approaches, and that a gulf may be opening in the subject between the academy and the general public. There is need now to show how these two pictures fit together, and it can be done by suggesting that academic scholars have recently and collectively established a framework within which early Stuart politics in general, and the background to the war in particular, make much better sense. This achievement has been a direct product of the dialectic of argument between revisionist and post-revisionist work in the period, and can now be explored in some detail.

Once again, the Great Civil War stands on its own as a watershed. The origins of the Second and Third Civil Wars, and of all the tangled politics and intellectual and religious ferment of the late 1640s, are hardly a matter for controversy: they were the direct consequences of that first gigantic struggle. Furthermore, that struggle still dominates the study of the preceding four decades of English history. When all necessary strictures have been made against the folly of reading history backwards, and of projecting the divisions of the 1640s into the early part of the century, it remains true that the first attempt of the Stuart dynasty to rule England ended in a failure more absolute than that of any other royal house, before or since. This inevitably directs attention to the questions of how stable the English polity had been between 1600 and 1640, and whether it had been dominated by features that propelled it towards disintegration, whether such features had been present but were long muted or marginal, or whether they appeared suddenly in the years immediately before the breakdown. In providing a better picture of the reasons for

that breakdown, scholars have focused on five distinct components of the early
Stuart state, each illustrating different aspects of the historian's work.

* * *

The first component is structural and functional, and its revelation represented
the greatest early victory of revisionism. It was a practical weakness in the early-
seventeenth-century English state, which was driving it towards breakdown and
impelling its rulers to desperate measures. The detection of it by historians represented a (literal) textbook case of how pioneering research into archival sources
could force the rethinking of a long-established historical orthodoxy, and it was
one to which Conrad Russell, in particular, drew attention.[1] In the mid-sixteenth
century, the English monarchy possessed a system of government finance which,
although based on much smaller resources and less ruthless extractive processes
than those followed by the new superpowers of France and Spain, was still efficient.
By 1600 it was the most backward in Europe, with the single exception of the
Scottish state with which it was about to be combined. The change had occurred
simply because it had been allowed to run down, in a period of inflation and
expensive warfare which required that more than usual attention should have been
paid to renovating and overhauling it. The customs rates were left at the level at
which they had been fixed in the 1550s, and new commodities passing in or out
of the nation were ignored. Similar neglect of the other branches of the ordinary
revenue meant that by the 1600s the total regular income of the sovereign had
fallen by 40 per cent in real terms. At the same time the assessment rolls on which
depended the staple unit of war taxation, the 'subsidy' voted by Parliament, were
left unrevised in a half-century in which the value of money itself was falling and
taxpayers were becoming ever more efficient in evading payments under the existing system. The person who should have been most concerned about the problem,
Elizabeth's long-serving Lord Treasurer, William Cecil, himself enjoyed an income
of about £4000 a year, and returned for tax purposes earnings of £133 per annum.
This meant that during the course of this queen's reign, extraordinary grants of
subsidy from Parliament were needed to cover a quarter of the regular expenses of
government, and war taxation was adequate for less than half the actual cost of the
wars. Solvency was maintained only by extreme parsimony, by borrowing, by
defaulting on bills, by sub-contracting military operations to commanders, and by
holding the salaries of state servants at a level that forced them to take fees and
bribes, obtain unpopular rights to license economic monopolies, and embezzle
state revenue, in order to make a worthwhile profit from office. Onto this collapsing system, at the opening of the seventeenth century, was thrown the burden of
the newly conquered kingdom of Ireland, a discontented, impoverished and
divided land which functioned in a structural sense as an independent state and in
reality as a colony of the English Crown and part of its political spoils system. To
ensure its own security, the government in Dublin needed regular subsidies from

England, which by 1610 accounted for about two-thirds of the annual deficit of the English royal revenue.

The fault for this mounting crisis can be laid firmly with Elizabeth herself. A case can be made that in the early decades of her reign her government was too preoccupied with carrying out a religious reformation, and in the later decades with a major war, to afford the time to reform the fiscal system or the risk of tax revolts if it were made more efficient. It could also be argued that the same period saw a considerable increase in local taxation, which reduced the resources to be tapped by central government and took up some of the latter's burdens. In the last analysis, however, nothing can excuse the queen's own constant neglect of the matter or can remove the conclusion that it may be attributed ultimately to her own pathological dislike of change and her indifference to the problems of her successors. She certainly ensured that the latter would be tremendous, and that a foreign king, James VI of Scotland and I of England and Ireland, would be faced with a financial system in desperate need of overhaul and an English political nation which was completely unaware of the difficulty and so not disposed to believe in it. The new burden of the subsidies to the Irish government met with equally little understanding and sympathy in England, and indeed it has plausibly been argued that Elizabeth's military pacification of Ireland was itself an expensive mistake, as that realm would have been both loyal and cheaply administered if left to its native lords and medieval Anglo-Norman settlers.[2]

James's decisive bid to get the necessary reforms through a Parliament was made in 1610, and failed because of mutual distrust between him and the House of Commons. The government only survived by imposing new customs duties on its own authority, which was an act of dubious legality and created an enduring source of resentment and argument between the Crown and the MPs of successive Parliaments. When Charles I succeeded in 1625, he was not awarded the normally automatic right to levy customs dues, until the matter was constitutionally settled; which it never was. Instead, he attempted to fight wars with both France and Spain in the later 1620s, and failed in them largely because the system of war taxation had further decayed, to a point where only a minority of the sums expected could actually be raised. The inability of MPs to appreciate the scale of the crisis contributed mightily to a further embittering of their relations with the king, and his decision to rule without them during the 1630s.

The discovery of this sequence of events rendered untenable the traditional account of early Stuart history. In that account, Elizabeth had featured as the wise and successful ruler against whose record the failure of the Stuart kings seemed the more glaring. Now she became a selfish and negligent politician who had bought peace for herself largely at the price of trouble for all those who survived her, both rulers and ruled. James and Charles could now be regarded not as wilful petty tyrants, anxious to increase their own power by trampling over the conventions of English politics and stretching their royal prerogative, but as men who had been handed an almost unworkable state machine and got the blame when they tried to explain that there was something wrong with it. Their own actions, and the trouble into which they got with English Parliaments, became much more intelligible, and to be viewed with a far higher level of sympathy. This, at any rate, was the revisionist case, and those who criticised it were able only to point out that the personal failings of the Stuarts made a difficult situation much worse. James was a spendthrift who ran a court and government notorious for greed, profiteering and scandal, and so made belief in the reality of the financial problem far harder. Charles was destitute of most of the political skills that might have won over Houses of Commons, and the diplomatic and military bungling of his regime compounded the weakness of his war machine. It is difficult to argue credibly, however, that neither of them would have done considerably better had they not been put in charge of a financial structure which was in the process of disintegration.

This discovery reinforced a sense of paradox that had been appearing in early Stuart historiography since sustained research into the local government of the period had commenced with the boom in county record offices. On the one hand this was now revealed as a period of backward, fragile and weakening central government, its fiscal system in advanced decay, its war-making capacity badly atrophied and the partnership between the monarch and the other parts of Parliament breaking down. On the other, government as a whole was growing larger and more active and the range of its services greatly extending, with a growing sense that public policy objectives extended far beyond dynastic ambition. The centre was becoming steadily more efficient in communicating its priorities to the provinces, through ever more numerous and elaborate chains of command. In every respect, institutions of governance were becoming more active.[3] The picture, therefore, was of a weak and dysfunctional early Stuart state which also engaged in ever more ambitious projects of social reform and control, with considerable success.

This does seem to have been the actual situation, however lop-sided it may appear now. The fiscal and military capacities of the monarchy were in a woeful condition, while its capacity to mobilise money and people to relieve poverty and famine, carry out measures against plague, and provide justice, were probably the most highly developed and effective in Europe. This result was achieved largely because, in a kingdom where local office-holding was unsalaried and in the hands of established social and economic elites – at every level – the measures to relieve social problems were those for which people were prepared to pay and to work. It helps to explain why the Civil War was, in so many respects, a local event, as this tradition of powerful parish and county government was mobilised for the evident needs of defence, usually in the cause of the warring parties, and sometimes in that of neutralism. It also, however, gives the conflict a pivotal importance in the process by which central government overhauled and improved its military machinery. In this perspective, the 1620s saw the effective collapse of the Tudor state, and the 1630s the final attempt to repair it, in the measures of Charles I's

Personal Rule. The failure of these precipitated the war itself; indeed, Conrad Russell has argued that the continued inability of Parliament to provide the necessary reform of the king's revenue gave him a powerful incentive for desperate measures; having outlawed the expedients by which he had kept the books balanced in the 1630s, and failed as yet to substitute other sources of income, the Commons had condemned the government to still greater problems.[4]

In the course of the war, sheer military necessity forced both parties to tax the wealth of the nation effectively and heavily, in a manner never attempted before, and to erect a powerful complex of armed services upon it. The insecurity of the succeeding parliamentary and republican regimes ensured the maintenance of this efficient new system, and for that reason there is something like an agreement among scholars that the period between 1640 and 1660 solved the essential problems of the English fiscal-military state, and laid the foundations for the ability of the future United Kingdom to achieve world power.[5] Two additions to this view can be suggested here. The first is that built into it is usually an acknowledgement that the conversion of first the English and then the British state into a first-rank military force was a long process, and what was commenced in the 1640s was not approaching anything like completion for half a century after that. There is less unanimity on what, precisely, was left incomplete. To one authority on the subject, the essential overhaul of the system was made by the 1650s, and substantially finished by the early 1670s, while to another, the Restoration period left the government with a diminished access to resources for making war, and the decisive development came in the 1690s. This consisted of the provision of efficient credit institutions to complement the reforms already made in taxation and administration.[6] Both views have merit, as they emphasise different features of the state as important. The problem can be summed up here as one of acceptance and consent; that the Civil War demolished the remnants of the Tudor state and created the machinery that would make England a major military power, but the succeeding fifteen years proved that it had not made that machinery politically acceptable. This achievement was indeed left until the period between 1688 and 1714.

The other observation is that, in accordance with the general tendency to concentrate on parliamentarians, historians have underestimated the contribution of the royalists to the improvement of English fighting power. The benchmark for the transition from military backwardness to military efficiency has generally been fixed at the creation of Parliament's New Model Army in 1645, the force that won the war and went on to provide the subsequent basis for the spectacular English military achievements of the following eighteen years. What might be suggested is that the New Model represented the digestion of lessons originally taught by the king and his supporters, into a form linked to good leadership and the economic power and population base of London and south-eastern England. Parliament's system of assessment for war taxation was itself based on that developed by Charles's government in his Personal Rule, for its controversial levy of Ship Money.

The Self-Denying Ordinance, whereby the parliamentarian forces were purged in early 1645 of all their aristocratic generals and many of their greater gentry, was preceded by a series of measures by the king, instituted within a year of the war's beginning. By these, he replaced local aristocratic commanders with men who had proved their worth as soldiers and were normally strangers to the regions placed under their military control. The social alteration was to some extent masked by his ability to promote his new warlords to peerages, thereby giving the illusion of a continuity of noble power.[7] The royalists were also responsible for three major innovations in military technology. When fortifying towns on the borders of their territory, they gave them earthworks of the latest European type, proof against cannon shot and with bastions for flanking fire, providing defences of a sophistication that Parliament was only to build subsequently. They introduced cavalry tactics developed by the Swedish king Gustavus Adolphus in the previous decade, of breaking the enemy by force of impact on the first attack, instead of sending in successive lines reliant on pistol fire and disengagement. Finally, they gave English siege craft the tactic of mining, the blowing up of fortifications by explosive charges placed in tunnels beneath. These novelties were partly the result of the fact that Charles was able to recruit more experienced officers than Parliament at the war's beginning – the last two were proposed by his German nephew Rupert – and partly of his need to compensate for his initial relative lack of arms, munitions and money. They helped to bring him very close to victory, or a compromise peace, at the end of the first full year of fighting.

Since the nineteenth century the war and its aftermath have often been celebrated for their contribution to the development of parliamentary democracy and civil liberty in England. It is clear enough, however, that it also played a vital part in a parallel process, which in combination with the first was to lead to subsequent national success and of which liberals (more nervously) should be equally conscious: a massive increase in the power and efficiency of central government. Such a perspective goes far to justify the traditional periodisation of English history. It makes the Civil War pivotal, but also clearly divides the Tudor and Stuart ages, since Elizabeth created the problem in the fiscal–military state apparatus and the new royal dynasty had to deal with it and so face a host of new political difficulties.

* * *

If one role of revisionist historiography was to direct attention to this major functional issue, the critics of revisionism played a very useful part in redirecting it to the importance of the way in which people thought about government. They were most effective in concentrating upon the pervasive and enduring importance of ideology in national and local politics. Johann Sommerville proved that rival and incompatible theories of the origin of political power circulated in early Stuart

England, linked to the writings of Continental thinkers. Some emphasised that the source of such power was in the deity himself, and was delegated by him directly to monarchs, making resistance to the latter equivalent to heresy or mortal sin. Others expounded a concept of government as a contract between ruler and ruled, embodied either in custom or in natural law. Sommerville made the point well that many Civil War parliamentarians believed that they were fighting against a long-term royalist plot to subvert traditional checks on the power of the Crown, and could draw on many statements and actions by the Stuart kings and their support-ers to justify this opinion. To him the crucial feature of royal reactions to the func-tional problems of the state was that many people believed that they flouted the law, and that they were based on an assumption that the Crown could override any civil rights in an emergency. As contemporary advocates of stronger monarchy argued exactly this claim, practical royal responses to fiscal and military difficulties were interpreted by their critics as matters of major constitutional principle.[8]

Richard Cust and Thomas Cogswell extended such insights into the realm of practical politics. The former revealed how written summaries of national news cir-culated widely in England in the early seventeenth century, almost always reflect-ing a viewpoint hostile to that of the royal court. Both writers highlighted the fact that Charles I genuinely did have different views of the role and duties of Parliaments from many or most of his subjects, expecting them to be docile instru-ments for his will while they also regarded him as having an obligation to redress their grievances through legislation. Both emphasised the failure of his govern-ment to explain its point of view adequately to the public. Cogswell also illustrated the ways in which an incompetently conducted foreign policy led during the 1620s to the alienation of large numbers of English commoners who had acquired a keen sense of patriotism formed around traditional civil rights and the Protestant religion. Both historians demonstrated that Parliaments were widely viewed as champions of popular rights and interests against a greedy and corrupt court, and suggested that a polarisation in English politics was already visible from the reign of James, and became much more obvious as soon as Charles succeeded.[9]

Between them, these three authors also acknowledged that there were qualifica-tions to be made to these points. Once again, a pattern worked much better in the case of the Civil War parliamentarians than in that of the royalists, for it was quite easy to trace a self-conscious development of the politics of the 1620s into those of the former party. The royalists, by contrast, included many people who had been equally identified with criticism of the court and royal government, and so the divisions of the earlier period were not, in fact, a direct preparation for those of the war. Furthermore, whereas the court and royal government did represent a readily identifiable group of people with particular ideas, their critics were a continuously altering network of individuals and factions who drew on a common language. These complications were enlarged by 'revisionist' historians responding to earlier charges that they had undervalued the ideological element in early Stuart politics.

Kevin Sharpe pointed to the number of thinkers in England during the period who cannot be fitted into either side of the polarity of ideas that was allegedly developing. He emphasised the manner in which from King James downwards virtually all people accepted that the monarch was at once the representative of the deity and bound to respect the existing laws. What existed were not two clearly opposed positions but a common stock of ideas on which different people drew in different ways for particular purposes in the tensions generated by the structural problems of the state.[10] Conrad Russell greatly developed this last point, to illustrate that the Civil War royalists and parliamentarians were people who were interpreting the same political traditions in different ways, to tackle the fundamental question of whether the existing authorities in Church or state could be trusted any longer.[11]

Glenn Burgess went on to suggest a completely different scheme of rival political ideas from that posited by Sommerville, Cust and Cogswell, which rejected the Victorian model of an ideological clash between Crown and Commons, court and 'country' on which the latter had been based. He used the new theory of discourses, taken by historians from literary critics, to suggest that under James I political thought was expressed in England in three different languages, those of common law, civil law and theology. Of these, it was the first that got into trouble in the crises resulting from the increasing financial breakdown of the Crown, which created a situation for which the traditional language had no remedy: the monarch was surviving by stretching his accustomed powers in new ways and playing by rules that could no longer be easily understood. It was Charles I's actions that caused more anxiety than his professed beliefs, and by 1642 the law itself did not seem adequate any longer to defend people against perceived threats to their liberties and religion. Burgess identified the pamphleteering of the Civil War itself as designed more to argue rhetorical cases than to establish basic principles, and again he discerned three different languages in it. The first was a rhetoric of the need to ensure that the king received good advice, the second one of the need of royal government to guarantee peace and good order to subjects, and the third one of the need for godly rule. These were appropriated, in different measures, by the warring parties.[12]

Kevin Sharpe likewise drew on the insights provided by the new literary theories into the history of political thought. He produced a picture compatible with that of Burgess, of an early Stuart polity in which people saw the state as an organism rather than an artifice, and struggled to cope intellectually with the severe strain that practical political difficulties were placing on traditional ideals. As there was no general agreement over what was amiss with the state, conflict inevitably resulted over the policies that might restore it to efficiency and harmony, but clearly opposed views did not develop until the Civil War itself.[13] At the opening of the new decade, Alan Orr fished in the same waters of published and spoken argument, and came up with yet another framework of interpretation. According to this, early Stuart English politics were neither consensual nor concerned primarily with common law, but centred on the emerging issue of the relationship of sovereignty with ecclesiastical government. In Orr's reading royal policy in the 1630s alerted many observers to the fear that churchmen were being encouraged to erect a state within a state, which had to be prevented by restoring control of religious affairs firmly to Parliament.[14]

That the same body of material could be read in such different ways strongly suggests that there is no single and obvious structure of thought and disputation in it. None the less, the debates over it have served a useful and productive purpose, in bringing together the functional breakdown in royal government identified by revisionism with the ideological arguments highlighted by its critics, and demonstrating how the latter responded to the former to turn the early Stuart period into a unique one in English political and intellectual history. Once again, the importance of 1603 and 1642 as dividing lines is restated, although the conclusions drawn from the political thought of the age between are not as neat, and offer rather less common ground, than those concerned with the structural problems of the state. It is relatively easy, and conclusive, to count sums of money and chart the development and decline of governmental institutions, providing that sufficient records for such exercises exist. The history of ideas is inevitably more fluid and impressionistic, because it deals with entities that themselves possess both those characteristics.

* * *

The third major component of the new framework was, like the first, initially given prominence by Conrad Russell. His instinctual understanding of the nuts and bolts of politics – the latter being traditionally his family business – led him to take interest in another functional problem of early modern European states, highlighted by the work of scholars of continental Europe: that of multiple monarchies. These were associated especially with sovereigns such as the Habsburg rulers of the Austrian or Spanish territories, to whom dynastic accident had bequeathed an assemblage of different hereditary possessions. It could be argued (and was by Russell) that the early seventeenth-century Stuart monarchies were potentially a more explosive assemblage than most because of their religious composition: it was simply not possible to find a single recipe for government that would give equal satisfaction to religious cultures as polarised as the Counter-Reformation Catholicism that was spreading in Ireland and the extreme Protestantism that had been established in Scotland. Another influence on Russell's perceptions was exerted by the new outpouring of works by Scottish and Irish historians, created by the expansion of higher education in those nations as in most parts of the western world during the mid-twentieth century. At times they impinged directly on perceptions of English history, most obviously in the case of James VI and I. Only the separation of national histories that had obtained for most of the century, and the relative sluggishness that had characterised the writing of that of Scotland, would have allowed such a dual character to survive as long as he did. To Scots, James VI was one of the most able and successful of monarchs, while to the English James I was a buffoon, a physically ungainly figure with ridiculous intellectual and political pretensions who soured relationships between the monarchy and its subjects. It was a Scot, Jenny Wormald, who brought the two together dramatically in 1983. She showed how much of the English view was a caricature based ultimately on traditional dislike and contempt for Scots, and how many of James's difficulties resulted from his attempt to operate an English political system that was very different from his native one.[15] During the late 1980s Conrad Russell delivered a succession of high-profile lectures that drew attention to the importance of relationships between the kingdoms of England, Scotland and Ireland in bringing about the collapse of Stuart rule in all three by 1642. These initiatives culminated in his two big books at the opening of the next decade.[16] It is likely that the new vigour of Irish and Scottish historians of the period would have attracted the attention of English colleagues in any case, but there is little doubt that Russell single-handedly turned a perspective that took in the whole archipelago into one of the major themes of Stuart historiography. As a tactic in the debates between the revisionists and their critics – however peripheral such a consideration may (or may not) have been to the author's own concerns – it was brilliant, for it outflanked the latter at many points and reset the whole subject in a new framework.

It was also decisive in building up what was pretty well an unassailable case: that it was impossible to understand the English Civil War without understanding what was going on in Scotland and Ireland, and that the three kingdoms constantly interacted with each other in the period between 1639 and 1642, and indeed between 1639 and 1660. Russell drew attention to the serious strains that were inherent in the union of crowns made between three such different states. In his persuasive reading, these had been kept under control by James's combination of skill and laziness, so that nothing had been done either to accentuate them or to remove them. It had been Charles's equally characteristic mixture of determination and ineptitude, expressed through a programme to strengthen royal government in all three realms and to bring them under a tighter set of common policies, that had exploded the tensions. His Personal Rule over England was brought to an end directly because of a Scottish rebellion against his attempted reforms, which not merely lost him control of his northern kingdom but of the government of England. The Scots had invaded England itself, defeated his forces and forced him to call the Long Parliament in England and to follow its wishes. More than anyone before, Russell brought out the way in which the demands that the Scots made on their allies in that Parliament embittered relations between the latter and the king to the point at which a genuine settlement between them became impossible, while also producing divisions in the Parliament itself. These developments provided a context for the Civil War, but it was the Irish who detonated it.

Some of their Catholic leaders, inspired by the success of the Scots and frightened by the militant Protestantism which the Scottish victory had made dominant in Britain, launched a rebellion of their own. It was the question of who could be trusted to command the army sent to crush this that finally ruptured relations between Charles and his opponents in England and precipitated war there. In the Russell perspective, the remarkable fact was not that Stuart government broke down in the English kingdom in 1642, but that it had survived longest there.

Conrad Russell's own work finished with the coming of the Civil War, but it was perfectly plain that his conclusions could be extended to cover it, and arguable that only the traditional neglect by historians of the royalists had limited the application of such an exercise. There has been a tendency among specialists to overstate the part played by Parliament in obtaining its own victory, concentrating above all on the achievements of the New Model Army. While it was certainly this body that won the war, the biggest single element in the king's defeat was that the Scots weighed in against him when he had a real prospect of winning. Their intervention gave Parliament the resources of a complete extra kingdom, the only one to share a land frontier with England across which troops could easily be moved. As the north of England was controlled by royalists, and had been the launch-pad for Charles's war effort, this meant that his forces were effectively being stabbed in the back and forced for the first time to fight on two fronts. The army that the Scots sent into England at the opening of 1644 was the largest ever fielded during the whole Civil War, immediately giving the parliamentarian cause in the north a superiority of three to one and acting as the decisive factor in the loss of most of the region to the king within eight months. Ever after that, the total manpower available to the royalists was smaller than that at the disposal of their enemies, while the wealth and extent of their territory were much inferior. In most battles, and all the biggest, the king's men were henceforth facing superior numbers and were defeated as a result.

It is true, however, that if Parliament called on Scotland, to some extent Charles called on Ireland. The latter was, admittedly, a much less considerable asset. For one thing it lay across a sea patrolled by Parliament's navy, while for another it was already badly divided and damaged by its own civil war, produced by the Catholic uprising. None the less, the king managed to ship over much of the royal army of Ireland to assist him. It could not be a balance to that of the Scots, because it was much smaller – 6700 men as opposed to about 22 000 – and had to be brought over in parties to scattered points instead of arriving as the Scots did in a single hammer blow.[17] This said, the quality of the soldiers who came was very high, bolstering the royalists at several points and giving Prince Rupert the nucleus of the field army with which he came very close to defeating the Scots and their allies in the north. Had Charles been skilful enough to persuade the Scots to remain neutral, Rupert's new army might well have provided him with the edge needed to win the war in England. Furthermore, Charles used Irish resources with much more spectacular effect to reverse the balance of power in Scotland. Eight months after the Scots intervened in England, an Irish royalist, the chief of the Macdonnels, shipped some of his clan over to reinforce the Scottish royalists and make an uprising possible in the Highlands. They were superb fighters, who made a partnership with the king's general in Scotland, the marquis of Montrose, which eventually achieved control of the country. Though their supremacy was brief, it forced much of the Scottish army in England to return home, preventing the Scots from sustaining their influence in English affairs and enabling Parliament to complete its victory with its own New Model Army and claim most of the credit for the king's defeat. Scottish patriotism has tended to obscure both the vital importance of the Macdonnel expeditionary force and its character as an intervention by Irish Catholics, but both have recently been emphasised.[18]

Mark Stoyle's interest in the role played in the war by Cornish and Welsh identity has highlighted a further potential for a truly 'British' perspective on the war, and one that also has important implications for an understanding of its strategic aspects. The relative neglect of the royalists has hindered a proper appreciation of something that has always been acknowledged by military historians: that it was the particular loyalty manifested towards the king by the Cornish, and especially by the more strongly culturally differentiated west Cornish, that made possible the royalist conquest of most of the south-western quarter of England and brought Charles close to victory. What needs to be emphasised in addition was that without the Welsh the royalist war effort would probably not have got off the ground in the first place. When the king raised his standard at Nottingham, his supporters were scattered across a wide area of northern, midland and western England. It was the almost solid adherence of Welsh-speaking Wales to his cause that put a loyal hinterland behind Shrewsbury, making this latter town the ideal place in which to gather soldiers raised in the north-west and the midlands, as well as in Wales itself, and weld them into a field army.

In the initial form in which Conrad Russell cast it, the concept of a 'British dimension' to the study of the Civil War proved to be immensely attractive to historians, and a perspective that encompassed all three kingdoms was soon applied to many topics in sixteenth- and seventeenth-century history. Three reasons may be suggested for this. One was that for specialists in fields such as that of English history in the 1640s, where debates had become complex and the evidence intractable, it opened up a new front on which to operate, restoring mobility and offering new archival discoveries as well as new viewpoints from which to understand old problems. It possessed an almost perfect combination of the familiar and the exotic. To scholars already versed in the sources for the Civil War, Irish and Scottish collections of documents, usually in publication, were already well-trod hunting grounds. They had, however, been used as a source of information on English affairs, with a whole hinterland of native warfare and politics that English historians generally understood only in outline. Nor had there hitherto been any greater mutual understanding between those of Ireland and Scotland themselves. British schoolchildren had generally been taught the Greek and Roman 'classics', and English literature from Chaucer, but nothing of the very rich literary tradition of medieval Ireland. England was geographically closer to France than Ireland, and the impact of French culture on the English had been continuous and tremendous from the time when the Normans came to rule them. At times the relationship between France and Scotland had been even closer. In the mid-twentieth century, educated British people still peppered their conversation with French words, and French was normally the first foreign language taught in schools. German, Italian and Spanish were the usual runners-up, with Irish nowhere in sight. The conceptual gap between the islands had actually widened in the twentieth century, as the emergence of an Irish Republic self-consciously based on alternative ethnic, religious and cultural models encouraged the British to detach their own history. By what may have been a knock-on effect, knowledge of Scottish history also declined markedly among experts in seventeenth-century England. A resurgence of interest in both other nations during the 1980s and 1990s therefore represented both a reclamation of lost ground and a voyage of discovery, each enterprise facilitated by the fact that most of the source material was in English.

A second reason for the popularity of the new perspective was that it offered marvellous opportunities for collaboration, especially between English historians and their growing number of colleagues in the universities of Scotland, Northern Ireland and the Republic of Ireland. In particular, it provided perfect subjects for an aspect of academic culture that boomed in the 1990s: the conference, with a collection of papers from its proceedings subsequently edited and published by the organiser or organisers. Young scholars were afforded an opportunity in these to present work to a large, and usually international, audience, and to get it into print without running the gauntlet of the more competitive and congested channel of academic journals. Established historians could be lionised and have the opportunity to meet colleagues in congenial circumstances. At best, such a large and dynamic concentration of experts might produce genuine breakthroughs in understanding of a subject. These occasions were good for the morale, and the *curricula vitae*, of almost everybody involved. It is not surprising, therefore, that whether or not they derived directly from conferences, most of the key publications on relationships between the three Stuart kingdoms put out in the 1990s took the form of edited collections of essays by different contributors.[19]

A third incentive to the new approach was that it offered participants the chance to participate in a major set of topical debates and to make contributions to contemporary political issues. In the mid-twentieth century, when the Westminster Parliament was still the focus for a relatively well United Kingdom, and incorporated a Crown that was still the focus for colonies and dominions and increasingly of a Commonwealth, it made sense to concentrate on its trials and triumphs. During the 1990s, devolution of power to Scottish and Welsh representative assemblies, and increasing co-operation with the Irish republic over the problems of Northern Ireland, refocused attention onto the relationships between that Parliament and other bodies within the British Isles. The 1640s represented an occasion on which such relationships were especially important and dynamic, and decisive for the history of the archipelago. At the same time, instinctual linkages between the British and the Continent seemed to diminish. This may seem a pre-posterous suggestion concerning a period in which the Channel Tunnel physically attached England to France and the swelling power of the European Union prom-ised the incorporation of the United Kingdom into a federation including all of its eastern neighbours. None the less, it is notable that the French influence on British culture lessened notably from the 1980s. French film-makers, intellectuals and nov-elists had made a considerable impact on the British during the central decades of the century, but now they became much less prominent in Britain unless they had been taken up in the United States. The globalisation of world culture in the late twentieth century was essentially an Americanisation of it, aided enormously by the developments in information technology that had been pioneered in and exported from the USA. French words were tending to fade out of the smart talk of the British by the opening of the twenty-first century, and to be replaced by Americanisms. Transactions with powerful continental European states no longer necessarily seemed to be the most important and obvious external links of the English or the British. Indeed the growing power of the European Union itself encouraged movements for local self-government and cultural separatism that could be comprehended under the umbrella of the Union's common economic and legal policies. Relations between the component parts of the British Isles, therefore, assumed a new importance and interest at the end of the century.

For all these reasons what was initially called 'the British problem' replaced the question of the causes and nature of the Civil War itself as the main focus of seventeenth-century English historiography, sucking much of the life out of study of the war itself. The conflict was losing its own identity, and becoming only one facet of what was increasingly termed 'The War of the Three Kingdoms'. This was the reason why the 350th anniversary of the Civil War, between 1992 and 1996, attracted so little attention from its established academic experts: most of them were away exploring archipelago-wide perspectives that were radically different from the parochial celebrations so manifest among the English at large.

The shift initially caused some disquiet within parts of the academy. Little of it was manifested by those who had so recently been the most avid critics of revisionism, and who tended to annexe the three-kingdoms perspective to their textbooks and otherwise continue to concentrate on the social and cultural devel-opments within England that were their main interests.[20] There were some scat-tered objections from other English scholars, who pointed out either that the three states had only influenced each other's affairs closely at exceptional moments, or that relations between England and Continental powers still counted for more, most of the time, than those between it and the other parts of the archipelago.[21]

The most forceful and natural critique was, however, made by some Irish and Scottish historians, who feared initially that the sudden interest in their nations manifested by English or English-based historians amounted to a new form of exploitation by members of what had traditionally been the dominant partner in the United Kingdom. The use of Scottish and Irish records made by Conrad Russell was, after all, quite explicitly and honestly to solve problems in English history, even though that of the other states was to some extent illumined by the process.[22] There was indeed a tendency in the early 1990s for editors or authors of books on seventeenth-century English topics to add a chapter on 'The British Dimension' or 'The British Problem' as a new appendage to otherwise conventional treatments of subjects. That certainly gave the impression of treating Scottish and Irish material as an enrichment of English history. Furthermore, the shorthand of 'British' to cover the whole of the archipelago, however convenient, posed obvious problems for the Irish and those sympathetic to them, and such approaches tended also to lump Scotland and Ireland together without emphasising that the differences between them were at least as great as the similarities. By defining a 'British' dimension simply as a non-English one, the new historiography threatened to produce an Anglocentricity as crass as the old kind that had ignored the other nations.[23] By the latter half of the decade, however, such insensitivities were disappearing, and a genuine sense of partnership and mutual benefit was being achieved between scholars of the three nations. It was becoming generally accepted that different emphases worked best for different problems in the period, and for different types of history such as central, provincial, political, social, intellectual and economic. A comparative approach was most suited to some, a collective one to others, and a separatist one to yet others, within a broad framework of awareness of what was going on in all parts of the islands.[24] A three-kingdom perspective on early Stuart history, and to the crisis in which the early Stuart polity ended, is now a professional commonplace.

It comfortingly combines the two different sorts of historiographical approach represented by interest in the functional breakdown of the early seventeenth-century English state and in its political ideologies. On the one hand it can be read as a matter of practicalities, by showing how developments in the different kingdoms had an impact on each other; an approach summed up by Conrad Russell's famous image of the three realms functioning like billiard balls. In addition, it can be treated as an episode in the history of ideology and culture, by looking at the stereotypical images that inhabitants of the three states constructed of each other and of different cultures within each, and how these influenced mentalities and drove political and military events. However it is deployed, the three-kingdoms perspective has the further effect of reinforcing the status of the year 1603, when the triple union of crowns was effected, as a major dividing point in the history of all three states.

* * *

The fourth aspect to the origins and nature of the Great Civil War to have been highlighted and clarified by recent debates also concerns ideology, but of a particular kind: religion. It focuses on the Church of England during the early seventeenth century. The main scholarly tradition from Gardiner onward was to regard that period as one of increasing religious repression by a Crown determined to impose conformity on its subjects, through the agency of a national faith that it directly controlled. In this view, the Civil War shattered that control, providing England with a period of toleration that permitted the permanent establishment – enduring through a resumption of persecution by the restored Stuart kings – of a remarkable and creative diversity of belief. If the villains of the story were James and Charles and their bishops, the heroes were the more radical Protestants, or puritans, who resisted them and fought their way to power and freedom in the course of the war. As enemies of monopoly and repression in all forms, the puritans also acted as the champions of civil and political liberty. This epic represented the creation myth of Victorian Liberalism, with its close association with Dissent, a term embracing all those Protestant churches existing outside the national religion by the nineteenth century. The same myth also made an appeal to two other great traditions. One was American nationalism, which focused from the late nineteenth century onward on the Pilgrim Fathers – apparently archetypal puritans – as the founders of the tradition of freedom and enterprise that was to flower into the USA. This was largely a consequence of the War Between The States, forcing the victorious North to find its own image of national origins, which obscured the inconvenient truth that the story of the American colonies had begun in Virginia. The other force was Marxism, which took up the Liberal myth in this as in most respects and merely reworked it to provide social and economic underpinnings. This process turned puritans into a progressive force in commercial as well as political and religious matters, the solvent that finally removed the middle ages from England and prepared the way for modernity. As the twentieth century wore on, the secular consequences of puritanism tended to be stressed even more strongly, their religion being represented as a conduit or even a gloss for bourgeois individualism and liberalism, or of the control by inferiors by village elites drawn from the middle levels of society.[25]

As three intellectual currents had united to give this story its momentum, so three, characteristic of the late twentieth century, were to demolish most features of it. The most obvious was revisionism, which posed a direct challenge to it, breaking most of the apparent connections between puritanism and economic and social progression and reconfiguring puritans as conservative and otherworldly thinkers, instinctually opposed to virtually all aspects of what has come to be regarded as modernity. The second was the collapse of Marxism as an intellectual force in the 1980s and the transformation from economic into cultural historians of scholars who instinctually sought for long-term processes in social and political change. The new sense that ideas might have an independent life of their own directed attention back to their history, and religious ideas were the most strongly expressed, and certainly the best recorded, in this period. This invited a new and much more thorough examination of the debates within, and concerning, the Church of England in the eighty years before the Civil War. It was work that was, moreover, of practical convenience. Works of theology not only represented another trove of source material that had hitherto been either untouched or under-used, but one that was concentrated in the great metropolitan and university libraries. Much of it was increasingly available in the new medium of microfilm, which rendered research expeditions unnecessary.

The third, and least easily demonstrated, of the three new intellectual currents was an uneasy recognition of the power of religious feeling even within the modern world, and its potential as a focus for identity when other groupings such as class, local community and (perhaps) nation were weakening. The resurgence of both Islamic and Christian fundamentalism in various parts of the world, the appearance and continuation of sectarian violence in Northern Ireland, the domi-nation of Middle Eastern politics by relations between Israel and its neighbours, and the explosion of religious hatred as a badge of ethnicity in the Balkans, have all driven home the point. Instead of being the narrators of history as a rational and controllable process, academic scholars have had to reckon with the power of unreason as well as that of contingency: of faith, fashion and mood.

As a result, the history of religion in England during the Elizabethan and early Stuart period has been one of the most dynamic and heavily populated fields of research since 1970, and the names of those who have contributed to it represent practically a roll-call of those working on the period in general.[26] The result of such a concentration of energy has been, almost inevitably, a great deal of con-flicting opinion, with much disagreement even over the terms to be applied to different religious movements or factions. None the less, there has also been a gen-uine amount of agreement building up, however implicit in many respects, over the general course of events. The starting point for this is the settlement of national religion made by the newly established Elizabethan regime in 1559, a rushed com-promise only produced by arresting the key members of the existing episcopacy. It created a Church of England that was Catholic in its administrative structure and its use of vestments for clergy, and Protestant in its royal leadership, its form of worship and its emphasis on preaching. As such it was the least Protestant of the world's reformed Churches, and its only obvious and inherent virtue was that it contained enough elements of both Protestantism and Catholicism to deter the adherents of both faiths from taking desperate action to oppose it. Both hoped that it would be altered, to bring it further into conformity with their ideals, and nobody seems at the outset to have expected it to remain in the half-baked form forced on it by expediency in 1559; but that is exactly what it did do. Furthermore, it acquired perhaps the vaguest and most hazily defined theology of any Christian Church. To some of the greatest questions of Christianity – whether humans can win salvation by their own efforts, whether clergy have a sacred status that sets them off from laity, whether the Church of England is an improved variety of Catholicism or something utterly opposed to it, whether the royal supremacy over the national religion was vested in the monarch alone or the monarch in Parliament – it returned ambiguous answers. That this should be so may be attributed primarily to Elizabeth, and specifically to two aspects of her nature. The first was her genuine reluctance to enquire into the beliefs of her subjects and to call them to account for these (as opposed to their actions); a stance adopted explicitly in contrast to the lethally effective enquiries of her sister and predecessor, Mary. The second was that same pathological dislike of change that produced the decay of the fiscal system. There is no clear evidence that the Church constructed in 1559 conformed exactly to the queen's own wishes and preferences, but after she had governed it for a few years she became rigidly opposed to any alteration of it.

This was, automatically, going to disappoint most, if not all, of the committed and enthusiastic Protestants among her subjects in the first half of her reign. If the 1559 settlement immediately produced a division between the Protestants and Catholics in the nation, which grew clearer and more bitter with time, another split occurred within English Protestantism, within seven years of the making of the settlement. Most of Elizabeth's own advisers and leading servants, including the majority of the bishops and privy council, attempted for almost twenty years to persuade her to carry out further reformation. They were, however, ultimately prepared to accept her determination to change nothing, and to observe the regulations laid down for religious observance in 1559. Other English Protestants were not. Collectively, the label of 'puritan' can be conveniently and justly applied to the latter. It began as a term of abuse, but then so did virtually all of the labels that have traditionally been applied to parties, radical religious denominations or political pressure groups in early modern England. Puritans were never a party and only intermittently, and partially, a movement or a pressure group. They differed markedly over what they found unacceptable in the Elizabethan Church, some disliking vestments, some ceremonies, some the retention of cathedrals and powerful bishops, and others varying mixtures of these, including the lot. They were also found on a spectrum of activism, from the few who separated themselves from the Church on finding the queen completely opposed to further reform, and a much greater number who mounted public campaigns to achieve the latter end, to many more who ministered to provincial parishes while quietly ignoring certain parts of the liturgy or the requirement to wear the surplice, or attended divine service with qualms that were only aired privately, in prayer and discussion groups of like-minded people. Many puritans engaged also in campaigns for the reform of society – closing alehouses and theatres, abolishing traditional communal festivities or separating them from the Church, relieving the poor, and rigorously punishing sexual transgressions – but not all of those identifiable with a wish for further religious reform can be found automatically supporting the social campaigns, and the latter were promoted by many people who were apparently contented with the Church as established.

By the last decade of Elizabeth's reign the queen's obduracy had crushed the public campaign for further reformation, while leaving many puritans of the quieter kind among the clergy, supported by a much larger number of laity at all social levels and biding their time in hope of new opportunities. Her determination, and long life, had also enabled the appearance of a new generation of members of the Church who had grown up with it and did not regard it as inherently anomalous or regrettable. They themselves differed greatly in their attitudes to the various components of it, to foreign Churches and to domestic Catholics and Puritans, but were united by an acceptance of the established religion of 1559, shading increasingly into positive enthusiasm for certain aspects of it. During the last decade of the reign, however, a third tendency was starting to appear within the Church of England, even more amorphous and less of a coherent movement than puritanism but still very significant. At present no agreement at all exists among specialists over what to call it, and it is proposed here to retain for it the traditional umbrella term of Arminianism, which was not only in origin a piece of abuse but an inaccurate one, seeking to identify some members of this tendency with a Dutch heresy to which they never directly subscribed. Again, the quality of injustice and inaccuracy is shared by many other terms for groups that have passed into enduring usage (Lollard, Whig, Tory and Leveller being obvious examples), and so the traditional one is continued here because of its familiarity and the lack of a really convincing and popular alternative.

Whereas puritanism sprang from a single basic reaction, Arminianism was produced by two. One consisted of people who, left to their own devices, would have been happy as Catholics but preferred to keep their jobs, incomes and personal safety intact by conforming to the reformed Church; they therefore wanted to preserve or augment those features of it which were closest to Catholic practice. The other reaction appeared among Protestants of the generation coming of age in the 1580s and 1590s who, now that the reformed religion had clearly defeated its opponent and claimed the genuine allegiance of the great majority of the queen's subjects, were happy to emphasise those same features or to reduce some which were most obviously opposed to Catholicism. Even less than puritans did people in the Arminian tendency agree on what exactly should be done. Many wanted a greater emphasis on ceremonies and sacraments than on preaching and the Bible, many more longed for a greater physical beauty and ornamentation in the parish church itself, others were concerned with emphasising the descent of their religion from that of late medieval England and playing down its links with foreign Protestants, while still others were interested in promoting a theology that held out the hope of salvation to the majority of members of their Church, with an acknowledgement that to some extent they might win it by their own efforts.

The Church of England emerged into the seventeenth century as one of the most successful varieties of Protestantism. In the course of Elizabeth's reign it had penned a committed belief in Catholicism into about 5 per cent of the population, and left this relatively small number of die-hards both geographically scattered and bereft of any firm popular base of support. It had converted the parish churches from settings for ritual into preaching houses and had produced a new national identity, passionately supported at all ranks of society, which made the reformed religion a badge of patriotism. It had also created a national faith which was extraordinarily versatile, open-ended, dynamic and fast developing, providing for many different styles of worship and belief within an overall framework that had integrated major aspects of the old and the new. That last feature, however, is more of a virtue to modern than to early modern eyes. Another way of regarding the same situation would be to recognise the Anglican Church of the early seventeenth century as the most badly defined, slackly controlled, deeply divided and volatile form of state religion in Europe. The differences between puritan and Arminian could seem great enough to make them essentially different kinds of Protestant religion, and it was by no means obvious that any single institution could accommodate them both indefinitely. Furthermore, they were operating within a uniquely febrile religious atmosphere. Anybody who made it to the age of sixty in 1640 had lived through the whole of the first generation of conversion to the new religion – the overwhelming majority of adults in England at the accession of the Stuarts had possessed parents or grandparents who had adhered to Catholicism – and the nation was gripped by the enthusiasm and insecurity that accompanies major conversion experiences. In this particular case, both were increased by the fact that early Protestantism was a religion that was identified very strongly with a belief in the approaching end of the world and the judgement of all humanity. Very many people in early Stuart England were disposed to regard any significant events, personal or national, as signs from the deity himself intended to direct them towards salvation, and the strong possibility that they were living in the last days of the cosmos greatly strengthened the hopes and fears attendant on such scrutiny. It was an extraordinarily unstable and combustible religious culture, and as so often in the annals of humanity its people proved capable of fulfilling their own prophecies: in the 1640s they created an apocalypse.

They were aided in doing so by the distinctively fragmented nature of religious geography within the boundaries of the Church of England. The late medieval Church had been to a great extent a patchwork of local loyalties, with particular saints and shrines representing the main foci of devotion for individual parishes or districts. These cults were, however, comprehended within a common form of religion. The English Reformation had left behind it a different sort of quilting effect, as it made different forms of Protestantism prominent or dominant in different areas. East Sussex contained many puritans, west Sussex very few. The West Riding of Yorkshire was a notable centre of populist, evangelical Protestantism, while the East Riding had a much more conservative and ritualist form of reformed religion. The latter was even more true of Herefordshire, but that still developed a dynamic network of puritans in the north-west of the county, centred on the Harley family. Lancashire preserved more Roman Catholics than any other shire, but had a notable enclave of puritanism in the south-east and a stronghold of more ceremonious English Protestantism in the south-west. Even with individual parishes, puritans often formed a self-conscious and closely knit minority. Again, this pattern provided a religious culture of fascinating and exciting variety; but it also meant that should these differing strains of religion ever turn on each other, then the nation would shatter, along rifts that ran not between regions but through counties, towns or even villages, and produce a civil conflict of extraordinary complexity and divisiveness. As suggested, English Protestants in the 1640s generally retained enough sense of common identity to save them from regarding each other as self-evidently damned and demonically inspired; but the divisions still ran deep enough to inspire a good number to kill each other without compunction.

The result of all these recent insights has been a restructuring of the periodisation in which Tudor and Stuart history has traditionally been conceived, in a way that does not match that so neatly represented by the three perspectives characterised above. In the traditional ordering, the Reformation achieved its decisive victory in the mid-sixteenth century, and the Elizabethan settlement simply imposed an enduring structure upon it, which was maintained with considerable success until the Stuart period. Then it was destabilised, partly by the heavy-handed and misconceived policies of the kings and partly by the continuing dynamic force of puritanism, propelled by economic and social change. With the decisive conversion of the bulk of the subjects of the English state to Protestantism now redated to the reign of Elizabeth, the bloc of time between 1560 and 1640 has assumed the status of a distinct and strongly marked epoch in English, Welsh and Cornish religious and cultural history; indeed, within the study of those kinds of history, the expression 'early modern England' seems increasingly to be confined to those years. The accession of the Stuarts makes only a minor dividing line within them.

One very good reason for this lies in the success that scholars have generally come to accord to James I in his management of the Church of England. Driven by his characteristic mix of shrewdness, laziness, pacifism and genuine intellectual curiosity and generosity, he carefully maintained and encouraged the diversity of English religion in a state of dynamic equilibrium. On arrival he allowed the puritans to renew their campaign for reform, and used it as a lever to induce many minor changes in the Church. None, however, amounted to the most important of the requirements of the puritan lobby, and the king and his bishops employed the subsequent enforcement of the slightly altered national regulations to identify and remove the most obdurate of the puritan clergy, amounting to about 1 per cent of the nation's ministers. Those who were prepared to bend or ignore aspects of the prescribed liturgy without creating a fuss were once again left in peace: and some features of the mainstream brand of national religion promoted under James would certainly have appealed to them, such as its emphasis on preaching, on links with foreign Protestants and on the Bible. Indeed, the definition of puritanism that holds good for Elizabeth's reign may not do so for that of her successor, as agitation for further reform of the Church was either crushed or placated and became less visible. Instead, it is more customary to identify Jacobean puritans by a style of piety that they shared with those who had led such agitation before and were to do so again in later years: strenuously concerned with personal salvation, acutely aware that the majority of humanity was doomed to damnation, and holding the authority of Scripture to be absolutely paramount.

James also promoted leading members of the Arminian tendency to high office, but ensured that until the end of his reign they were outnumbered by deans and bishops who represented the mainstream of Anglican belief and practice as it existed at his accession. He employed Arminians partly as a means of providing a choice of styles of worship, and partly as a mechanism by which he might threaten the mainstream churchmen if they attempted to impose policies on them. He accordingly left a Church that was just as riven with suspicion and hostility between different kinds of cleric, but whose members co-operated very well for most of the time in the work of preaching, administration of sacraments, and pastoral duties. The English state had achieved the remarkable combination of the most diverse Protestant culture and almost the most ramshackle fiscal and military structure of any in Europe, with the greatest degree of internal peace.

In the broadly consensual picture that is building up among specialists, this unsteady equilibrium was unbalanced by Charles I, who gave power to elements of the Arminian tendency in it because of his own desire for a Church based on order, dignity and beauty. The result, in his Personal Rule, was to make Arminianism so thoroughly unpopular that the Long Parliament forced him to abandon it. The result was not, however, a return to the Elizabethan and Jacobean status quo, because the sufferings of the puritans under Arminian rule had convinced them that further reformation of the Church was essential to their own safety and that of English Protestantism. In any case, they were being pushed in this direction by the Scots who had brought down the Personal Rule, and it was the tension that resulted between them and those who wanted to revert to the Elizabethan compromise which provided one of the major lines of division between the Civil War parties.

It has been stated that this summary of events is one that would probably be endorsed in essentials by most of those writing and teaching the history of the subject in universities at the present time. It may be added that most of them would also probably make qualifications or challenges to aspects of it, but that does not vitiate the broad amount of consent that it seems to command. There are, however, three problems with it, in ascending order of importance. The first is that ideal types such as 'puritan' and 'Arminian' may be hard to identify among real individuals on the ground, because even a diverse and shifting set of characteristics such as those defined above may not correspond to the manner in which particular people combined strongly marked attributes from different categories. It is easier to find archetypal puritans than members of the other classifications of belief, largely because they tended to define themselves self-consciously. Peter Lake has, however, made three very effective cautions in his study of a 'classic' London puritan minister of the 1620s and 1630s, Stephen Denison. One is that the individual components of belief and attitude in the puritan mind-set do not in themselves add up to it: what made a puritan was their integration into a dynamic whole. Another is that puritan attitudes did not translate automatically into social or political equivalents: they could be orthodox, clerical and authoritarian in one context and populist and libertarian in another, according to their treatment by current political authorities. The last was that a common stock of puritan thought could be used for very different religious purposes, on a spectrum with total conformity to the national religion at one end and radical separatism at the other.[27] Christopher Haigh had more problems when examining the identity of the Leicestershire parson Thomas Pestell, an ideal subject for study in that Pestell got into a mesh of political and religious troubles in the course of Charles I's Personal Rule that resulted in our knowing more about him that almost any other parish clergyman of the early Stuart period. Haigh found that he defied all historiographical labels: he combined the 'classic' features of a puritan, Arminian and 'mainstream' Jacobean churchman, and his friends and foes straddled contemporary ideological divisions.[28] This inevitably invites the suspicion that many or most of the other clergy of his time would be equally difficult to classify if we only had the information with which to form a judgement.

Such an anxiety need not represent a serious threat to historical interpretation: after all, human beings are perennially capable of constructing ideal categories of person, which inspire intense loyalty or revulsion, while recognising that individuals whom they know personally do not fit the types particularly well. It does, however, raise some particular difficulties when considering the second problem with the model of religious history sketched out above. This concerns the argument built into it that, by making a version of Arminianism dominant in his Church, Charles I was responsible for destabilising the Elizabethan and Jacobean compromise and accentuating the divisions in English religion in such a way as to make them a cause of civil war. The problem with this view is that in behaving as he did, Charles was probably more typical of his time than either of his predecessors. Everybody who supported the Church of England during the first eighty years of its existence seems to have done so with some misgivings or dislikes with regard to certain aspects of its nature and composition. Virtually every thinking person involved in it believed that it needed to be improved or tidied up, and it was Charles who undertook the work. His obvious difficulty was that the Church contained contrasting opinions as to what needed doing. Any attempt to exert greater central control over it was going to worry a lot of people, and any attempt to define or enforce beliefs and practices was going to worry a lot more. The differences of style and ideal within it represented not a contest between forces working for repression and uniformity and those working for tolerance and pluralism, but between equally intolerant people who thought that their opinions should be prescribed and enforced on all. In the 1620s Puritans fought hard to eliminate the Arminian tendency in the Church, in the 1630s they complained bitterly when the Arminians harassed them in return, and in the 1640s they joyously seized the opportunity to persecute Arminianism as strenuously as possible. Their actions throughout were, in their own terms, both absolutely consistent and in harmony with the overwhelming opinion of the age. The latter held that if a government was not put there by the will of the Christian God, then it could not be a proper government, and if it was a proper government, then all its subjects needed to believe in the state religion. To tolerate a wrong religion was to deny the will of God, a very dangerous step to take as its consequences could be eternal damnation. The great crisis of conscience faced by anybody in Christian Europe during the early modern period was what to do if the religion of one's own state seemed to be going wrong: all solutions to it agreed that some withdrawal of co-operation with that religion was needed. It can certainly be suggested that by acting as he did Charles pushed the Church into a new phase of its development, and raised the stakes of religious politics. It is much more difficult to argue convincingly that, with such divergent and mutually hostile forces at work in English religion, it would have been possible to maintain the Jacobean balance much longer in a society that did not have any principled and instinctual commitment to diversity.

The greatest single problem that hangs over the current model of interpretation of English religious politics in the period, and which incorporates the first two, is the question of whether, by backing the Arminians, Charles automatically made the wrong choice. This is in turn related inseparably to the issue of the success and popularity of his Personal Rule, a matter which highlights vividly three of the main preoccupations of a historian: historiography, periodisation and source material. The historiography currently has the following shape. Ever since the time of Gardiner's great Victorian narrative, the Personal Rule has generally been treated as a time of unpopular, inefficient and at least potentially despotic government, never viable in the long term and brought to an end by public opposition. This picture was challenged directly on all counts by Kevin Sharpe, in a series of works culminating in his huge book of 1992.[29] The views of other authors on the period over the past one and a half decades have generally represented either dissent from, riposte to, or qualification of, his arguments.[30] It seems therefore as if Sharpe stands at one end of a spectrum of attitudes; but nothing simple can be concluded from this pattern, because his research has been the most comprehensive and cohesive to date.

The periodisation matters because of the manner in which the Personal Rule ended. There is no doubt whatsoever that it failed, because the Long Parliament which met in November 1640 proceeded to condemn both its fiscal and its religious policies, and drove the royal councillors and servants most closely associated with them to death, prison or exile. It was brought to an end, and the calling of the Parliament enforced, by the king's war with the Scots who had rebelled against his attempts to reform their own national religion; and here lies the crux of the problem. In the Gardiner view of events, the Scots merely liberated and gave expression to an English discontent that had long been increasing. In the Sharpe view, their rebellion ruined royal policies in England that had been enjoying a reasonable amount of success. Charles's defeat by them was completely unprecedented, as former crushing victories of the Scots over the English had been few and taken place on Scottish soil itself. This was an invasion of England by a Scottish army which had carried all before it and remained in occupation of key English resources while dictating the terms of a truce. In itself such a disaster would have severely shaken public confidence in the royal government, but in addition the Scots won the propaganda war, causing many of the English to believe that Scottish opposition to their common monarch was intended to rescue the traditional liberties and Protestant religion of both nations against an attempt to subvert them. In the Sharpe view, therefore, the Personal Rule is not one period but two, dividing sharply when the Scottish uprising began in 1637 and transformed the 'natural' course of events.

Any possibility of resolving the matter depends heavily on the evidence for public opinion during the years before and after that key date, and it is not sufficient to the task. The two greatest expressions of such opinion in seventeenth-century England – Parliaments and newspapers – are missing from the 1630s, and the manuscript newsletters that function as a major source for political historians of the preceding two decades are much rarer then. In default of such bodies of material, we depend on chance survivals of remark, usually in private papers, or in those cases where Crown policies produced local controversy. Neither shows any conclusive pattern. It is easy to find cases of puritans who were alienated, but these are precisely the people whom one would expect to be, and who seem to have represented a self-conscious minority in the population as a whole. It is also likely that the retrospective and literary nature of puritan piety would encourage those who practised it to leave more records than others, and notable that a number of undoubted puritans, as Kevin Sharpe has noted, left private records that do not complain of the regime. The points at which the latter provoked protests or commotions testify either to particular local circumstances which made the religious innovations harder to accept, or to a division of opinion. It is probably impossible from this evidence to construct a convincing general picture of what the majority of his subjects thought of what the King and his servants were doing, and how precisely the conflict with the Scots altered their views.

When this is said, however, it is still possible to suggest that Charles's adoption of a version of Arminianism as his religious policy had a fundamental structural defect that was almost inevitably going to provoke serious opposition to it, and also helps to explain the divisions that later beset the Long Parliament over religion and fed into the Civil War. The defect is the more apparent in that Kevin Sharpe himself, generally the advocate of the viability of the Personal Rule, has drawn attention to it:[31] Charles's Church of England seemed to work against the interests of the ruling elites of the English state. Its policy of renegotiating leases of Church lands formerly made on easy terms, of driving harder bargains for such leases in the future, and of attempting to increase the tithes paid to clergy, threatened the pockets of landowners and seemed to mark an attempt to claw back some of the material profits that they had made from the Reformation. Its policy of repairing and beautifying churches sometimes involved the removal of family pews installed by the dominant families of the parish. The anger or impatience with which the king and his leading churchmen responded to gentry petitions against ecclesiastical initiatives, such as those sent from Somerset against the continuation of church ales (parties to raise money for the parish) or from Kent against the restriction or abolition of foreign Protestant congregations, suggested that the powerful laity were to be excluded from having a voice in local religious matters. The admission of leading churchmen to the royal prerogative courts of Star Chamber and High Commission meant that nobles and gentry found clerics sitting in judgement upon them for a range of offences concerning order, morality and political opinion. In general, Charles's ambition to create a Church that was wealthier, more powerful and more independent of the laity (while also more closely controlled by the monarch and kept to a greater degree of conformity and uniformity), could only be achieved at the expense of the leaders of secular society.

Such a policy was likely to be particularly risky in the kingdom of England, where the Crown relied to an unusual extent on the voluntary co-operation of local lay elites to get its business done. It also, however, flew in the face of contemporary Continental European trends, which were for monarchies to strengthen themselves by making mutually profitable alliances with local lay elites at the expense of the remainder of society. Charles was attempting to knit Church and state more closely together in a stronger combination without cutting his nobility, gentry and urban oligarchs into the deal. This would do much to explain both the hostility of most of the Long Parliament to the religious innovations of the 1630s and the readiness of many peers and MPs who had not been associated with puritanism to support further reforms of the Church that diminished central control. It would also explain why the same national elites eagerly supported an intolerant Episcopalian Church with an emphasis on ritual and beauty (very similar to that of the Personal Rule) as soon as it was presented to them on terms that enhanced their social and political power: which is how the Restoration religious settlement of 1661–62 was made.

* * *

Taking all these elements together – the crisis in the fiscal–military state, the way in which it rebounded on political thought, the problems of co-ordinating a triple monarchy of such varied nature, and those of such a dynamic and fissiparous Church – it can be seen that historians during the last two decades of the twentieth century have mapped out a network of interlocking tensions that between them amply explain the outbreak and nature of the Great Civil War. Real progress in understanding has been made, even if different experts emphasise different parts of the network of factors. The problem that has beset them most keenly has been to show how exactly these tensions interacted to produce the conflict in different regions and at different levels of society and government; and a resolution of it may ultimately be beyond their powers, given the state of the evidence. If the war may be likened to a physical explosion, then historians have acted like efficient forensic chemists in building up a convincing picture of the component parts of the mixture that created the combustion. They have been less successful in determining how and why exactly that mixture was manufactured and detonated, a process that demands different skills that rely far less on straightforward forensic analysis; and the harder in that none of the suspects can actually be interviewed. History has long been perceived uneasily as a discipline lying somewhere between an art and a science, and investigation of the Civil War represents a case study of that unstable identity.

The simile of an explosion, however, incorporates the question of responsibility for the disaster, and here again a consensus has appeared among specialists. It supplies the fifth element in the framework of causation recently constructed and represents another major area of historiography: the role of the individual in producing great changes. The most prominent, powerful and influential individuals in this period were monarchs, and the process of revisionism has had a dramatically divergent impact on the reputations of the two involved in this case. James I has indeed become a lot more like James VI of Scotland, being generally recognised as a shrewd, intelligent and competent sovereign rather than as a pedantic and despotic buffoon. It remains true that the two kings are not quite the same, for James's rule over England was clearly less of a success than his government of Scotland. He was too unused to English ways, too old when he succeeded to the throne, and suffered from increasing ill health as well as some basic personal faults that were more apparent in the circumstances of the southern kingdom. He was financially extravagant, indulgent to his courtiers, and bad at explaining himself and at promoting a good image to the public; an especially grave set of defects when following a mistress of parsimony and of public relations such as Elizabeth had been. On the other hand, he faced problems of government that Elizabeth either had not known or had neglected or even produced, and it seems generally agreed that he left a realm that was perfectly amenable to management and improvement by a successor of equal or greater ability.[32]

Instead, it got Charles I. The traditional historiography that descended from Gardiner had cast him either in the role of an aspiring tyrant or of a woolly-minded and not very attractive man who fell foul of social and political changes that were beyond his ability to control. Revisionism, with its emphasis on central political events and short-term factors in historical outcomes, has in general only magnified his shortcomings. Since the end of the 1980s a succession of historians have returned deeply negative judgements on Charles. Conrad Russell declared that 'I find civil war without him almost impossible to imagine.'[33] Michael Young portrayed the king as somebody to whom menace and violence were the instinctual solutions to political problems; he 'was just plain scary'.[34] L.J. Reeve found a man simply unsuited to public life, chronically unsure of his own abilities and with a dislike of both politics and administration.[35] Christopher Durston has held him directly responsible for creating conflict between the Crown and the other parts of Parliament, and between his subjects: the principal author both of his own misfortunes and of those that beset his nations.[36] Recent parallel work by Scottish historians has held the king directly responsible for provoking the rebellion in their country that brought down the Personal Rule. Ignoring plenty of intelligent and informed advice to the contrary, he relentlessly pursued political and military policies of his own that led directly to disaster.[37] He has the record of being the only Stuart monarch of the triple kingdom to turn most of his ancestral nation against him, rather than making it a source of strength for rule elsewhere. Austin Woolrych has combined these verdicts in his overview of Charles as monarch of all three kingdoms.[38] They go far to uphold the decision of the New Model Army and its collaborators to execute him in 1649 as a 'Man of Blood', responsible for all the miseries that had been inflicted on the English since his accession.

There is a considerable irony in the label of blood-guilt, in that left to his devices – which he more or less was for the first fifteen years of his reign – Charles I was one of the gentlest of monarchs. He did not permit a single political execution in any of his three kingdoms, showing a distaste for taking life unique in any effective ruler of England alone for well over four centuries, and probably since history began. He threatened people collectively and individually, and put some of them in preventive or punitive detention, but he did not kill. The first death warrant that he signed in a political cause was of his own minister, the earl of Strafford, and forced upon him by the Long Parliament in the face of his bitter opposition. In the course of the Civil War, while the same Parliament continued to put English and Irish politicians to death – the notable English victim being Archbishop Laud – he again sent nobody to the scaffold. His reign did contain the local conviction and execution of a number of Catholic priests, under the existing penal laws, but the total was small compared to those achieved in that of his father and tiny in proportion to the figures notched up under Elizabeth. His marriage to a Catholic queen ensured that the religion of Rome had a foothold at court that gave some security to its adherents there. Unlike every Tudor sovereign, and James, he did not burn anybody to death for holding Protestant opinions that were deemed heretical by the prevailing Church. His regime may have put severe pressure on puritans, but this mostly took the form of admonition; the number of clergy actually deprived of their benefices came to less than a quarter of those dispossessed in his father's first decade of rule; and was minuscule compared with the purge commenced by Parliament during the Civil War. Furthermore he allowed the continued existence of a sanctuary for puritans in his dominions, represented by the colony of Massachusetts. When a trio of them deliberately sought martyrdom, by attacking the regime's religious policy as vehemently and publicly as possible, the king's prerogative court sentenced them to lose their ears rather than their heads; although this was enough to provoke an outcry sufficient to deter the government from any further spectacles of the sort. The execution of people accused of witchcraft went into steep decline during Charles's 'effective' reign, at least partly because of direct discouragement from him and his bishops, and might have ended altogether had his power not be broken. Instead the Civil War allowed it to reappear on an unprecedented scale in Parliament's quarters, and to gain a new lease of life that would postpone its disappearance for a further half-century.[39] From these perspectives, the king has good claims to be regarded as a liberal humanist hero, and his opponents in the Long Parliament as bloody-minded bigots.

Nor do his ideals, as expressed through his Personal Rule, seem to be especially offensive to a modern mind. He and his most prominent servants wanted a more efficient system of local government that offered his people greater security against plague, famine, poverty and invasion. They wished to protect commoners against encroachments made on their economic rights by the rich and powerful, although that policy could be subordinated to the need to reclaim large areas of forest and fen in order to increase the food supplies of an overpopulated nation. They defended the traditional games, revels and recreations of ordinary people against those who tried to abolish them in the name of a better regulated and more godly society. They attempted to improve the efficiency of the navy on which the safety of the realm and its trade depended. They desired to have a Church in which the buildings were better repaired and more attractive and the clergy better behaved, paid and educated. Their watchwords were unity, peace, order and efficiency, and they did produce a realm that was envied by the Europe of the time for its tranquillity and prosperity. It was such considerations that caused Kevin Sharpe, looking back over the first two-thirds of the reign from the catastrophes that commenced in 1641, to suggest that the king 'may even have been right'.[40]

All told, Kevin has been Charles's best friend over the past twenty years. As well as making his sympathetic study of the Personal Rule, he has examined the workings of the monarch's own mind rather than wholly concentrating on royal actions and their effects. In doing so he has made sense of the apparent paradox that Charles was both one of the most calamitous of rulers and one of the best trained. In his reading the king attempted to become the ideal sovereign portrayed in the writings and teachings of his father: curbing proud oppressors, giving justice to the poor, defending innocent mirth and recreation, keeping a temperate and devout court, being a faithful and loving husband and devoted father, dressing moderately, being pious and virtuous in habits, keeping promises, and seeing the realm as a single community with which the royal honour was bound up.[41] There is actually no contradiction between this picture and that drawn by Charles's many recent detractors; the problems of the reign were essentially the result of the king's attempt to put these excellent principles into practice.

The crucial issue, highlighted by all the recent studies, was that he was a conviction politician of heroic inflexibility, who happened to be bereft of virtually all basic political skills. He could neither understand other people nor manage them, and had chronic difficulties in explaining or projecting himself. As a result, the execution of his designs ultimately aroused confusion, fear and doubt to a degree that automatically sabotaged his dream of a more united set of realms developing in harmony with a stronger and more effective monarchy. There was nothing inherently wrong with his hectoring and steamrollering responses to opposition and his determination to drive through plans for the improvement of his realms that were badly understood by many in them. He might actually have succeeded had he possessed the insensitivity and conviction of a true egomaniac. He pushed most of the Scottish political nation into rebellion in 1637–39 in the full realisation that with the resources of England behind him he could probably crush the uprising militarily. He indeed succeeded in raising a powerful and well-equipped army without needing to call a Parliament, and accompanied it to the Border. Had he launched it at the Scots, he might well have carried all before him and had the British Isles at his feet, to be remodelled according to his ideals. Conversely, he could have been completely defeated, forcing him to give the Scots peace on their own terms (as he did the next year) and leaving him to rebuild the prestige of his government in England without having to face a Parliament. Instead his nerve gave way and he accepted the Scottish offer of a truce and further talks, even though his forces were larger and better supplied and he had supporters in arms in the northeast of Scotland and no rebels to fear at his own rear. He had not expected to meet with such determined opposition from his northern subjects, nor that they would raise so strong an army to meet him, and he was equally taken aback to discover how little enthusiasm his counsellors and generals (especially the all-important commander of his vanguard) had for the war. It is the clearest mark of Charles's failings as a leader that he could repeatedly be perplexed by the results of his actions; and this particular episode, at Berwick in June 1639, was the turning point of the reign. The king's authority in his three kingdoms never recovered from it and began to unravel continuously thereafter. The monarch portrayed by Kevin Sharpe and by the more hostile recent authors are perfectly compatible figures: Sharpe himself added to the other condemnations of the king's practical abilities a blunt statement that Charles 'was no politician'.[42] The distinction between this monarch's virtues and vices is the classic one between principle and practice.

Furthermore, as Conrad Russell has also emphasised, had Charles been a ruler as absolutely incompetent as Edward II, Richard II or Henry VI, there would have been no Civil War. It was the king's identity as a man of conviction and conscience that made him operate far more effectively as leader of a party than of a nation.[43] Although his eventual defeat in the war may be blamed on errors of political, diplomatic and military judgement, he was faced with remarkably complex choices in all spheres of operation, and the fact that the struggle lasted as long as it did and that he came close to winning it, or bringing his enemies to terms, must reflect in part on his abilities. He learned from earlier mistakes to become a constant and practised communicator, explaining his aims and policies carefully to his people. As a commander in chief, he was dedicated and energetic, marching with his army on major campaigns and efficiently chairing councils of war. In three successive campaigns, between 1642 and 1644, he and his military advisers transformed an initial position of weakness and disadvantage into one in which they were able to fight on equal terms and, in each case, achieve notable successes. They almost pulled off the same trick in 1645, till they fatally threw away the opportunity, and the war, in a fit of overconfidence. Once defeated, he never yielded to the temptation repeatedly accepted by the next three generations of his dynasty, and by his grandmother Mary, Queen of Scots, of fleeing to safety and ignominy abroad. Instead he remained in England, and in captivity, and stuck by his principles and his friends, resisting tremendous pressure from his former foes, many of his former supporters, and his wife, to sacrifice beliefs and loyalties in order to increase his chances of returning to power. Instead, with remarkable courage and consistency, he attempted to pull off the trick of appealing to public opinion while dividing his enemies and winning many of them over, without making any large political concessions. It was precisely because he came so close to success that he was put to death.

None of this palliates his repeated failure as a monarch, and his curious mixture of strengths and weaknesses only made him more dangerous to his subjects. None the less, there are two other perspectives that can be taken on his career – and rarely are – which cast it in a kinder light. One was that he would probably have fared far better in a range of alternative roles. It could be argued, for example, that had his elder brother Henry survived to become king, Charles would have made an excellent duke of York. His innate sense of loyalty, and of family connections, is likely to have kept him as a reliable supporter of the reigning monarch, while he would have been a valuable patron of art and architecture. With Henry tending more to evangelical Protestantism, Charles's taste for aspects of Arminianism could have maintained the existing balance in the Church. It could also be suggested that he might have made a greater success as ruler of peoples who were more in sympathy with the style of monarchy that he represented. The unusually heavy reliance of the English, Scottish and Irish Crowns upon the consent and co-operation of their subjects, and the unusually divided and varied attitudes and beliefs of those subjects, called for the very qualities in which Charles was most lacking. By contrast, his religious, aesthetic and political instincts would probably have made him a reasonably effective ruler of a Counter-Reformation monarchy. Certainly he would have fitted the position of the prince of a small Italian state with credit, and quite possibly would have coped well had he been born to be a Habsburg sovereign of the Spanish or Austrian lands.

The other line of extenuation, which does not depend on counter-factual hypothesis, is that his opponents, though usually greatly superior in their grasp of practical politics, were actually less realistic than the king himself. Certainly Charles was often infuriatingly obtuse and difficult to handle, but he did listen to advice and he could be persuaded into new courses. Instead his critics in English Parliaments, both in the 1620s and the 1640s, and in Scotland in the 1630s, repeatedly treated him with a provocation and insensitivity that were guaranteed to bring out the very worst in his nature and call forth the most negative possible reactions from him. Nor did they collectively behave much better than he when they had gained power. To win the war against him, the parliamentarian leaders repeatedly committed and magnified actions for which they had roundly condemned him in the past. The same politicians who failed to bring him to terms in 1646–47 wantonly provoked the New Model Army to mutiny in the latter year, while the army itself then failed spectacularly to co-operate with successive Parliaments. The king's opponents in the 1620s did not understand the crisis in the state financial and military system that was limiting his ability to function effectively and driving him to desperate courses. Many of those in the 1640s believed in the existence of an international Roman Catholic conspiracy to subvert the Protestant religion and the liberties of free peoples, of which their monarch was a collaborator, a tool or a dupe, and in particular that the Irish rising of 1641 was a part of this design and that the king had abetted it. This was wildly wrong, and was a fantasy based on a view of the world, and a brand of religion, that depended on suspicion and hatred. Charles can be blamed fairly for failing, as ruler of these people, to understand and deal constructively with their emotions; but nothing that he wanted or believed was as completely out of touch with reality as they were.

He did not die because he had made war on his people or threatened their liberties. He was put to death by a group of English – the New Model Army and its political allies – which had come to realise that he could never be trusted to accept the settlement that they wanted for the country. That settlement incorporated a very radical brand of puritanism, tolerating the existence of extreme Protestant groups who wanted to worship outside the national Church, that was not just rejected by Charles but by the great majority of the people of each of the three kingdoms. It was precisely to prevent it that the king had carried out his desperate gamble of putting together an alliance that represented between its constituent parts most of the inhabitants of the island of Britain, and was defeated in the Second Civil War of 1648. To get rid of him, his enemies had to remove two-thirds of the traditional institution of Parliament, the monarchy and the House of Lords, and purge the Commons down to a minority. Ever after, the regimes produced by this act had to place constant limitations on the expressed will of the nation, by binding political qualifications on its elected representatives and subjecting them to further purges, summary dissolutions, and severely restricting their constitutional powers. In the end, they destroyed themselves in a welter of in-fighting and defections, and the first elected national assembly since 1640 that represented anything like the will of the electorate proceeded to restore Charles's son.

The last battle of the English Civil Wars was not, as is commonly claimed, that at Worcester in 1651 at which Charles II was defeated after his invasion of England with a Scottish army, to avenge his father and restore the traditional constitution. It was at Winnington Bridge, in August 1659, where the republic's army crushed the rebellion of Sir George Booth, one corner of a nationwide alliance of former royalists and parliamentarians intended to bring back the monarchy and Lords. It involved about 5000 men, making it a full-scale pitched action of medium size by the standards of the earlier conflicts.[44] The last military event of the wars came only in April 1660, when John Lambert rallied a few hundred horsemen at Edgehill in the midlands. The place for the rendezvous was intended to frame the whole period neatly, as indeed it did, for it was the scene of the first battle of the Great Civil War, almost eighteen years before. Lambert's troops were to form the nucleus of an army designed to prevent the restoration of the Stuarts, but before reinforcements could reach him he was routed and captured by a larger body of soldiers loyal to the provisional government. There were other republican conspiracies after that, spanning the first seven years of the restored monarchy, and intermittent bloody fighting continued in Scotland throughout the remaining four decades of the seventeenth century. None of the English plots, however, succeeded in getting a party of soldiers into the field, and the Scottish troubles were largely self-contained. England enjoyed a quarter-century of often tension-ridden internal peace before a new cycle of serious violence began in 1685.

To end the English civil wars in 1660 instead of 1651 is to make a significant historiographical argument. It changes the perspective on the 1650s from one that treats the decade as a period of recovery under strong and successful government, engaged in interesting constitutional experiments and bestowing an unprecedented amount of liberty of conscience, to one that portrays it as taken up with continuing political instability, religious confusion and tension, and continued bloodshed, as a succession of republican regimes struggled and failed to achieve either popularity or constitutional legitimacy. Fear of just such an outcome played a very large part in the readiness of the majority of those peers and MPs who had fought the king in the Great Civil War to come to terms with him after the Second Civil War. The soldiers who prevented such an outcome then failed completely to prove that an alternative had been viable. The divisions of the 1650s were just as bitter as those in the 1640s, though different in kind as former royalists and parliamentarians closed ranks against republicans and sectaries, and arguably more long lasting. The result was, ultimately, a still more interesting, varied and culturally dynamic English society than that of the early Stuart period – judged by the criteria of modern liberal humanists – but only at the price of a lot more suffering and killing, lasting almost another hundred years.

In the last analysis, the issues that divided Charles I and his executioners in 1649 are barely accessible to the modern imagination. The soldiers who insisted on his trial shared, with varying degrees of enthusiasm, a view of the world powered by the sense of constant intervention by an omnipotent god, to whose direct intervention their victories could be credited. Many of them hoped to be numbered among the saints who would reign in his name at the end of the processes of history. Charles himself died because he believed in the same cosmology. In his reading of it, he held his royal title at the direct dispensation of the deity, and would earn his reward of eternal salvation only if he subjected himself wholly to the divine will. His executioners agreed wholly with both parts of this proposal, but read the signs differently; what to them, and the army behind them, had been heavenly reproofs and warnings to the king, followed by evidence of outright divine repudiation of him, had been to Charles a systematic testing of his faith. To the king, a willingness to abandon his concept of how the English state should be – with a uniform national religion and a legislative and judicial power vested in monarch, Lords and Commons, and both remaining under ultimate royal control – was to risk the perpetual damnation of his soul.[45] His refusal to surrender his principles of divine order, which he saw as his means to salvation, marked him for his enemies as a man irrevocably damned.

This is a view of human life, and of history, that is no longer shared by the overwhelming majority of the inhabitants of the United Kingdom; it places a greater conceptual gulf between the chief actors of 1649 and the present-day British than between the latter and the modern Chinese. It is entirely possible to make a leap of imagination and to conduct a process of research that permits an understanding of Charles and his executioners. It may well be also that differences of temperament, interest and tradition will induce some writers and readers of history to accord more sympathy to the monarch or to his opponents. As far as the present day is concerned, however, the only rational response to an invitation to choose between them, in terms of political, civil or philosophical principle, is an abstention.

4 Oliver Cromwell

One of the more neglected categories of source-material for the English historical memory consists of the 'A to Z' street maps of towns and cities on sale at motorway service stations. A perusal of the indexes of these suggests that Cromwell has more streets named after him than any other character in the story of the nation: and few of them are major thoroughfares in the civic and commercial hearts of the communities. Most are in residential neighbourhoods, suggesting that he has a particularly strong place in the affections of ordinary people. This makes his tenure of the tenth position in the polling for the 'Greatest Briton' in 2002 appear unexpectedly low, but it was still sufficient to confirm his status among the subjects of the contemporary United Kingdom as the most celebrated and admired personality of his age. His position in the traditions of the wider Anglo-American community is indicated by the fact that during the past forty years he has been the only character from his century to be made the hero of a full-scale cinematic blockbuster with an all-star cast.

His celebrity is certainly understandable, for, if not exactly a story of rags to riches, his career represents a spectacular rise from almost total obscurity to supreme power that is unique in the history of the British Isles. It was also very swift – just fourteen years for the whole process – and accompanied by the glamour of striking military victory. He was a soldier who won every field action in which he engaged, and which included most of the largest battles in seventeenth-century British history. This sort of career is far from rare in world history, but Cromwell represents the only case of it within this archipelago. In itself, his success does much to explain the admiration with which he is treated at the present day. In a society based on the principle of meritocracy, he is the outstanding past home-grown example of it. None the less, his reputation is generally held to depend as much upon what he represented as what he did, and how he used power as well as his achievement of it. He is regarded as a conviction politician of exceptional probity, serving ideals that still compel the respect of the present day and in some respects prepared the way for modern democracy and civil liberty.

Upon closer inspection there is something very odd about this situation. After all, for virtually the whole period since Cromwell's death, his nation has been governed in a manner to which he and his party came to be very much opposed, and which they did their utmost to remove. Ultimate executive power has been vested in a hereditary monarchy, descended from the royal family which he strove permanently to exclude. Legislation has been a process shared between an upper house based on a traditional hereditary aristocracy and a lower one elected by qualified commoners and with sole power over its own membership once in position. This was the very system destroyed by the revolution that brought Cromwell to major political and military power. The national Church has been one with bishops, cathedrals and a pronounced element of ceremony and physical decoration, in which Protestants of his hue have had no place. If anything, the national forms of politics and religion that have obtained for most of the intervening centuries have borne a closer resemblance to those proposed by Charles I and his supporters in 1642 than those associated with the man who came to be their greatest enemy.

It is true that reforms in the nineteenth and twentieth centuries produced an electoral system for the House of Commons that was presaged to some extent by the measures carried out by Cromwell and his allies. It is also true that in recent years the hereditary element in the Upper House has been reduced to an extent that makes it more similar to that which was briefly established in the 1650s, while the office of Prime Minister has been enhanced to the point at which in some respects it resembles Oliver's one of Lord Protector. There is no evidence, however, that any of these measures were inspired, either consciously or subconsciously, by those of the mid-seventeenth century. Indeed, the culture of modern Britain has grown ever more unlike that which characterised Cromwell's rule. The United Kingdom now contains the most secular society in the Western world, and it has long been one of the least militarised. It would be hard to find a character from its past who personifies it less than the man who rose to power as the leader of a godly army. Current relationships between the constituent states of the British Isles depend heavily on mutual understanding and co-operation; the very reverse of that imposition of English control by direct conquest which was one of Oliver's most obvious achievements. Whereas other military heroes of his nation displayed their prowess against foreign foes, he led armies only within the British Isles, and the blood that his soldiers spilled was almost wholly that of their fellow subjects in what had been the triple kingdom of the Stuarts and was to be the United Kingdom of the later British monarchy. In strictly logical terms, Cromwell is not a heroic progenitor of contemporary Britons but the polar opposite: the exemplar of the very things that modern Britain has most conspicuously avoided: militarism, religious fundamentalism, English chauvinism and civil discord. The people whom he most closely resembles in the current English-speaking world are the extreme right wing of the American political spectrum: they alone share to the full his mixture of evangelical Protestant piety, association with republicanism, admiration of redemptive violence, and willingness to override constitutional and legal norms which are perceived as having been corrupted into a shelter for evil.

His current popularity is also remarkable in that it is a relatively recent creation. As Timothy Lang and Blair Worden have demonstrated between them, for almost two hundred years after his death his dominant reputation was that of a self-seeking adventurer associated (in varying degrees) with usurpation, destruction, desecration and religious fanaticism leavened by hypocrisy. There were voices raised in his favour, but they tended to be self-consciously opposed to the norm. His transformation into a hero took place under Victoria and was largely produced by two mighty and interlinked forces of the age, the Liberal Party and the Dissenting Churches. Both were new powers in national politics and sought for figures in the past who might be employed as ancestors and precedents for themselves. Cromwell's faith, moral earnestness, political pragmatism, imperial associations (because of his govern-ment's conquest of Jamaica) and undistinguished but respectable social origins all fitted him for such a role. In a succession of works, but above all the densely researched volumes of Gardiner, he was presented as a truly national hero, rather than that of a party. None the less, the works were produced by various different kinds of Liberal, and the enduring contention over his reputation was neatly illus-trated by the controversy over the proposal to erect a statue of him outside the House of Commons to commemorate the tercentenary of his birth. It was eventu-ally paid for not by public funds but from the private pocket of the Liberal party leader, Lord Rosebery.[1] This division of views was slow to die away. In rural areas, the old dominant image of the Lord Protector as a vandal and a bogeyman, well established in local folklore by the eighteenth century, was still recorded in the first half of the twentieth. As late as 1960 the naming of yet another Cromwell Gardens, on a newly built housing estate at Wallingford in the Thames Valley, was voted down by the borough council on the grounds that it honoured a 'malefactor'.[2] It seems likely that this reaction was connected to the fact that Wallingford had been one of the last royalist fortresses to surrender at the end of the Great Civil War; although Cromwell himself had not been involved in its reduction.

What a Lang or a Worden needs to do now is explain the fortunes of Oliver's reputation in the period since the mid-twentieth century, when controversy has been replaced by something approaching a consensual admiration. In large part this development has been due to the increasing dominance of the writing of his-tory by university-based professionals. It is notable that, as interest in the Civil War has undergone a relative decline in recent years, preoccupation with Cromwell himself has, if anything, intensified. Since 1990, he has been the subject of three new full-length studies, by Barry Coward, Peter Gaunt and J.C. Davis, while yet another has been commissioned from Martyn Bennett. John Morrill has edited an important collection of essays devoted to Cromwell's career, while he has featured prominently in major textbooks on the period from Derek Hirst and Austin Woolrych. Laura L. Knoppers has examined the way in which Cromwell was represented in propaganda works by his supporters and opponents.[3] All of these are fine works by talented historians, and all have contributed – in some cases very significantly – to knowledge of their subject. What is striking is the una-nimity achieved by this relatively large number of different scholars. All have essentially endorsed and repeated the verdict passed by Gardiner: that Cromwell was a great and admirable individual who dominated and determined the politics of his age and was ultimately a political failure. He achieved neither his vision for the future of his nation nor any settlement of its affairs, not because there was anything inherently wrong in what he desired but because the bulk of his compatriots were not yet ready to recognise its worth. There is a double conundrum in this pattern. One part of it is, as has been said above, that in many respects Gardiner's tragic hero seems a figure peculiarly ill-suited for celebration by the modern British. The other is that, as has been said much earlier, Gardiner's view of British history was one that became a major target of the revisionists of the 1970s. Somehow, while that portion that dealt with the early Stuarts has been subjected to sustained and largely persuasive challenge, that concerned with Cromwell has been endorsed, and sometimes by the same historians.

Certainly a historiographical drift seems to be setting into Oliver's image at a level below that of professional scholarship. The overwhelming majority of the undergraduates whom I teach arrive at university with a vague and unthinking impression of him as a national hero. On examination their opinion is revealed to be a compound of different sources. Most obvious is the opinion of the historians whom I have cited, and of their predecessors in the late twentieth century who generally wrote in much the same style. Sometimes these are read directly at school, and more often they are filtered through teachers, textbooks, sixth-form conferences and television programmes. To the many who have been taken on visits to the Houses of Parliament, the sight of the statue planted by Rosebery, right before the entrance to the Commons, conveys a solid and silent impression of Cromwell's assured centrality in our constitutional history. To top this off, there is the Hollywood film, rescreened at regular intervals on television channels.

There may indeed be a simple explanation for this situation: that Gardiner's portrait was actually perfectly correct, and that recent research has only served to reinforce it. On the other hand the favourable attitude taken by recent specialists towards Cromwell makes a rather obvious fit with the tendency of the same historians to concentrate interest and sympathy upon the parliamentarians of the Civil War; in fact it is a chronological continuation of that tendency. The absence of any Tory-Anglican-royalist tradition among academic experts in the period certainly works towards this end. It might be suggested also that the generation that underwent its formative experiences in the Second World War, and dominated universities between the 1960s and the 1980s, would have certain points of contact with the New Model Army and its leaders. Both had, after all, gone through a gruelling struggle, which at points seemed likely to end in their destruction, against ideologically opposed enemies who could be identified (in the modern case inarguably) with political tyranny and moral evil. Both emerged into a scarred and battered postwar England with a commitment to reforms that would ensure that the defects of the pre-war world would never reappear. Such a hypothesis, however, fails wholly to account for the persisting and strengthening favour accorded to

Cromwell by younger historians, and for the manner in which Victorian perceptions could be overturned in the case of early-seventeenth-century English history
but reinforced in that of the middle decades of the century. It seems that there is
another factor at work here, and one related directly to the way in which historians are trained to practise their discipline: the condition of the surviving evidence.

* * *

The rehabilitation of Oliver's reputation in Victoria's reign really began with the
edition of his letters and speeches by Thomas Carlyle that appeared in 1845. As
Lang and Worden noted in their study of the historiography, this served him better than any straightforward biography would have done. By speaking in his own
voice (admittedly garnished with Carlyle's irrepressible editorial tendency to shout
support for Oliver and abuse at his opponents), he provided the best possible
defence against the charges of hypocrisy, ambition and treachery that had commonly been levelled at him by authors after the Stuart Restoration had swept away
the last remnants of his regime. Cromwell could be a marvellous user of words, at
once apparently artless and colloquial and gifted with a talent for telling and ringing phrases. Carlyle's edition presented readers with what was effectively a spiritual
autobiography, by a devout and dedicated leader faced with extraordinary challenges, opportunities and temptations. Together with *The Pilgrim's Progress* and
Paradise Lost, it takes its place as one of the three classics of puritan literature.
Subsequently augmented by S.C. Lomas, and then apparently replaced by Wilbur C.
Abbott's massive series of volumes that further enlarged the same material, they are
also the starting point for any modern biographer.[4] Effectively, for most they seem
to have been the finishing point as well. The now standard portrait of Oliver as a
tragic hero, of mighty powers, high ideals and infinitely good intentions, struggling
with an impossible task, is the one that he presents in person. John Morrill, reflect-
ing on the book that he had edited on Cromwell, could declare that its subject 'has
proved one of the most accessible and open of Englishmen. In seeking to make
sense of him, the essays in this volume have quite properly allowed him to speak
for himself. They have not been insouciant or uncritical; but they have projected an
image he projected of himself.'[5]

Quite so, and the issue of whether it actually is 'quite proper' to allow a historical personality to speak for himself is one that needs to be argued rather than
assumed. John Morrill was too good a historian to be unaware of the problems
involved, or to shirk them. Later in the same essay he noted the discrepancies
between Cromwell's projected image and that formed of him by many of his contemporaries, and concluded that he was 'one of the best-known and least easily
understood of the great men of history'.[6] Elsewhere, in the same year, he published
his concern that the ready availability of Cromwell's letters and speeches could
have 'inhibited rather than enhanced' a thorough examination of his life and

thought, and 'encouraged scholars to dash off biographies rather than to research them properly'.[7] It is by no means obvious, however, that even a thorough examination and proper research will necessarily overcome the problem of understanding Oliver, rather than merely understanding what he wanted people to think of him. The test case here may be that of Blair Worden, who has repeatedly been cited since the 1980s as the person most likely to make such a breakthrough. This opinion rests primarily on three important essays which he published in 1984 and 1985, which between them made a very revealing study of the meaning of Cromwell's words. Thanks to these we now comprehend much better what Oliver and some of his contemporaries signified when they spoke of liberty of conscience, or of providence, or of the fear of attracting divine disapproval.[8] What they provide, however, is insight into the way in which Cromwell employed and manipulated a set of images and ideas, without any consistent and detailed consideration of questions of sincerity, opportunism, context, moment and possible differences between his usage and that of others. As such, they are (thus far) brilliant contributions to intellectual and cultural history rather than biography in the conventional sense of the term.

It is revealing and – given the biographical tradition outlined above – almost shocking to discover how different the perspectives taken on the subject can be by scholars who are not primarily concerned with the man himself. As yet no experts in literary criticism have examined the letters and speeches as texts, and compared views on the manner in which they use rhetoric and trope, and whether they can be read against the grain of the explicit messages. It may still be significant that one author in that tradition, considering events in the First Protectorate Parliament of 1654–55, could refer casually to the impossibility of knowing how far Cromwell's words could be believed and describe him as 'a paradigm of self-fashioning'.[9] A historian attempting to make sense of developments at the opening of the next Parliament, of 1656–58, has reported on the absence of good information on which a history of central politics in it could be based. In default of it, Cromwell's biographers have tended to assume that his own role was very important, if not pivotal, but the hints and rumours that survive suggest that events were driven by a division between his civilian and military advisers. He himself appears as a withdrawn, aloof and enigmatic figure.[10] One of the most remarkable new perspectives has been taken by Sean Kelsey, in his study of the Commonwealth of 1649–53. His sympathies lie with the civilian government of the regime, represented by the purged Parliament which transformed England into a republic and the Council of State that it appointed. This approach has led him into a view of the state's army and its commanders, including Cromwell, that is startlingly and refreshingly hostile after the implicit support and extenuation that most authors have given to them. Previous work had portrayed the Parliament as a body caught between a radical army and a conservative nation, and generally faulted it for failing to satisfy either. Kelsey's is the first to argue that the army itself, which had created the regime by purging the Parliament down to a minority prepared to establish a republic, pushed it into an impossible position. The soldiers had no clear or coherent vision of the reforms that they wished to have adopted, and were divided over particular courses. They demanded that the new regime be both radical and popular, and these were actually incompatible targets. Kelsey almost casually exposes the determination of the army to retain overall control of the political process, and of Cromwell to retain control of the army, and the ruthlessness and cunning with which they manoeuvred in order to obtain these ends.[11]

Even when concentrating on Oliver's own words, without selection and when their context and intended meaning are absolutely clear, it is perfectly possible to draw diametrically opposed conclusions from them. An example of this may be provided in the form of one of his earlier known letters, written to a friend and fellow parliamentarian in the immediate aftermath of the biggest battle of the Great Civil War, Marston Moor. It was the first really large action in which Cromwell had borne a command, and he had played a decisive part in the complete victory achieved by his cause. His purpose in writing, however, was not merely to announce a personal and a partisan triumph but to break a piece of terrible news to his correspondent:

Dear Sir,

It's our duty to sympathise in all mercies; that we may praise the Lord together in chastisements or trials, so that we may sorrow together.

Truly England and the Church of God hath a great favour from the Lord, in this great victory given to us, such as the like never was since this war began. It had all the evidence of an absolute victory obtained by the Lord's blessing upon the godly party principally. We never charged but we routed the enemy. The left wing, which I commanded, being our own horse, saving a few Scots in our rear, beat all the Prince's horse. God made them as stubble to our swords, we charged their regiments of foot with our horse, routed all we charged. The particulars I cannot relate now, but I believe, of twenty-thousand the Prince hath not four-thousand left. Give glory, all the glory, to God. Sir, God hath taken away your eldest son by a cannon shot. It brake his leg. We were necessitated to have it cut off, whereof he died. Sir, you know my trials this way; but the Lord supported me with this: that the Lord took him into the happiness we all pant after and live for. There is your precious child full of glory, to know sin nor sorrow no more. He was a gallant young man, exceeding gracious. God give you his comfort. Before his death he was so full of comfort to Frank Russel and myself he could not express it, it was so great above his pain. This he said to me. Indeed, it was admirable. A little after, he said one thing lay upon his spirit. I asked him what it was. He told me that it was, that God had not suffered him to be no more the executioner of His enemies. At his fall, his horse being killed with the bullet, and I am informed three horses more, he bid them open to the right and left, that he might see the rogues run. Truly he was exceedingly beloved in the Army, of all that knew him. But few knew him, for he was a precious young man, fit for God.

You have cause to bless the Lord. He is a glorious saint in Heaven, wherein you ought exceedingly to rejoice. Let this drink up your sorrow; seeing these are not feigned words to comfort you, but the thing is so real and undoubted a truth. You may do all things by the strength of Christ. Seek that, and you shall easily bear your trial. Let this public mercy to the Church of God make you to forget your private sorrow. The Lord be your strength; so prays

> Your truly faithful and loving brother,
> Oliver Cromwell[12]

This is one of his more famous letters, but has been given here in full so that a closer reading can be made of it. It is typical of most of his personal missives in its rough, vigorous, idiomatic style, its fervent piety, and his tendency to use military victory automatically to exalt and justify his cause. Its fame is due to its publication by four successive editors, for the original disappeared after a sale in 1917. It can plausibly be read as a supreme illustration of the humanity of the author. Faced with the task of informing a friend of the sudden, violent and painful death of his son and heir, Cromwell begins with the good news: the tremendous victory won by their common cause. He then moves on to disclose the tragedy, in staccato sentences that betray his emotion. He reminds his friend, obliquely, of the recent loss of his own eldest son (of sickness contracted while serving in a garrison), establishing a bond of grief between them. Then he gives comfort, in the way most needed by a devout puritan such as his correspondent, by assuring him that his child is destined for the perpetual bliss of heaven. He piles on the further consolation that the boy expired in certainty and joy, consoled both by salvation and by victory and aided by them to overcome his physical pain. Given the cultural values and expectations within which Cromwell and his friend operated, and the perennial human needs of bereavement, Oliver could hardly have done better.

From a different point of view, it is an appalling piece of writing, vividly illustrating the dehumanising effects of war. The people whom Cromwell and his comrades have been killing were virtually all fellow Englishmen, against whom they could hardly have imagined committing acts of violence only three years before. Yet already the royalists are rendered inanimate ('stubble') or demonic ('His enemies') or criminal ('rogues'), and all this poor, mutilated, dying boy can regret – at least in Oliver's depiction of him – is that he was not able to slaughter more of them. All this civil strife, which others at the time were calling 'unhappy' or 'unnatural', is hailed joyously as part of the natural and cosmic order, decreed and cheered on by God Himself. Furthermore, Cromwell's definition of righteousness is remarkably narrow. He is not rejoicing in the victory of Parliament, let alone that of a broad-based British alliance in which Oliver's East Anglians had co-operated fully on the battlefield with Yorkshiremen and Scots alike; something which is only acknowledged with a reference to 'a few Scots in our rear'. Instead his concentration is wholly upon 'the Church of God' and 'the godly party', by which he emphatically does not mean the Church of England and the parliamentarians in general, but his particular faction within both, of a minority of extreme puritan radicals. None of this diminishes the letter as an exercise in consolation, but it is one that has been straitjacketed within a narrowly sectarian mentality.

This example may prove the point of how difficult it can be to reach a common view of the man even when his behaviour is consistent and the evidence is unambiguous; and neither of these factors obtain in much of the later part of his career. None the less, recent studies of him have, as said, tended to be remarkably consensual, and to endorse a portrait of him that is rooted in Victorian historiography and based largely on his self-image. It is time to take a closer and more critical look at that image.

* * *

On trawling through the editions of Cromwell's letters and speeches, it is easy to extract many phrases that would win applause from modern liberals, democrats, patriots and meritocrats; the constituency which he, in his Victorian reworking as a national hero, is generally held to represent. There are, indeed, many more examples of such phrases than are current in most of the surviving utterances of his contemporaries. He honours the traditional ranks of society while valuing personal qualities above social status: thus, he manages to be anti-establishment and anti-aristocratic while leaving people their titles and their property. He talks of the need to preserve both the civil liberties of the nation and the liberty of conscience to citizens of differing religious views. He repeatedly urges the British to unity, reconciliation and a common effort to sustain and promote national greatness. At the same time he calls for measures to relieve the victims of persecution abroad. He excoriates tyranny, intolerance and bigotry. His religious devotion and love of Scripture are palliated for many modern readers by the apparently personal, enquiring and non-denominational nature of his faith. The latter is also rendered more palatable to present-day tastes by the almost total absence of Satan from his utterances. Oliver's cosmos is not one divided by an epic contest between mighty forces of good and evil, but ordered and directed throughout by an omnipotent, benevolent and just deity whose directions and purposes should engross the whole attention of true believers. Its lack of dualism may help to explain one of the most attractive aspects of his personality to modern observers: his willingness both to forgive defeated foes who had shown repentance and conversion, and to recognise genuine piety in individuals to whose ideas and loyalties he was opposed in most respects. Also appealing to present tastes is his lack of interest in particular forms and structures of religion and his enquiring focus on the nature of divine revelation.[13] In other respects, his own words do him less than justice, for they conceal his love of beauty (save in the case of language) and of fun. Recent biographers have added to the earnest Cromwell of the public image a private man who enjoyed music, dancing, art and practical jokes.[14] In all these respects he can be made into the perfect historical figure: a person from an earlier age who still seems to speak directly to our own.

A closer examination reveals some anomalies in this portrait. Blair Worden and J.C. Davis have done much to elucidate the concepts of liberty current in the mid-seventeenth century and show how they differed from those that have prevailed in the last two hundred years. Like almost everybody of his time, Cromwell did not believe in toleration as a virtue in itself. A *de facto* freedom of worship was achieved in the late 1640s and 1650s because all those Protestant groups who now wished to practise outside the Church of England were driven to make common cause with each other and with the parliamentarian army. They did so most reluctantly, because of the fear of being wiped out by the majority in Parliament who wished to establish an intolerant presbyterian system. The alliance between the independent churches and the soldiers persisted because they remained unpopular minorities within British society. In this situation Cromwell and his colleagues ensured liberty of conscience for groups who shared a common ancestry in pre-war puritanism. The aim was to provide a temporary toleration of their diversity in order to give them time to resolve their differences and rebuild a properly reformed national Church. Once that was accomplished, those groups left outside it (mainly Catholics and Episcopalian Anglicans) could be persecuted more effectively. Freedom, to Oliver and those who thought like him, was not identified with individual or corporate rights, but with co-operation with the true will of God. Tyranny was defined as the repression of the godly, not as repression of human beings in general.[15]

Cromwell's utterances are therefore soaked in a language of virtue that is uncompromisingly partisan. They repeatedly use the word 'honest' as a shorthand for radical puritanism, as to Oliver a commitment to such piety was itself proof of sincerity and probity. This forms the context for one of the most admired quotations from his letters, defending his recruitment policy to his horse regiment in 1643: 'I had rather have a plain russet-coated captain that knows what he fights for and loves what he knows, than that which you call a gentleman and is nothing else.'[16] It is easy to understand how such a plea for a combined patriotism and meritocracy has appealed to the nineteenth- and twentieth-century British, but the context of the original letter – which, as in the case of the one after Marston Moor, now exists only in printed editions – puts a different gloss on the passage. What Cromwell wanted his captains to love and fight for was the cause of radical reformation of the national Church. As he declared earlier in the letter, employing his usual code, he sought 'honest, godly men', and puritans of this hue were not common in the upper ranks of county society. The gentry with whom he was dealing were suspicious of them not merely because they were of lower birth but because of a belief (which was to prove well-founded in subsequent years) that some of them might wish to do away with the Church altogether.

This charge – that he was employing and encouraging 'Anabaptists' – was one which Cromwell had repeatedly to face during the following fourteen months, and he employed various strategies to counter it.[17] One was simply to deny it, another to gloss over the religious issue by emphasising the intrinsic ability and loyalty of his men, as in the case of the letter above. A third was to declare a strictly legalistic interpretation of the need to fight the Civil War, avoiding the issue of religion. This was expressed most clearly in September 1644, when he grumbled over the accusations of religious extremism and heterodoxy still levelled at him and his officers and announced that he regarded his part in the conflict as motivated only by 'the authority of the Parliament to maintain itself in its just rights'. This is one of the very few statements by Cromwell to have been read against the grain by a historian, Glenn Burgess, who has set it in a succession of declarations made by puritans in the course of the war, by which they denied a religious motivation for their support of Parliament and insisted on constitutional grounds. This was to counter royalist charges that they aimed at a fundamental subversion of the Church and to occupy the moral high ground of custom and legality, representing themselves as defenders of the established order.[18] Burgess added in most of these cases the personal motivation was very clearly religious, and the declarations a tactical reformulation, although a sincere one. This is certainly true of Cromwell, as is revealed by his private letter after Marston Moor, which emphasised the primacy of religion in his cause, and was made starkly clear to all a year later, after the decisive victory at Naseby. Emboldened by the total defeat of the king's own army, he asked of the House of Commons that his men be granted the 'liberty of conscience' for which they were fighting.[19]

Even in this early stage of his public career, therefore, Oliver was no straightforward holy warrior but somebody who manipulated language to conceal, extenuate and promote his aims, and those of his faction in the parliamentarian party. This pattern remained true for the rest of his life. He talked and wrote a great deal about God, but not all of the time. Many of his surviving letters are purely functional, and if they mention his deity at all, it is in a routine farewell. Religion saturates his language whenever he is attempting to extol or defend his public actions, or is musing to friends about political difficulties. This is natural enough to any devout Christian of his age, seeking to inspect the apparent workings of providence, but would be especially necessary to somebody in his particular position. His rapid rise to power consisted of participation in a rebellion against the traditional source of political and moral authority, the monarch. In a century when all legitimate government was presumed to rest on divine right, it was important for Oliver to demonstrate to himself and to others that his apparent position as a rebel and a usurper was taken in strict accordance with the will of providence. In the last analysis he always appealed simply to the military defeats sustained by his opponents, but as a conscientious puritan he was also obliged to consider Scripture in more detail for messages that his course was divinely ordained. This gave his speeches, in particular, a sermonising quality of a sort rare for a lay politician.

It also turned them into perpetual exercises in self-justification. Their consistent tone is summed up perfectly by a report of one made to the corporation of London in 1658, which is the more striking in that it was written by an admirer and with no intentional irony: 'He represented unto them how eminently God had owned and prospered him in the great work in which he stood interested for the establishment of righteousness.'[20] The problem here was the hazy boundary between righteousness and self-righteousness: in seeking repeatedly to justify the ways of God to humans, he could give the impression – and, as shall be discussed, commonly did – of taking the name of God to justify all that he did himself. In seeking to convince the world that the Almighty had 'owned' him, he needed also to annihilate rival sources of divine authority. The most bitter and indignant of all his public declarations were those issued to opponents – whether Irish Catholic bishops or Scottish Covenanters – who likewise appropriated the language of godliness for their cause.[21] To the former he argued Scripture, in the manner of Protestants confronting the traditions of Rome, while to the latter he reversed tactics and declared that the Bible was not a plain guide: 'Precept may be upon precept, line upon line, and yet the Word of the Lord may be to some a Word of judgement, that they may fall backward, and be broken and be snared and be taken.' When Scripture was quoted against him, Oliver was very quick to rule that its apparent authority could be illusory. Likewise, among his own supporters he was careful to ensure that nobody could claim any direct mandate from their deity. It was customary from 1647 onward for army officers to respond to political dilemmas with prayer meetings at which they asked for the divine spirit to guide them in reaching a decision. After one of the first of these, Lieutenant-Colonel Goffe made the mistake of reporting what he felt that God had told him personally, and was forced to apologise by Cromwell, who insisted that nobody at these gatherings could actually claim to speak on behalf of the deity.[22] This was certainly in accordance with Oliver's sense of religious propriety, but it also eliminated the risk that one of his subordinates could assume the status of a prophet.

In the last analysis, Cromwell's argument for providential blessing was based on the principle that might is right, and he had accordingly to work very hard to cloak this potentially unpalatable truth. The plain fact of his military career was that, providentially or not, he almost never fought an enemy who was superior in number and equipment to his own forces at the moment of contact. With only one exception, at Dunbar in 1650, his victories depended on the fact that he made full use of odds that were already in his favour. At other times, it is true, only his own talent as a commander and the ineptitude of his enemies ensured that his numerical supremacy was gained: at Preston, in 1648, he faced an enemy army that was much larger than his in total, but took it in the rear and by surprise when it was strung out on the march. He could therefore overwhelm each segment of it consecutively, concentrating all his forces against smaller units. It was rhetorically necessary, however, for him to represent all his victories as actions won against foes who were superior in material terms but lacked the favour of God: only by this means could a clear divine dispensation be claimed for the result. Thus at Worcester in 1651 it is clear to the historian that Cromwell had concentrated 28 000 men against 12 000 royalists, enabling him to attack them simultaneously from two sides at once and enjoy numerical superiority on both. Furthermore, when the king's men attempted a counter-attack, on one flank, they were not only outnumbered at that point but having to move uphill and over open ground on horseback against an enemy covered by hedgerows and ready to receive them with concentrated fire. To complete the hopelessness of their situation, the constriction of the terrain meant that they could only deploy some of their force at any one time.[23] When reporting his inevitable triumph to Parliament, Cromwell conceded that he had been able to engage the enemy on two fronts at once. However, he also made the royal army out to be 16 000 strong, while failing to state his own numbers, and declared that leaving only a small force on the far side, it had launched almost its whole strength at just half of his army. This enabled him to imply that he had still been given a victory against more powerful foes.[24]

Another example of the same process is represented by his famous recollection of the battle of Naseby, made a month later in a letter to an MP which was published as a pamphlet and presumably written with that purpose in mind. Cromwell was intent here on answering his critics in his own party, whom he described as 'malicious' individuals 'who swell with envy'. He described how he 'saw the enemy draw up and march in gallant order towards us, and we a company of poor ignorant men', and went on to say how the certainty of God's favour to his cause gave him confidence of victory.[25] In reality his 'company' consisted of a superbly cohesive and well-equipped cavalry wing in an army that outnumbered its enemy by a ratio of over one-third; this superiority was one reason why the New Model had taken the risk of engaging the king in the first place. On Cromwell's side of the battlefield, the odds were nearer two to one in his favour, and he was facing an enemy struggling to attack him uphill across broken ground, against whom his greater numbers could tell to maximum effect.[26] It may well be that in details of these reports he was being perfectly sincere; that he genuinely thought the king's army at Worcester to be larger than it was, and that he was initially impressed by the sight of the one marching to attack him at Naseby. None the less, the consistency of his strategy in maximising the marvellous element in his successes, and the polemical reason for doing so, are both very clear.

In other respects tactical considerations demanded inconsistency. An example of this has already been given, in his assertion or undermining of Scriptural authority in exchanges of propaganda. A more extended one consists of his attitude towards the toleration of Roman Catholics. It first became a matter of public importance in his invasion of Ireland, and at two points of particular ideological delicacy. One occurred when he was negotiating for the surrender of the town of Ross, and its Irish governor asked for toleration of the religion of its Roman Catholic inhabitants, on the grounds that Cromwell had by then often declared his commitment to liberty of conscience. He received the tart answer that 'if by liberty of conscience you mean a liberty to exercise the mass, I judge it best to use plain dealing, and to let you know, where the Parliament of England have power, that will not be allowed of'.[27] Oliver thus both refused discussion of the point and pushed off responsibility for it onto his government. He had to do better three months later, when the Catholic bishops urged the Irish to greater efforts to resist his invasion, as a threat to their religion, liberties and nationhood. In his public declaration of reply, he deployed two arguments against them. The first was based on the Bible, and standard Protestant polemic: that clergy of their kind were not justified in Scripture and that they were followers of the Antichrist predicted in the Book of Revelation. The second was narrowly legalistic: that the mass was forbidden in Ireland under the laws of Queen Elizabeth and that he was only executing the latter. He also proclaimed[28] that he had come '(by the assistance of God) to hold forth and maintain the lustre and glory of English liberty in a nation where we have an undoubted right to do it; – wherein the people of Ireland (if they listen not to such seducers as you are) may equally participate in all benefits, to use liberty and fortune equally with Englishmen'. Like most of Cromwell's pronouncements, it was more distinguished by rhetoric and indignation than careful reasoning. Within eight months he was to lecture the Scots on the fallibility of Scriptural interpretations, while Elizabethan laws in both England and Ireland had equally forbidden liberty of worship to radical Protestants, and he campaigned successfully to have them repealed. He never specified the 'undoubted right' of the English Parliament to rule Ireland, when the latter was technically a separate kingdom, linked to England only by the fact that the same royal family wore both crowns: and Cromwell's Parliament had just deposed that family. Finally, by terming the Catholic clergy 'seducers', he tried to turn the historical tables on them by representing them as the newly arrived and illegal religion rather than conservers of the traditional faith of the Irish. As an exercise in logic, it was deeply flawed, but the polemical battle was of little consequence when he had the resources to win the military one, and did.

Unhappily for Oliver, the problem did not go away with the conquest of Ireland, but returned to trouble him when he was Lord Protector in England, and as a consequence of his foreign policy. In 1654 his government took the decision to launch an unprovoked and undeclared attack on the colonial possessions of the Spanish crown. For once we have an insight into how such a major policy decision was reached, in the form of notes taken on the debates over the issue among Cromwell's inner ring of advisers. They commenced with the practical problem that the successful ending of a war with the Dutch, started by the purged Parliament, had left a large battle fleet to be paid off or redeployed. With most of Europe still failing to co-operate with the regicide British republic, it was resolved to increase fear and respect for the latter among foreign nations by attacking one of the great monarchies. Spain was chosen, for three different reasons. First, it was the most intolerantly Catholic of all the great powers, neither allowing Protestants among its own subjects nor permitting English merchants to practise their own religion while in its territory. Second, it seemed easy and profitable to attack, having a rich and extended colonial empire which seemed to present a soft target. Third, it was already overextended in a major war in Europe, and there was an apparent chance that it would not be able to muster the resources to oppose an English attack on its West Indian islands. The notes only occasionally distinguished different speakers in the debate, but it is clear that Cromwell approved of the arguments given above, and at one point he is clearly identified as a speaker. It came when the most powerful and talented of his military supporters, John Lambert, opposed the whole scheme as too risky, suggesting that peace and financial retrenchment would provide a better chance of securing the newly established Protectorate within the British Isles. Cromwell answered him directly, with the argument that the need to win prestige in Europe, and Spain's combination of intolerant Catholicism, tempting wealth and apparent vulnerability, suggested that divine providence was leading them into such a course.[29] The record of the discussion provides a wonderful insight into Cromwell's mixture of piety, pragmatism, aggression and opportunism.

He got his way and the result was a celebrated disaster, the first major defeat of his cause. His expeditionary force was beaten off the richer Caribbean islands, and he found himself locked into a major war with Spain for which he needed more resources than his government currently possessed. His predicament propelled him towards a partnership with two different entities: a Parliament, which would vote him war taxes, and the crown of France, which had its own war with Spain and could be persuaded to join forces with him. France, however, was itself a major Catholic monarchy, although one that granted some freedom of worship to Protestants, and so any alliance with it had to be carefully packaged at home. In September 1656 Cromwell met the Parliament, and presented it with an account of his foreign policy designed to meet both his needs. His government's first public manifesto, recognising the existence of the new conflict, had defended it primarily on legal grounds, that Spain claimed an unreasonably large amount of the New World and in any case had provoked a breach by breaking the terms under which it had agreed to deal with English merchants.[30] The Protector preferred now to bang the drums of emotion. First he informed the MPs that Spain was the bitterest and most inveterate enemy of both their nation and of the Protestant religion, which meant, quite simply, 'whatsoever is of God'. Anybody who doubted that the conflict now in progress was not 'providential', was not 'well acquainted with Scripture and the things of God'. He then broadened his attack to take in 'any state that is Popish', and declared the Pope himself to be the Antichrist. This enabled him in turn to attempt to whip up feeling against the English Roman Catholic community, as a Spanish fifth column: 'they are a great part of your danger'. He extended his catalogue of villains further, to incorporate the English royalists, whom he treated as dupes of the Catholics. In brief, the current enemies of his government were 'all the wicked people of the world, whether abroad or at home', and the only sure means to save the nation from them was to vote it a lot of money. Oliver was, however, careful to make one major exception to his blanket condemnation of the adherents of Rome, and that was, of course, the French. They alone, for reasons or in ways that he did not bother to specify, were Catholics and yet not really under the Pope's authority.[31]

Three months later, as the Parliament still debated the measures to be taken in response, he wrote to the Italian churchman who was currently the maker of French royal policy, Cardinal Mazarin. The two of them were moving towards measures of co-operation against the Spanish, but the current sticking point was that Mazarin, as a pious if practical Catholic, felt that he could not make a partnership with the Protestant English state unless he could improve the position of its Catholics. In responding, Cromwell cast not a single glance at his recent characterisation of the latter as servants of Antichrist and friends of the Spanish. Instead he regretted that political considerations made a public declaration of toleration for them impossible; as indeed they did, not least because Oliver himself had worked so hard to inflame the feelings of the English in precisely the opposite direction. He pleaded to Mazarin, however, that Catholics had fared better under the rule of his Protectorate than under the Commonwealth that had preceded it, as their fines had been less stringently collected and he had intervened to save some who had been convicted under the laws that criminalised their worship. This claim was true, as historians have demonstrated that, despite his occasional recourse to the rhetoric of bigotry, Oliver's government had indeed enforced the laws against English Catholicism with a notable lack of rigour.[32] What was peculiarly Cromwellian about the manner in which he reported the fact to the cardinal was that he dressed it up in a different language of righteousness and probity, boasting that he had 'plucked' many Catholics from 'the raging fire of persecution, which did tyrannise over their consciences, and encroached by an arbitrariness of power upon their estates'. He could never resist claiming the moral high ground, even when this involved jumping with considerable agility from one peak to another.[33] The results were effective: an Anglo-French military alliance was slowly concluded, which resulted in some notable victories and territorial gains for both states.

This constant manipulation of the language of godliness according to the practical needs of the occasion was not lost on Cromwell's contemporaries, although it is unlikely that more than a very few were aware of its full extent. In his systematic vilification that set in after the restoration of the monarchy, he was sometimes accused of being a canting hypocrite, pretending piety in order to further his own designs, and this became one component of the hostile portrait that dominated historiography until the nineteenth century. There is no doubt that it is unjust, and that his writings prove the passionate sincerity and intensity of his personal faith. As John Morrill has noted, however, most of those who found fault with him before the Restoration likewise admitted the genuine nature of his religiosity, and their charge against it was more subtle. They suggested that while seeking good ends – a pious and well-governed nation – he showed too much opportunism in the means and eventually became somebody capable of deluding himself that whatever promoted the success of his own government was the will of God.[34] It is suggested here that, although the evidence cannot conclusively prove this accusation, it contains much to support it. There is no doubt that he consistently sought to reshape English religion and social behaviour in conformity with the views of the radical puritan minority of which he was one. There should be equally little that in this cause he manipulated the language of godliness and fashioned representations of events with a confident lack of scruple. The first quality raises problems for straightforward characterisations of him as a national, rather than as a sectarian, leader. The second makes it equally difficult to endorse automatically an image of him as a politician of exceptional probity.

* * *

These suggestions demand an analysis of his attitudes towards what have been viewed, in his time and since, as more secular matters. Although in his early days Cromwell could, as shown, use a language of strict defence of legal rights and obedience to known laws to justify his actions, once in supreme power he was blatantly honest in his contempt for them. John Morrill has aptly summed him up as 'a divine right revolutionary', concerned with neither constitutional propriety nor accountable government and equipped with 'a maverick attitude to civil rights'.[35] This aspect of Cromwell's make-up has not, however, received proportionate attention in the other recent studies. It came to the fore, significantly, as soon as he encountered serious opposition in his newly acquired capacity as the nation's Lord Protector: when the first Parliament called under the constitution that had appointed him failed to co-operate with his government. In his opening speech to them he had emphasised that under that constitution they now possessed the power, and the freedom, to settle the nation. A week later he called them back to inform them that when he had called the Parliament 'free' he had meant so only on condition that it worked with his regime, and so he now needed to 'magnify' his own constitutional powers to ensure that they could not continue unless they agreed to do so. He quoted the proverb 'necessity hath no law', and added that his necessity was 'manifest'.[36]

On facing his second Parliament two years later he harped on this theme from the beginning, defending the actions of his regime in the interim as essential, 'the grounds of Necessity for justifying of men's actions being above all considerations of justification, of instituted law.' He added that 'if nothing should ever be done but what is according to law, the throat of the nation may be cut while we send for some to make a law'. Urging them to their business he informed them that 'you must not expect that men of hesitating spirits, under bondage of scruples, will be able to carry on this work'. He poured scorn on critics who 'cry up nothing but righteousness and justice and liberty'.[37]

As he preached, so he practised. Most celebrated, and commonly extenuated by historians, was his government's habit of holding political critics in preventive detention for long periods. He referred to this himself in the speech just quoted and it is easy to accept the excuse always provided: that to try them would probably have meant exposing them to worse penalties, whereas a confinement that had no legal status could be terminated as soon as the prisoners promised to behave better. It remains true, however, that the practice of detention without trial, to silence critics and neutralise their activities, is one that has long caused unease among the British and which they have repeatedly attempted to ban; and it was technically illegal by the time that Cromwell began to apply it. More striking, and less often considered, are other aspects of his regime's attitude to the forms and processes of the law.

It was roughest in the spring and summer of 1655, when confidence had been shaken by the total failure of the first Protectorate Parliament and by a royalist rebellion. Within a month the government replaced five judges, a purge without precedent under the old monarchy and one necessary to ensure that it had judicial leaders compliant enough for some of the measures now in hand. One of these was to try the royalists captured after the rebellion. The latter had turned out to be a pathetic affair dispersed by a single horse troop. Less than four hundred rebels had turned out at the height of the rising, and it seems that less than half of those were still in arms when the showdown came. Many of these were put on trial, and the government felt confident enough to leave the verdicts to a jury. Thirty-nine of the accused were sentenced to death, of whom fourteen or fifteen were executed and the rest transported to the plantations of the West Indies. At that point, however, the government halted the proceedings, and proceeded to add to the transportation party not only all those who had been acquitted but some who had not yet been tried: the jury had clearly been too scrupulous. Another of the legal measures of the period was to try a merchant who had challenged the regime's right to collect customs dues, given the failure of the Parliament to endorse its constitutional authority. Clearly he could not be allowed to win, but the method used to cow his defence – of arresting the lawyers who had agreed to act for it – disturbed legal experts who had hitherto loyally supported the regime.[38] The Protectorate certainly took the lives of only about a score of its opponents, making it a merciful government in absolute terms, but these executions were still significant in view of the tiny amount of armed resistance that it actually encountered. It is still more worthy of notice that its leader could both boast of his record in over-throwing tyranny and defending civil liberty and express open contempt for the known laws and due legal processes.

Cromwell chose instead to justify his actions in two different ways. One, which has been touched upon, was simply to invoke a divine mandate for whatever he was currently trying to do. He adopted this tactic in small and personal matters: in 1651 he wrote to an old friend and ally, Lord Wharton, who had withdrawn from public life because he could not accept the abolition of the monarchy and House of Lords in 1649. Rather than engage in constitutional arguments, Cromwell informed Wharton that for him and those like him to have such scruples was just a way of denying God: of finding a way 'to reason yourselves out of His service'.[39] He also employed the same argument on the grand scale. He described the purging of the first Parliament called by the Protectorate as an expedient given to him by the Almighty. When the Parliament still failed to work with his government, he dismissed it with a furious attack on those who suggested that he obtained politi-cal ends by intrigue and manipulation, when all he did was the will of God: indeed he went so far as to accuse anybody who doubted the legitimacy of his regime of blasphemy: 'To say that men bring forth these things when God doth them – judge you if God will bear this?'[40] When greeting his next Parliament, he contrasted the 'men of hesitating spirits' whom he was damning for legal and constitutional scru-ples, with 'men of honest hearts, engaged to God'. Explicitly he informed it that since the necessities of his government were sent by divine providence, anything done in the name of those necessities was done in accordance with divine will.[41]

Cromwell also, however, appealed to a different source of authority, and one that resonates as favourably with modern liberals as his religiosity did with those under Victoria: 'the people'. When his first Parliament as Protector questioned his author-ity, he informed it that 'if my calling be from God, and my testimony from the people – God and the people shall take it from me, else I will not part with it'.[42] To his second Parliament he thundered 'I am by the voice of the People the Supreme Magistrate.'[43] Significantly, he abandoned this line as soon as this second Parliament seemed willing to work with him, justifying his position thereafter in terms of the recognition which it had given him. He never defined whom he meant in his appeal to populism, and it is difficult to see how such a claim could plausi-bly be justified. The Protectorate was established not by any popular voice, vote or will, but by the officers of the army that Cromwell commanded, to what the lead-ing historian of the event has recently summed up as 'general silence and indiffer-ence' on the part of the public.[44] The Protector's invocation of the latter, if it were not simply bluster, can be accounted for only in terms of the argument put forward at times by or on behalf of the army in 1647–48, that in some way it represented the true feelings or interest of the nation better than an elected Parliament had come to do. The matter must be left open because Cromwell, as usual on these public occasions, preferred not to subordinate rhetoric to reason.

Cromwell's century was one in which vituperative language was common in politics, and at times he engaged in it to the full. In one speech to the first Protectorate Parliament, he described the royalists as 'like briars and thorns' and some religious radicals as 'differing little from beasts'. He was also capable, when there seemed need, of misrepresenting the views of opponents. In 1654 he boasted that the Protectorate had been established to rescue the nation from 'men of Levelling principles' who had attempted 'to make the tenant as liberal a fortune as the landlord', something that had been advocated (and only subject to some interpretations) by the most marginal and powerless of the radicals who had written or spoken during the whole period since the Civil War.[45] If abuse and misrepresentation are two of the classic weapons of the able and less than perfectly scrupulous politician, then so is an ability to repackage a programme to put it past a new audience, and here again Oliver was a master of the art. In 1653 he and his officers expelled the remnant of the Long Parliament and justified the fact partly on the grounds that it had repeatedly failed to enact measures of godly reformation. On greeting its successor, the nominated Parliament, he delivered the most radical of all his speeches, using language that verged on the apocalyptic as he urged its members to take up the work in which their predecessors had failed. After the implosion and collapse of this body, and the substitution of the Protectorate, his spin on the issues changed. When he met the next Parliament, in September 1654, he was actually inviting it to enact the same reform programme, of liberty of conscience for radical Protestants who wished to worship outside the national Church, encouragement of a 'godly ministry' within it and of unity between it and the independent churches, and reform of the legal system to make it cheaper and simpler. His language was, however, completely different. Faced with a more conservative body, he presented the measures as a means of safeguarding and stabilising society in the face of threats from irresponsible radicals.[46] To state this is not to deny the possibility that these sleights of hand were unconscious, and that he had genuinely misunderstood opponents and come to take different views of matters himself. None the less, they are very striking.

They need to be taken into account with another of his traits, to which J.C. Davis in particular has drawn full attention in recent years: that he was an inveterate networker. Throughout his career in public life, he worked devotedly at bringing people together to discuss concerted action and to agree on a common view of affairs, dissolving differences and doubts by sustained private debate of the issues. This was related to another characteristic of his career that has been highlighted by Davis; that his rapid rise was greatly assisted by powerful connections provided for him by family relationships and religious affiliations. He may have arrived in the Long Parliament as an obscure minor gentleman, but he was still related to fifteen other MPs and had important noble patrons.[47] Cromwell's love of consensus reached by discussion is connected to another aspect of his nature to which less attention has been drawn by historians: that in essence he had no ideas of his own. Throughout his political career the blueprints to which he worked, the programmes that he espoused and the measures that he supported or enacted were all suggested by others. This pattern afforded him the tactical advantage that others could be blamed each time that things went wrong, but he does not seem to have had much option in the matter. In part it was related to the fact that he was never trained to have a theoretical or scholarly mind, something which occasionally expressed itself defensively: in 1656 he extolled university students 'who instead of studying books, study their own hearts'.[48] It does seem also, however, that there was nothing in him that could be trained, and that with all his energy, charisma and power of nature, he was really designed to be an executive agent, carrying out the plans of others. This may be, indeed, why he placed such an exceptionally heavy stress upon the will of providence in human affairs, thereby raising above the level of particular human beings the dominant trend of his political life.

A rare illumination of Cromwell's habits of thought and action is provided by the shorthand notes of what have become the most famous private discussions in which his party ever engaged: the Putney Debates of late 1647. These were meetings in which leading army officers talked over the future of the nation with a selection of their most radical critics among their own soldiers and in London. In the course of these discussions some of those present delivered several of the most ringing statements ever made in a pre-modern age about the workings of representative democracy. None of the latter were contributed by Cromwell. Indeed, of all the individuals prominent in the discussions he is the only one apparently to have no theoretical opinions at all. Instead he intervened frequently, lengthily and passionately to achieve conciliation, unity and moderation. Repeatedly he expressed respect for the views of the radicals and held out hope that they might be achieved – including a repudiation of the authority of the king and the House of Lords – while urging caution, delay and a waiting on events at the present time.[49] If this was typical of his way of proceeding – and it perfectly matches his behaviour in the earlier debates in the council of army officers at Reading[50] – then it provides one obvious reason why he became the figure who strove to hold together the alliance of different groups that had created the republic, and to function as its leading figure.

It also explains, however, how he managed to achieve a reputation for deviousness, insincerity and unreliability among those whom he seemed to encourage and then disappointed their hopes. Such a reputation was attached to no other prominent person in his party. The outburst of the London civilian radicals known as 'Levellers', in 1649, is famous: 'You shall scarce speak to Cromwell about anything, but he will lay his hand on his breast, elevate his eyes, and call God to record; he will weep, howl and repent, even while he doth smite you under the first rib.'[51] Less commonly quoted, more restrained and still more pertinent is the comment of the sectarian leader John Rogers, being interrogated by the Protector and others of his government in 1655: 'every man almost that talks with you is apt to think you of his opinion, my Lord, whatever he be'.[52]

The post-Restoration caricature of Cromwell represented a man consumed by personal ambition, who cheated and manipulated his way to supreme power as an objective in itself. This, as every recent biographer has agreed, cannot stand up to investigation. It was so unlikely that Oliver would end up running the country, until the early 1650s, that he can hardly have had any long-term aim to do so. All his various elevations were offered to him by others, and once made Lord Protector he did his utmost in his speeches to Parliaments to refute suspicions that he had actively sought the office and regarded it as anything other than a trust and a burden. Indeed, from the moment that he rose to national eminence, he carefully avoided any of the measures that would reinforce charges of self-seeking, and which indeed represented the traditional rewards of high appointments. Although he was granted huge estates for his services by the Long Parliament, and resided in former royal palaces as Protector, he never attempted actively to maximise the material profits of power. By contrast, he could haggle fiercely over private transactions, such as the value of the dowry awarded to his son and heir Richard, on marriage.[53] Nor did he display any dynastic ambitions, keeping Richard out of public affairs, and devoid of any military or political experience, until the end of his own life when (too late) it became evident that a hereditary Protectorship seemed to be the most popular solution to the problem of finding his successor. Although he submitted to a considerable element of ceremonial pomp in his second installation as Protector, again in deference to apparent public opinion, he continued to project a plain and unpretentious self-image from day to day.[54]

As in the matter of piety, so in that of ambition, the charge that was most often made against him during his lifetime was more subtle than that prevalent after the return of the monarchy, and deserves more attention. It was of a man who commenced with fine ideals but who came to use and abandon people for his own political ends and to believe that the essential goodness of his own regime justified virtually any tactics in the struggle to defend and promote it. In this vision he was a good person who became corrupted by power to associate his retention of it automatically with the will of providence and the promotion of virtue. Once again, it may be suggested that, while the nature of historical evidence makes such a view impossible to prove, there is much in the record that sustains it.

* * *

Thus far, the emphasis has been mainly upon Cromwell's words, evaluated at times in the light of his actions. Any further consideration of him has to reverse the balance, and make an analysis of his actual behaviour at key moments of his political career. That career really became continuously significant from 1647, when the army of which he was second-in-command entered national politics as a propelling force. The apparent form that it took was to react to events made by others, observing developments until it became obvious that the soldiers were collectively going to take a certain course, and then supporting them in it. He played no recorded part in encouraging the agitation in the New Model Army in the spring of 1647, which led it to refuse to disband as the Long Parliament now wished, and to turn on Parliament with a programme of its own demands. Instead he appears to have struggled to reconcile the two bodies, throwing in his lot with the army when it became apparent that a breach was inevitable. In the autumn, as described, he worked hard to preserve the unity of officers and men, striving both to avoid alienating the political radicals who had surfaced among them and to restrain them from any immediate action. His behaviour in 1648 is consistent with this pattern. Having fought hard and decisively to defeat the army's enemies in the Second Civil War, he expressed his personal support for the demands within it to bring the king to trial, and perhaps to execution, and for the purging of Parliament to bring that about, should it be necessary. He himself, however, took no lead in the matter. He also privately expressed his reluctance to put such drastic measures into action, preferring to wait until their absolute necessity became clear and referring to himself as 'a poor looker-on'.[55] He arrived at London, the centre of the crisis, only when positively ordered to do so and when the purging of Parliament had already begun. Thereafter he played a shadowy role in events until the actual trial of the king, when he served faithfully on the tribunal which condemned Charles, and he subsequently became the leading soldier of the new republic. Throughout, he held consistently to the view that the army's will needed ultimately to be done, but only by proceeding as cautiously as possible in an attempt to maximise support for its actions.[56]

This picture is coherent, convincing and fits the known evidence; which is how historians traditionally like to have their history. Only those who are most determined to admit of alternative explanations are going to have any trouble with it. Once that admission is made, however, there are slight shadows on the record. One is the general concern that if Cromwell had engaged in any clandestine manoeuvres to help the course of events along, such necessarily secretive actions would not have left any trace in the historical sources. In the absence of such a trace it is impossible to do more than recognise the doubt, but there are two specific incidents which have long given pause to specialists in the period, even though they have generally paused no more than briefly. One concerns the most dramatic of the army's moves in its confrontation with Parliament in mid-1647, its seizure of the person of the king. What is certain is that the origins of this coup lay in a series of discussions between Cromwell and various army officers and sectaries held at the former's lodgings in London when he was still attending the House of Commons. Alarmed by rumours that the leaders of Parliament were intending to send Charles away to Scotland, to lead a coalition of forces designed to destroy the army, Cromwell and his confidants agreed to replace the king's guards with soldiers loyal to themselves. In the event, the commander of the party sent to prevent the king's removal, Cornet Joyce, went much further and brought Charles to the army's own quarters. Joyce later insinuated that Cromwell had instructed him to do this, which Oliver vehemently denied. Both traditional and recent analyses of the incident have chosen to believe Cromwell, and to accept that Joyce, though a very junior officer, acted on his own initiative in the belief that the king was about to be snatched back from him by armed force, and he needed to get Charles away to greater security. This was, indeed, the line taken by Cromwell's fellow commanders at the time.[57]

The second incident is the escape of the king from the army's custody in November of the same year. Charles's custodian was Cromwell's cousin, Edward Whalley, to whom Oliver sent a letter warning of a likely attempt by radicals upon the king's life. Whalley showed this to Charles – probably at Cromwell's suggestion – and his royal prisoner then fled, to refuge on the Isle of Wight. The governor of the island was another of Oliver's kinsmen, Robert Hammond, with whom Cromwell kept in close touch, and Charles's decision to appeal to him for protection turned out to be fatal. It limited his freedom of movement, and as soon as the king began to deal with the army's enemies, Hammond locked him up until he was taken to London to be executed. Cromwell's enemies later charged that he had frightened Charles into flight and directed him towards a death-trap. The possible motivation for such a trick is debatable: on the one hand, the king's presence had become an embarrassment to Oliver in his attempts to hold the unity of his army together, while on the other, Charles could be a much greater danger to that army if at large. If he were not at large, but trapped and discredited in Wight, then of course the danger would evaporate. On the other hand, there is no solid evidence that Cromwell played any part in the king's decision to flee and, even if he had done anything to put Hammond and the island in Charles's mind, there was no guarantee at all that the king would act on it and not escape out of the reach of both Parliament and army. For these reasons recent authorities have tended to acquit Oliver of any responsibility for the event.[58] In both cases – of the king's seizure by Joyce and of his flight – the existing evidence weighs on Cromwell's side, and that is what historians have to work on. It is still interesting, however, that his enemies – however embittered and retrospective – thought him the sort of man on whom such charges could plausibly stick, and there remains a tiny chance that either of both were correct. If they were, of course, then the Cromwell of the standard history books is a very different man from the one of reality. It may seem harsh to admit of such doubtful evidence, and it is possible to argue that the reputation of any public figure could be impugned by such an approach. What is significant here is that contemporaries did not make the same charges against most other politicians; there was something about Cromwell that struck some of them as particularly slippery.

Once the republic was established, Oliver gradually found himself, yet again, in the uncomfortable position of mediator between a Parliament and an increasingly angry and disappointed army. After the end of his military campaigns, in late 1651, he applied himself for eighteen months to the dual role of trying to persuade the purged House of Commons to enact the reforms that the officers wished and to reconcile the latter to giving the MPs more time to do the work. This balancing act collapsed famously on 20 April 1653 when he hurried to the House with a file of soldiers, having met their officers and announced (according to an eye-witness) that the Parliament could no longer be relied upon to do what they wished and that some 'unbiased' men were needed instead. He listened awhile to the debate in progress, and then interrupted it by saying something rude about the ceremonial mace and many ruder things about the MPs, and having them all ejected from the chamber. He then met the soldiers in the capital again and (somewhat at variance with what he had told them that morning) insisted that on entering the House he had no intention of expelling its members but that he had been overruled by 'the spirit'; he left characteristically open whether by this he meant his own loss of temper or divine guidance. This was, he went on to say, because the Parliament was 'designing to spin an everlasting thread'.[59]

The traditional interpretation of this episode was clear and consensual: that Cromwell had discovered that the MPs were attempting to pass a bill, with great speed, to fill up the vacant seats in their own House rather than call a new Parliament as they had promised to do to him and the army. Then, in 1971, Blair Worden demonstrated conclusively that the bill concerned had actually been for new elections, as the army had hitherto wished.[60] That immediately raised the question of why, in that case, Cromwell had so violently prevented its passage and made it the occasion for the termination of the whole Parliament. In the intervening years, historians have proposed a number of plausible explanations, none of which seem susceptible of absolute proof in the existing state of evidence.[61] The intention here is not to evaluate or to add to their suggestions, but to look harder at why certainty in the matter is so elusive. The most important reason is that Cromwell himself destroyed the evidence. The document that would have resolved, once and for all, what the MPs were actually up to was the bill under debate, and Oliver himself removed it when the House was cleared by his soldiers. To prove his case against it, he need only have quoted it in official statements; instead, it disappeared completely.

This left his word to be weighed against others in subsequent recriminations, and so it is important to look in detail at what he said. His immediate self-justification, to the meeting of soldiers, has been quoted: he wrapped it in a characteristically striking and opaque metaphor, which suggested that in some way the MPs were attempting to perpetuate their own power. Two days later he and his council of officers issued a formal declaration to extenuate themselves. It held up the number of military victories that they had won as proof of God's particular favour to them, and accused the MPs of attempting to fill up their House by recruiting extra members of the same kind as themselves, who would not give 'the people' 'a due liberty'.[62] This seems fairly clear if (as Blair Worden has proved) dishonest, but when

Cromwell faced the next (nominated) Parliament, over two months later, he stated both that the true reason for the expulsion 'hath never been yet thoroughly imparted to any' and (for reasons never given) was better explained verbally than in writing. He then repeated the charge that the Parliament had intended only to recruit itself, denying the people the right of choosing their own representatives. He added immediately, however, the accusation that it had also intended to deliver 'our liberties' into the hands of old enemies: which hardly sat well with a project of reinforcing a House committed to republican government. Apparently observing the confusion, he commented that to explain this in detail would be 'to rake into these things too much'. He then veered into berating the expelled MPs for failing to encourage the work of godly reformation (for which his talk of 'liberties' was generally a code), and suggested that their proposed 'New Representative' would have been no better. A gap of logic had now opened between his declarations that the Parliament had intended merely to fill itself up and that a 'new' one had been planned. Again, he appeared to acknowledge it, admitting for the first time that the MPs had not actually said that they intended to perpetuate themselves, but that they spoke of 'continuation'. He hinted at what may well have been the crucial issue: that the MPs were unwilling to hand over power to an interim government approved of by the army. His one unequivocal assertion, on which he left the matter, was that he thought that he had reached an agreement with some of the House to lay the bill aside until further talks had been held with the soldiers; and had been furious to find that they were not doing so.[63]

In subsequent years, and to other Parliaments, he harked back uneasily to his action. Addressing his first one as Lord Protector, he repeated the charge that the purged Parliament had intended to fill itself up indefinitely by supplying its vacant seats. He then introduced a new element to his argument, accusing it of planning to do so with a scheme to make some of its members eligible for re-election in successive new Parliaments, each sitting end to end and representing the supreme authority in the state. The revolution of 1649, which he had supported, had explicitly vested ultimate power in elected assemblies of the people, and it had always been normal for experienced parliamentarians to seek re-election to new Parliaments. Cromwell did not explain why electoral sovereignty had suddenly become so threatening.[64] Two and a half years later, confronting another body of MPs, he took a fresh crack at the subject and admitted that the bill on which the purged Parliament had been working was not one to fill up its existing membership. Instead he accused it of having gone to the opposite extreme, by dissolving itself immediately and substituting a succession of assemblies, elected every three years and controlling all branches of government. Instead he and the army wanted power to be vested for a time in 'some worthy persons' who could be trusted to run the nation. Having begun by justifying his action in terms of protecting the rights of the people to choose its representatives against the ambitions of a self-seeking oligarchy, Cromwell seemed to have reversed the whole thrust of his argument to acknowledge that he was trying to establish an oligarchy which could be relied on to protect the interests of himself and his party.[65] One of the baffling aspects of this succession of shifty, guilty and clumsy excuses is that none of the MPs whom he had expelled, many of whom thereby became his bitter opponents, attempted to make a systematic answer to them. He should have been an easy target, but was allowed to get away with rambling around the subject unchallenged. The conclusion is inescapable that they did not do so because they also had been acting in ways which would not bear public inspection: Cromwell was saved by the fact that everybody concerned in the matter had something to hide.[66] Thus the evidence for the matter runs out, with a strong smell of sleaze hanging over it.

The problem with Cromwell's attempts to bang the drums of populism was that he tended to elide two different groups under the common, ringing and admiring, label of 'the people'. One was the people of the nation, and the other the minority of radical puritans within it whom he tended to characterise as 'the people of God'. He clearly hoped that at some future date they would indeed become one, and his problems (and those of his regime) derived from the fact that they were not and that 'his' people were not only heavily outnumbered but unpopular, at all levels of society. In confronting this situation, Oliver tended to work simultaneously towards three goals, representing different shades of practicability. The most desired and the least likely was that the two would actually become one, with the majority of the English and Welsh enthusiastically adopting his own particular brand of religion. A lesser and more feasible objective was that the 'godly' would control the nation and set the tone of its life. The bottom line, which his regime had secured and to which it was committed, was to ensure freedom of worship for Protestant radicals until a broad and thoroughly reformed national Church could be achieved.

The step taken after the expulsion of the purged Parliament was the one most clearly designed to achieve the second objective and also which most clearly recognised the distinction between the two definitions of 'people'. Almost immediately after they had issued the declaration defending the expulsion on the grounds that the MPs had intended to perpetuate a corrupt oligarchy hostile to godly reform, Cromwell and his officers set about installing a worthy oligarchy committed to reforming the nation. The implosion and collapse of that body, the 'nominated' Parliament, in December 1653, was arguably the true turning point in Cromwell's public career. Until that moment he had remained convinced that, once in control of affairs, the 'honest' people of the country would produce the society and polity that he and his allies desired. His actions hitherto had consisted of clearing out of the way more and more of the traditional institutions and elites as they proved to be impediments to the work. In mid-1653 it was handed over to as convincing a group of the pious and well intentioned as he and his officers could choose, and the result was the disintegration of the resulting assembly amid bitter quarrelling. From that moment onward, the course of Cromwell's policy turned to the construction of institutions that might control and balance the divisive forces in human nature as well as enacting the policies that he and his officers desired. After that, also, he was prepared to envisage the restoration of traditional institutions and elites, and make compromises with them, in order to guarantee the freedom that radical puritans had already achieved.

The fate of the nominated assembly is itself, however, another Cromwellian conundrum of an absolutely typical kind. He refused to attend it himself or initially to take a leading part in the Council of State that it appointed; an ostentatious gesture of lack of personal ambition that also kept him clear of the problems of the new regime and of any implication in its possible failure. By December 1653 the divisions in the assembly had reached the point at which the majority sabotaged it by withdrawing from it and resigning its power to Cromwell himself. A body of soldiers then arrived to drive out the more radical minority that had remained. Some of the army officers were ready with a new constitution, that appointing Oliver as Lord Protector, which they had already shown him. Cromwell expressed his complete innocence of involvement in the planning or execution of any of these developments, and his surprise at them. Any interpretations of his behaviour must be made on a spectrum between two extreme views. One is of a man extraordinarily cut off from political reality, not keeping a close eye on events and allowing his soldiers to be used for a dramatic coup without his permission or knowledge: which is how Oliver presented himself. The other is of one quietly following and colluding with developments, while claiming detachment from them. The spectrum of possibility is not, however, one that stretches between genuine innocence and complete implication. For somebody as prominent and as habituated to politics as Cromwell, to have become cut off from developments would have had to have been a deliberate tactical ploy. The spectrum runs between two different sorts of political manoeuvre.[67]

Three key episodes may suffice to exemplify the problems of understanding Cromwell's role as Protector. The first is one which should perhaps do more than any other to establish his credentials as a hero to modern liberals: his decisive role in the readmission of a Jewish community to England. The process began in October 1655, with a formal petition for this step lodged by Menasseh ben Israel, a Jewish intellectual visiting from Amsterdam where the Dutch state already tolerated his religion. Cromwell showed clear favour to Menasseh, giving him lodgings, inviting him to dine and encouraging his petition. He may actually have hinted to him that he should undertake the mission in the first place. Cromwell carefully referred the petition to his Council, while expressing support for a favourable decision. There followed a considerable controversy in print, with anti-Semitic views predominating and the Protector himself being accused of having taken bribes from the Jews. He attempted to build support for readmission by convening conferences of his councillors with lawyers, clergy, scholars and merchants in December to talk the matter through, but failed to secure agreement. It had become clear that he could, if he wished, declare a readmission to be legally valid under his own executive powers, but this is exactly what he did not do. Instead, he declared that he and the Council would pronounce on the matter in due course and then did nothing, so that the exchange of published views died away for lack of an issue with which to deal. When opponents of readmission lobbied him, he spoke soothingly to them and so allayed their concern. By February 1656 the public seemed to have lost interest in the matter.

The government newspaper, however, continued to deliver a subliminal message in favour of the Jews by highlighting their sufferings under Catholic governments, especially that of Spain. At the same time Cromwell permitted the continued residence of a Jewish community in London that had disguised itself as Spanish and Portuguese immigrants, and whose trading interests he had begun to favour as soon as he had become Protector. In March 1656 the leaders of this community petitioned him for written confirmation of their right to private freedom of worship and to a cemetery for their faith. Again, the Protector declined to take any formal responsibility for a decision, referring the matter once more to his Council, which once again failed to agree. The legal ruling on which the readmission hinged was taken ad-hoc on 16 May, by an action of the Admiralty Commissioners regarding the goods of one of the London Jewry, which had been seized from him as a presumed Spanish subject residing in England after it had gone to war with Spain. It returned them after he had described himself as a Jew, and so, in effect, recognised the right of those of his race and religion to live in the capital. Thereafter they practised their faith and established a cemetery as if their petition had been granted, and experts have generally considered that they would not have dared to do so without tacit encouragement from the Protector. He quietly arranged for Menasseh to be rewarded with a pension, but when he met his next Parliament in September, he declared that his government had given liberty only to 'men that believe in Jesus Christ – that's the form that gives the being to true religion.' He was disassociating himself in public from a policy that he had apparently pursued with resolute determination in private. Under his clandestine protection, English Jewry was allowed to enjoy an informal toleration that rapidly became an accepted part of metropolitan life.[68]

It is just possible that the policy concerned was not, in fact, a coherent one; that he took a number of unrelated and unthinking actions, and that he gave no clandestine encouragement to the Jews in London. It is far more likely – and has been accepted by all historians of the matter to date – that he pursued a consistent aim to success through various changes of tactics. Having failed in his initial attempt to achieve a legal readmission, because of unexpected opposition in his Council and from public opinion, he proceeded to outflank both. With what looks like real brilliance, determination and duplicity, he diverted attention from the issue, allowed the Jews to enjoy in practice what he could not accord them in law and concealed his own part in the process. What is not, and cannot be, agreed, is why he went to this trouble. One possible explanation is that he was swayed by theological factors.[69] Many puritans in early seventeenth-century England had been led by study of the Bible to a new appreciation of Hebrew culture, and some had been influenced by the Scriptural prophecy that the Second Coming would be preceded by the conversion of the Jews. By 1650 a tradition of support for the readmission of the latter to England, based on their place in the cosmic drama, had been firmly established among some radical puritan thinkers. It was upon that tradition that Cromwell himself drew to justify his own support for the policy. In a private letter written in late 1648, he listed the Jews among the 'godly people' who needed to unite in order to make a perfect society. When he met the nominated Parliament of 1653, he recommended a consideration of readmission to it on the grounds that others thought it a precondition for the reign of Christ. He seems more openly to have adopted this as his own position at one of the conferences to discuss the question in December 1655. One witness recorded that when most of the clergy present proved hostile, he reminded them that the conversion of the Jews was a Christian duty as well as one of the events of the apocalypse. The same source also noted that, when he encountered further opposition, Cromwell first agreed that the Jews were the most despicable race on earth and then swung the argument round to ask why, in that case, anybody should consider them a danger. If accurate, this is a wonderful snapshot of Oliver's supple use of logic in the pursuit of agreement.[70] Most historians of the issue, however, have emphasised another motive which the Protector certainly possessed for adopting his stance: that the Jews whom he was protecting in London were secretly serving him as an intelligence network in his operations against Spain, as well as army contractors and loan managers. There is no doubt that they were very useful to him in this capacity and that he would have been reluctant to lose them.[71] It is impossible to determine which consideration was uppermost in the Protector's mind during this period, but the practical one must at least have powerfully reinforced the pious one.

The second episode is one with which the admirers of Cromwell have always had great difficulty: the collapse of the system of Major-Generals. This was instituted in 1655, as a solution to problems of finance, security and godly reformation in the wake of the royalist uprising early in the year. It established a system of local militias, recruited from the supporters of the regime and paid by a new tax levied on former royalists, who were supposed to be the people whom these forces were designed to watch. The latter were commanded by high-ranking army officers, the Major-Generals concerned, who were each assigned a region in which they were also given a general oversight of local government, with a view to encouraging the moral reformation and improvement of society. The failure of the tax to support the system was the main reason for the calling of the Parliament of 1656. Three months after this convened, the military men in the House attempted to persuade it to give legal recognition to that tax. They encountered considerable opposition, many regarding the measure as unjust and divisive, and it was eventually defeated in a straight vote on 29 January 1657. The rule of the generals and their militias automatically collapsed with that decision.[72]

Cromwell's role in all this remains complex, controversial and largely mysterious. His part in the inception of the system is unknown, because we do not know exactly how or by whom it was conceived; all that can be said is that he gave full formal support to its establishment but does not appear to have been the driving force behind it. On meeting Parliament in 1656 he expressed strong and unequivocal commitment to it and implied that it was now a permanent feature of government. He claimed (subsequently) to have been surprised by the attempt to have it recognised by the MPs, and to have played no part at all in the eventual failure of this process. In the early stages of the debates, the army officers believed themselves to be reassured by him that he was on their side. Remarkably, however, he did absolutely nothing to help them, when his position as Protector would have weighed in powerfully on their side. Still more remarkably, opposition to the measure was actively supported by some of his civilian advisers, whom he might have restrained, and also by quite obscure relatives of his, who seem unlikely to have acted without believing that they had his approval. That support seemed to be signalled, spectacularly, when a cousin of his visited him shortly after speaking against the tax on royalists, and was rewarded with the gift of a rich cloak. Christopher Durston, who has made the most detailed study of the episode, concluded that the Protector seems to have become a confused and dithering individual, reacting passively to events and not really understanding what was going on and why.[73] The virtue of this interpretation is that it conforms exactly to the image that Cromwell tried to present of himself. It is, of course, the one that he also projected of his conduct at the time of the collapse of another constitutional initiative to which he had initially given full support, the nominated Parliament.

The problem with it is that this Cromwell cannot really be the same man as the one who manipulated his government and his people, so cleverly, to ensure that a Jewish community remained in England. Explanation for his behaviour is only credible in terms of two different models. One is that he made an ostentatious gesture of disengagement and constitutional propriety, by leaving Parliament free to reach its own decisions in a matter that did not question the fundamentals of his regime. The other is that, realising the strength of the opposition to the tax, he actually decided to change sides and encourage his civilian clients and relatives to join the attack. Neither is susceptible of proof, given the state of the evidence, but both acknowledge that Oliver abandoned his military colleagues and allies in order to win favour with a Parliament at a time when constitutional legitimacy and effective sources of taxation were needed more than ever. If so, the tactic was effective, because on the day after the tax on royalists was voted down the Parliament agreed to supply a large sum of money for the war against Spain.

It also, however, resolved on a far more controversial and celebrated measure: the offer to the Protector of a new deal whereby he secured the gains of the republic – most of all, liberty of conscience for radical Protestants – in exchange for a return to something like the old constitution of a monarchy and two Houses of Parliament. The first and most symbolically weighted clause in this package was to make Cromwell king, and one of the best-known episodes in English history is that of his long hesitation over the offer, from 24 February till 8 May, which ended in his firm rejection of it. One aspect of the recent historiography is the way in which those scholars who have dealt with the affair have striven to rule out the primacy of external influences on Cromwell's decision. In their reading, it was based primarily on his own deepest beliefs and instincts, which told him that kingship had become an accursed thing in England and he could not accept it in an act of mere expediency.[74] Consistent with the general pattern of recent scholarship is the fact that this view was part of the rehabilitated image of the Protector as national hero developed under Victoria. Both literature and art celebrated the offer of the crown as the moment when Cromwell faced his greatest temptation, and passed the test.[75] Predictably, it is also the image presented by Oliver himself: of a personal decision, taken on grounds of conscience.[76]

Any consideration of the issue should take as its starting point the Protector's first recorded expression of views on it, made when a deputation of army officers visited him on 27 February to request him to reject the whole package. Two versions of his reply to them survive, but they differ only in details and agree on two fundamental points. One was that he blamed them for all the failures to reach a political settlement over the past four years and disclaimed all personal responsibility for them; in some cases with evident injustice.[77] He suggested that the offer now being made by the Parliament was likely to be the best chance that they would get. The other point is that he urged them in particular not to quibble over the restoration of the monarchy, reminding them that the original plan drawn up by military leaders for the Protectorate would have appointed him king: he described the title as merely 'a feather in a hat', not worth arguing over.[78]

This should have done the trick, but it did not, for it did not address the crucial point that the Protectorate had been designed by the soldiers, to achieve their desired reforms, while this constitution was offered by civilians, to limit the influence of the military in political life. Instead of winning over the army en bloc, the speech divided it. During the following two months Cromwell continued to be lobbied to refuse the Crown, as some of the independent churches, aware of the hostility towards themselves harboured by many MPs, added their pleas to those of the soldiers. By 3 April he had decided to reject the kingship, only to find that the Parliament insisted on it as an intrinsic part of the new deal. The Protector now found himself trapped between the two, equally determined, bodies of opinion and struggling to find a way out in discussions with both. At one point he admitted directly to a deputation of MPs that he owed his position and the victory of his cause to 'the godly of this nation', and he would not do anything to distress them. His language had changed, however, to mirror that of 'the godly' themselves. He described the reasons put to him for acceptance of kingship as based on expediency, the force of which he acknowledged, but those against it as reflecting the apparent judgements of God. On 13 April, famously and sonorously, he declared that 'I would not seek to set up that that providence hath destroyed and laid in the dust, and I would not build Jericho again.'[79] The ringing phrase is often repeated in histories: what is not remarked is that something which had been a feather six weeks before had suddenly acquired the size and weight of a ruined city. Cromwell was signalling to the opponents of kingship, who were all or virtually all-radical puritans, that whatever he decided to do he had heard and understood them. It can hardly be coincidental that, having abandoned the Major-Generals in January, on 21 April he went out of his way to praise the excellence of their work in another speech to a parliamentary deputation.[80]

On 6 and 7 May, according to his secretary John Thurloe, Cromwell told some MPs that he had decided to accept the title. Thurloe was certainly in a position to know what the Protector was doing, though not what he was thinking, and it is significant that Oliver's remarks seem to have been made informally and off the record, as if to give a final test to opinion. If so, he certainly brought results, because his three greatest army officers informed him that they would cease to serve him if he became king. Then he heard that Pride, the colonel who had supervised the purging of the House of Commons in 1648, had raised a petition against monarchy from regiments in the London area and was taking it to Parliament. Cromwell announced his final and formal refusal of the crown before it arrived at the House. Recent proponents of the view that he was swayed primarily by his own conscience have argued that since the army was divided, he could easily have swept aside this opposition had he been determined to become king.[81] This suggestion is susceptible to two replies. The first is that there is absolutely no evidence that Oliver ever sought the crown as an end in itself. Rather, he was prepared to accept it as a means of achieving the working relationship with an elected Parliament that had hitherto eluded his regime: and this is exactly what he urged upon the officers on 27 February. He refused it when he became convinced that the political price to be paid for it would itself be high enough to risk the stability of his government.

The other reply is that nobody is in a position to state with confidence what would have happened if the Protector had accepted the title and so gravely offended sections of his army. It is worth remembering that two years later his son and successor Richard resolved to brave the course from which his father had recoiled: of making a working relationship with a Parliament in the face of open disapproval from some army officers, and trusting to the fact that the army was apparently divided in its opinions. To his horror, he found that the junior officers and ordinary soldiers overwhelmingly followed the lead of his critics, and he fell from power. It is impossible to say whether or not the same thing would have happened to Oliver had he pressed forward in the same manner. What is very clear is that he was always nervous, as he repeatedly emphasised in his speeches to Parliaments, of discontent among the military on whom his own tenure of office ultimately depended. When he dissolved the Parliament which had offered him the crown, a year later, most observers attributed this to the fact that the divisions that had opened in the Parliament were unsettling the soldiers.[82] How far Oliver's actions and words in April and May 1657 were propelled by expediency, and how far they proceeded from a genuine change of heart produced by the pleas and threats of the 'godly party' who had been his traditional constituency of support, is simply impossible to say. What is apparent is that he was turned aside from his preferred course of accepting the crown, by pressure from this constituency, and in his wholly accustomed manner he articulated the alteration in language that re-established his credentials as a servant of providence. Such a conclusion would also explain why he subsequently felt able to accept the title of 'Your Highness', a royal robe, a royal sceptre, a royal household, and the work of creating knights and a hereditary peerage, without any sign of repugnance. There remains, however, a possibility that he never considered acceptance of kingship as a practical prospect, and played off the different groups against each other with considerable skill until he secured a compromise over the package offered by Parliament. If so, then there was even more of the fox in his nature than contemporaries and historians have thought; and it is even more significant that, after all that tactical brilliance, the compromise concerned proved a failure.

In considering Cromwell's career as a politician, it may be worth bearing in mind that his formative experiences in public life, and the source of his subsequent prominence, lay in his career as a soldier. As soon as he began to command armies himself, his tactics were marked by a consistent pattern: he avoided head-on attacks. Instead he aimed always to take the enemy by surprise, either in the rear or the flank or by a diversionary assault. It would be rather odd if, having manifested an instinct for this behaviour on the battlefield, he did not prefer to operate in similarly oblique ways in the political arena. It is certainly clear that he extended to the latter another trait that he had first displayed in war: a special care in his selection of subordinates so that he built up a clientage of officers who were both inherently capable and loyal to himself.

Here may lie the main functional reason for the collapse of the Protectorate and then of the republic of which it had formed one government. In the full-blown, Victorian, representation of Cromwell's career, he could hardly be said to have failed at all. That career reached its emotional climax with his refusal of the crown, representing the supreme moral victory of his life. Thereafter (in this view) the constitution that he subsequently agreed with the Parliament, and which represented a compromise with its wishes, proved unworkable because of the short-sighted and quarrelsome behaviour of certain MPs and the suspicions of the army. None the less, the last year of the Protector's life, though barren of domestic achievement, was marked by glorious victories abroad as his new alliance with France decisively defeated the Spanish and brought England the port of Dunkirk. He could die, therefore, with both his own integrity and his record as a national leader intact, literally fitted for heaven. His disappearance left his unworthy successors – his inept son Richard, his greedy and selfish generals and the blinkered republican politicians who had become some of his most bitter opponents – to squander his inheritance and bring about their own downfall and the restoration of the monarchy. In secularised form, this has been very much the message of the recent biographies and textbook studies: that Cromwell was indeed a failure, judged by his own aims, but a heroic and admirable one who was betrayed more by the temper of his times and the inadequacy of those who followed him, than by his own actions.

When considering such conclusions it is crucial to look at the men whom he chose to serve and succeed him. There is no doubt that Cromwell himself attached a great deal of importance to such choices. Henry Reece has shown how, throughout the 1650s, he selected and appointed all the higher officers of the army himself, from the rank of colonel upwards. In doing so, he increasingly mixed and balanced radical puritans promoted from the army of the 1640s with talented newcomers of more moderate religious and political views, sometimes former royalists. There was no consistent swing towards moderates in his appointments: rather, he was carefully mixing and matching people of different inclinations who were characterised primarily by their devotion to himself.[83] It has long and generally been recognised that he followed the same policy in his selection of political advisers, whether formal councillors or court favourites: they were a mixture of army officers and civilians, of godly radicals who had helped to bring about the end of the monarchy, House of Lords and monopolistic national Church, and of people (usually civilians) who had never been involved in those events and clearly thought that they had been taken too far. In both the military and civilian spheres he showed a strong preference for his own relatives, by blood or marriage, and in both he sometimes upheld this inclination over considerations of talent: his son-in-law Charles Fleetwood and his cousin Henry Lawrence were promoted to very high offices in the army and the Council respectively without showing more than average abilities of leadership and administration.

This pattern obtained in other areas of government as well. The work of Jeffrey Collins and J.C. Davis has revealed how close a personal interest the Protector took in the personnel of the national clergy: he made 40 per cent of all recommendations for appointments to new benefices himself, and his candidates were very seldom rejected. All were good preachers and pastors, but their views regarding doctrine and Church government varied considerably, and they showed a considerable variation in their responses to the subsequent restoration of the monarchy, bishops and traditional festivals and ceremonies.[84] To govern conquered Ireland, Cromwell initially retained Fleetwood, who had been installed by the purged Parliament, and who favoured a radical restructuring of religion and society using army officers and members of independent churches as his agents (the two groups heavily overlapping). As soon as he became Protector, however, Oliver began to undermine his son-in-law by sending out his own younger son Henry to command the army. This cut Fleetwood off from his own power base, and also hampered his plans for reform because Henry did not share belief in them and preferred a more conservative programme of settlement, using the established Church of Ireland and the main Protestant gentry families. Fleetwood gave up and returned to England in 1655, but Cromwell took two years to appoint Henry in his place and then undermined the latter's power in turn. He did so partly by failing to support his initiatives from England, partly by leaving the extent of his son's independent authority badly defined, and partly by dividing responsibility for the government hazily between Henry and a Council that was still full of Fleetwood's supporters. By listening to the appeals of both but doing nothing decisive to gratify either, he ensured that the two groups of clients remained balanced against each other, that he could not be blamed personally for the results of any major policy initiatives in Ireland, and that the powerful army of occupation in that country could never be used against him.[85]

Whether Oliver himself intended all these results is, of course, impossible to prove. It is entirely possible that they were achieved unconsciously or accidentally. The undoubted fact that in his speeches he tended to talk like a radical at one moment or in one context, and as a conservative or a moderate at another, may reflect a proportionate conflict of rival impulses in his own thought. It is also quite possible, though equally beyond proof, that his adoption into his service of people with a range of views and backgrounds represented to him a microcosm of that reconciliation and settlement of the nation under the Protectorate that he called for in some of those speeches. In default of any demonstrable knowledge of his actual thoughts and motives, a historian can only judge by the results. In the short term, he succeeded in holding together a relatively broad-based administration that retained the support of the army and the obedience or loyalty of the civilian population. The question of how much longer he could have done so, in the face of growing tension between his military and civilian supporters and between defenders and critics of the established Church in the nation at large, and the continued failure of his government to achieve a stable financial and constitutional basis, must remain a matter for speculation. It does, however, seem hard to deny that his structuring of Irish government prevented the pursuit of any consistent policy for the settlement of the land – deliberately or not – and so wasted one of the best opportunities that the English and the Protestant Irish had ever possessed for the long-term solution of its problems. Likewise, on his death he left an English regime that was run by men deeply divided amongst themselves and suspicious of each other, and with no common commitment to a particular set of either ends or means. Their only common factor had been loyalty to himself, and when he was removed, there was nothing to hold them together. He must take some of the responsibility for installing a structure that could not survive his passing.

This is directly linked to his own lack of constitutional vision, and his reliance on the blueprints of others. He was emphatically not the man who brought about the transformation of England into a republic; as seen, he was carried along, often passively, by a general tide of opinion in his army and for three years after the great events of 1648–49 he acted as the main executive agent of the new Commonwealth rather than its steersman. The general who came closest to being an ideologue and a precipitator of events during this period was his son-in-law Henry Ireton. Ireton, however, died in 1651, and his place as the most effective thinker in the army was taken by John Lambert, a dashing military commander and the architect of the Protectorate. As such, Lambert was for two years the obvious successor to Oliver, but the latter reacted to him with increasing suspicion and disfavour. The younger man was effectively cast off as an adviser when the Protector began trying to co-operate with Parliament in 1656–57, and he resigned rather than accept the compromise with the MPs that resulted. Cromwell greeted his passing with obvious relief, despite the fact that it stripped the regime of the one man who combined intelligence, charisma, popularity with the common soldiers and real constitutional vision.[86]

One of the hallmarks of a truly dedicated statesman or stateswoman is a dedication to the long term, and to building structures that will last into new generations. For somebody who allegedly exemplifies the conviction politician, Cromwell displayed remarkably little sign of this. Having frozen out Lambert, he introduced his own son Richard into national life, giving him military commands and political appointments and thus putting him forward as a possible successor. What he did not do was to start to build a solid body of support for Richard in the army or the civilian administration, or to model either in such a way as to ensure that particular policies would be promoted or safeguarded on his own death. He did nothing to reduce the ideological rifts and personal animosities among the people whom he was leaving to take over his responsibilities. Even on his deathbed he took no measures at all to care for the state after his passing, and may actually have expired without even naming a successor. His only recorded concern during his final period of consciousness was for his own soul.[87] This is a dramatic indication that, at some point in his career as Lord Protector, Cromwell genuinely lost interest in what would happen to the cause that he served when he himself was not bound up with it. His behaviour may be described as a pious resignation to the ways of providence, but he had put in place the material with which providence would have to struggle, and during his life had repeatedly taken actions that would help the achievement of what he perceived to be the divine will.

* * *

It seems that any future biographer of Oliver Cromwell, and any future historian of the period that he dominated, will have to form a picture of him within a field contested by three different images. One is the now familiar textbook and cinematic image, formed by Victorian Liberal and Nonconformist politics but resting ultimately on the man's own self-portrait. Authors vary in their degree of emphasis upon his religiosity and in their inclination to find fault as well as virtue in him, but there is still a substantial agreement on the main features of the picture: a man of noble ideals and great abilities as soldier and statesman, thwarted in his dreams by the temper of his age and yet achieving enough to point a way to democracy, meritocracy, liberty of conscience and national greatness for future generations. It must be emphasised that this view of Cromwell is still viable, but to retain credibility it must be argued more carefully than it has been hitherto and matched far more carefully against the views of his contemporaries and what can be reconstructed of actual military and political events.

The second picture has recently been articulated most obviously by Christopher Durston: that of an excellent soldier who was out of his depth in politics and so ended up reacting to successive events as Protector with an alternation of dithering, evasiveness and impulse, preventing coherent or successful government. This view also can be supported by the available evidence. The third perspective on Cromwell was taken by myself in 1990,[88] and in the past few years it has apparently been endorsed by Sean Kelsey. It also faults him as a statesman but credits him with considerable abilities as a practical politician and propagandist, drawing in large part on the qualities that had made him a victorious soldier. It recognises that he was a person of sincere piety and high ideals, who was carried to supreme power by a combination of talent and accident, without initially having any ambitions to secure such a position. This image also, however, emphasises that he was seriously flawed with regard to both means and ends. While attempting always to speak a language and to take up positions of exceptional moral probity, he manipulated words, actions, laws, rights and people with ruthless lack of scruple. This habit was to some extent forced upon him by his position as a sectarian leader attempting to turn himself into a national one, and as somebody who had seized power by armed force in the face of both constitutional legitimacy and the popular will and was trying to reconcile himself with both. His reputation for deviousness, however, itself functioned to undermine the acceptance of his regime, while his political machinations left it acutely vulnerable as soon as he himself was removed. In the last analysis, according to this view, he became incapable of separating his own interests, and survival in power, from those of the cause that he served and from the will of God.

This chapter has done much to reinforce that last picture, but it does not conclude by recommending it. Instead, what has perhaps emerged most strongly is a paradox of historical writing. Biographers of Oliver Cromwell possess what on face value ought to be a marvellous combination, of a dominant historical figure who has left a treasury of apparent insights into his thoughts and actions, represented by his written and spoken words. That is no doubt why there have been so many biographies, and why most have been produced with relative speed. The problem, which has been highlighted here, is what happens if historians cease to trust what Cromwell has been trying to represent, and yet are equally bereft – at most points – of any more objective and reliable authorities. In that case, do biography and history remain possible at all? The most obvious answer seems to be that they do so only by providing a plurality of possible Cromwells, of the kind suggested above. A less obvious and less comfortable one is that the heroic Cromwell is likely always to prevail, simply because he wrote and spoke the script for such a character so well and because of the coincidence that it contained so many phrases that resonate with the modern age.

5   Charles II

For five years I shared an apartment in Bristol with King Charles II, being the period between 1983 and 1988 in which I consistently worked upon a biography of that monarch. In pursuit of that project we also went on many excursions together, not merely over the British Isles and parts of continental Europe, but to the far side of the world. It was thus a relationship more intimate and sustained than many friendships with the living, but at the end of that span of time, and when the book was written, I knew him less well than any of my friends in the present world. This chapter is an exploration of that paradox. In part it is the story of the creation of a history book, which may illustrate for many readers more clearly than before the manner in which such work is carried out, and how it has altered during the last three decades of the twentieth century. It also, however, has other purposes: to examine the historiography of Charles himself, and to use it to reflect upon the difficulties of writing biographies of early modern politicians, and of making sense of early modern political history in general. For some time leading literary scholars of the period, and especially new historicists, have emphasised the personal in their work. Historians, by contrast, have tended to erase it, even while a more cultural and less fixed sense of the nature of scholarship has started to creep into their discipline. To bring myself as well as my subject to the centre of the stage may be to effect a move which enables an interrogation of the ways in which biography and history are written, and how those ways have changed and are changing.

In a sense, writing lives of English monarchs was a family business in my part of the academic world, for three of them had been produced by members of my department at Bristol University in the couple of decades before I started work on mine. I was also aware, however, that there was a contrast between their situation and my own, summed up in the words with which one of those predecessors, David Douglas, opened his famous biography of William the Conqueror. Publishing in 1964, he noted that an invitation to deliver the Ford Lectures at Oxford University had 'impelled me to bring to a conclusion certain studies in Anglo-Norman history which had occupied much of my leisure for more than twenty years'.[1] From one viewpoint he was speaking wholly literally, because the main business of term-time, then and now, is considered to be teaching, and research is confined to those 'leisure' periods when a university-based scholar is released from these contractual duties. From another, it evokes perfectly the spirit of a now vanished age, with its suggestions of an unhurried genteel erudition. It was not considered imperative for academics ever to write books at all, and a major enterprise such as a royal biography was commonly worked up to gradually, as Douglas did, so that it crowned a career devoted to the slow and patient accumulation of the expertise required to speak with confidence and decision on the subject. The twenty years which he mentioned had not been the length of his own career, for when he published his life of William he was already an emeritus professor looking back on four decades in the profession. It was simply the period which he had devoted to studying the Conqueror's reign. Likewise, when my other predecessor at Bristol, Charles Ross, produced his lives of Edward IV and Richard III, he waited until he had been at work for over two decades before attempting even the first of those.[2]

In view of this my own decision to undertake such a book when I was not yet thirty years old, and had been engaged in research for just seven of those years, might seem like a piece of personal hubris. Although elements of the latter may have been present, it reflected far more obviously the greatly increased pace of activity in the academy, and the increased expectations of young historians, which developed during the 1970s. In 1978 John Miller had brought out a biography of Charles's brother and successor, James II, in a manner which had reflected the new fast-stream style of career trajectory. He had begun by obtaining what had now become the usual first-step qualification for an academic job, a doctoral thesis. Its subject had been the relationship between Catholicism and politics during the reigns of Charles and James, and he had gone on immediately to develop it into a first book. The whole process had taken him five years, and he then proceeded without slackening to make some of his existing material the take-off point for his work on the biography, which was out in another half-decade.[3]

I had followed the same route, save that I had inserted another book between that based on the thesis and the life of Charles, and both these first two works provided launch pads for different parts of that third book. The earlier had been devoted to the royalists in the Civil War, and the second to the period 1658 to 1667. Both enterprises had introduced me to Charles, and just a year's hard labour would close the chronological gap between them and give me material covering more than half of his life span. Three more years, and I would be able to cover the entire reign. That I should think in terms of such breakneck speed was typical of the confidence and energy of my academic generation, but it matters also that I was urged into the project by three scholars who were older and much more illustrious than myself. Their suggestions were supported by respected editors working for two of the nation's most prominent academic presses, who felt themselves that such a book was needed and that I was the person to write it, in the time frame proposed. Attitudes in our profession were changing indeed. Their continued alteration may be summed up by the introduction to a still more recent study of a Stuart monarch, Tony Claydon's profile of William of Orange which appeared in 2002. He informed his readers that 'after nearly a decade and a half studying the 1690s,

I very much hope this book will be my last to concentrate on William III'.[4] Forty years before, scholars had considered a lifetime of research a suitable preparation for such a major study; by the new century fifteen years could be regarded as too long. My own one fell just on the later side of the watershed between the age of leisured and genteel erudition and that of restless and impulsive exploration.

In my decision to write a life of Charles it also counted for a great deal that, largely because of accident, a tradition had emerged by which biography was the major form by which English politics in the Restoration period had been studied. Since 1950 three full-length studies had been published of leading ministers of Charles II, each one of which had either made the name of the author or represented his most-respected book;[5] and now there was Miller's life of James II. To produce one of Charles himself would be to build upon the example and the information furnished by these forerunners and crown the structure which they represented. Over the same period, the art of biography itself had become established as one of the most popular and most highly regarded forms of scholarship. The public clearly liked the idea of getting to know historical characters and enjoying the natural story which a human life usually represents. Political history, although often criticised or challenged, was still the paramount form studied in schools and universities, and the idea of character as a decisive force in it was generally accepted. The combination of the two circumstances was to invest the writing of biographical studies with especial prestige as a branch of literature, both inside and outside the academy, with its own manuals and conduct books. The author of one of these, Robert Gittings, defined the genre as 'poetry with a conscience' and declared that since the early twentieth century, 'no good biographer has dared to be less than an artist'. He went on to assert that 'the biographer must suffer, not dully but acutely, not only the wrongs but all the experiences, triumphant or disastrous, of the subject whose life he attempts to recreate'. The same sense of utter absorption and self-identification came through in the words of Stephen B. Oates, recalling the writing of his study of Abraham Lincoln: 'I became so immersed in his life that I got depressed when he did; I hurt when he got hurt.' Another noted practitioner of the genre, Jean Strouse, declared that biography had now taken the place of the novel, giving its audience the same large slices of life in which questions of character, motivation, morality and social pressure could be explored in depth, with the additional excitement that the story being told was a true one.[6]

The notion of the biographer as an artist sat uncomfortably with the positivism of traditional historical scholarship, with its emphasis on objectivity, the independence of the data and a strict policing of the imagination. The two were commonly reconciled by a sonorous phrase much heard in academic circles during the 1970s, the notion of the 'definitive life'. At its most practical, this signified the first biography of a subject to establish, as well as could possibly be accomplished, the complete record of their origins, upbringing and career. More often, it was used loosely to convey the idea that a good enough scholar could write the life of somebody so well that there was no need to do the job again, and that the resulting book could take its place permanently as a solid building-block in the edifice of knowledge of the period concerned. It was part of the optimism and high seriousness of that febrile decade that academics could tote such an ambition as one to which any responsible and well-motivated historian should aspire.

Lurking behind all these precepts and incentives in the particular case of Charles II was a general assumption among professionals that a good, let alone a definitive, biography did not exist for this particular monarch. Such a consensus had been achieved despite the fact that no less than fourteen studies of Charles, some of them celebrated, had been published since the beginning of the century. That so much quantity could be associated in the minds of apparent experts with so little quality was the product of a cleavage in attitudes to the king, which reflected not just the fortunes of his historical reputation but a division between the writing of academic and non-academic history.

* * *

I first encountered Charles myself in a dog-eared children's encyclopaedia which was handed on to me when I was six years old, in the late 1950s. It may itself have been a decade or two older. It included sections on English history, and that on the Restoration was headed, uncompromisingly, 'How England got back its Monarchy, and with it a Bad King.' Behind this judgement lay over a hundred years of respectable scholarly tradition. In 1848 the most popular historian ever to write in Britain, Lord Macaulay, declared that Charles's one ambition had been to remain 'a king who could draw without limit on the treasury for the gratification of his private tastes, who could hire with wealth and honours persons capable of assisting him to kill the time, and who, even when the state was brought by maladministration to the depths of humiliation and to the brink of ruin, could still exclude unwelcome truth from the purlieus of his own seraglio, and refuse to see and hear whatever might disturb his luxurious repose'.[7] The Whig politician Macaulay was explicitly comparing him to the eighteenth-century kings of France, whose indolence and incompetence had apparently prepared the way for the French Revolution; in this way Charles and his brother could be made the equivalent backdrop to the Revolution of 1688 in England, which Macaulay was about to celebrate. In constructing this picture, however, he was drawing upon satires circulated in Charles's lifetime, which were in turn inspired by stereotypical ancient images of effete tyrants whose realms crumbled about them as they indulged themselves. It was Charles II who was being characterised in these words, but it was also, interchangeably, Sardanapalus, Nero, or Elagabalus.

At the opening of the twentieth century Macaulay's collateral and spiritual descendant, George Macaulay Trevelyan, had a different take on Charles, although one which was equally hostile. His monarch was just as lazy but actively dangerous: he 'was plotting an overthrow of our religion, our liberties and even our racial independence', by introducing Catholicism, despotism, and a subservient alliance with the foreign power which most perfectly summed up both in Charles's generation: France. Only England's good luck and his own ineptitude thwarted him. Patriotic readers of Trevelyan would not be surprised to find that this despicable king was not really British, his features being marked by 'thick, sensuous lips, dark hair and face of a type more common in Southern Europe'.[8] His Charles was, in fact, a stage villain.

Three years before Trevelyan wrote, another respected scholar, Osmund Airy, had published a biography of the monarch and produced a third form of stock character by which, damningly, to represent him. Under his pen Charles became the type of the upper-class wastrel, talented and intelligent, but so fatally flawed by his taste for pleasure that he wasted every gift and opportunity and came to a sad end. Behind the picture of this monarch stood Dorian Gray and all the other doomed genteel anti-heroes of late Victorian and Edwardian fiction. The conclusion to Airy's life of Charles bears comparison to the lushest of such writing: 'He left his country in anxiety, not in grief. ... His guide was not duty; it was not even ambition: but his guide was self; it was ease, and amusement, and lust. The cup of pleasure was filled deep for him, and he grasped it with both hands. But pleasure is not happiness. There is no happiness for him who lives and dies without beliefs, without enthusiasms, and without love.'[9]

After all this caricaturing, it seemed likely that as the writing of history became more self-consciously academic and professional, in the course of the twentieth century, so judgements on Charles would become more moderate and balanced. So they did, but just sufficiently to make their overall negativity more impressive. In the 1930s the three great writers of textbooks on the Restoration period, Sir Keith Feiling, David Ogg and Sir George Clark, all examined the reign of Charles, and all awarded him a lower second class. They agreed that he was a superficially attractive, intelligent and able man, but unprincipled and lazy, with a facade of facile goodwill and an obsession with dissimulation.[10] Summing up a century of scholarship in 1938, the American historian Clyde L. Grose conceded that in a crisis Charles could show himself to be 'among the abler kings of Europe'. As head of state, however, he was 'marked neither by high principle nor striking accomplishment', as head of the Church he was 'a liability of the first order', and Grose concluded that 'the convincing biographer who would portray Charles as a great and a good king must have consummate literary skill and generous blindness to facts'.[11]

As the century passed its zenith the academic verdict actually got harsher. In 1966 Kenneth Haley produced a short study of the king for the Historical Association, and summed him up as 'respected by few, trusted by scarcely anyone, and held in awe by none'. His reign was 'one long series of hand-to-mouth expedients', and to Haley he could not 'convincingly be built up into anything like

a great monarch'.[12] The 1970s, the immediate backdrop to my own work, provided
three judgements by leading academic colleagues. James Jones allowed that Charles
developed into a 'formidable, even intimidating, monarch', but that his 'indolence
and inconsistency ... created serious political and governmental confusion and
weakness'. John Miller, in writing the life of his brother James II, took a swipe at
him as 'a weak king, struggling to minimize the effects of his own idleness and
indecision', and John Kenyon thought him a ruler who 'squandered all his
chances', did not apply himself to governing, and near the end of his reign 'lapsed
into petulant and indifferent senility'.[13]

Whether muted or strident, the underlying negativity of the scholarly tradition
is patent, and seems to have derived from two conditioning factors. The less important is that by definition the authors of academic books tend to be highly motivated, self-disciplined people habituated to consistent hard work, especially that
concerned with reading, writing, and documentation. It is possible that they have
found something instinctually offensive about a king who was notoriously bad at
paperwork, cultivated an air of lazy affability, and was averse to the pursuit of long-
term goals and sustained policies. None of them were like Charles, but rather a lot
of their more irritating university pupils may have been so. The more important
factor – by far – is that few of the king's contemporaries rated him very highly as a
monarch, and most of them who have left records complained of exactly those
apparent defects as a politician which were highlighted by the historians. Although
the prevailing tone of the academy since the nineteenth century has been liberal
or socialist, perhaps perpetuating the Whig prejudice against Charles, the negative
judgements on him have been made by historians who themselves spanned the
political spectrum.

All this being so, it is now important to emphasise with equal weight that at the
time at which I started work on him, the popular reputation of this king was as one
of our most admirable and engaging of monarchs, a dearly loved success both as
ruler and as man. The fact that this should be so is a testament to the sheer vigour
and resilience of historical traditions which operate both outside the academy and
outside the world of political historians. This one was relatively late in developing,
being heralded only in 1917 with the publication of a life of Charles by a prominent Conservative politician and military man, Sir Henry Imbert-Terry. Tories had
always tended to like Charles better than others had done, naturally enough in
view of the fact that the origins of their party lay in a rallying of support to him
during the last six years of his reign. Furthermore, many of the best-known anecdotes to illustrate the king's amiability had been published (and perhaps invented)
by some of them during the long period in which they were out of office under the
first two Georges: effectively, to construct a picture of a cultivated, witty and wise
Tory monarch with which to embarrass the personally boorish and politically Whig
Hanoverians. None the less, Imbert-Terry wrote in self-conscious lone reaction
against the hostile Victorian and Edwardian consensus, and did so by a revisionist

reading of selective episodes. His Charles was a king struggling successfully with huge problems, who was merciful, civilised and shrewd, and whose apparent indolence and undoubted untrustworthiness were carefully deployed political tactics. His difficulties with his Parliaments were ascribed to his being ahead of his time, in his fundamental belief in religious toleration and his equally consistent and enlightened wish for an entente with the French. Despite those difficulties, Sir Henry managed to assert somehow that he was also very popular with the common people.[14]

This book was to provide a constant source of ideas for what was to come, but seven years elapsed before the rehabilitation of the king became a major literary industry, and it did so as part of a general reaction against what was supposed to be Victorianism. To the period succeeding upon the horrors of the First World War, that of the Restoration, with its apparent exuberant celebration of pleasure after the gloom and militarism of the Civil Wars, Revolution, and Interregnum, provided a role-model. By its very nature, history written directly for a popular audience tends to reflect and address the anxieties and hopes of societies at large, more directly and effectively than that produced by the academy. In this fashion, Charles became the royal patron of the Roaring Twenties, and no less than six biographies of him appeared between 1924 and 1933. None were the work of academics, and most were written by literary men who produced novels, plays or digests of popular history. They tended to avoid a close analysis of the political episodes of the reign, concentrating instead on the more romantic adventures of his exile, his relationship with the arts and sciences, especially the theatre, and his personal life. There is no doubt that he was shown to his best advantage in all of these, and a sustained composite picture was built up of a monarch who was clever, perceptive, witty, tolerant, gallant, kind-hearted, loyal and brave: one of the most able kings to rule in Britain and by far the most attractive and entertaining. Proof of how loud a chord this image sounded with the book-buying public is provided by the way in which the major publishing houses competed with each other to put out works which propagated it. Allan, Hodder and Stoughton, Cassell, Routledge and Duckworth had all entered the fray by 1933,[15] but Longmans, Green, and Co. emerged as the clear victors, when they signed up a young writer called Arthur Bryant.

His biography of Charles, published in 1931, was the book that made his name, going into ten reprints within four years. He went on to become one of the British public's favourite writers of history, and to win a knighthood, by sustaining the skills which he had revealed in this opening work. His view of the king was essentially that of the popular biographers of the 1920s, but he brought to it three important additions. First, he was simply a much better author. All of his predecessors in the genre had been literary people of some competence, writing what passed for history in the manner of a novel, but the power of Bryant's prose was outstanding. It was not just that he used words well, but that they were driven by a personal vision of seventeenth-century England as a rural paradise, a land of marvellous natural beauty in every season, populated and embellished by happy, boisterous and essentially free people, who were organically linked to their terrain, their ancestors, and each other. Like most writers with this concept of the English past, he accompanied it with an implied sense of the comparative ugliness and spiritual poverty of the present. There was something inherently conservative, if not reactionary, in his characterisation of the traditional England as a society of 'country squires and parsons, of yeomen and cottagers and ragged, cheerful squatters, making their own wares and their own pleasures after the manner of their ancestors'.[16]

The second comparative virtue of Bryant's book was its sustained use of primary source material, even if virtually all of it was printed and it was not submitted to any rigorous analysis. The third was that it gave full scope to Charles's political career, as well as his social persona and cultural achievements. Bryant made consistent and explicit the claim that had already featured in Imbert-Terry's study: that in some way Charles both truly understood his people and was truly loved by them, and had the best interests of his nation at heart. The villains of the tale are the 'politicians' who filled his various Parliaments, and who somehow managed to interpose themselves between sovereign and subjects in such a way as to make life dreadful for both, starving Charles of money and thwarting his attempts to institute religious toleration.

This scheme of things allowed Bryant to bring his story to a happy ending, in the last four years of the reign when the king dispensed with Parliaments altogether. His skill and patience in bringing this about now afforded his realm 'a wonderful prosperity', amid which he 'was now master of as great a power as any King of England has wielded – the sweeter that it was founded, with little help of arms or money, on his people's love'.[17] Bryant did not cite hard evidence for this popularity; it was assumed as natural. Nor did he consider other aspects of those final years which are patent enough in the record: that without Parliaments the regime could neither legislate nor raise war taxation, so that England was paralysed both as a legislature and as a military power. They were also a period of sustained persecution of religious dissenters, when Oxford University had, for the only time in its history, issued an index of books which the English should not be allowed to read, when members of the parliamentary opposition were purged from all levels of government, and when the Church of England was articulating a theory by which royal power was legitimated not by the monarch's subjects but by his leading clerics. For Bryant it was enough that the king had at last achieved his alleged ideal of 'a united nation, in which no divisions of creed or faction should impede the course of government';[18] in other words, in which parliamentary democracy had been suspended. Remembering that the book was published at a time of economic crisis, when such democracies were collapsing in many parts of Europe in the face of calls for national unity obtained and enforced by charismatic leaders with a populist message and a determination to crush constitutional opposition, there is much in it now which chills the blood of a liberal as well as a historian. Truly its success was in large part due to its ability to capture the mood of an age.

After its appearance anybody producing another life of the same king in the near future had to be either very stupid or very canny, and the latter quality was manifested by Dennis Wheatley when his study of Charles came out in 1933. It cashed in on the success of Bryant by repackaging some of the same material with a renewed concentration on the monarch's private life and some freely admitted 'imaginary reconstructions' supported by vivid pictorial illustrations. Wheatley had just established what was to be a long career as one of the world's most popular writers of 'thriller' fiction. He simply turned the monarch into a historical prototype for the heroes of his own novels of espionage: a charming sexual predator and master of deceit, who was quick-witted, fundamentally decent and thoroughly patriotic. To Wheatley, Charles was 'undoubtedly the cleverest and perhaps the greatest man, who ever sat upon the English throne'.[19] His contempt for, and distrust of, democracy was more obvious than Bryant's had been, and he remained till the end of his life an unrepentant admirer of fascism.[20] Like many of the radical right-wingers of the time he represented his attitudes as a rejection of outworn conservatism as well as of socialism: thus, he explicitly declared the revisionist view of Charles taken by himself and Bryant to be a repudiation of both Victorian puritanism and 'the arctic douche of school-taught history'.[21]

With the success of these two books, and especially of Bryant's, the revisionist view became the standard one accepted by the general public. That it was not a right-wing genre alone was amply proved in 1939 when George Bernard Shaw staged his play 'In Good King Charles's Golden Days', in which the wise, worldly, easy-going and tolerant monarch of the new popular histories became something approaching an ideal philosopher king. This was also the Charles found in a stream of historical novels and on the silver screen, as the century wore on towards its midpoint; a pair of genres worthy of study in their own right, but needing a greater investment of time and other resources than that available for the present chapter. Academic historians reacted to his presence with occasional outbursts of bitterness. Clyde Grose's remarks about biographers, quoted earlier, were both barbed and aimed directly at Bryant and his fellows. John Kenyon lashed out at the 'mattress and chamberpot school' of history, which made the king 'the darling of frustrated romantics'. Kenneth Haley commented sadly on how ubiquitous the Bryant image of him was among lecture audiences outside universities.[22] That these comments between them spanned the period from the late 1930s to the late 1960s indicates well how impervious that image was to academic opinion. It was sustained partly by the successive reprintings and editions of Bryant's book, but also by the fact that popular history had a momentum and tradition of its own, and new publications embodied and sustained an admiration of Charles which was now part of it, and which readers expected. At the end of the 1970s that admiration was reinforced when two of the finest contributors to the genre in the late twentieth century, Lady Antonia Fraser and Richard Ollard, simultaneously published new studies of him.

The former brought out a full-length biography, based on fewer sources than those used by Bryant but including a few items never used by an author before. In general it represented a moderate and elegant restatement of the now familiar pop-history image. Her Charles was a king who had 'inherited a country war-torn and poor, divided, restless and suspicious. He left behind a country outwardly at harmony.' Once again, political purges and religious persecution were simply brushed out of the picture; indeed, neither would have featured much in the works on which she relied. Once more, also, the king was asserted to have been beloved of his ordinary subjects, without recourse to the local records which might have tested that opinion. The assumption was simply that because he seemed so attractive and human a person, this must have been apparent to all: 'witty and kind, grateful, generous, tolerant, and essentially lovable, he was rightly mourned by his people'. Like her predecessors, Lady Antonia assumed that because Charles had lots of mistresses, he had to have been exceptionally attractive as a lover, and her added assertion that he had 'a general respect for women' carried more apparent weight in proceeding from a female writer. Indeed, there was a hint of hormonal throb in her comment on his 'curling and sensual mouth, so beguiling in our day'. That comment also pays tribute to another conventional aspect of the pop-history image of him to which she gave renewed emphasis; that he was somehow a more modern and progressive figure than most of his contemporaries.[23]

Richard Ollard's study consisted of an extended sketch of Charles's personality, based on the usual published texts and concentrating overwhelmingly on material drawn from his life before the Restoration and so avoiding most of the harder questions concerning his performance as a ruler. He recognised that historians had differed considerably in their estimation of Charles both as man and as sovereign, but declared comfortably that 'the national consciousness has never had any doubt. Charles II was the best of company, gay, carefree, pleasure-loving, tolerant'.[24] As his own survey bore out that impression, and added a verdict on the king as tireless and masterly in his conduct of business, he clearly valued what he appeared to consider a timeless national opinion over those of academics. At the close of a decade in which iconoclasm and revisionism had swept universities, Ollard could represent the amateur historian as the true custodian of the public memory.

The pop-historical image of Charles, like the much less favourable one embedded in the academic histories, persisted because it appealed to certain habits and instincts possessed by the literary sub-culture concerned. Its main virtue was simply that it was so appealing: the vision of the king developed in the 1920s made him a strongly marked and seductive personality unique in the annals of British monarchy. He was a sovereign like no other, and one who shone out in that traditional, picture-book concept of the national past which conceived of it in terms of a succession of rulers with definitive characteristics, nicknames and anecdotes attached to them. This was why the essentially static nature of the popular historiography of Charles after Bryant made perfect sense: the public bought books like that by Lady Antonia Fraser because they already had a vague notion of how the king should be and wanted to read about it in more detail and in a form which offered the greatest ease and pleasure. The much more limited and consistent set of sources used by the popular historians, in comparison with the academics, made the reproduction of the stereotype all the more likely. As for these authors themselves, it can be suggested that this image of Charles made a personal appeal to them because it seemed to represent the sort of person whom they themselves would like to meet, in the drawing rooms, dinner parties and literary lunches which many of them frequented.

The dichotomy between the academic and the non-academic views of the king was sustained without any response to changing bodies of supporting evidence. The popular accounts, from Imbert-Terry onward, often made great play with the calendars of treasury books edited by W.A. Shaw from 1904 onward, in the prefaces of which he revealed the fact that the financial settlement made upon the Crown by the Parliaments after the Restoration produced a revenue smaller than that intended. This landed Charles with an acute problem in which the MPs did not believe, and Shaw went on to argue that many of the troubles of the reign could be blamed upon this error, of which the king was the innocent victim. The favourable revision of his image also drew on the successive editions of the Pepys manuscripts produced by the naval historian J.R. Tanner, which showed the monarch to have taken a keen and intelligent interest in the administration of his navy. Neither, however, made much impression upon the academic authors, as they counted for little beside the existing quantity of contemporary evidence for Charles's shortcomings. Likewise, the pop-historians did not change their attitudes in 1975 when an academic, C.D. Chandaman, overturned Shaw's verdict by proving that the financial settlement produced a steady surplus after a decade, and that better management and better relations with Parliament would have enabled Charles to survive until that point without serious difficulty.[25] A writer like Fraser simply used details from Chandaman's book while ignoring its main polemical thrust.[26]

When academic publishers and senior colleagues encouraged me into my own work upon the king with the recurrent observation that no 'good' biography of him existed, they were therefore making a heavily loaded statement. It was effectively a further declaration of hostility in a polarisation of the subject which had lasted for more than sixty years, and in which I was now to make my own intervention.

* * *

As far as I was concerned, my professional position made only two demands upon me in the production of the biography, and both were broad and ill-defined: that

I write a fuller and better-documented account of the life and reign than anybody had published before, and that in the process I say some things about it which seemed to my peers to be both important and new. My own hope was to aim for a higher target, by turning out a book which was scholarly enough to satisfy my colleagues and readable enough to appeal to the general public, so getting the best of both the traditions of work upon Charles. I was not committed by inheritance to follow either of the latter. My training and employment in the university system made me regard the hostile, academic body of writing as my parental one; but nobody who had grown up in the western world during the 1960s and 1970s was under an obligation to respect her or his parents. If I overturned the negative judgements upon Charles and restated the popularly accepted one, with better evidence, then I was carrying out an act of scholarly revisionism as dramatic and praiseworthy as any other. As a child I had imbibed the hostile attitudes to the king, as expressed in that tattered encyclopaedia, but in my teenage years I had greatly enjoyed the books of Sir Arthur Bryant and Dennis Wheatley. I cannot say what my school would have made of Charles, for like most in Britain at that time (and since) it ignored the Restoration period.

Furthermore, I did have some slight relationship with the main representatives of the popular tradition. I admired the elegance of Richard Ollard's prose, and had cited his sketch of Charles in my book on the Restoration as one of the best things ever written upon the king before his return from exile.[27] Sir Arthur Bryant was, as said, a hero of my adolescence. The patriotism which had almost led his writing into some questionable political assumptions in the early 1930s showed to its best effect when deployed against a fascist enemy in wartime (as did that of Wheatley), and his concept of England was also well suited to the nostalgic and conservative atmosphere of the 1950s. It was much less concordant with the following two decades, and he had written much less during them. At the opening of the 1980s, however, he bounced back with a projected three-part national history for a new generation of children, and the first volume of this, published in 1984, was sent to me for review by the main history magazine read by the general public. I made plain my belief that Sir Arthur had lost none of his talent as a writer, but also expressed concern that he was recreating for the present age, completely unrevised, the opinions and prejudices which English people had held about their past during his own youth. The implicit racism, sexism, and bellicosity of the whole package did not seem to me necessarily to be the best lessons for the young readers of the new Britain, let alone the outdated nature of most of the knowledge offered in it.[28] In publishing this I fully expected that the old lion would reply in kind, if he noticed me at all, and that an interesting exchange might ensue. Instead, he died. I was aware that he had been severely ill before commencing the trilogy, but was also uneasily conscious of the impact which a bad critical reception of a beloved project can have upon the health of somebody already delicate; and I had not heard of any reviews more favourable than mine. As a result I felt that I owed

Bryant something, and when I wrote my biography I took no direct issue with any of his work, and lauded its literary qualities in my introduction.

My debt to Lady Antonia Fraser was much more straightforward. I had been unable to trace one of the couple of new sources which she had used in her biography, and so I wrote to her asking for information on its location. She replied that she possessed a copy and offered to loan it to me; it duly arrived by post and proved to be very useful. In return, I invited her to lunch at a restaurant of her choice, an act of great daring on my part as I had never before extended such an offer to a celebrity, and also in view of the size of a young lecturer's salary. She accepted with warmth and grace, and in person she was as charming and clever as reputation had made her; I was so nervous that I forgot to take off my scarf throughout the whole meal. I was also impressed by the way in which, when we spoke of Charles and his contemporaries, she regarded them almost as personal acquaintances, while I still saw them more as inhabitants of an age far removed from our own and approached only through the filter of surviving documents. The occasion only enhanced my opinion of her, and I determined to treat her in my own book much as I had Sir Arthur; to pay respect to her work in its preface and to avoid any specific criticisms of its style and approach.

There was thus no inherent reason why I should not have been the person who tried to make the favourable view of Charles acceptable in the academy, but in point of fact there was never any such hope; before I started work on the biography I already disliked him. I had got to know a lot about him while writing my preceding book on the Restoration, and my belief in the pop-history image had withered away as I did so. In large part this was simply because to write that book I had to immerse myself in the political history of the 1660s, and on doing so I encountered in Charles all the opportunism, inconsistency, recklessness and distaste for sustained hard work which had drawn such negative judgements upon him from predecessors who had concentrated upon the same materials. Furthermore, an important aspect of my book was its heavy use of provincial records to illustrate the way in which government policy was made and executed. They testified amply to the relief and rejoicing with which the overwhelming bulk of the population had greeted the return of the monarchy, but also to the speed and depth of disillusion in the monarch who had returned, at all levels of society. They spoke for a rapid and widespread impression that Charles was a debauched spendthrift who neglected public business and disgraced his office; I could find no trace of the popularity so consistently and confidently proclaimed for him by the non-academic authors.[29]

It made still more of a personal impact on me that I found the realities of the data to be so much at variance with the pop-history image of Charles as a king of exceptional kindness, tenderness, generosity and affability. My book ended in the closing stages of the year 1667, with an act which even an admirer of his like Richard Ollard had regarded as graceless: Charles's dismissal of his old and loyal minister the earl of Clarendon, as a scapegoat for policies which the latter had opposed, and his subsequent support for a legal attack on the old man which forced him to flee the country in fear of his life. Writers such as Ollard, who had a particular affection for Clarendon, represented this as an uncharacteristic lapse on the part of the king. I felt differently on both counts. Clarendon seemed to me a politician (and a historian) with both great talents and great failings, who to some extent brought his fate on himself. On the other hand, I found Charles's treatment of him to be wholly in character for a ruler who had always turned with absolute ruthlessness and petty spite upon anybody who defied him or crossed his will and then became vulnerable to his malice.

Other cases of this trait in action from the period 1660–67 were those of Archibald Johnstone and Sir Henry Vane. The former was a Scottish zealot who had humiliated and annoyed Charles by preaching at him about his sins and those of his parents in 1650. When the Restoration occurred Johnston bolted for the Continent, from where the king's persistent enquiries led to his extradition three years later. The Scot had gone completely mad in exile and represented a pathetic sight from which both the king's English and Scottish advisers recoiled in pity. Charles, however, was determined on his death, and secured it. Vane was an English republican, who had refused to beg for the royal mercy after the return of the monarchy, or to express contrition for what he had done. The king's reaction was to pass his Lord Chancellor a letter demanding Vane's death as soon as possible, which was obtained by keeping the jury without food or drink. The old republican was beheaded on the anniversary of the great defeat of Charles's father at Naseby, with musicians placed under the scaffold to drown out his last words.[30]

These acts of vengeance disturbed me less than the king's treatment of his own wife, Catherine, and of Quakers. Unlike some of Charles's Victorian critics I felt no disapproval of his adultery in principle. What shocked me were the details of his behaviour towards his queen shortly after their marriage, when having enjoyed the honeymoon and declared his approval of his bride – above all, significantly, of her docility – he attempted to impose his most recent mistress on her as her first lady of the bedchamber. Catherine objected strenuously to this insult, whereupon he turned against her both in private and in public, deprived her of all her own maidservants, returned his affections to his mistress, and sent relays of churchmen and ministers to bully his wife into surrender. After two months of tearstained refusal, the lonely and miserable girl gave in, but Charles continued to treat her with coldness and contempt for a year afterwards, in which he paraded his mistress and his illegitimate children with an openness which he had avoided previously. As for the Quakers, I was aware that by the early 1660s they had become the religious movement which has persisted ever since: devout, pacifist, and committed to witnessing on behalf of a much more radical, and democratic, form of Christianity than any which had been seen in England before their time. As such, they were deeply unpopular with much of English society, and especially with the social elites.

I did not feel any personal impulse towards their sort of religion, but having read their tracts and letters extensively for my book I did respect their honesty, courage, and dedication. Accordingly, it pleased me to find for myself what had always been claimed for Charles by his admirers; that he initially regarded them with more geniality and tolerance than most of his subjects and attempted to stem their persecution. The evidence suggested that he did so more because he found them amusing and because of their fervent expressions of loyalty to him as God's chosen instrument, than because of any attachment to toleration in principle; but his behaviour seemed agreeable enough. I was accordingly startled to discover what preceding work upon him had missed; that the royal attitude changed violently at the end of 1663. A few Quakers had become involved in a tragicomic plot against the government hatched by a spectrum of religious dissenters in the North, propelled by the ineffectuality of the regime to halt escalating persecution of nonconformity in the provinces. The number of plotters was tiny, and their plan was called off; but not before it had leaked. Charles found it convenient to inflate grossly the size and danger of the conspiracy as a ploy to rally support for his increasingly unpopular rule, but he also seemed to regard himself as personally betrayed by the participation of even a handful of Quakers in the affair. He encouraged a new act of Parliament to outlaw all religious meetings outside the established Church, and then urged its execution upon the Quakers with personal malice.[31]

I was therefore faced with the prospect of writing the life history of a person with whom I already lacked sympathy; but this did not deter me. I felt that it would be interesting to test the charge often levelled against biographers, of being in love with their subjects, by seeing if it was possible to produce a perceptive work by tackling a person for whom I felt no warmth. The Charles whom my book on the Restoration seemed to be revealing was in many ways a more interesting man and ruler than the one of the stereotype; and furthermore there was no guarantee that my view of him would remain constant. It was possible that a thorough treatment of his early life would reveal experiences which would amply explain the less agreeable characteristics which he had manifested by the 1660s, and better qualities which had been corrupted by those experiences; in which case my story would take on a tragic tone. It was equally plausible that in later life he had matured and mellowed, and become the admirable figure of the pop-histories; in which case the story would become one of redemption. At any rate, I was fascinated enough to proceed; and fascination, rather than sympathy, is arguably the essential quality to bring to such work, empowering the writer with the curiosity and delight needed to undertake it.

The pattern of research for the project took shape slowly between 1983 and 1985. My book on the Restoration had been produced by two and a half solid years of reading followed by one of constant writing. I was anxious not to repeat that experience in a hurry, for by the time that I was into my ninth month of constant authorship I felt like a slave chained to an oar in a galley, who was expected to pilot the ship and keep a log-book at the same time. As that book had amounted to 150 000 words, and the biography would be closer to a quarter of a million, I had to find a different way of operating. Accordingly, I resolved to carry out the research for each chapter separately, and to write it, before proceeding to work on the next. This would provide a constant alternation of research and writing, to keep both fresh. Furthermore, I decided to concentrate in alternate months on the biography and on a completely different programme of research, on the history of seasonal festivals. That would enable me to advance slowly on a broad front, taking care each year to publish an essay in both fields to signal to my colleagues how I was faring. The result would be to double the amount of time spent on my life of Charles, but to ensure that I supported the strain of the project better, and perhaps gave it more thought and patience than would otherwise have been the case. I lived according to this programme from October 1983 to November 1984, and then a meeting wrecked my whole plan.

It hinged upon a conversation which I had conducted in the Sphagetti House Restaurant in London in November 1982, after delivering a seminar paper at the Institute of Historical Research. Four well-known historians came out to eat with me, and we discussed our respective future ambitions. I had been wondering whether to follow my book on the Restoration by retreating to the period of my first work, the 1640s, and investigating a particular problem there. One of the company told me that he had already resolved to tackle that subject, and asked me in the nicest possible way to leave it to him. This was wholly in accordance with the beliefs about our discipline shared by most academic historians in the 1970s. Not only was it assumed to be possible and desirable to produce 'definitive' histories of specific phenomena, but it was also implicitly thought that two good scholars of the same subject, working at the same time, would duplicate all or most of each other's work. It was therefore considered to make sound professional sense to divide up the territory so that different research projects would not collide or overlap. Having honoured this convention, I turned to John Miller, the biographer of James II, who was one of my other companions that night. I asked him if he intended to undertake a matching life of Charles, and he told me that, having already provided his opinion of that monarch while writing about his brother, he saw no point in doing so. I resolved at that moment to take on the job myself. Over two years later John Miller came to Bristol to address our student history society, and during that visit told me that his new project was a biography of Charles. Quite understandably, he had completely forgotten our exchange in that restaurant, and changed his mind in the interim.

We were both shocked to learn that we were now working in tandem, and at once set about a new partition of the subject to minimise the degree of overlap and competition involved. There was no doubt that John was formidably well qualified for the commission which we had both now undertaken: he lived in London, close to the main archives and libraries of relevant material, had a splendid knowledge of just those decades, the 1670s and 1680s, in which I was a novice, and was an older and more celebrated scholar than I and so would have better claims to research funding and study leave. My only hope in trying to match him was therefore to write a very different sort of book. We rapidly agreed that he would concentrate on the period after 1660 and on the workings of the regime in England, with a full consideration of foreign policy. I would cover the whole life, keep the king fairly firmly at the centre of events, and include his relationships with Scotland and Ireland. This conformed neatly to our existing interests and intentions, while appearing to give me the bigger job. It also had the effect of convincing me that my former plan of leisurely progress and alternate study of the ritual year had to be scrapped. It would have been foolish for me to get into a race with John, when I had no real idea of how long either of us would take to finish, but it was important to get my book out within a year on either side of his, to avoid having to revise my own extensively to take account of his findings and agenda. From that moment onward I began to work flat out on the biography.

* * *

Historians rarely write about the practical business of going about their work. Much of what follows is intended for general readers who may wonder how it is accomplished, although some of the details have important implications for the historiographical reflections which follow. The experience of research itself was altering during this period, and in retrospect the changes were to mark part of a major shift in the expectations and activities of historians in Britain between the 1970s and the 1980s. Each time I commenced a chapter, I would of course read through everything relevant which was obtainable in my own university library. The next port of call after that was always the nearest national copyright collection to Bristol, the Bodleian Library at Oxford which also possessed one of the greatest deposits of manuscripts and tracts. After Oxford would come the great national collections of the capital, above all those housed in the traditional handsome eighteenth and nineteenth-century premises of the British Library and the Public Record Office. There was always a thrill in working in spaces where not only generations of famous historians had laboured before, but also Karl Marx, Darwin, and the whole roll-call of scholars whose researches in London had helped make them famous. It also helped that the two were situated a short walk apart, so that in a gap in document production at one of them, it was easy to pop over and carry on reading items kept at the other. In the time during which I worked on the biography, this system began to break down under increasing demand. At the Library bundles of famous pamphlets which had simply been produced for me when I was working on my doctoral thesis were now available only on microfilm to spare the originals; and the microfilm readers were often all busy, or the films themselves impaired or badly wound. Much worse and more fundamental was the increasing demand placed on the same number of staff by a proportionately growing number of academic readers. Crises began to occur in which the supply of books was disrupted for days on end, and I once witnessed an altercation in which an irate foreign scholar threatened to smash the spectacles of the person at the issue desk if his order did not arrive by the end of the afternoon. By the end of the 1990s both collections were rehoused in new buildings on opposite sides of London, and the happy tradition of flitting between them, and the strong sense of historical continuity in the use of them, were gone.

More than a pattern of working vanished in those years. When I entered the university system in the 1970s, its writers of political history not only shared a belief that knowledge and understanding of the subject could be straightforwardly advanced, but that the printed records were a facade behind which the solutions to major questions were hidden in handwritten manuscripts. The main quest of such historians in that period was to seek out these treasures and reveal their contents to the world for the first time, giving the process of research the combined excitements of an archaeological dig, a detective story and a quest-romance. Such expectations hovered just as thickly around the celebrated metropolitan deposits as any others. It was accepted that the serried rows of catalogues of the manuscripts held by the British Library contained items which had never been properly read, and the importance of which was not yet appreciated, by experts in most areas of political history. As for the Public Record Office, a legend circulated among professionals that it contained a room piled high with unedited seventeenth-century papers. What was certainly true was that major collections of state documents from that period had not until the 1970s, been touched by historians. In 1977 a veteran historian at Oxford told me how, on first ordering up one of the bundles of papers from those categories, he found inside it a mouse's nest containing the skeleton of its last occupant. He wondered whether a biologist might tell him in which century the mouse concerned had lived and died. By the 1990s this world was gone. The remaining classes of document had been worked through – though the importance of individual items could easily be missed – and nobody was talking any more about unexplored rooms in the Public Record Office; the space-age architecture of the buildings on its new site at Kew did not lend themselves to such stories in the manner of the Victorian towers of the old one in Chancery Lane.

The archives and libraries of the capital posed a particular problem for myself: I had no convenient base in the city, and so work there had to be carried out on day-visits. The sprawling geography of London, and its distance from Bristol, meant that rail journeys were the fastest and most efficient means of travel, but they were also the most expensive. To travel later in the day meant a lower fare, but also less time before the library or record office closed; so it might not be a saving at all. In this situation, there was an almost irresistible temptation to push as hard as possible at each set of records, keeping breaks for food or drink to an absolute minimum, throughout the hours of public admission. This was a sensationally tiring and stressful way of working, and one in which the potential for missing information and making errors was maximised. I was always worn out by mid-afternoon, and used to fight fatigue and lapses of attention by chewing gum, the only occasion in my life when I had resorted to this habit. My worst labour was over the Baschet transcripts, the copies made by a Victorian antiquary of despatches sent home by foreign ambassadors to the English court, above all the French. These were records of crucial importance to the interpretation of Charles's reign, and to read them in London was infinitely preferable to having to do so in Paris or other Continental cities. It did, however, mean slogging through thick bundles of pages written in early modern French, hour after hour on visit after visit; and the gum really came into its own then. Once there was a young woman standing in front of me who was reading a series of medieval rolls all through the day, with unflinching concentration. I wondered how she could muster the self-discipline to do so, until she turned round and I saw her mouth, like mine, was chewing away rhythmically.

The quest-romance for the unedited manuscript was an even stronger theme of work in provincial archives. The happiest hunting-ground for English historians during the 1970s was the county record office, an institution which had come into its own during the mid-twentieth century as private and public archives flowed rapidly into the comprehensive local collections established in the care of shire councils. They had the delicious prospect of reading through large quantities of fresh material, commonly in attractive premises and with the aid of friendly and attentive staff, which at the least opened up wholly new perspectives on familiar subjects and at best supplied crucial new pieces of evidence to solve long-standing questions and revise common assumptions. The charm of many old provincial towns added to the attractions of such research. My first two books had been heavily dependent on it, but my work on the biography took place during a period of transition in which many of the advantages of the provincial offices were wearing away.

For one thing, they were becoming overcrowded, and for a particular reason: the boom in interest among ordinary people in searching out and reconstructing the details of their family trees. Why this should have become so much more popular in the late twentieth century is an interesting historical question in its own right, and one deeply bound up with changing attitudes to the past. I was, however, more concerned with the results. During the time in which I carried out research in county record offices I saw them gradually fill up with people, usually elderly and overwhelmingly from the lower middle class, poring over documents for clues as to the identity and fortunes of their ancestors. This new pressure on the resources of the offices coincided with the cuts in local government spending brought in by the Thatcher ministry. Staff became more tired, harassed and impatient, and more resentful of historians needing to work through long sequences of papers. Spare seats in reading rooms became harder and harder to find and prior reservation of places turned into a requirement in most offices. By the end of the 1980s some were starting to charge admission fees.

This process went in tandem with a change of attitude to the archives themselves. In the 1970s record office staff generally regarded their deposits as existing to be at the service of the public, among whom academic historians were treated as an aristocracy. Two decades in which scholars took full advantage of this situation brought home to many archivists how fast the physical condition of manuscripts could deteriorate under the impact of frequent inspection. Increasingly, their duty seemed more to be to preserve the records for some hazy future rather than to submit them to the mauling of present-day consumers: historians had shifted from being the main people whom the system was there to serve to being the principal vandals against whom its treasures were to be defended. More and more documents were declared to be unfit for production. The excuse commonly supplied with this was that they would be made available on microfilm or subjected to conservation programmes, but the lack of funding meant that such work was only carried out in a small minority of cases. At times the result could be maddening. In 1985 David Underdown published his celebrated and controversial book on the English Civil War, *Revel, Riot and Rebellion*, based mainly upon local records in three western counties. One of these was Dorset, and in 1991 I went back to its record office to check comprehensively through the sources which he had used in order to evaluate some of his conclusions. I was informed that a third of them, including some of the most important, were now classed as too delicate to be available to the public; I had absolutely no way of making up my own mind upon the arguments based upon them by my predecessor.

The alteration in service can be illustrated well by the case of the first county record office which I ever visited, that of Northamptonshire. I arrived there on a summer day in 1977, to find it housed in a sprawling russet mansion set in a luscious parkland on the outskirts of the county town. As I entered the grounds the perfume of their flowers struck me in the face. The office was small, but I was one of only three people in it and the staff greeted me merrily, with real interest in me and my work. The documents which I wanted were produced immediately and I was left to make what I wished of them. When I last worked at the same institution, it was on another summer day in 1991. The office had moved into new concrete, glass and steel buildings on another part of the town's rim, and although they were more spacious they were also crowded with readers. The staff – all new faces to me – were coldly formal and distant, and I was only permitted to order documents in limited quantities and at spaced times. Some were now declared too delicate to be produced, and all those which I was allowed to see could be read only when covered with a polythene sheet and were issued only after a treble process of signing and checking. It must be stressed that by that date the Northamptonshire Record Office was one of the most attractive, for at least the staff were polite, I was not charged for my work, and the manuscripts were delivered fairly quickly. There is small wonder that this was the last period in which I conducted extensive research in provincial archives.

The most romantic aspect of the quest for the undiscovered manuscript did not, however, concern public collections. It lay in the big country houses still owned by the heirs of the politicians whom historians were studying. There, it was believed, hidden away in muniment rooms and private libraries – essentially the natural habitat of the papers concerned – could be the evidence to determine key issues of policy-making. Up till the 1970s important new documents were indeed discovered in such places, and in the 1980s the thrill of the chase remained for scholars working in them. It was true that the actual experience of many stately homes, and especially those with famous manuscript collections, was more prosaic. It involved driving up to a huge stone palace such as Longleat or Chatsworth, calling at what was very much a tradesman's entrance, being met by the household archivist and paying a fee, and receiving the documents in a usually Spartan side-room reserved for the purpose. Given the pressure of scholarly interest on these archives, things could hardly be otherwise. Only in homes less frequented by historians, and owned by unusually sociable and informal aristocrats, was a researcher treated to lunch by the magnate in person and a good conversation regarded as payment enough for the intrusion: such a house was Mapperton, home of the earls of Sandwich.

It may be a coincidence that these happy exceptions were thickly concentrated in my own region of the West Country, or it may be that my residence there made it easier to establish such personal contacts. Three in particular stand out from the rest. One was at a mansion even more rambling and semi-ruinous than the norm, lying in the fold of a hillside. The roof contained twenty-seven attics, none of which harboured any political papers but which were instead the roosting-place of four species of bat. The owner and I donned boiler suits to explore them, jumping from rafter to rafter with the curry-powder-and-snuff odour of guano everywhere. The second remarkable experience was at a large manor-house which was at that time the home of a single shy elderly gentleman, who slept and ate alone in the cold, echoing rooms, surrounded by paintings of ancestors whose names he could no longer recall and photographs of children who had grown up and moved to work in London. He simply did not know what books or manuscripts were in the library, and I found myself rooting through a treasury of first editions, correspondence and notebooks centuries old, grown with white mould and tumbled over shelves, cases and floor. I rediscovered one of the most famous letters of the English Civil War, which had been published fifty years before and supplied historians with some of the most poignant words ever to express the conflict. At some point after its first discovery, somebody had used it as a bookmark and it had lain enclosed in the volume concerned ever since. My host was delighted to have it thus located, and I was pleased to have also found a set of documents of real value for my book on Charles. We thus both parted cheerfully and affectionately, as I drove away northward and he retired into his world of burglar alarms, priceless and superfluous period furniture, rows of watching portraits, and silence.

The third case was the most spectacular, and in a small way changed national history. It concerned Ugbrooke Park in Devon, home to the Barons Clifford of Chudleigh who were descended from one of Charles II's Lord Treasurer. During the nineteenth and early twentieth centuries, historians had made a number of major discoveries there relating to the greatest puzzle of the reign, the Secret Treaty of Dover, in which Charles had promised Louis XIV of France to convert to Catholicism, use French troops to quell opposition to this step in Britain, and launch an unprovoked joint attack on the Dutch state with the purpose of destroying it. Historians had endlessly debated the king's motives in negotiating this agreement, without reaching any consensus. The English copy, and various supporting documents from the secret discussions, had been concealed at Ugbrooke by the first Lord Clifford, and their successive discovery and publication between the 1830s and the 1950s had provided the debate with some of its key pieces of evidence. Near the end of 1983 a friend and senior colleague in Stuart studies, John Morrill, told me that he had heard a rumour that further finds might be made at the house, and that its collection was now once again accessible to scholars after a long period of closure. I accordingly wrote to the heir to the estate, Captain Thomas Clifford, and was courteously invited to call upon him.

My visit took place in mid-January 1984, when snow was lying on the slopes of Dartmoor above the valley in which Ugbrooke lies. I walked down that valley, to come upon the mansion after a sudden turn of the road. It was a large crenellated building, with the family banner flying from one tower, and nobody else in sight. The sense of trepidation grew stronger upon me as, repeatedly knocking and calling, I made my way through the front gate into the courtyard, and then through a door into the corridors beyond. It was removed completely when I was greeted in the depths of the house by Captain Clifford and his wife, with the utmost friendliness. I found myself seated before a log fire with a half-bottle of hock and a crystal glass, chatting about history and ghosts while my hosts hunted out documents for my attention. 'This', I thought to myself, 'is what I call research.'

The manuscript holdings of Ugbrooke were indeed magnificent, and largely unexplored. The muniment rooms were crammed, and looking at some of the collections outside my own period, I noticed letters signed by eighteenth-century Popes, Napoleon's foreign minister Talleyrand, and George Bernard Shaw. I thought it possible to write a good article on the local dimension of Catholic Emancipation from the contents of one shelf alone. The Stuart state papers included some abstracted by the first Baron from the policy-making documents of Oliver Cromwell. The Secret Treaty itself, and the notes on the negotiations, was preserved in a chest safely lodged in a vault, and they all looked as if they had been written in the previous week. They enabled me to write an essay for publication in an academic journal, setting out my own interpretation of Charles's motivation in making the agreement.[32] This was, however, only the beginning of my association with the manuscripts, and with the Cliffords, because my visit helped catalyse an existing feeling on the part of the family that it would be wise to raise further money for the restoration of their house, by selling the Stuart political papers in such a way as to make them immediately accessible to the nation. The resulting talks lasted more than three years, and culminated in what I was told at the time to be the greatest sale of state papers in the history of the world. The Secret Treaty and its supporting documents were auctioned at Sotheby's in July 1987, and eventually ended up in the British Library, with the treaty itself permanently on display to the public. The process taught me a great deal about how the market for artistic and literary treasures operates, and how to manage the mass media. It also afforded me the much greater prize of a lasting friendship with the Cliffords of Chudleigh.

When all these stories are told, it must be admitted that I never did find a document in private hands which completely overturned received opinion concerning any historical event. The fruit of all my researches in country houses, including Ugbrooke, was to furnish many additional pieces of information which could be combined with those from printed sources and public archives to build up a better picture of the reign, stage by stage. There was just one moment when it seemed as if things might have been different; when Captain Clifford showed me, and a representative of the British Library, the original locking despatch box of his ancestor the first Baron, which doubled as a writing-desk when the minister was travelling. It had been in this that the Secret Treaty and its associated documents had made the journey to Devon. Two of the three drawers were empty, but the lowest was jammed, and this turned out to be because it was still full of seventeenth-century papers; which presumably had been there ever since the first Lord Clifford had put them in. My eyes met those of the man from the Library over the top of the box, as we realised simultaneously that we just might be in the historiographical equivalent of the position of Columbus. With Captain Clifford's permission we levered the drawer carefully open; but the manuscripts concerned turned out to be routine Treasury records, presumably the last through which the Lord Treasurer had checked before his resignation, retirement and sudden death. Again, they were of incidental interest in rounding out historical knowledge, and there was a shiver in realising that we were the first people to see and touch them for over three centuries, but they told us nothing dramatically new.

In my record of success in hunting through private collections, I was more fortunate than many of my fellow historians during the same period. During the 1980s it became generally believed that, at least where the medieval and early modern periods were concerned, there was nothing more of outstanding importance to be discovered in the archives of stately homes; or at least in those which were accessible to scholars. By the 1990s academic interest had largely moved away from them.

When all these developments are taken into account, it may perhaps be better understood why, by the end of the twentieth century, specialists in Tudor and Stuart political history were ceasing to regard the discovery of unused manuscripts as the highest ambition of their calling, and archives were no longer necessarily seen as the natural focal points of their research. Instead, interest was moving back to printed works, and the re-evaluation of sources long known and used in national collections, and extending into new areas such as artistic representation. It was becoming much more common for historians of the period to make detailed case studies of particular incidents, resting upon the thorough theoretical analysis of a restricted body of evidence, than to attempt the grand panoramas produced by archival material analysed in bulk. In large part these developments were the result of general shifts in the climate of historical research, produced by the impact of cultural studies, anthropology and postmodernist attitudes to the nature of enquiry. It could be argued, for example, that archival records marginalise the public voice and sphere. In part however – and this is an issue hardly ever openly discussed – they were reactions to the growing practical problems of archival research.

* * *

From the moment that I decided to concentrate solidly on the biography, almost four years were needed to finish the job. I do not think that there was a day during this time, including Christmas, on which I did not put in some work on the book, and it was completed in the summer of 1988. I wrote the death-scene of the king in a library in Oxford, penned the end of the conclusion in a hotel in Edinburgh, and produced the last words of all, the climax of the introduction, on board a ferry sailing to Dublin; which, together with sheer relief, explains the euphoria of that final passage. Whether it was good for my health or my humanity, the intensity of this rate of progress should have given me the ability to immerse myself in Charles's career to the point at which, like the authors of the manuals for the writing of biography, I could live and breathe with my chosen person. In fact I could not. It had become clear to me that an ideal subject for a biographer is somebody who has left a body of published written works, a diary of personal thought and opinion maintained over many years, a large number of surviving letters, medical records relating to her or his health problems, and a set of memoirs, and was closely observed from childhood onwards by other people who knew her or him well and wrote down their impressions. Very little of this was true of Charles: no authored works, no diary, no medical records and no memoirs. His letters were few, and rarely betrayed personal opinion or discussed the making of policy, and for periods, especially in his childhood, he does not feature in records at all or can be observed only from outside. He certainly fascinated his ministers and courtiers in retrospect, so that a number of them wrote character-sketches of him; but this was because he baffled them, quite deliberately as part of the arts of dissimulation and deceit which he practised to make himself feel more effective as a monarch. Furthermore, the inherent beliefs and instincts of a king ruling 300 years before were so very different from my own that although hard research could bring me to understand them, I could never share them. I certainly built up a portrait of Charles with certain consistent characteristics, but to get inside of him would have required leaps of imagination based on insufficient evidence, and my professional vocation – as I conceived of it – forbade me from taking them.

What was abundantly clear by the time that I had covered his life up to the Restoration was that there was no sharp alteration in his nature as a result of his experiences in exile. As soon as Charles emerges into the full light of history, which is effectively during his final years as prince of Wales and his first few as king, all the characteristics which he was to display in maturity were already obvious: the charm, the rash impulsiveness, the opportunism, the aptitude for face-to-face business but dislike of paperwork, the love of adventure, intrigue and the pursuit of multiple policy options, the physical courage and moral cowardice, the capacity for producing political and military disasters and then escaping from them, and the vicious streak which appeared when he was thwarted or rebuked. As I pushed steadily into the new territory of the 1670s and 1680s, I found that nothing changed, save that one trait became more accentuated than before. This was Charles's habit of assuring ministers and courtiers of his full confidence to their faces and then laughing at mockery of them by others, or ordering their dismissal, behind their backs. Whether this stemmed from his addiction to intrigue and subterfuge, or the sense of leadership and power which he bolstered in himself by keeping loyal servants feeling insecure, or from his dislike of direct confrontations, I could not tell; a classic case of being able to identify the qualities of the man accurately while remaining incapable of explaining them. The results were clear enough, and nothing in his earlier life prepared me for quite the pitch of tragicomedy to which this characteristic brought Charles by 1682, when he bolted down the back stairs of his palace to avoid facing in person a Scottish minister whom he was resolved to dismiss simply because the man's enemies at home had been complaining about him.[33] My patience with those pop-historians who had spoken of the king's obvious attraction for women wore especially thin when I learned the true story of how he came to seduce his principal mistress during the last years of his life, Louise de Keroualle. Louise had not wanted to be a royal bedfellow at all, but somebody else's wife. What doomed her was the fact that Charles lusted for her, his minister Arlington urged her to submit in order to secure a protégée who shared his master's nights, and Louis XIV wanted to have a Frenchwoman placed beside his English cousin. In the end she gave in because unless she did so she had no prospect of either a court office or a husband in either England or France, with both monarchs set on pushing her into the arms of one of them. Being impoverished, she simply had no option,[34] and so her future life was narrowed irrevocably to that of a royal whore, although a rich one. I would not have reacted so strongly to the recovery of this story from the records, had the relationship of the poor girl with Charles so often been represented as another demonstration of the charm and sexual attraction of the king. Nobody had spotted the squalid play of power structures involved.

Such episodes as this were characteristic of the lack of romance which I found in a court and a period which had been so effectively romanticised in the popular histories; my view of them corresponded, in fact, very accurately to the portrait of both drawn in the mercilessly disparaging verses of the satirical poetry for which the age had always been famed. The brutality, dishonesty and cynicism of its politics, taking their character in large part from the monarch, impregnated my book in such a way as to make me at times the literary heir of Rochester and Marvell rather than of Macaulay or Trevelyan. As ways of writing a biography went, it did give consistency to my portrait of the subject and provided a better explanation of the events of his reign than had been furnished before; in this sense I reinforced the tradition that a hostile or equivocal biographer could produce as effective a result as any other. I did recognise virtues in Charles: his winning manner, his love of novelty, his fidelity to old servants who never disobeyed him and to his family, and his good judgement in choosing ministers and military commanders. I also defended him against some weaknesses with which others had charged him: of being too profligate with money and easy-going with his courtiers. Both acts, however, made the greater emphasis upon his shortcomings as a ruler seem all the more tragic. None the less, after a couple of years, I began to find the experience of working constantly upon a monarch whom I disliked, and with an atmosphere of intrigue and insecurity which I found uncongenial, genuinely depressing. There was no escape by writing the political history of the reign in Scotland and Ireland. In the former, I became used to the pattern whereby the nation's leading men operated like gladiators in a Roman arena where only one man could be the winner: as regularly as if by a mechanical process or a law of nature, allies would turn upon each other as soon as they had destroyed the predecessors whom they had worked together to undermine and replace. As for the Irish government of Charles, it became as monotonous to me to observe how one viceroy after another was recalled and replaced because of manoeuvres by rivals and enemies at the royal court which had little to do with the objective quality of the manner in which each governed the land. By the end it had become clear to me that had I written the cultural history of the period instead of concentrating on explaining its political events, then I would have had a more pleasant time as well as encountering a slightly more appealing face of its monarch.

If my attitude to history changed during these years, then so did my attitude to historians. I had written my book on the Restoration as a personal narrative history of the period, avoiding if at all possible any tendency to correct my colleagues and predecessors and to oppose their views. This was because I had acquired such an aversion to academic infighting as I had witnessed it during the 1970s that I was determined to attempt to show that history could be written without recourse to it. I cited the views of other authorities in footnotes but left it to an informed reader to infer whether and how I differed from them. Thanks to the elephantine pace of academic publishing, although I completed it in September 1983 the book did not appear until July 1985, by which time I had written a quarter of my book on Charles. The reviews convinced me of two lessons to which I have adhered ever since. First, that unless I lit up the main points and arguments which I was trying to make in the literary equivalent of neon, then even informed and conscientious readers were likely to miss them. Second, that what I had intended as courtesy, in not engaging directly with my peers, was taken by some of them as neglect or undervaluing. Henceforth in my writing of the biography I increasingly proceeded by reference to the published views of predecessors, and in my footnotes set out my differences with them at every point. This tactic appeared to work; at least I got no more complaints about neglect, and only one reviewer of my book on Charles felt that I had been too hard on fellow-historians.

That book was published by Oxford University Press in November 1989, and brought me all the more obvious rewards that I might have desired: it received generous reviews in both academic journals and the popular press, earned good royalties for a scholarly work, and ensured my immediate promotion to a Readership, the upper-middle grade of my profession in Britain. It was the first thing which I had written to be extensively noticed in national newspapers, and taught me what a mirror a long book can become for its readers, especially those having to write impressions of it against the short deadlines which the national press imposes. Christopher Hill, one of the most celebrated of Britain's Marxist historians, declared that I had proved that the English Revolution had transformed England into a parliamentary monarchy. The right-wing scholar Jonathan Clark felt, on the contrary, that I had demonstrated the viability of absolute monarchy in the late Stuart period, while the Conservative politician Enoch Powell was as positive that my book revealed the beginning of a party system dependent on the doctrine of ministerial responsibility.[35] The contrast between the work's reception in Scotland and Ireland was also a lesson to me. As said, I had taken care to treat Charles fully as ruler of both those kingdoms as well as (more conventionally) of England, and therefore to make the biography into a work of their history also. Scottish academics received it with delight – it got an especially good review in *The Glasgow Herald* – and the result was to foster personal relationships between myself and the equivalent scholars of a land which I dearly loved. My affection for Ireland was as great, but the much more tightly knit and insular nature of academic history in the republic meant that my book was more or less ignored there. It strengthened my connections with colleagues in the British province, but in the south it earned me only one (appreciative) letter from a private reader and, much later, a request to examine a thesis in the period.

The most negative reviews were written, significantly, by the two individuals who represented the current generation of pop-history biographers of the king: Lady Antonia Fraser and Richard Ollard. Their remarks clarified, very helpfully, the contrast between their attitudes and those of an academic author. Lady Antonia declared that my book 'succeeds admirably as a work of history but fails, finally, as a biography'. To her it presented a 'panoramic picture', but with an inevitable loss in 'the field of human relationships', especially that between Charles and his wife; it was 'a big, fat work of history ... struggling to get out' of the biographical form. To her, the classic question of such a biography was, 'what was King Charles II really like?'. She conceded that I had attempted to answer it, but did not feel satisfied by the result; which was reasonable enough because I did not feel that it could be wholly achieved given the state of the evidence. Once again, she sounded the personal note in her relationship with the king, referring to his 'fine, cynical, swarthy, sexy face', and declared that of all the characters in history, he was the one whom she would most like to meet, and to interview. The essential difference between us was that my time with Charles had convinced me that even were it possible to resurrect him from the dead, and persuade him into a conversation upon anything like equal terms and those which we would mutually comprehend, neither of us would get straight answers out of him. We would find him as affable and elusive as the courtiers who kept his company regularly for years, and expressed their bafflement in their memoirs and letters. Fraser and I were agreed that an ideal biography of the man ought to succeed where they had failed; we were divided by her belief that somehow one could be written.[36]

Richard Ollard made a broadly similar point, but with more acerbity. He noted the unprecedented depth of research behind the book, and then challenged the notion that contemporary records – or indeed any solid documentary proof at all – were necessary to make assertions about the past. The impressions of observers, and even the judgement of close hindsight, were enough to him to furnish plausible evidence of a fact. Once again the personal note was sounded: when considering a point at which I had rejected certain allegations concerning the king's earliest sexual experiences, because they consisted only of gossip repeated years later by untrustworthy sources, Ollard declared that 'one can surely see that sardonic phiz crease into a grin'. The point that one obviously cannot, because the 'phiz' concerned had turned to dead bone very long ago, weighed less with me than the self-conscious archaism of the term, which reflected the patrician elevation of Ollard's own style. This was, indeed, his other quarrel with me; that my own mode of writing was too dull, crude and crowded for him: it 'would sooner satisfy the examiners than sacrifice to the Muses'. In this context it is interesting that the academic reviewers had generally praised my book for the vivid and accessible manner in which it was written, and done so in plain and everyday English themselves. There were clearly different norms and expectations in operation here, each probably valid in their own way. The cumulative message of Ollard's piece was very clear; that no amount of academic industry and thoroughness counted for much to him in comparison with mannered literary flourishes, intuitive leaps of imagination, and a sense of cosy and confident personal familiarity with a received image of a historical figure.[37]

Both reviewers, therefore, to some extent restated the view of Charles which had been presented in the popular biographies since the 1920s; but to the time of writing, that has been its last appearance. It is possible that my book succeeded in bringing the harsher portrait of the king which had always obtained in the academy to that general public which had hitherto been apparently largely impervious to it. At any rate, no book of the 1990s included the wise, kindly, perceptive, tolerant and generous ruler of the alternative tradition. From time to time I was made aware of the resentment felt by ordinary people at my apparent destruction of this monarch. At the beginning of the decade this was usually expressed in muttered comments from elderly people at the end of public lectures; by the end it more often took the form of indignant emails from Americans.

* * *

These complaints disturbed me considerably less than the implications of some of the studies of late Stuart history which were published alongside and after my book, and which focused much more sharply some of the concerns which had troubled me during the writing of it. They began with the work of a young historian of the Restoration period called Paul Seaward, whom I had met in Oxford when he was a postgraduate student just commencing research. In 1982 he had heard me give a seminar paper based on my work for my own book on the Restoration, and written to me subsequently to say that he had intended to write a thesis upon the Cavalier Parliament during the early 1660s. Having now realised that I was already engaged with the subject, he asked whether he should leave it to me and choose another; this being wholly in keeping with the prevailing academic convention, noted above, that two scholars should avoid working simultaneously in the same area. I made an immediate decision to scrap that convention, telling him that my own study was a broad one of the whole period between 1658 and 1667, and that if he concentrated wholly on parliamentary affairs in some of those years, then the sharper and more restricted range of his vision would certainly throw up perceptions which I would miss. I therefore urged him to continue with his original project, offering to furnish such help to him in it as he desired. The result was a friendly and respectful relationship between us, and his doctoral thesis was duly passed in 1985.[38]

My book on the Restoration was, of course, published in the same year, and on comparing the two, I noticed one very striking difference between them. Both of us had considered the practice of the Cavalier Parliament during its early years, of passing acts which gave the government new or renewed powers while limiting their operation to a set term of a few years. I bracketed this pattern with other actions of the Parliament concerned which thwarted royal policy or amounted to a refusal to allow the revival of institutions which had strengthened previous rulers, and suggested that it had been intended to restrict the potency of the restored monarchy. Paul had offered the alternative opinion that the fixed terms given to these statutes were not politically motivated, but indicated trial periods for what were essentially experimental measures. What was clear to me was that only one of us could be correct, but the state of the evidence did not permit a resolution of the difference. No MPs at this period had left diaries or letters in which the motivation behind individual measures was described, and in default of them he had guessed at one explanation and I at another. As the issue was an important one, I found this state of affairs interesting and frustrating. In my life of Charles II I drew specific attention to the divergence in our views, and invited fellow historians to debate and determine it.[39] Paul's thesis was duly published as a monograph in the same year as that in which my biography appeared,[40] and I looked forward keenly to seeing how informed colleagues would cope with the problem which was so starkly raised. None of them did. Paul's book got excellent reviews as mine did, and, as far as I could discover, nobody considered what to me was a troubling question as to how an important aspect of political history could possibly be settled.

Then there was the problem of Charles's religion. As everybody knew, he was received into the Roman Catholic Church upon his deathbed. Many previous authorities upon his life and reign had concluded from this that he had long desired such a step, and been constrained from taking it only by the very obvious obstacle – well proved by the reaction to his brother's public conversion – that it would outrage most of his subjects. There was a string of evidence, referring to his whole lifespan from childhood onward, to support this belief. In the course of my own research, I decided that all of it was either fraudulent, distorted or equivocal, and that up till his deathbed, where his reception into the Roman Church was accepted but not proposed by him, there was no sign of any genuine desire for such a change of religion on his part. One reviewer of the book, John Morrill, expressed a fear that I might have been 'overschematic' in 'arguing away' the evidence for a long dalliance by the king with this faith;[41] and I thought that this might be true. I subsequently tried again, working over all the data once more, and more intensively, in an essay published in 1996,[42] and reached the same conclusion. This time I put it in a firmer context, by suggesting that like most European rulers of his day he saw religious questions primarily in terms of the preservation and furtherance of his own power at home and abroad. The labyrinthine nature of his religious policies derived partly from his tendency to make any policy in this manner and partly from the fact that he was restored to rule three kingdoms with quite different religious traditions, none of which was entirely at his command. I published this essay in the explicit hope that it would encourage debate, but none ensued and I was left wondering whether the silence was due to a general acceptance of my case or the lack of any other historian sufficiently interested in the matter. What kept the latter troublesome for me was that undoubted deathbed conversion: if all the evidence of his life powerfully suggested that Charles lacked personal piety and had an essentially secular and pragmatic view of religious affairs, why did he bother to make it at all? I had done my best with the issue, but ultimately it seemed to be another insoluble puzzle of the reign.

My concern deepened as other historians continued to publish upon aspects of Charles's life and rule. A full-length study of him as reigning monarch actually appeared as I was still at work upon my own, and was delivered by one of the dominant figures in the historiography of the period, James Jones. It made a sharp break with existing tradition, being a book by a distinguished academic which took a favourable view of the king's talents as a ruler; in this respect its author had changed his ideas markedly since the previous decade. He argued indeed that Charles was both selfish and careless, but added the assessment that he could learn from mistakes and keep his nerve in a real crisis.[43] The effect upon me was one of stimulation rather than concern. I thought it a very clever book, which summarised difficult issues with a magnificent clarity and provided fine assessments of several of Charles's contemporaries. It concentrated, however, overwhelmingly on the last six years of the reign and was limited to making somewhat daring interpretations of the most accessible and well-known published sources. I found that I disagreed with 108 separate statements, and having praised the virtues of the book and signalled my differences with it in a review,[44] I could debate those differences in detail when making my own assessment of the king.

Very different issues were raised by John Miller's study of Charles, which eventually appeared almost exactly two years after my own.[45] It was a colossal work, concentrating in such detail upon the years after 1668 that it provided almost a week-by-week narrative of them. When it became clear that my book would appear before his, John told me that he was resolved not to read it until after his own was published, so that he would be making a completely independent assessment based upon equally detailed research. He had kept faithfully to this resolution, and it was remarkable and gratifying to discover how completely we had agreed on most issues including, critically, the character of the king. We had detected and documented to equal effect his intelligence and charm, his lack of long-term plans or deep inclination to Catholicism, his reprehensible and maladroit treatment of ministers, and his lack of aptitude for business and atrocious ineptitude with paperwork. In brief, John confirmed my generally low opinion of Charles as politician and statesman. In addition, he highlighted certain aspects of some personalities and measures which altered my opinion of them, while generally sharing my views upon most. Significantly, he instinctually made my interpretation of the behaviour of the early Cavalier Parliament, and not that of Paul Seaward, while not spotting, or at least not commenting on, the problem of the sources.

Where our views did differ was in our treatment of gossip. Like most early modern royal courts, that of Charles II abounded in rumours concerning the king's attitudes and intentions, and his unusually intense love of secrecy and duplicity made them even more numerous and feverish than was usual in such establishments. I had simply discounted most of them, on the assumption that the individuals who originated and propagated them were not sufficiently well informed to be able to judge accurately of such matters. John had believed most of them with the same instinctual ease, producing a picture of Charles as an airhead of a king who altered his plans almost daily in tense political and diplomatic situations. It was of a piece with this approach that he also believed literally most of what Charles said in his private conversations with French ambassadors, whereas I had suspected strongly that he was attempting to manipulate the French along with everybody else. As a result, John's king was not just a much more volatile man than mine, but a much more timid and pessimistic one.

On the other hand, John attached much less significance to a source which I had thought the most important and reliable in providing insights into the king's true opinions and real input into policy-making: the notes taken of debates in the Privy Council's Committee for Foreign Affairs. This was effectively a forerunner of the cabinet, the meetings of the king with his most favoured and trusted royal advisers in which most major governmental initiatives were discussed and resolved upon. Given Charles's love of informality and dislike of written records, the survival of these rough jottings of the opinions expressed by the king and every other person present, made by the committee's secretary, seemed to me to represent a rare example of solid historical evidence of how policy was made. John now undermined that apparent solidity. For example, at a debate in early 1672 Charles professed himself to be very sceptical of the arguments for religious toleration, and only agreed to issue a declaration of it when pressed to do so by most of those present. I had used this as one refutation of the assertion in the pop-history view of Charles, that he was naturally tolerant. John Miller suggested that the king's apparent reluctance was a sham, and that the exchanges between him and some of his advisers had been carefully rehearsed to give an impression to the others that reasoned argument was winning him over to a policy to which he was disposed in any case.[46] There was absolutely no way either of proving or of refuting such a view, but the reliability of the whole source, as a unique insight into how policy was actually made, hung upon it. Likewise, there was no final means of determining whether John or I had the sounder instinct with regard to the court gossip and the king's conversations with French ambassadors. Colleagues would either be unable to choose between us or do so on a basis of instinct or prejudice; and so the areas of the reign which had to be left permanently baffling were now much enlarged.

They now became extended still further, to include the major question of whether Charles's political preferences and decisions were to any significant extent influenced by his mistresses. I had thought that they were not, unless the women concerned were allied to politicians to whom the king was inclined to listen to anyway, while John Miller considered that the mistresses could be potent figures in their own right, and five years later an American scholar, Nancy Maguire, supported his view.[47] This time an umpire was at hand, in Sonya Wynne, who concluded that the state of the evidence was so bad that it was hard to tell whether Charles was influenced by any courtier, and that he would have been exceptionally reluctant to admit susceptibility to the power of a woman. She agreed with me that it could not be claimed that his bedfellows ever changed his mind about a policy, and that there was no real proof that they guided him on matters about which he had no strong opinions. Where she differed from me was in doubting whether, given the king's love of secrecy, any evidence would have remained had he indeed been swayed by them; in which case the problem was insoluble.[48] I had to agree that she was correct.

The ripples of disquiet spread wider in my mind in the course of the 1990s, as I observed the parallel, far more populous, and sometimes far more heated debates taking place among specialists in the reign of that other early-modern English king whose rule was characterised by unstable court and ministerial politics and dramatic alterations of policy – Henry VIII.[49] It was becoming increasingly obvious that the disagreements concerned were based largely upon the fact that the differing historians were relying upon rival assessments of events left by different foreign ambassadors and courtiers. The latter were drawing contrary conclusions from personal observation of the same developments, and at this space in time it was probably impossible to determine who was correct. Different perspectives again were obvious to scholars who depended more heavily upon government records and formal correspondence between leading royal ministers and councillors; and these were in turn limited and possibly misleading. In most cases the participants in the controversies were filling in the gaps in already selective citations of evidence with intelligent reconstructions of possible sequences of events. The first specialist in the period to draw public attention to this problem, Steven Gunn[50] suggested that it might best be met by a broader perspective which would allow historians to understand 'what was normal in early Tudor politics, and what were the processes of long-term change within them'; but it has yet to be demonstrated that such an understanding, even if one could be consensually achieved, can actually determine how policy was made, and political careers furthered or ruined, in specific instances.

Comparable difficulties were developing in a third major area of early modern English historiography, the origins of the English Civil War. During the 1990s the dominant figure in it, or at least the one who determined much of the direction of debate, was Conrad Russell. He had opened the decade with a pair of major books on the subject, and an important suggestion in one was that negotiations between Charles I and the Long Parliament in early 1641 had been masterminded by a particular clique of peers who came close to achieving the sort of compromise political settlement which would have averted the war. It subsequently became noted that the evidence for this consisted once again primarily of gossip, rumour and opinion reported at second and third hand, which had been crafted together to provide a possible narrative of events. In this case also, the narrative concerned was not invalidated, but shown to be apparently incapable of ultimate proof.[51]

Back in the 1970s it had been generally assumed that the existence of an unprecedentedly large number of professional historians, working with a novel intensity and energy, would disinter such large quantities of new information from the archives that it would be possible to provide better answers than ever before to some of the classic questions of Tudor and Stuart political history. Now that the work was being done, and the information was pouring in, it was becoming obvious that the source material was often much more intractable than had formerly been supposed, and that it was getting harder than ever to determine why political events had followed particular courses. Where historians were thin on the ground, as in studies of the reign of Charles II, their differing interpretations appeared side by side. Where they were more thickly clustered, as in research into the reign of Henry VIII, they were more prone to collide.

My own experiences had also made me sensitive to the problems of writing biographies of early modern English politicians, and so I was particularly interested in those experienced (and more important, acknowledged) by John Guy when he published his study of Thomas More in the year 2000. Here should have been an ideal subject for the genre: a royal minister of exceptional prominence who had left large bodies of published work, familial letters and official papers. In all three he had apparently set forth his own beliefs concerning statecraft and religion, and he had in addition been made the subject of a memoir written by somebody who had known him in both public and private life. John himself was not only one of the leading historians of Tudor England but had been engaged with the study of More for over a quarter of a century. He now declared that he no longer believed that a 'truly historical biography of Thomas More can be written. The sources are too problematic'. He had found that confident statements concerning most aspects of his subject's career could only be made by privileging one set of disputed assertions over others. More's own words could never be trusted, because he made a habit of concealing his inner feelings, of blending truth and dissimulation indistinguishably, and of crafting even ostensibly private statements in such a way as to deliver a particular image of himself to contemporaries and posterity. The records of his domestic and family life were largely created by 'the equivalent of spin doctors', and John Guy's conclusion was that 'there is an historical Thomas More, but no one really knows where he can be found.'[52] It is worth appreciating the irony that this negative verdict could only be reached with such clarity because the sources for More's life are comparatively so rich.

It is a sign of the toughness, adaptability, enterprise and general good health of my profession that colleagues responded swiftly and silently to the challenges thrown up by these difficulties. It was also entirely in character that rather than debating the problems, they tended to celebrate the attractions and achievements of the courses into which necessity was to some extent forcing them. One of the latter was simply to abandon the study of high politics altogether, for the booming new field of cultural history. Another, more attractive to those whose careers were already rooted in political studies, was to take new approaches. Specialists in Tudor topics, where the crowded and dynamic nature of research had made the drawbacks of traditional approaches so obvious, were in the forefront of these. John Guy proposed that the best way to understand the politics of the period was to study its political literature, and so try to reconstruct the relationships between people, institutions and ideas.[53] His pupil Stephen Alford lauded the shift from emphasising the administrative, bureaucratic and constitutional dimensions of Tudor history to a preoccupation with language, iconography and literary forms. He believed that the politicians of the time might be better understood by comprehending the political culture within which they operated.[54] Steven Gunn, while making his frank analysis of the shortcomings of prevailing analyses of court politics, suggested that a more fruitful alternative approach was to analyse the structures of the groupings which engaged in them.[55] In each case it was implied or declared that these new perspectives promised a way of achieving a better engagement with the problems of political history and better solutions to the questions embedded in them. A less triumphalist but still sympathetic way of viewing these developments is to suggest that experts are increasingly giving up hope of understanding exactly how and why policy was made, and of penetrating the counsels of rulers and ministers. Instead they are confining themselves to the externals of the subject: to studying what contemporaries thought was happening, how governments presented what they did, and the context in which political actions took place. It is no accident that research into early modern court politics is giving way to the new phenomenon of 'court studies', the exploration of the structures and cultural milieu of royal and princely households.[56]

The sleepier and more sparsely populated world of late Stuart historiography responded more slowly and in a more understated way to the same tendencies. No more biographies of its monarchs were produced during the 1990s, but two studies were made of the greatest European contemporary of Charles and James, Louis XIV. The one which attracted the most academic attention and applause was by Peter Burke, and this concentrated wholly upon 'the public image of the king. ... the place of Louis XIV in the collective imagination', rather than on the 'real' personality, thoughts and actions of the monarch.[57] Eight years later Ian Dunlop produced a more conventional biography, but one which still remained content to portray the king in public, without attempting to penetrate his private thoughts or feelings.[58] The political histories of Charles II's reign followed the same trend. Most striking and explicit in this regard was John Spurr's study of the 1670s. He began it by declaring generously that the previous half-century had seen the publication of four outstanding books upon the reign, two of them being the lives of Charles by myself and John Miller. He then noted that they occasionally conflicted on points of interpretation, 'and even detail'. Rather than trying to resolve these conflicts, or to worry about their implications, he chose to give relatively little attention to the machinations of the government, and to concentrate upon what the public knew or thought they knew of them, and upon reconstructing the culture and atmosphere of English politics in the decade; in which tasks he succeeded splendidly.[59] He had, effectively, turned to aspects of political life which could be properly studied, and in the process dealt with one major issue of importance for biographers of the king. His study of public opinion was so thorough that it left no doubt as to the tremendous extent of the distrust inspired by this monarch and his governments, and the destructive and divisive effect of it upon national life. In the same year John Miller himself published another study of the politics of Charles's reign. In large part, unsurprisingly, he repeated the views which he had already expressed in his earlier work, including the biography, but he also was shifting to looking at the reception, effects and reputations of policies. He reinforced the growing sense of the corrosive impact of royal unreliability and opportunism upon the nation, but at times he was now prepared to state that the king's motivations remained a mystery.[60]

These issues were illustrated spectacularly well by a study of an early modern British monarch which appeared at the opening of the new century and seemed at first sight to buck the trend: David Starkey's life of the young Elizabeth I.[61] This was a work by an experienced and prominent academic who also enjoyed tremendous success in the mass media, and it accompanied a television series which he wrote and presented. It deliberately adopted the style of the traditional popular biography, abandoning footnoted references for bibliographical guides kept to the rear and telling the story as a 'historical thriller'. In the manner of the popular biography he presented his subject as a heroine, and admitted to having 'fallen half in love' with her himself; thereby emphasising the spiritual bond between author and subject which had lain at the heart of the idealised tradition of biographical writing. The result was excellent history, which scooped both markets by impressing colleagues as well as achieving major sales among general readers; but for the sensitised it also highlighted the problems of the genre.

Where David Starkey added significantly to our knowledge of Elizabeth was in externals; most of all, in tracking the grants of land and office which she made, to see how she built up a power-base, and in noting the changes in royal ritual which signalled political and religious attitudes. His work was at its most speculative, and most controversial, when dealing with the core of his story, the personality and views of Elizabeth herself. One point at which those are particularly important to history, and intriguing to historians, came immediately before her accession to the throne. Two directly conflicting accounts have survived of her expressed intentions towards the national religion. Neither seems particularly reliable, the first being a recollection made years later, and the second a piece of gossip. A more timid or scrupulous historian might have reserved judgement, but Starkey decided firmly to believe in the truth of both, and reconcile them by declaring that the first account represented Elizabeth's official reply, while the second was a private encourage-ment to her Protestant supporters. His justification for this Solomonic judgement was that it was 'in character' for her.[62]

How, then, were the components of that character to be recovered? David Starkey's central thesis was that her role-model was her father Henry VIII, and the text which he used to unlock her developing views on both religion and family relationships was a translation of a poem by Marguerite of Navarre which she made at the age of eleven. He read it as evidence of her conversion to Protestantism, and of her devotion to a father whom she compared to God in his kindness and power. Each interpretation, however, has been challenged from the text itself. Patrick Collinson, the leading expert on Elizabethan religious history, read it as an evan-gelical tract, but not a Protestant one, while Anne Lake-Prescott had already pointed to a slip which Elizabeth had made while translating a line which com-pared the penitent soul to the daughter of a loving father. She had rendered 'father' as 'mother'. Starkey declared this to be a straightforward grammatical mistake, and dismissed any attempts to read psychological significance into it as nonsense. To do so, however, was to make an interpretation of the text which was itself arbitrary and suppositious, and ultimately not susceptible of proof. In other words, the source which he himself had identified as exceptionally important in providing insight into the future queen's character and opinions could be turned against him.[63] His solution to such difficulties was a wholly traditional and familiar one; to make a confident personal interpretation and to seek to pre-empt any objec-tions, leaving others the choice of accepting his view as read or preparing a case against it. This is the manner in which the writing of political history has pro-ceeded for centuries, and built into it is the assumption that such a process of dialectic takes us closer and closer to the truth. What may be suggested now is that with regard to some of the most important problems of early modern history (to cast the suggestion no wider), it may not.

An opposite solution to this problem, which has begun to surface in the writing of early modern history, is to suggest that it really does not matter anyway. One of those to articulate it has been David Cressy, considering the debates over two radical groups who were once thought to have existed within the ferment of English politics in the 1640s: the Ranters, who allegedly denied the existence of sin and of Hell, and prescribed for true believers a world of pure self-indulgence, and the Adamites who met and worshipped naked as well as condemning all religious hierarchies, liturgies and disciplines. The crux of the debates had been whether these people had been present in reality or had been invented as object lessons by hostile pamphleteers. To Cressy 'the key question. ... is not whether Ranters or Adamites really existed, but what the discourse in which they feature tells us about contemporary attitudes and alarms'.[64] This is certainly an interesting and valuable question, and has the especial merit of one which can actually be answered from the surviving evidence, which consists mostly of the denunciations of the heresies concerned. It also, however, represents another example of that retreat to externals which has been observed as characteristic of early modern historiography at the end of the twentieth century. The question of whether there really were people in seventeenth-century England who held and acted upon such sensationally radical ideas is surely just as fascinating and important, and it must as surely be a matter for regret if we have to admit that we may never answer it. Such an admission may well be the honest and realistic one, now that the evidence is being thoroughly evaluated for the first time. Just as we are increasingly conceding that we shall never know how or why some policies were made, or why rulers and their advisers sometimes acted as they did, so we may have to recognise that we shall never know what was possible to the people of this society. That recognition, however, ought to contain some element of regret.

A third position, between these last two, is to admit to the difficulties while hoping, vaguely, that more and better research will somehow solve them. This was adopted by Malcolm Smuts, when providing his overview of the causes of the English Civil War, which was quoted earlier. To repeat it, he summed up the problem as one of 'dealing with historical processes so complex that simple models of causation cannot adequately describe them. What is needed is more nuanced and closely textured analysis. Perhaps the most important example is the challenge of explaining relationships between religion, social change and politics.'[65] Few if any specialists would deny the accuracy of this analysis; what remains in doubt is whether the surviving evidence allows that challenge to be met, except in rare local or individual cases which may or may not be at all representative of norms. Smuts was honest and anxious enough to return to the issue repeatedly within a few pages. He acknowledged that 'no conceptual model has so far succeeded in providing an entirely satisfactory explanation for the sociological or geographical distribution of puritanism', and added immediately that 'the messiness of the evidence does not diminish the importance of the problem'. Again, both parts of the statement should command general assent, but the question which now hangs in the air is whether the problem can ever be solved. Two pages later Smuts considered the impact of printed discussion of politics and religion on the nation. He concluded that a dramatic increase in such discussion during the Civil War period was easy to prove, but that its impact 'is not easily assessed'. The question is begged once more: can such an assessment actually be made? Vexed by these uncertainties, at one point Smuts made a retreat to David Cressy's posture, by declaring that 'we cannot filter out all the myths and polemical distortions from the story of the Civil War. ... since many of these are integral to it. Knowing what actually happened can sometimes be less important than appreciating what contemporaries believed.' It is a matter of opinion, which further work may clarify, whether this represents a healthy shift of perception or an admission of defeat.

When I began to work on the life and reign of Charles II, I was living firmly in one world of professional historiography; when the book was published and reviewed, that world was altering, seemingly irrevocably, into another. In part the story of this transformation has been of the loss of a dream, the slow abandonment of the belief that an unprecedentedly large, dynamic and professional body of historians could solve many of the outstanding puzzles of the past, and provide a new depth of knowledge of it, by making a systematic recovery of the surviving evidence. Central to this concept was the straightforward and pragmatic exploration of archives, like the mapping of an unknown geographical territory. Thirty years of sustained work have been more than enough to reveal that in many cases both the questions and the sources are too problematic to sustain this belief. On the other hand, it has also been a success story, of how academic historians have been able to eradicate hitherto resilient popular stereotypes, and intervene in mass culture in such a way as to make their voices louder and more persuasive than at any time before. It has also shown how swiftly and creatively they have responded to the difficulties which their own work has thrown up.

Both considerations now beg the question of how a life of Charles II can now be written. It seems to me that there are two models available that confront the problems that I have discussed above, in a way that traditional biography does not. One is to accept the necessity of withdrawing to surface appearances, and of writing a book with a tripartite division. First, it would establish what were the stereotypes and conventions of good and bad kings that the people of Charles's kingdoms possessed. Second, it would analyse the way in which Charles tried to project himself to them, and consider the royal image that he developed and sustained. It would also ask whether there was any discernible distinction between his public image and that which he seemed to have of himself. Third, it would look at the impressions which others formed of him, at different levels of politics and society, and reach a conclusion on how far they diverged from the one that he sought to present. The interface between the two would permit an objective conclusion as to the overall success or failure of his reign. Whether or not we could ever get to know the man, we could certainly say something about his style of kingship. The second model would resemble the conclusion of the previous chapter, on Oliver Cromwell: it would present the known facts of the reign, episode by episode, and show how they might be used to construct entirely different interpretations of Charles's character, intentions and policies, and the way in which they interacted with others.

The problem, of course, is that neither of those blueprints match up to the traditional aim of biography: of providing a linear and coherent story of an important human's life, which enable the reader to feel that she or he is actually getting to know that person. Neither would it really palliate the lack of that sense of spiritual union with another being which is supposed to be the greatest experience of biography (and sex, and religion). If anything does palliate it for me, it is the realisation – more common to a person in later life than in youth – that to live with somebody for years and find that you never really knew them, and that ultimately their thoughts and actions are a mystery to you, is as tragically common an experience among living, speaking human beings as it is when dealing with one long dead.

6 The Glorious Revolution

The revolution of 1688 carries particular significance in the historiography of the Stuart period, for it was the key event of the Whig history of the nation which has come in for such ridicule and disdain in the second half of the twentieth century. Just as Alfred is the single English king to have earned the nickname of 'great', so this revolution is the only one in the national story to have attracted the common title of 'glorious'. To mid-Victorian Britain, it represented the pivotal moment when modern Britain's political and cultural framework was formed. After a succession of chapters which have highlighted the manner in which late-twentieth-century historians have both inherited and dismantled the agenda of their nineteenth-century predecessors, this classic item of Victorian historiography clearly invites examination. In that tradition it represented the constitutional and emotional climax of the struggles that had characterised Stuart Britain, and as such a consideration of it represents a natural conclusion to this book.

As is fairly well known, a genuine national consensus that the events of 1688 had actually been 'glorious' was only achieved a very long time after their occurrence, in the commemorations of their centenary. Having appeared, it was immediately subjected to very different interpretations, according to the particular political purposes of the writers concerned, and this situation endured for two generations.[1] Only in 1848, when developments in Europe concentrated the minds of the English once more on the nature of revolution, did Macaulay supply a definition which became more or less standard. To him the Revolution Settlement of 1689–90 represented the point at which the popular element in the English constitution finally prevailed over the monarchical one, and so gave British politics a remarkable stability and flexibility which had endured to Macaulay's own time (and indeed has continued to do so until our own).

It is important to stress that this view was never systematically refuted in either the late nineteenth or the early twentieth centuries. None the less, interest in the late Stuart period waned and public and professional attention was diverted elsewhere. The decline was not a steady one, for in the late 1930s the very eminent historian George Macaulay Trevelyan published a celebration of the events of 1688, but its overall progress was unmistakable and may be put down to three developments. One was the appearance of S.R. Gardiner's history of the first Stuart reigns and of the Civil War, which appeared to prove that the political changes of 1688–89 were only the climax to a struggle which had gone on since 1603, and in which the vital groundwork had been laid for the subsequent English polity. The second was Sir Herbert Butterfield's critique of the insensitivities of what he termed the 'Whig' attitude to history. Macaulay was generally taken to be the exemplar of the latter, and it is possible that the events which he admired tended to become tainted by association. The third, and most important, was the impact of the Marxist view of historical processes. In its softest form, as examined earlier, this suggested that major political changes must have profound social and economic causes. In its hardest, it held that there are specific shifts in the development of any industrialised society and that each can only happen once in its history. As the Civil War and subsequent English Revolution of the 1640s had been much more cataclysmic events than the 'Glorious Revolution', they seemed to many scholars influenced by such ideas to represent a more promising expression of these fundamental changes. Thus interest became concentrated far more heavily on the early seventeenth century, and even when the Marxist view of the Civil War was refuted (which took, as said, until the 1970s), the momentum of the debate over 'revisionism' has maintained that imbalance down to the present. In 1982 Angus McInnes issued a direct reproof to this state of affairs, by stating firmly that the 1680s and not the 1640s were the years of the true English Revolution.[2] The result was a complete silence, as early Stuart specialists ignored him and got on with their own concerns.

Nevertheless, the pace of research into the late Stuart period has accelerated as it has done in all others since the 1970s, and an important debate was created among its specialists. It began in 1972, when two established experts, J.R. Jones and J.R. Western, simultaneously declared that during the 1680s England was moving towards an absolute monarchy which was only prevented by the revolution of 1688.[3] They tried at the same time to distance themselves from 'Whiggism' by claiming that unlike Macaulay they did not regard the defeat of absolutism as inevitable; a plea which was somewhat unfair to the great Victorian as a large point of his narrative had been to portray constitutional monarchy in England as a fairy-tale princess rescued by William of Orange. Their argument has been discussed ever since with an intensity increased by the tercentenary of the revolution, and has only started to wane in the later 1990s as part of the relative loss of interest in political history. This debate has revealed a curious division between generations. Most of the specialists who established their reputations in the 1970s or before – Angus McInnes, John Morrill, Robert Beddard, John Childs, Jonathan Israel and above all Bill Speck and Lois Schwoerer – have agreed broadly with the Jones-Western thesis.[4] Most of those who have founded their careers since – Jonathan Clark, Daniel Szechi and Tim Harris – have tended to play down the importance of the events of 1688–90. By the opening of the twenty-first century, the dominant attitude was one of ambivalence. In 2001 Jeremy Black commenced a textbook on 'eighteenth-century Britain' in 1688, stating that 'in some respects' the whole hundred-year period after that date could be seen as one of the workings out of its events. He was still careful, however, to put the name Glorious Revolution firmly in inverted commas, and add that 1660 or 1694 might, from different perspectives, be considered more important points of departure. In 2000 Jonathan Scott's much more polemical and selective overview of seventeenth-century England had declared that the changes of 1688 broke the mould of Stuart politics for good and ushered in a genuinely successful period of state building which has endured to the present. At the same time, he found it necessary to question what was 'revolutionary' about the events of 1688–89, or of the 1690s, and suggest that no clear answer existed to this problem.[5] The major exception to the pattern of generational contrast has been John Miller, who from 1973 to 1990 challenged both the idea that England had a potential for absolute monarchy and that the Revolution Settlement changed very much.[6] Recently, however, he has slightly qualified his views on both.[7]

In the early chapters of this book, most of the emphasis has been on evaluating recent developments of scholarship in particular areas of Stuart studies. In this final one, dedicated to what was the 'classic' event of the whole period in much traditional historiography, the approach is more akin to that undertaken in the one devoted to Cromwell. Although it will conclude, as it began, with reflections on the status of the Revolution of 1688 as a part of national history, much of it will represent a personal intervention in current debates, and a situating of myself in the spectrum of current opinion.

* * *

The first part of the task must be to establish a personal view of the context for late Stuart politics. Conventionally, they have been regarded as forming a sharply defined period, with its own characteristics and preoccupations, and its own team of experts. Recently both Jonathan Scott and John Miller have, in different ways, challenged this tradition, by asserting that the crises with which it was marked were continuations and replays of those of the 1640s, which were in turn derived from early Stuart politics; in this way, they have emphasised the fundamental continuity of the century over its divisions.[8] My own judgement upon this argument is that it is half correct. In its favour I can repeat the conclusions of my book on the Restoration: that the events of 1640–63 had changed an enormous amount but settled nothing, because the basic issues which caused the turbulence of those years all remained unsettled.[9] I identified these issues as the tensions between executive and legislature, Church and dissenter and court and country. Following my work on Charles II, I would add a fourth: the strains in the partnership between the three realms of the British Isles. All in all, I would still stand by the last sentence of that earlier book: 'whatever had ended in 1660–62, it was not the English Civil War'.

Against the continuity thesis must be entered the major qualification that the period after 1660 contained novel features of political life, which between them created an atmosphere of chronic political insecurity of a sort which had not existed before 1640. The first of these was the fear of a repetition of the terrible bloodshed and disruption of the mid-century. The political elite of the nation were left conscious of the danger presented by either an irresponsible Crown or a turbulent populace, although it varied considerably within itself in the emphasis placed on one or the other. The experience of civil war and revolution had resulted in a sense that the cost of political error could be very high indeed. A second novel factor was one which should illustrate that social and economic forces, although not of primary importance to the causation of national events, could certainly play a supporting role. Until the mid-seventeenth century, the prices of agricultural produce had been increasing steadily for over a hundred years. From the 1640s onward, they first stabilised and then began to fall, dragging down the level of rents chargeable by landowners. With their incomes under pressure, the latter found the proceeds of office all the more important, potentially increasing both the Crown's power of patronage and jealousy and suspicion of those who profited from it. A third new sort of tension was the large scale of Protestant nonconformity bequeathed by the Interregnum and the Restoration Settlements. It proved relatively easy to drive dissenters from public office and to give magistrates powers to terrorise their meetings. It also proved impossible to eradicate them. Detailed research has indicated how flexible and ill-defined a phenomenon dissent was, and how badly equipped and personally reluctant local officials often were in dealing with it.[10] At all levels of government, policy swayed uneasily between persecution and toleration in the three decades after the Restoration.

These were all phenomena internal to the nation. In addition there were further novel strains derived from developments outside it. One was that both the nobility of Scotland and the Catholic majority in Ireland now seemed to recognise that their breach with the Crown in the 1640s had been disastrous to them, and were much more prepared to support it in British affairs. Another was the dramatic rise in the power of France, creating a situation in which the most formidable state in western and central Europe, apparently hostile to English religion, political ideology and trade, possessed the whole of the opposite shore of the narrowest strait of water which separated England from the Continent. A final, and tremendous, new source of tension lay in the public and permanent conversion of the heir apparent to the three thrones of the British Isles to the Roman Catholic faith. Here the fit between continuity and change is especially striking. As Jonathan Scott has emphasised, the long-term context of that development consisted of the dramatic progress of the Counter-Reformation over the past hundred years. In 1580 about half of Europe has been Protestant; by 1680 the proportion had been reduced to about one-fifth, and in no case had the reversal been produced either by a Catholic uprising or by a foreign conquest. The victories of Rome had all resulted either from the succession of a Catholic ruler to the leadership of a state or by the slow erosion of the rights of Protestant subjects by a dynasty which had continued to profess the older religion. The situation of England in the 1670s and 1680s was, however, still dramatically novel. Not only had the cumulative progress of Catholic recovery now reached a point beyond any achieved in the previous few generations, but the sudden expansion of French power and the equally sudden presence of a Catholic heir, established firmly within the structures of English government, created dilemmas for which there was no precedent since the victory of Protestantism in Britain during the previous century.

It is therefore very easy to support James Jones's belief[11] that the politics of the restored monarchy were peculiarly well suited to metaphors of disease and neurosis, being characterised by thoroughly unusual levels of fear, suspicion and opportunism and fraught by instability. There seemed to be a loss of any common sense of what the agreed rules of governance actually were. These are circumstances in which skilful rulers have commonly secured an extension of their powers, in order to meet a public yearning for stability and reassurance. Do I, therefore, also agree with Jones's other suggestion that absolute monarchy was possible in England at this time? This was contested most swiftly and fully by John Miller,[12] who pointed to the considerable contrast between social groupings, institutions and ideologies in seventeenth-century France and England to suggest that the potential for a French-style absolutism did not exist in the latter. His comparison is to some extent vitiated by two considerations. The first is that the most recent work by historians of early modern France has shown that its government was a far more complex and subtle affair than had been supposed, resting upon the consent of various local and national elites.[13] The second is that the French comparison with England was one of the least similar to have chosen. It is surely better to look at Protestant realms which had a strong tradition of national representative assemblies, such as Sweden, Denmark, Brandenburg, Saxony and some smaller German states. Nobody seems to have made this comparison systematically, but from the amount of information readily available for these countries[14] it seems that in each absolutism was achieved by a partnership between the ruler and the dominant social groups. In this, the former was entrusted with legislative powers and a standing army based on permanent sources of revenue, in return for guaranteeing the safety of the dominant religion and the economic and social interests of the upper class or classes.

Was there, then, any potential for this in England? One suggestion sometimes made to pre-empt this question is that there was no theoretical apparatus for an English absolutism.[15] This argument seems to me to be doubly faulty. For one thing, theory was not a necessary precondition for political action in seventeenth-century England. In 1642 king and Parliament found themselves at war with each other and then set about trying to find constitutional justification for taking up arms. In 1649 Charles I was executed, and then reasons were provided for having a republic, by writers who were often clearly half-hearted, and arguing from pragmatism. I am quite persuaded that the average Tory squire did not read English theoretical defences of stronger monarchy such as that by Sir Robert Filmer. I am equally unconvinced that the average Brandenburger or Swedish noble *did* bother to read a European equivalent like the works of Bodin or Bossuet. For another thing, it is quite possible to suggest that some ideological basis for absolutism actually was developing in late-seventeenth-century England. Mark Goldie has demonstrated that in the 1680s the Church of England developed the argument that the authority of the king derived not from the people but from the bishops, and that he only needed to defer to the latter.[16] It was, after all, Archbishop Sancroft himself who committed Filmer's classic treatise of absolute monarchy, *Patriarcha*, to the press.[17] Tim Harris has, with equal ability, pointed to the conditional nature of the loyalty offered to the Crown by the Tory laity (who included most of the greater landowners). The condition concerned was the willingness of the monarch to observe the existing laws and to defend the Church.[18] It does, to me, beg the question of what they would have denied to kings who consistently did both those things and then sought greater powers against foes at home and abroad, in the manner of other north-European Protestant rulers of the age.

Was there, however, an apparatus of stronger royal power being constructed under the restored monarchy whether or not the monarchs were earning the confidence of the political nation? Again, it is possible to answer in the affirmative. Western and Jones both pointed to the crucial importance of the fact that in the 1680s, for the first time, the English monarchy was enabled to support a professional standing army from its regular revenue. John Childs has shown that this army represented the same percentage of the national population as the one maintained by Louis XIV did of the population of France.[19] Western also emphasised that the army was supported mostly by taxes on trade, largely sparing the landowning elite in the manner of provision for Continental forces.[20] It had been unnecessary for a deal to be struck between Crown and gentry to effect this in England because a trade boom had provided the extra money anyway. Western also drew attention to the streamlining and greater professionalisation of the central bureaucracy. Perhaps even more interesting in this regard has been research which has shown how in the 1680s taxation was gathered more smoothly than ever before and its officials detached from local communities in a novel way.[21] This lends particular significance to Andrew Coleby's comment that James II's attempt to manipulate parliamentary elections simply represented the application of the new fiscal techniques to electoral problems, often using the same agents.[22]

These broad developments provide the context to the specific measures of the last part of Charles II's reign. Again, local studies have been important in revealing the dynamics of the campaign by which boroughs surrendered their charters to the Crown and received new versions with a revised list of corporation members. The process represented both an actual and a potential increase of royal power in towns and a shift of power within local ruling groups. We are now certain that it was driven on by provincial Tories allied with a set of 'hard-liners' on the Privy Council, a perfect example of a collaboration of Crown, Church and ruling classes for mutual benefit, of the sort which strengthened European monarchies.[23] As is well known, the same collaboration pushed forward a parallel effort to purge common political and religious opponents from county administration. In the same years the royal government engaged in a wholly unprecedented and carefully orchestrated drive to bring all of England's overseas colonies under direct Crown control. It was inspired by a clearly focused authoritarian and imperial vision.[24] The early Stuart state had been a ramshackle and even decaying entity in its military and fiscal aspects, while presiding over and encouraging an ambitious and highly successful enterprise in social control and reform directed against such problems as poverty, plague and hunger. The late Stuart state, operating in less tense economic circumstances and having sustained the shock of the mid-century political turmoil, had largely abandoned its interest in social paternalism, and concentrated instead on maintaining domestic security and building a much more efficient fiscal and military system.[25]

* * *

I would therefore agree with Macaulay that the seventeenth-century English polity contained a potential for either the monarchical or the popular element to become dominant, and that therefore events and personalities were all-important in determining what actually fell out. In this regard it is notable that England at this time was ruled by one of the most accident-prone dynasties in history. During the three hundred years between the accession of the Stuart family to the throne of Scotland and the succession of James VII and II, over half of its ruling members had died violently; perhaps a European record for the age.[26] This was the result, in most cases, of a disastrous mixture in these rulers of idealism, high ambition and political or military misjudgement. The succession of James VI and I to the English and Irish thrones itself had implications for the position of the monarchy in England, as Jenny Wormald, Conrad Russell, Neil Cuddy and others have recently stressed the suspicion felt by the political nation for a foreign king and its new concern for the extent of the royal prerogative. The creation of a triple kingdom itself increased that suspicion, for it at once relieved the English of a fear of attack by a foreign power based in the other realms and created one that their own monarch might use Scottish and Irish resources to overawe England. It is very significant, given this situation, that James I, Charles I, Charles II and James II all in different ways failed to conform to the ideal of what the political nation wished a king to be: a successful warlord and an upholder of the established laws and religion. Their failures in this fundamental regard make a contrast with the relative fortunes of (say) the Bourbons, Spanish or Austrian Habsburgs, Wittelsbachs and Vasas.

Of the four of them, James II has certainly received the worst press, both among professional historians and in the popular imagination. In a childhood schoolbook

I found a nursery rhyme by Eleanor Farjeon about the four kings, the first verse of which ended 'The fourth combined, as all may see, the vices of the other three.' His most recent biographer, John Miller, portrays him at best as a rather pathetic old man, while John Callow's yet more recent study of his career before acceding to the throne depicts him as a deeply flawed young one.[27] It is easy to gain the impression that James was like Edward II, somebody who would have made a mess of ruling under virtually any circumstances. Against this tradition can be entered a plea that he did have some virtues. He was physically very brave, as demonstrated spectacularly at the naval battles of Lowestoft and Sole Bay. He was good with money, loyal to friends, sober, industrious and a competent adminstrator. Even Macaulay, who hated and despised him, praised the care which he displayed towards the navy, acting as his own Lord High Admiral. One piece of faint praise often accorded to him, that he was honest, may be misplaced and a murkier truth actually more to his credit. He was certainly candid in very big things, such as his open conversion to Rome which almost cost him his succession to the throne, in the face of his royal brother's attempts to persuade him to conceal his change of religion.[28] He was also, however, perfectly capable of saying one thing to a man's face and another behind his back, as revealed by the way he lulled the marquis of Halifax into a false sense of royal favour in early 1685.[29] He could also change his mind on an issue to suit altered circumstances, as is illustrated by the way in which, at different points in his career, he inveighed with equal passion against religious tolerance and religious persecution. John Miller has demonstrated both that his adoption of a policy of general toleration in the course of his reign was initially the result of expediency not desire and that he was not telling the truth when he then declared that such a policy had always been his aim; although Miller allowed for an element of self-deception in this statement.[30] Such a capacity for duplicity is not necessarily a bad thing in a politician.

It matters more that James is commonly reckoned to have been stupid, and from Charles II to John Miller there have been plenty of informed commentators to make this charge. It needs to be treated with some care as, after all, a real fool could not have commanded fleets and run administrations as ably as James did. In the league of English royal stupidity he is not even in the same division as Edward II or Henry VI, belonging more to the category of the maladroit and overambitious which contains such figures as John, Henry III and Richard II. One could make a case that he possessed as much actual brainpower as Anne, George III and George V, all monarchs who kept their thrones and, in the first and last cases at least, enjoyed a well-deserved popularity. James is reckoned foolish, rather, because he pursued an extremely dangerous policy with obstinate determination, and failed in it. It may also be emphasised, in fairness to his critics, that he possessed an almost pathological tendency to make life hard for himself, demonstrated in both public and private affairs: it is characteristic, for example, that he was both repeatedly unfaithful to his wives and constantly tortured by guilt about it.[31]

When considering James's intentions as monarch it must be stressed that there is not a single source available to the historian in which these are reliably set out. Much, however, can be inferred from a comparison of his statements, and of observations upon him, and even more from his actions. There is every reason to endorse John Miller's opinion that, as an ageing man in fragile health, with his immediate heirs both Protestants, he was in a desperate hurry to use his tenure of the throne to improve the position of his fellow Catholics in his three kingdoms. Miller seems to me right again in insisting that James was not concerned with establishing royal absolutism, and to the evidence which he cites in his biography of the king, two more examples may be added. One is that the major campaign to renew borough charters, which James keenly supported in the last year of this brother's reign, was called off as soon as he took the throne and was able to throw all his energy behind Catholic emancipation.[32] The other is that in his spectacular purges of local government the king was wholly concerned with finding personnel to enact this policy of emancipation,[33] not to develop the functions of that government or to increase central control of it.

Now, however, John Miller and I begin to depart company again. I would put a very heavy emphasis on the fact that James was not interested merely in securing the toleration of Catholics, which involved granting them the right to practise and to advertise their religion without molestation. He could have secured this with almost no difficulty, because it was offered to him by virtually everybody who mattered: by the leading Tory politicians and by about two-thirds of Justices of the Peace and deputy lieutenants in 1686, and by William of Orange in 1687. All were prepared to accept that the penal laws against Catholic worship should no longer be enforced. The king, however, wanted in addition to give his co-religionists power, in the form of military, naval and administrative office. Not even the Pope or the leaders of the English Catholic community encouraged him in this scheme.[34] It seems to have been entirely his own idea, and the key to it is apparently contained in a statement which he made to the French ambassador in July 1685, that the ability of patronage to make converts was greater than all the arguments of priests.[35] To ensure the highest possible number of conversions to Rome before his demise, therefore, according to this logic, he set about trying to hand over large parts of the established structure of authority to Catholics, as fast as possible. The policy soon proved to be impossible to effect with the consent of any existing national body, and so he set out to achieve it not only with the maximum speed but the maximum crudity of means. It must have been apparent to him within a year that a gentle approach was going to get nowhere.

In the process he was aided by two other character traits, which together made him peculiarly suited to running amok in a constitutional china shop. One was a natural authoritarianism, so powerful that it is legitimate to suggest that, had he been a Protestant monarch, he would have put all his effort into enhancing royal power. During his brother's reign, when he was not able to do much to countenance Catholics, he was repeatedly associated, in rumour or fact, with such schemes.[36] As proprietor of the colony of New York, he stubbornly denied the requests of its settlers for a representative assembly of the normal colonial kind.[37] The French ambassador remarked of him that 'the only way to be in favour at court … is to follow his wishes blindly'.[38] His other trait was an insouciant disregard for the niceties of law and protocol. John Miller has noticed that in his dealings with the Pope he was as careless and contemptuous of the regulations of the Vatican, when they got in the way of his desires, as of the common and statute law of England.[39]

Lest anybody doubt the power to which the English monarchy had swelled in the 1680s, in comparison with that available to it in previous generations, it is instructive to note the extent of James's actions. When he asked the judges their opinion of his use of the dispensing power to relieve individuals from the Test Act which disqualified Catholics from public office, the result was just the same as in Hampden's Case which had challenged Charles I's right to levy Ship Money on the whole kingdom, fifty years before: seven to five in favour. This narrow majority, under James's father, had constituted a moral blow to the government, which could only try to hide its anger. James simply replaced four judges. He did, in fact, sack more judges for inconvenient political views in the course of his short reign than any other seventeenth-century English ruler, all of whom lasted longer on the throne than he. Even having eventually purged the bench three times over, he still could not get it to agree that he had the power to suspend a statute completely; but he proceeded to use that power all the same. He tried, quite deliberately and overtly, to control elections so as to reduce Parliament to a cipher for his will. In 1688 he charged the archbishop of Canterbury and six other prelates with sedition for refusing to support his suspension of the penal laws. Most significantly, the Crown's case was not that the bishops were wrong in stating that the king had acted outside the law, but in stating that he *could* act outside it, and the Solicitor General added a denial that any subjects could petition the sovereign about anything except in Parliament.[40]

James's enforcement of his will was as rough as his attempts to bend the law to it. In the first months of his reign, he personally ordered the execution of 239 of the rebels who had supported the rebellion of his nephew the duke of Monmouth. His judges at the 'Bloody Assize' which followed the rising had attempted to spare these men after the first wave of victims had gone to the scaffold, but James insisted that they be hanged, drawn and quartered as well.[41] He used his army to menace London and other cities and removed judicial business concerning its members from common-law to military courts.[42] Anthony Fletcher has found that James replaced between 75 and 90 per cent of JPs (effectively, the local political nation) in every county which had been studied until the time at which he wrote.[43] Since then the information has come in for Wiltshire, where the rate of dismissal was 95 per cent.[44] James also became the first English monarch to bring in Scottish and Irish regiments to secure England. The significant thing about all this is not just the passivity of the English (which could be attributed to his army), but that he found supporters, or collaborators, for all that he did. Eveline Cruickshanks has considered those drawn from the Tories, Mark Goldie has directed attention to his Whig and nonconformist allies, and Philip Norrey has given more emphasis to the local opportunists of neither hue.[45] All branches of government were kept functioning, and in several cases did so with unusual efficiency[46] until the eve of the Prince of Orange's invasion which launched the revolution. By mid-1688 affairs had, it was true, reached an impasse in which James could suspend laws but not alter them. This he hoped to achieve with a packed Parliament, which in the event never met. James Jones and M.J. Short have suggested that it would have given him success, John Miller and Bill Speck have suggested, with equal force, that it would not.[47] The matter must therefore be left in doubt, but the birth of a Catholic heir in mid-1688 meant that for James time suddenly seemed to be on his side rather than against him.

* * *

All this considers the reign in the context of English and Welsh affairs, but in that of the British Isles as a whole, it is still equally remarkable. In particular, it had a direct bearing on what has come, since the 1980s, to be known among historians of the early modern period as 'the British problem'. What is really problematic about this issue is that, as defined by the recent debates, it is actually a study of four different, though interrelated, phenomena.[48] The first and most obvious is that discussed in early chapters and pioneered by Conrad Russell: the interaction of the three kingdoms of the early modern British Isles. As Russell pointed out, multiple kingdoms, united by dynastic accident in one sovereign, were common in early modern Europe, but this was a very unusual set. England was the most centralised monarchical state in Europe, and had a society much more individualist, capitalist and socially mobile than was the norm for the age. Scotland was much closer to that norm, while Ireland represented the bizarre pattern of English government institutions imposed on an unusually fragmented society. The combination was much worsened by the effects of the Reformation, which succeeded in converting most of the English and Scottish, but not the Irish, and in establishing a different sort of Protestant Church in all three states. What proved to be fatal to the early Stuart monarchy, however, was the very unusual – indeed unique – circumstance that by 1642 it had failed to impose its wishes on the religious behaviour of the majority of its subjects in each realm.

The second model of the 'problem' is that most closely associated with the work of Steven Ellis: of an exercise in English state building. Until the 1530s the frontiers with which the English monarchy had been most concerned were those of its rich and prestigious French lands. In gaps between fits of activity on the Continent, however, it had expanded to acquire large zones of territory in Ireland, Wales and northern England that were generally left under the control of local magnates. It was in the 1530s that this pattern began decisively to change. France was growing too strong for English claims on former land there to be feasible. At the same time the Reformation created deep new ideological divisions across Europe in general and the British Isles in particular, and turned the western and northern English borderlands into potentially serious gaps in national security. They had, therefore, to be taken under direct royal control, a process that lasted over one and a half centuries and was only completed in the 1690s. By then, the native ruling elites of Wales and northern England had been brought into the metropolitan English system with full rewards, and their Irish equivalents disposed or taken over. Scotland was outside that system, but brought into co-operation with it by the common bond of Protestantism. The Scottish Reformation had depended initially on books printed in London, and in English. This crippled Scots as a literary language, so that after 1600 most Scottish publications were in English. In 1500 about 65 per cent of the people of the British Isles could speak any form of English, and that which they did speak was often a distinctive dialect. By 1700, 85 per cent could speak a Standard English, and Protestant elites, equipped with this common language controlled the entire archipelago and could harness its resources to create a superpower.

The third model of the 'British problem' has been emphasised by Scottish and Irish historians, but linked to the 'borderland' one by Steven Ellis. It depends on a different division of the islands, into English regions and those predominantly speaking a Celtic language. This ran through each of the three kingdoms, and by the sixteenth century made them the only states in the whole of Western Europe to have what their rulers regarded as a savage frontier. By this model, the creation of a British identity was one that depended on the destruction and downgrading of Celtic cultures. By 1600 Wales had been peacefully and successfully assimilated, because of the accident that the Tudor royal family had obvious Welsh blood. In the early to mid-seventeenth century the power of the Irish Gaelic chiefs was finally broken and they either fled or accepted English ways, at least as part of a dual culture. At the same time the bond between Irish and Scottish clans was much weakened, and after the 1640s it was severed. By 1660 only Scotland's Celtic hinterland remained more or less intact, and that is why it started to emerge as a major political and strategic problem after then.

The fourth definition highlights the stunningly anomalous position of Ireland. It has been emphasised, naturally enough, by Irish scholars such Nicholas Canny and Brendan Bradshaw, and assimilated to the three-kingdom model by John Morrill. Ireland was in the extraordinary situation of being an independent kingdom that was never visited by its monarchs. Between 1399 and 1689 none went there to be crowned, or took any oaths on accession to respect its laws. Its rulers were regularly deposed without their Irish subjects ever being consulted in the matter. Irish government was a carbon copy of the English one in every detail, but with a completely invisible ruler. This did not mean independence in practice, but treatment as an English colony. After the 1550s Irish institutions were usually worked by newcomers who treated land and office as an extension of the English political spoils system. The English themselves never seemed sure of what they were doing there. They never had a scheme for annexing Ireland to the English state, but they did speak of assimilating it to English ways. On the one hand they treated the native Irish as full subjects of their own Crown, with feudal titles and a right to formal justice. On the other, they equated them with tribal peoples in the Americas, as savages essentially different in quality, while the medieval English settlers of the land were regarded as traitors and backsliders in the work of civilising and converting the natives. They let the latter remain, unlike Native Americans, because they were already harnessed to the economic processes needed to exploit the land and less alien in their culture. At the same time they made almost as little attempt to convert or re-educate them, and often saw them as almost equally lacking in human rights. As a result, wars and rebellions in early modern Ireland tended to be much bigger and much nastier than those in Britain, with many more atrocities towards both soldiers and civilians, committed by all parties.

In all these contexts, and by all these models, the conquest of the British Isles by a radically Protestant British republic changed everything. As said above, it convinced the Scottish ruling elites that the English without kings were much more dangerous than the English with them. At the restoration of the monarchy, they set to work to bolster the house of Stuart as a rampart for the security of Scottish national identity and independence, and to strengthen royal control of government and Church as part of that process. Similarly, the same trauma convinced most Irish Catholics, of both Gaelic and English descent, that the monarchy offered them the best hope of a restoration to the land and office that they had lost, massively, with the Cromwellian conquest. The civil wars and revolutions of the mid-century also convinced the Stuarts that their policy had been misguided. It had been established by James VI and I, as a common framework for his new triple kingdom and as a means of assimilating Scottish government to approaches instituted by Elizabeth in England and Ireland. In Scotland, he based his rule firmly on the richest, most urbanised and most Protestant region of his realm, the central Lowlands. He officially stigmatised the Gaelic culture of the Highlands and Isles as barbaric and deserving of extirpation, and supported one of the clans most aggressively associated with the new Protestant faith, the Campbells. In Ireland he continued the Elizabethan policy of entrusting government to English politicians and adventurers, planting English and Scottish settlers on land confiscated from the native Irish, and pushing the medieval English settlers of the island, who had mostly remained Catholic, into a political limbo. This approach had the merit of consistency and coherence, and of appealing to the prejudices of the majority of the inhabitants of Britain.

It also backfired catastrophically under Charles I, when many of his English and Scottish subjects lost confidence in their ruler. It was the 'civilised' Scots of the Lowlands, and the Campbells, who rebelled against royal policy in the 1630s and aided the English Parliament against their joint sovereign in the 1640s. By contrast, many of the Highland chiefs remained loyal to their king, and under the command of the marquis of Montrose almost won back Scotland for him. The Irish Catholics, especially those of English descent, also joined in the attempt to re-establish the monarchy in all three kingdoms after it had been abolished by the revolution in England. This pattern, inevitably, left its mark on the later Stuarts. Charles II and James II had both learned from the mistakes of their father. They interfered in Scottish affairs as little as possible, reduced the number of offices given to Scots at the royal court to a tiny number, and more or less left Scotland to run itself under a succession of viceroys chosen from the native nobility. The main requirement of the latter was that they should keep the land from interfering in English affairs. At the same time they played on the sense of identity between the Scots and their own dynasty, and built up a body of support for themselves among the clans of the central Highlands. They cut down the Campbells – literally, as two successive chiefs were beheaded – and treated as bitter domestic enemies the most radical Protestants of the land, who resisted the reforms in the Church associated with the re-establishment of royal power over it. Located mainly in the south-west, they were submitted to increasing terrorism by royal soldiers, sometimes reinforced by Highlanders.

In Ireland, Charles temporised, by confirming in power the Protestant elites established there by the Cromwellian conquest and yet restoring a minority of Catholics to their land. He also veered away, most of the time, from the late Tudor and early Stuart policy of sending out English strangers to govern the kingdom. For much of his effective reign he relied on the duke of Ormond, the most powerful surviving noble of the Anglo-Norman conquerors who had ruled half the island for the English monarchs during the later Middle Ages. Ormond was a Protestant, but to appoint him was still a step back towards much older ways of governing the land. James took a further one, by placing in power another scion of medieval English settlers, Richard Talbot, whom he raised to the dukedom of Tyrconnel. Like most of his community, Tyrconnel was a Catholic, and set to work steadily and with great cunning and success to return administrative, judicial and military offices to his co-religionists. By 1688 this work was largely complete, and though most beneficiaries were ultimately of English descent, the new favour to the Catholic religion inevitably had some benefits for the natives as well. In that year also, as mentioned above, Irish and Scottish soldiers were brought into England to assist the royal army there in the task of securing the land against invasion or rebellion.

James's religious objectives had therefore led him to an almost complete reversal of the solution to the fourfold 'British problem' that had been attempted by the

Tudors and by his own father and grandfather. Like his abandonment of the role traditionally expected of their monarchs by the Protestant English, this action was at once reckless, precipitate and remarkably successful. It was likewise accomplished without rebellion, or even serious unrest. In its way, it represented a coherent and perfectly viable means of dealing with the multiple kingdom and its diverse cultures, even though it ran at odds to the whole trend of subsequent British and Irish history as well to that of the two generations preceding James's own.

* * *

Like all of James's policies it failed absolutely, because he was felled by a foreign army led by an alternative ruler. It is suggested here that this was the consequence of two serious weaknesses in his position. One of these consisted of his conduct of foreign affairs, which James virtually ignored in order to get on with his task at home. This was by no means necessarily a foolish policy. During the 1680s developments in Germany were leading slowly towards a major war between France and coalition of its enemies. Over the previous eighty years, England had always enjoyed greatest economic prosperity, and diplomatic influence, when it remained neutral while such great conflicts approached and then raged, able to trade with all the contending nations and be courted by all. This is precisely the course at which James aimed, and he realised that it would be most effective if he maintained a powerful navy, at once a deterrent to foreign aggressors and an inducement to would-be allies to bid highly for England's support. Unhappily, James's natural heavy-handedness and his complete preoccupation with domestic affairs meant that the policy was not carried through with the skill which it required to succeed. His refusal to reach a firm understanding with any foreign power, coupled with his blustering talk of using his fleet to punish his neighbours 'for insolences in all parts of the world',[49] left other nations resentful and nervous of England instead of hopeful or grateful.[50]

Nevertheless, it is crucially important to appreciate that James lost his throne, not because he provoked a foreign power so much as because that power contained the prince who had married his daughter and heiress presumptive. William of Orange shared with James the quality of pursuing an aim greater than personal aggrandisement: in his case a determination to throw back the power of France. He pursued this aim with ruthlessness, chicanery and trickery far greater than any ever shown by James, and with much greater intelligence. He had already decided to invade England by the beginning of 1688, to head off the potential threat to the succession of his wife to its throne, presented by the pregnancy of James's queen.[51] It may be suggested here that two developments made it essential for him to do so before winter. The first was the birth of James's son, which clearly removed Mary from the position of heir if the child were accepted as the genuine son of the king.

William had therefore to encourage rumours that the child had in reality been smuggled into the birth-chamber, and to strike before they died down or were successfully refuted. He did both. The other reason for moving fast was the impending convention of James's Parliament. If it met, then the Prince of Orange faced a serious two-way risk: if it either endorsed the king's policies, or forced him to back down over them, William's prospective pose as the saviour of English liberties would be severely weakened. The prince therefore convinced the Dutch Estates to support what had hitherto been a private venture, and furnish him with a full-scale, state-funded field army. He did so by deliberately misrepresenting to them information which he had received from England and France to frighten them into believing that James and Louis had secretly agreed to attack the Netherlands, just as Charles II and Louis had actually done almost twenty years before.[52] Once he had landed and seen an opportunity to claim the throne immediately, he frightened James into fleeing to France, as Robert Beddard has proved, by sending soldiers to chase him out of London.[53] In truth, however, James had to flee once William had won, not (I think) so much because he could not bear the idea of limitations on his powers, as Bill Speck suggests,[54] as because he would have had to betray not only his religion but his son, whom William had declared to be an impostor.

The Prince of Orange could hardly have succeeded so easily, none the less, without James's other major weakness: his own pessimism. It might almost be said of him as of the later French monarch Louis-Philippe, that he was 'allowed to fall'. The common picture of James II as a confident monarch forging ahead out of touch with all reality, until rudely awakened to it by William's preparations for invasion, is grotesquely wrong. The Exclusion Crisis left this king afraid of the majority of his subjects – one reason for the savagery of his retaliation after Monmouth's Rebellion – and as soon as he realised that the Tories and the Church of England would not support him in his most cherished schemes, he felt very much alone and in danger. His bitter remarks to the French ambassador Barrillon, to his courtiers, and to the Seven Bishops, all express this self-image, as does the fact that after issuing the Declaration of Indulgence he strongly refortified Portsmouth as a secure way station if he had to flee to France, and prepared Ireland as another prospective refuge. As soon as he learned that William was ready to attack, he went into panic and made concessions to the Tories which not only threw away his plans for a compliant Parliament but wrecked local government. As the Prince of Orange sailed, James left potential traitors at liberty in the hope that this would conciliate them. When his enemy landed, he dithered for two weeks and then gave up, abandoning first his army, then his government, and finally his country. Once gone, he remained a broken man, as later observers in Ireland and France agreed. In the last analysis, the tragedy of James II was that he was brave and foolish enough to undertake a heroically risky course for the sake of his religion, but not strong enough to see it through.

My comments on the results are brief and largely second-hand, representing no more than a feather in the scales of historical debate. I agree with the great Victorian legal historian Maitland that the events of 1688–89 constituted a revolution in the modern sense of a major and illegal upheaval in the state, for the Convention Parliament which offered the crown to William and Mary was not constitutionally summoned.[55] I agree with Bill Speck and Lois Schwoerer (and Macaulay) that the Revolution Settlement which followed decided that the power in the state would henceforth rest with the monarch-in-Parliament, not the monarch alone. I concur with them also that it decisively weakened the major royal powers to command the armed forces, determine the national religion and manipulate the enforcement of laws.[56] I support John Morrill's conclusion that the revolution not only established a new pattern of constitutional relationships but crystallised out the parties which dominated English politics for the next two centuries, created a new context for spiritual and moral imperatives and forced a redefinition of England's relationships with Scotland, Ireland and Europe.[57] It produced, in short, a new framework within which the various problems and tensions of the late Stuart English polity, listed earlier, could be resolved.

It follows from all this that, while I do believe in Jonathan Clark's concept of a 'long eighteenth century', I would commence it in 1690 and not, as he does, in 1660.[58] It also follows that I hold it irrelevant to any consideration of the importance of the Revolution Settlement that sixty more years had to pass before the opponents of it accepted its permanence,[59] and that twice, in the rebellions of 1715 and 1745–46, they may have come close to toppling it. I fully accept that the constitutional changes later in the reign of William III were even more far-reaching than those at the beginning, but insist that the former were the product of those earlier changes. The same consideration must be applied to the undoubted fact that a further half-century of constitutional development followed from both. Nor can it alter my position that the reforms of 1689–90 left many tensions in English, let alone in British or Irish, politics, and created an entirely new set.[60] The revolution of 1688 seems to have been both a real watershed and a real point of demarcation, determining the crucial issue of the balance of constitutional power in national life. The fact that its outcome does seem to have hung so much upon personalities (as outlined above) and contingency (represented by the changes of wind which enabled William's invasion force to set sail, and to land safely in Devon) fully justifies the epic treatment of it made by historians such as Macaulay and the use of it as an object-lesson in the way in which the accidental, providential and wonderful can all operate in human affairs.

* * *

The events of 1688 therefore provide a perfect example of the sort of material which can help historians meet one of the great challenges of their profession: of turning history into stories with the carrying power of myth. This is, of course, exactly what the classic Whig historians such as Macaulay set out to do, and succeeded in doing. There is no doubt that the 'Glorious Revolution' is tailor-made for the articulation of what Sir Herbert Butterfield characterised as 'the Whig interpretation of history': 'the tendency in many historians to write on the side of Protestants and Whigs, to praise revolutions provided that they have been successful, to emphasise certain principles of progress in the past and to produce a story which is the ratification if not the glorification of the present'.[61] It is equally well suited to that sensationalisation of the past which is the most consistently successful means of preserving an interest in it and a sense of identification with it on the part of the general public, including the sophisticated and informed public. The most popular written works of history have consistently been those which have met Macaulay's hope of equalling the impact of fashionable works of fiction, while by far the most important contemporary medium for mass communication, television, makes extensive and successful use of history in a format which depends heavily, and often literally, on its inherent potential for drama. This needs to be borne in mind when considering Butterfield's assertion that the 'Whig' way of writing it tends to overdramatise events.[62] Such reflections throw into especially sharp relief the obvious fact, highlighted at the opening of this chapter, that Butterfield was making these remarks to attack this sort of historiography, and that the success of his criticisms among his profession may have done much to diminish the reputation of the revolution of 1688 together with those of the historians who had eulogised it. As made clear earlier in this book, the term 'Whig' has become the most ubiquitous term of abuse and condemnation in the discipline. How, then, in a world of postmodern historiography, is it possible to emphasise the importance of the events of 1688, and tell their story with zest, without falling into the trap of being 'Whiggish'?

One answer to this question would be to deny the need for it, by suggesting that Whig history actually has merits. The criticisms made of it, like most which the twentieth century has mounted against Victorian liberalism, reflect the sheer success of the latter. When Macaulay wrote his history, he was facing not the triumph of constitutional monarchy and religious toleration across Europe but its exact opposite, the crushing of both by the monarchies of Russia, Prussia and Austria, in partnership with many lesser despotisms such as the Papacy and the Bourbons of Naples. The stridency with which he lauded their triumph in England owed much to his sense of its essential fragility. It was the progress achieved by both during the later nineteenth and early twentieth centuries which made the celebration of their historical achievement come to seem to some observers complacent and unthinking, in a manner to which Butterfield quite rightly took exception. Only for a short period, in the 1930s, was their victory apparently reversible, and that called forth Trevelyan's eulogy on the Glorious Revolution.

Having said that, Butterfield's famous essay itself embodies some significant ironies. One was that he specifically excepted from his criticisms those historians who openly and consciously express prejudices in their writing and use them to leaven their perceptions and give emotional colour to their prose. His objection was to those who recognised no such partiality in themselves and spoke as impersonal and objective judges. By this reckoning, Macaulay himself, who wrote as a self-conscious partisan, should be held up for admiration. A second irony is that, like so many critics of historiography, Butterfield committed the faults of which he himself was complaining, in apparently complete lack of awareness that he was doing so. In retrospect it is clear enough that his own conservative and Christian beliefs, and hostility to the established social and academic elite, set him at odds with the tone of much of the history being written in the early twentieth century and led directly to his attack on it. In making that attack, however, he himself wrote with the air of an impartial and objective critic, calling for a better standard of professional work and a more perfect recovery of objective truth. A third irony is that in subsequent decades his increasingly overt identification with a humane and evangelical Christianity led him to write history himself that corresponded to the criteria which he had condemned earlier as Whiggish.[63]

When these points are recognised, the admiration long accorded to Butterfield's essay remains justified, for it represented a passionate plea for a greater pluralism in representations of the past, and an enhanced sense of the subjectivity of judgements upon it, which current historiographical theory thoroughly endorses and which are certainly reinforced here. How, then, might a pluralist history of the 'Glorious Revolution' be produced which still does justice to the epic quality and importance of the events concerned and the colour of the personalities? It may be suggested here that five entirely different approaches all do equal credit to it in separate ways. The first is the Whig version, especially in its most raw and blatant form, as represented by Macaulay. If it has been proposed earlier that William of Orange was less of a chivalric hero, and more of a scheming and ruthless politician, than Macaulay believed, then William may be none the less admirable for having been less of the lion and more of the fox; only provided that the historian is prepared to identify openly with either the declared principles for which the revolution was effected, or its actual short- and long-term results, or both.

The second approach, which is also traditional but has been hitherto much more muted, is simply to reverse the sympathies. In that case the revolution turns into a disaster, William into a villain, and James into a tragic hero of the classic kind, noble in his objectives and brought low by personal flaws and unscrupulous enemies. This case is not easy to make for England, even if James's conversion to the cause of religious toleration, although belated, is accepted as genuine and lasting. The roughness of his treatment of constitutional proprieties makes him an unlikely proponent of liberalism, and there have been no modern historians prepared to argue for the virtues of absolute monarchy in itself. Even a Catholic apology for

James is vitiated by the facts that the majority of English Catholic leaders thought his policies unwise and that they resulted in a disaster for Catholicism. When such a defence has been attempted for him, as by Hilaire Belloc, it has only succeeded in appearing the more eccentric and unrealistic as a result.[64] Where the tragic view of the revolution becomes very easy and convincing to sustain is in the writing of Irish and Scottish history. The crushingly negative consequences of it for national independence and religious liberty in Ireland, at least as far as the majority of the Irish were concerned, and (in the slightly longer term) for the Gaelic society and culture of Scotland, have always been obvious. William of Orange naturally enough reversed the approach taken to the 'British problem' taken by James and restored that instituted under the Tudors. The Irish Catholics were crushed in a series of bloody battles and placed firmly beneath the rule of a Protestant minority, while Highland culture was once again officially stigmatised. Royal favour in Scotland was returned to the more radically Protestant Lowlanders – permanently producing a Presbyterian National Church – and to the Campbells. In the long term, the identification of many Gaelic clans with the cause of James and his successors led directly to the destruction of the Highland Scottish way of life and eventually to the clearance of many of the people.

The Whig version of events could only assimilate this aspect of the story by declaring it to be a necessary evil, permitting the dominance of English and Protestant rule which eventually led to a pluralist society within which Catholics and Gaels themselves could find an equal place and share in the wealth and prestige of the common British achievement. Ability to make this case with conviction has waned steadily through the twentieth century as it has become plain that such a society has failed, at least in the form in which the Victorians tried to establish it. Most of Ireland became independent in 1922, in a form which explicitly negated the achievements of the revolution, while the rest has been convulsed with violence which has drawn explicitly upon memories and images of it. The devolution of self-government to Scotland, amid the reappearance of a separatist Scottish nationalism, has also undermined confidence in the benefits of a political upheaval which led by knock-on effect to Anglo-Scottish Union. It is entirely possible to combine the perceived negative impact of the events of 1688 on Ireland and Scotland with a story of how the high expectations of them in England were largely dissipated in political muddle and corruption, and the growing unpopularity of William, to make a convincing case for the revolution as at best a narrowly nationalist or sectarian victory, or at worst a harrowing tale of the betrayal of high ideals.[65] At the present day it is indeed only possible to present its story as an unequivocally glorious achievement by confining one's vision to Britain, or even to England; but that narrowing of focus is easily achieved, and the fragmentation of the British polity may make it still more easy. Furthermore, it may be chronologically as well as geographically uncoupled from the negative views, by arguing that although the wars of 1689 to 1691 in Scotland and Ireland were a consequence of the revolution, they were different phenomena. In 1688 both those nations remained at peace, and so there were no parallel upheavals in them to divert attention from the extraordinary developments in England.

The third approach is also a tragic one, but based on an altogether different, and more generalised, attitude to human affairs. It accepts the two basic postulates of the positive view of the revolution – that it was a major and decisive event, and that its consequences were beneficial – but places them within a framework of contemporary desire and expectation. By this reckoning, all the protagonists were personal failures, and the happy result was produced by a series of interlocked errors. The Whig coalition of the early 1680s strove to avert the succession of a Catholic monarch to the throne, and helped instead to ensure that it occurred upon a wave of loyalism. James II was determined to make Catholicism a potent force in the political and religious life of the British Isles, and helped instead to ensure that a Catholic monarch never ruled in them again, and that his co-religionists were long excluded from power, and weighed down with social disabilities, all over the archipelago. William of Orange, who was first and foremost a Dutch patriot, invaded the islands to secure their resources to help his nation in beating the French. His rule over them established a framework of government which helped to raise Britain to a pitch of power which eclipsed that of the Dutch for ever. The Tories strove to obtain a strong and revered monarchy and an intolerant Church, and ended up helping to bring about a constitutionally limited Crown and a legalised religious dissent. Archbishop Sancroft worked for the extirpation of nonconformity and for a powerful Church of England operating in partnership with an unprecedentedly potent monarchy. Because of his inability either to obey all of the commands of James or to accept his deposition, he ended up in schism with a much-weakened national Church. This view of the revolution is at one with a broader perspective on the Stuart period as one of high political stakes, high ideals and ruined hopes; a span of history at once very important, very dramatic and terribly sad. It drives home the truth that the future is generally least tractable to those who desire most ardently to mould it. It makes the revolution into a tragedy in the true, ancient Greek, sense of the word. In an age in which sectarian celebrations or denigrations of these events have become more or less unacceptable in the academy, it is the one which comes closest to investing them with a profound sense of the religious; of the lack of capacity of humans to order their own affairs.

The fourth approach is one that has appeared only recently, being prominent in the work of Jonathan Israel, Jonathan Scott and Tony Claydon, and draws attention to the European context of the revolution.[66] Between them they have emphasised that the invasion of England was undertaken by the leading Dutch politician, with Continental objectives in mind and equipped with the professional army of the Dutch state, recruited from many nationalities. Likewise, the subsequent full-scale conflict in Ireland was one theatre of the European War of the League of Augsburg, with a French army reinforcing the Irish and both being beaten by

William's large multinational one loaned by his native state. Their work has, however, deeper implications or arguments. It suggests that the problems of the Stuart multiple kingdom were essentially insoluble by domestic forces, and were decisively resolved by the appearance of a foreign prince schooled in different ways. William's firm personal Protestantism, his hatred of France and his long habituation to working with representative institutions, all combined to restore trust between ruler and ruled in England based on an unprecedented and enduring co-option of Parliament into the process of government. For the first time, popular fear of popery and arbitrary rule could operate in favour of the monarchy and not against it, and it could be said that a Dutch troubleshooter had solved the difficulties of the triple monarchy by applying foreign methods to it. This is a perspective with a great deal of obvious sense and it is possible that, in the era of the European Union and of powerful multinational corporations, it may acquire widespread acceptance and appeal among the British public. So far, however, it is not yet familiar outside a small group of professionals.

The fifth approach is to recognise that prominent historical events change their image and form with time: that the revolution of 1688 was a different phenomenon to the people of that age than it was to the Victorians, and can be to us. What was 'glorious' about it to contemporaries was that it preserved or rescued a set of identities built militantly around religion: a Protestant one for the British as a whole and their ruling elites in Ireland, and a specifically presbyterian one for the Scottish supporters of William and Mary. It enjoyed two different new leases of life from the end of the eighteenth century onwards, when it became a rallying-point for Irish Protestants facing a resurgent Irish nationalism, and also a symbol of the achievement of constitutional monarchy, religious toleration and representative democracy for the British. The present day lies in the shadow of those recreations of it, but rather uneasily. It has become obvious that the only possible long-term solution to the problems of Northern Ireland lies in reconciliation, and a diminution of sectarian politics. In Britain, the Victorian celebration of 1688 has waned along with the end of a sense of identity with the nineteenth century. It retains only a vestigial power to inspire or to provoke, although that power is not yet spent: reading the attacks made upon the concept of the revolution as a decisive event, made in the early 1990s, it is hard to resist a suspicion that they were sharpened by the schoolmistressy tones of the Conservative Prime Minister, Margaret Thatcher, repeating tritely the Victorian eulogies of it to mark its tercentenary.

It is this perception which calls into question the relevance of the revolution to the present day. Pieces of history, like living humans, get on if they have powerful friends and relations or else a widespread popular appeal; if they underpin or reinforce the identity of surviving interest groups and seem to speak directly to major aspects of the present. In this respect the revolution of 1688 fares relatively badly. The political party which was the most obvious beneficiary and heir to it, the Whig, disappeared in the late ninteenth century, and the direct successors of the Whigs, the Liberals, declined to a minor force in the early twentieth. The party that replaced them, the Socialist, found its heroic progenitors in the 1640s, if it looked to the seventeenth century at all, rather than the nineteenth, for historical roots. The tendency of Americans to regard the events of 1688 as a vital prerequisite for their own Revolution and War of Independence has waned with the reconstruction of American identity upon a supranational and multicultural basis. The very ease and relative bloodlessness of those events in England can count against them in national and world memory: they left no battlefields, no martyrs, no memories of prolonged and heroic struggle. The relative impression made on recent national consciousness was well pointed up by the contrast in the processes of commemoration in 1988 and 1992. In the first of those fell the tercentenary of the Glorious Revolution, and the response was a high-level, decorous, and rather stilted one: a government-sponsored exhibition at the Banqueting House, Whitehall, a speech by the Prime Minister, as mentioned, and a set of academic conferences and publications on both sides of the Atlantic. Four years later fell the 350th anniversary of the outbreak of the English Civil War, with no interest displayed by central government and comparatively little by academics, but (as discussed earlier) a huge groundswell of excitement and activity on the part of city and county councils, local museums, amateur historians, the mass media at all levels, and re-enactment societies. There is no doubt that it was the latter anniversary which seized the attention and involved the energies of the general public much more extensively, and with much less encouragement from political and intellectual leaders. For the reasons stated above, the 1640s had an imaginative presence at the end of the twentieth century which the 1680s had lost. They apparently contained the 'people's' war and revolution, whereas the changes of 1688 were very much those made by rulers and leading politicians.

None the less, the main thrust of this chapter has been to argue for the revolution of 1688 as a major and formative event, with huge issues at stake and a high level of inherent drama in its story. To put forward this argument is itself to contribute to ongoing historiographical debate, but it is also to suggest that the revolution has enough intrinsic importance to make its appropriation likely by the future. It may turn out to be a piece of history which has had its day, but the mere fact that it received a large measure of official recognition at its tercentenary, while lacking an obvious linkage to current power-blocs and preoccupations, illustrates the grip which it still has on the national memory, however attenuated. It may be that it will have more periods of glory, in the centuries to come, to replace the two which it has enjoyed already; but I personally hope that it does not. This is simply because of the great cause to which it has always been linked in the minds of the British: of parliamentary democracy. Whenever that form of government seems in serious danger – as in the late 1840s and in the 1930s – the events of 1688 become glorious in response. Whenever it seems secure, mundane and to be taken for granted, they tend to retreat into the remote and unemotive realms of history, and their more destructive and partisan aspects become more obvious. If the glory of 1688 has truly had its day, then it may be because the world has become a safer place for representative institutions.

7 Conclusion

Lecturing to my class of undergraduates, in the Cambridge of the mid 1970s, the future Sir Geoffrey Elton was generally sanguine about the future of the writing of early modern English history. If he worried about the prospect of it being taken over by Marxists, as described earlier, then this was a perceived threat to a thriving concern. One foundation of his confidence consisted of a huge quantity of raw source material; when a student asked him if there might soon be nothing new for historians of Tudor and Stuart England to say, because there would be no evidence left untapped, he replied that there was so much left in the archives that up to a century would be needed to read through it all. Elton was famed as one of the chief proponents of empiricist history, a tradition that depended at least partly on the notion that the sources should speak for themselves; but even he emphasised that they only spoke to the right people. Here again he had cause for optimism, for the mid-twentieth century had made considerable progress towards the creation of an unprecedentedly large cadre of university-based historians operating within a common career structure and rigorously trained in the necessary skills of decipherment and analysis.

Geoffrey Elton's estimate of the likely rate of progress through the unread documents was, it is true, based on an academic culture in which historical research had been relatively slow and intermittent. The basic duty of a university teacher was to teach, with authorship viewed as an optional extra, although a desirable one and generally essential for promotion. Academics who did write history were expected to justify their privileged position by achieving the greatest possible expertise in a particular subject area. They were encouraged to begin by making careful and detailed studies within it, acquiring a knowledge that could build up until they eventually attained the magisterial expertise that entitled them to publish broad surveys and textbooks. This patient, laborious and meticulous way of proceeding was reckoned to carry the best chance of producing work so well researched and considered that it could stand for all time: the much-prized definitive study of a topic. The quality of research was to be judged by the handful of other experts in a given area, whose duty it was to submit all publications within it to inspection, criticism and challenge or approval. As in certain species of horned beast, all-out combats between dominant figures in a particular territory were actually quite rare, but could be spectacular and savage occasions when they did occur. In all this way of proceeding, academic historians were often conscious that, far from being the monarchs of their discipline, they often featured as its poor relations. Much of the history written in the United Kingdom in the mid-twentieth century was still produced, as it always had been, by members of the wider literary world, generally wealthier, better connected, faster working and more famous than university staff, and capable regularly of publishing books that academics themselves took seriously.

Between 1970 and the end of the century, this world of scholarship disappeared almost completely. Onto it were thrown the strains of the great enlargement of British higher education, commencing in the 1960s and continuing to the present, combined with the cumulative underfunding of it that began in the 1980s. One result was to produce a record number of professionally trained, university-based historians who were expected to carry out and publish research as consistently as they taught students, and at maximum speed. This was institutionalised in the late 1990s, when departments began to be funded according to the quantity and quality that they could turn out within set spans of time; the targets set utterly destroyed the old ideal of patiently accumulated expertise. This sudden frenzy of work, imposed within a blatantly competitive framework, ought to have had three catastrophic effects on the writing of early modern English history. One would have been to consume, almost to extinction, the surviving stock of untapped source material: a process equivalent to the demolition of Anglesey's copper mountain in the late eighteenth century or the slaughter of the North American bison in the late nineteenth. A second should have been to have increased tension and acrimony between scholars working on the same subject to the point at which the profession was riven by constant feuding at all levels. Alongside this unhappy state of affairs, non-academic experts in the period might have been expected to prosper still further, able to explore sources and ideas without such pressure of time, criticism and (increasing) teaching burdens, and well placed to cash in on a swelling public interest in the national and global past.

At first it might seem that all these consequences were coming to pass, and the story of 'revisionism' in early modern English history, examined in this book, was in large part an immediate manifestation of them. In the event, however, the situation that resulted, and endures at the present, came to represent virtually the opposite state of affairs. Preoccupation has shifted from the discovery and exploitation of sources to the different ways in which they might be understood. Relations between historians in particular fields have become less instead of more adversarial, with a heavier emphasis on co-operative and interdisciplinary ventures. As the growing use of the past as entertainment in the mass media has produced an unprecedented number of television and radio programmes about history, it has been academic experts who have dominated them, almost to the exclusion of all others. Works of history produced outside universities have virtually become relegated to the status of light reading.

There are a number of different factors that account between them for these, apparently paradoxical, developments. One is a direct consequence of the increased pace of research and the much larger number of professionals engaged in it: a much greater sense of the fragmentary and inscrutable nature of historical evidence. Until the 1980s there was still a widespread impression that history was essentially a jig-saw, and the recovery of it largely entailed the rediscovery of missing bits that could then be fitted into what was already known of a particular period, theme or event to produce a fuller picture. At times this is actually how the process of research felt, and does feel, but there is now a much greater sense of how much of the jigsaw has been lost for ever, and how difficult it is to build up a picture from the pieces that survive. Indeed, the latter do not preserve fixed and objective images, but refracted impressions, that are by their very nature, though in varying degrees, partial, blink-ered and untrustworthy. Their interpretation and use may not, after all, be best effected by a standardised disciplinary training in source analysis, so much as by importing theories and techniques from the social sciences and literary criticism, engaging in collaborative ventures of investigation and discussion and celebrating the capacity of different scholars to achieve differing perceptions.

This development has been reinforced by the consequences of the long-term underfunding of British higher education. There are no longer many obvious prizes for which academic historians can compete, and an unprecedentedly large number of them now have to share such honours as there are. If the carrots have generally been removed from the profession, the sticks have been greatly multiplied in the form of financial penalties for underachievement, falling directly on departments and universities rather than individuals. In this hard climate, there has been a nat-ural and salutary tendency for historians to band together for protection. At the same time, the profession has shared with the entire globe in the twentieth century the loss of a true sense of an immanent past. What this means in blunt language is that until various points in that century (differing according to one's nation, region and social status), the skills and knowledge of parents and grandparents were still of some utility to a new generation, as they had always been since human beings evolved. By the turn of the millennium, the pace of technological change and its solvent effect on social and ideological forms meant that the past no longer lived on in the present in everyday and unthinking ways: it had perished. The sense of its loss, and of a new need to contact and reclaim it, is probably the main expla-nation for many of the cultural phenomena of late twentieth-century Britain, such as the appearance of re-enactment societies, the quest by ordinary people for their family histories, the burgeoning of a self-conscious 'heritage' industry, and the explosion of television and radio programmes about the past. It has also affected historians, including those of the Stuart period. There has been a sharp decline in the sense that the people of the latter were essentially our own selves in period costume, and that the emotions and ideologies that they embodied have direct rel-evance to the present day and indeed can be continued in it: the early 1970s was the last great flowering of that sort of imaginative connection. It has been replaced by a much greater impression of seventeenth-century people as representing a different society and culture from our own, in the manner that a traditional people in a different continent do. It is no wonder that the discipline of anthropology has recently provided some of the most heavily used of the techniques and insights to be applied to the writing of domestic history.

Another contributory factor to the current state of historical studies in general in British universities, and of Stuart studies in particular, has been the growth of social and cultural cohesiveness within the profession. The nature of the educational processes through which all members of it now pass, the salaries and lifestyles that it commands, and the demands of the job (now standardised, regulated and strengthened as never before, by government requirement) all tend towards the production of a more homogenous body of historians. The classic academic expert in the Stuart period is now somebody who is lower middle class in social and economic characteristics, socialist or liberal in political attitudes, and agnostic or atheist in religion. As a group, historians of the Stuarts, like historians in general, have become markedly less patrician, considerably less male and much more diversely provincial in origin. As a result they are more likely to be united by a common training and common work conditions, and much less likely to overlap with national political, social and cultural elites and to reproduce the loyalties and divisions of the latter. The new pressures of their job leave them with little time for commitment to external causes and enthusiasms. It is much less likely now than it was forty years ago that a member of a history department will know what the personal political or religious views of colleagues actually are. For much of the twentieth century, experts in early modern England differed over historical issues of class, religion and politics that had direct and obvious implications for the present and future of their own society. The sort of controversy that has divided, and divides, them in recent years has been over where the earl of Northumberland happened to be on 30 July 1647, how far early churchwardens' accounts accurately reflect parish financial arrangements, and whether the first Whigs and Tories can meaningfully be described as political parties. All of these examples actually have important implications for how we view aspects of the past, but they do not have the same immediate sense of connection with the present. The effect of these changes on the writing of Stuart history, both in broadening and in narrowing the vision of practitioners, has been one of the main themes of this book.

Creeping around the work of historians of seventeenth-century England, and confronted at times in the pages above, there has been a final great development of the years since 1970: a relative loss of faith in political institutions and processes as the unifying and defining factors of a society and a nation. The devolution of government within the United Kingdom, the progressive integration of the latter into the European Community, and reforms in the constituent units of Parliament and discussion of much more radical transformation of them, have cumulatively weakened the attachment of the British to constitutional arrangements that had formerly seemed both uniquely effective and the end product of a heroic history.

More generally, in an age in which technology has turned daily life into an experience of accelerating change, national institutions are coming to seem as mutable and transitory as all other human constructions. This last phenomenon is, of course, global, and the others are shared to some degree by most other European states, while the USA is engaging in its own quest for a means of preserving the union of a uniquely multicultural and multiracial superpower within institutions and traditions created for only some of its component groups. All this has tended massively to reinforce an interest, among historians and others, in cultural habits and assumptions as the true bonding or limiting forces of national groups, of which political life is merely one expression. Such an interest has, as suggested earlier, both diminished the traditional national emphasis on the great events of the Stuart period and conditioned the form of recent work upon them. It is also a ripe field for an application of reflexivity in its own right, to match that attempted here in the realms of political and religious history: but that is an enterprise for a different book.

Notes

▦ 1 Revisionism

1. Derek Hirst, 'Parliament, law and war in the 1620s', *Historical Journal*, 23 (1980), p. 455.
2. For just such a view, see Austin Woolrych, 'Shifting perspectives on the Great Rebellion', *History Today*, 52 (2002), pp. 46–52.
3. Samuel Rawson Gardiner, *History of England from the Accession of James I to the Outbreak of the Civil War* (London, 1883–84), vol. iv, p. 36.
4. Peter Lake, 'Retrospective: Wentworth's political world in revisionist and post-revisionist perspective', in J.F. Merritt (ed.), *The Political World of Thomas Wentworth, Earl of Strafford, 1621–1641* (Cambridge: Cambridge University Press, 1996), pp. 252–83.
5. J.P. Sommerville, *Royalists and Patriots: Politics and Ideology in England 1603–1640* (London: Longman, 1999), pp. 264–5.
6. David Cannadine, 'Historians in "the Liberal Hour"', *Historical Research*, 189 (2002), p. 345.
7. John Rowland Phillips, *Memoirs of the Civil War in Wales and the Marches 1642–1649* (London, 1874), 2 vols.
8. Ronald Hutton, 'Clarendon's history of the Rebellion', *English Historical Review*, 97 (1982), pp. 70–88.
9. Alan Everitt, *The Community of Kent and the Great Rebellion* (Leicester: Leicester University Press, 1966); and *The Local Community and the Great Rebellion* (London: Historical Association, 1969); J.S. Morrill, *The Revolt of the Provinces* (London: Allen and Unwin, 1976).
10. G.R. Elton, 'A High Road to Civil War', in C.H. Carter (ed.), *From the Renaissance to the Counter-Reformation* (New York: Random House, 1965), pp. 325–47.
11. It is actually possible that none of them shared his attitudes, but whereas I know that some did not, I am not sure about others who subsequently became less prominent.
12. Paul Christianson, 'The causes of the English Revolution: A reappraisal', *Journal of British Studies*, 15 (1976), pp. 40–75; Conrad Russell, 'Parliamentary history in perspective 1604–1629', *History*, 61 (1976), pp. 1–27.
13. John K. Gruenfelder, 'The electoral patronage of Sir Thomas Wentworth, Earl of Strafford, 1614–1620', *Journal of Modern History*, 49 (1977), pp. 55–74; Paul Christianson, 'The peers, the people, and parliamentary management in the first six months of the Long Parliament', *Ibid.*, pp. 575–99; Clayton Roberts,

'The Earl of Bedford and the coming of the English Revolution', *Ibid.*, pp. 600–16; Mark Kishlansky, 'The emergence of adversary politics in the Long Parliament', *Ibid*, pp. 617–40; James E. Farnell, 'The social and intellectual basis of London's role in the English Civil Wars', *Ibid.*, pp. 641–60.

14. G.R. Elton, 'Tudor government: The points of contact: I. Parliament', *Transactions of the Royal Historical Society*, 5th series 24 (1974), pp. 183–200; 'II. The Council', *Ibid.*, 25 (1975), pp. 195–214; 'III. The Court', *Ibid.*, 26 (1976), pp. 211–28.

15. Kevin Sharpe (ed.), *Faction and Parliament* (Oxford: Oxford University Press, 1978).

16. Conrad Russell, *Parliaments and English Politics, 1621–1629* (Oxford: Oxford University Press, 1979).

17. Roger Lockyer, *Buckingham* (London: Longman, 1981); Anthony Fletcher, *The Outbreak of the English Civil War* (London; Arnold, 1981).

18. Paul Christianson, 'Parliaments and Politics in England 1604–1629', *Canadian Journal of History*, 16 (1981), p. 107.

19. Usefully summarised and analysed by J.H. Hexter, 'The Early Stuarts and Parliament', *Parliamentary History*, 1 (1982), pp. 203–7.

20. He struck back instead in 1985, in the preface to the second edition of his classic work, *The Causes of the English Revolution* (most easily read now in the 2002 Routledge reprint, pp. 165–81). It was notable that to do so he drew heavily on the work of other historians produced over the previous seven years, showing what his other later publications made clear: that this great scholar had moved to the social history which had always come more naturally to him.

21. Conrad Russell, pers. comm. March 1991.

22. George Bernard, pers. comm. 5 October 1998.

23. John Morrill, 'The religious context of the English Civil War', *Transactions of the Royal Historical Society*, 5th series 34 (1984), pp. 155–78; 'Sir William Brereton and England's wars of religion', *Journal of British Studies*, 24 (1985), pp. 311–32; 'The attack on the Church of England in the Long Parliament 1640–1642', in Derek Beales and Geoffrey Best (eds), *History, Society, and the Churches* (Cambridge: Cambridge University Press, 1985), pp. 101–24; Kevin Sharpe, 'Crown, Parliament and locality', *English Historical Review*, 399 (1986), pp. 321–50; 'Ideas and politics in early Stuart England', *History Today*, 38 (1988), pp. 45–50; *Criticism and Compliment* (Cambridge: Cambridge University Press, 1987).

24. Paul Christianson, *Discourse on History, Law and Governance in the Public Career of John Selden* (Toronto: Toronto University Press, 1997).

25. Derek Hirst, *Authority and Conflict* (London: Arnold, 1986).

26. David Underdown, *Revel, Riot and Rebellion* (Oxford: Oxford University Press, 1985); Ann Hughes, *Politics, Society and Civil War in Warwickshire, 1620–1660* (Cambridge: Cambridge University Press, 1987); Thomas Cogswell, *The Blessed*

Revolution (Cambridge: Cambridge University Press, 1989); Richard Cust, *The Forced Loan and English Politics* (Oxford: Oxford University Press, 1987); J.P. Sommerville, *Politics and Ideology in England 1603–1640* (London: Longman, 1986); Stephen K. Roberts, *Recovery and Restoration in an English County* (Exeter: Exeter University Press, 1985); L.J. Reeve, *Charles I and the Road to Personal Rule* (Cambridge: Cambridge University Press, 1989).

27. Richard Cust and Ann Hughes (eds), *Conflict in Early Stuart England* (London: Longman, 1989).

28. Ann Hughes, *The Causes of the English Civil War* (London: Macmillan, 1991).

29. G.R. Elton, *The Parliament of England 1559–81* (Cambridge: Cambridge University Press, 1986).

30. Mark Kishlansky, *Parliamentary Selection* (Cambridge: Cambridge University Press, 1986).

31. Kevin Sharpe, *Politics and Ideas in Early Stuart England* (London: Pinter, 1989); John Morrill, *The Nature of the English Revolution* (London: Longman, 1993).

32. Conrad Russell, *The Causes of the English Civil War* (Oxford: Oxford University Press, 1990); and *The Fall of the British Monarchies 1637–1642* (Oxford: Oxford University Press, 1991).

33. Kevin Sharpe, *The Personal Rule of Charles I* (New Haven: Yale University Press, 1992).

34. Glenn Burgess, *The Politics of the Ancient Constitution* (London: Macmillan, 1992).

35. Peter Lake, review of Russell, *Causes*, and *Fall*, in *Huntingdon Library Quarterly*, 57 (1994), pp. 167–98; Cynthia Herrup, 'Revisionism: What's in a name?', *Journal of British Studies*, 35 (1996), pp. 135–8; Derek Hirst, *England in Conflict* (London: Arnold, 1999); David Underdown, *A Freeborn People* (Oxford: Oxford University Press, 1996); Merritt (ed.), *The Political World of Thomas Wentworth*; Christianson, *Discourse on History*; Sommerville, *Royalists and Patriots*; Andy Wood, 'Beyond post-revisionism?', *Historical Journal*, 40 (1997), pp. 23–40; Hughes, *Causes of the English Civil War* (2nd edn, 1998); Norah Carlin, *The Cause of the English Civil War* (Oxford: Blackwell, 1999).

36. Kevin Sharpe, 'Print, polemics and politics in seventeenth-century England', *Journal of British Studies*, 41 (2002), p. 232.

37. A.G. Dickens, *The English Reformation* (London: Batsford, 1964).

38. Christopher Haigh, *Reformation and Resistance in Tudor Lancashire* (Cambridge: Cambridge University Press, 1975).

39. Christopher Haigh, 'The continuity of catholicism in the English Reformation', *Past and Present*, 93 (1981), pp. 37–69; 'The recent historiography of the English Reformation', *Historical Journal*, 25 (1982), pp. 995–1007; 'Revisionism and Catholic history', *Journal of Ecclesiastical History* (1985), pp. 394–406; 'The Church of England, the Catholics and the people', in Christopher Haigh (ed.), *The Reign of Elizabeth I* (London: Macmillan, 1984), pp. 195–220.

40. Margaret Bowker, *The Henrician Reformation* (Cambridge: Cambridge University Press, 1981); J.J. Scarisbrick, *The Reformation and the English People* (Oxford: Blackwell, 1984).
41. Robert Whiting, 'For the health of my soul', *Southern History*, 5 (1983), pp. 68–94; 'Abominable idols', *Journal of Ecclesiastical History*, 33 (1982), pp. 30–47.
42. Christopher Haigh (ed.), *The English Reformation Revised* (Cambridge: Cambridge University Press, 1987).
43. Glyn Redworth, 'Whatever happened to the English Reformation?', *History Today*, 37 (1987), pp. 29–36.
44. For example, Patrick Collinson, *The Religion of Protestants* (Oxford: Oxford University Press, 1982); *The Birthpangs of Protestant England* (London: Macmillan, 1988); Diarmaid MacCulloch, 'The myth of the English Reformation', *Journal of British Studies*, 30 (1991), pp. 1–19; *The Later Reformation in England* (London: Macmillan, 1990); *Building a Godly Realm* (London: Historical Association, 1992); John Guy, *Tudor England* (Oxford; Oxford University Press, 1988); Robert Whiting, *The Blind Devotion of the People* (Cambridge: Cambridge University Press, 1989).
45. Patrick McGrath, 'Elizabethan Catholicism: A reconsideration', *Journal of Ecclesiastical History*, 35 (1984), pp. 414–28; Geoffrey Dickens, *The English Reformation* (2nd edn, 1989).
46. Christopher Haigh, *English Reformations* (Oxford: Oxford University Press, 1993).
47. Eamon Duffy, *The Stripping of the Altars* (New Haven: Yale University Press, 1992).
48. Christopher Haigh, review of Alexandra Walsham, *Providence in Early Modern England*, in *English Historical Review*, 115 (2000), p. 965.
49. Ethan S. Shagan, *Popular Politics and the English Reformation* (Cambridge: Cambridge University Press, 2002), p. 5.
50. Alexandra Walsham, *Providence in Early Modern England* (Oxford: Oxford University Press, 1999).
51. Shagan, *Popular Politics*, p. 7.
52. J.C.D Clark, 'Eighteenth-century social history', *Historical Journal*, 27 (1984), pp. 773–88; *English Society 1688–1832* (Cambridge: Cambridge University Press, 1985); *Revolution and Rebellion* (Cambridge: Cambridge University Press, 1986).
53. Written by Peter Watson for *The Observer Review*, 31 January 1988. This interview contains most of Clark's most outspoken statements upon the political context of his work.
54. Mark Kishlansky, in 'Symposium: Revolution and revisionism', *Parliamentary History*, 7 (1988), p. 331.
55. For example, the four contributions to *Ibid.*, pp. 328–38; Joanna Innes, 'Jonathan Clark, social history and England's "Ancien Regime"', *Past and*

Present, 115 (1987), pp. 165–200; Jeremy Black, 'England's "Ancien Regime"', *History Today*, 38 (1988), pp. 43–50; Ronald Hutton, review of *Revolution and Rebellion, History Today*, 37 (1987), pp. 54–5. The letter was, of course, published in *The Observer*, in reply to the article above.

56. In addition to the 'immediate' reactions above, compare the tone of various textbooks on the period produced during the following years: Paul Langford, *A Polite and Commercial People: England 1727–1783* (Oxford: Oxford University Press, 1989); Jeremy Black, *The Politics of Britain 1688–1800* (Manchester: Manchester University Press, 1993); Geoffrey Holmes and Daniel Szechi, *The Age of Oligarchy: Pre-Industrial Britain 1722–1783* (London: Longman, 1993);

57. J.C.D. Clark, 'The strange death of British history', *Historical Journal*, 40 (1997), p. 800.

58. Alan Macfarlane, *The Origins of English Individualism* (1978); *Marriage and Love in England* (1986); *The Culture of Capitalism* (1987). All published in Oxford by Blackwell.

59. J.C. Davis, *Fear, Myth and History: the Ranters and the Historians* (Cambridge: Cambridge University Press, 1986).

60. Examples of such irenic writers in the early Stuart field were Gerald Aylmer and Barry Coward.

61. That was my own fate, for much of the 1980s.

62. Christopher Coleman and David Starkey (eds), *Revolution Reassessed* (Oxford: Oxford University Press, 1986).

63. This was David Starkey, reviewing Peter Gwyn, *The King's Cardinal* (London: Barrie and Jenkins, 1990). I regret that although I have preserved a cutting of the review, it did not include details of the journal in which it appeared; I did not at the time conceive that I would write on the subject.

64. Derek Hirst, 'Unanimity in the Commons, aristocracy and the origins of the English Civil War', *Journal of Modern History*, 50 (1978), p. 50.

65. Kishlansky, *Parliamentary Selection*, p. xi.

66. J.S.A. Adamson, 'Politics and the nobility in civil war England', *Historical Journal*, 34 (1991), p. 215.

2 The Great Civil War

1. Charles Carlton, *Going to the Wars* (London: Routledge, 1992), pp. 201–9.

2. *Ibid.*, pp. 209–11.

3. *Ibid.*, p. 211.

4. C.V. Wedgwood, *The King's War* (London: Collins, 1958: a Fontana paperback in two editions, 1966 and 1968).

5. I wish that I could remember the authors of most of the 'pop' histories and novels about the war that I read between 1966 and 1970, when still at school; I got through at least a score. Some were works from the earlier part of the

century that remained popular, often reprinted and available in most public libraries, of which the most celebrated was Margaret Irwin, *The Stranger Prince* (London: Chatto and Windus, 1937). A classic example of a historical work from the period itself, that used most of the narrative devices of fiction, was Frank Knight, *Prince of Cavaliers* (London: Macdonald, 1967).

6. W.C. Sellar and R.J. Yeatman, *1066 and All That* (London: Methuen, 1930. Quotation from 1965 Penguin edition), p. 71. The popularity of the work during the 1960s may have had something to do with the fact that the latter, like the early 1930s, was a period much given to questioning militarism and jingoism, and to throwing off the traditional assumptions of British culture. It must, however, also have gained relevance from the continued teaching in British schools of the sort of history that the book was designed to lampoon, reinforced by a generation of masters whose great formative experience had been the Second World War, an event which for them reversed the apparent lessons of the First World War.

7. J.S.A. Adamson, 'Eminent victorians: S.R. Gardiner and the liberal as hero', *Historical Journal*, 33 (1990), pp. 641–57; Raphael Samuel, 'The discovery of puritanism 1820–1914', in Jane Garnett and Colin Matthew (eds), *Revival and Religion since 1700* (London: Hambledon, 1993), pp. 201–48; Timothy Lang, *The Victorians and the Stuart Heritage* (Cambridge: Cambridge University Press, 1995); Blair Worden, *Roundhead Reputations: The English Civil War and the Passions of Posterity* (London: Allen Lane, 2001), pp. 215–95.

8. Blair Worden, review of David Norbrook, *Writing the English Republic*, *Times Literary Supplement* (29 January 1999), p. 5.

9. Review of John Morrill *et al.* (ed.), *Public Duty and Private Conscience in Seventeenth-Century England* (Oxford: Oxford University Press, 1993), in the *English Historical Review*, 108 (1993), p. 983.

10. In each case based on a PhD thesis: P.R. Newman, 'The royalist armies in northern England 1642–1645' (York University, 1978); Ronald Hutton, 'The royalist war effort in Wales and the West Midlands 1642–1646' (Oxford University, 1980); Martyn Bennett, 'The royalist war effort in the North Midlands 1642–1646', (Loughborough, 1986). Some of the most significant of the publications to which they gave rise were P.R. Newman, *The Battle of Marston Moor* (Chichester: Anthony Bird, 1981); *Royalist Officers in England and Wales, 1642–1660* (New York: Garland, 1981); 'The Royalist Officer Corps 1642–1646', *Historical Journal*, 26 (1983), pp. 945–58; and *The Old Service* (Manchester: Manchester University Press, 1993); Ronald Hutton, *The Royalist War Effort 1642–1646* (London: Longman, 1981); Martyn Bennett, 'Contribution and assessment: Financial exactions in the English Civil War', *War and Society*, 4 (1986), pp. 1–11; ' "My plundered townes, my houses devastation" ': The Civil War and North Midlands life 1642–1646', *Midland History*, 22 (1997), pp. 35–50; 'Dampnified villagers: Taxation in Wales during the First Civil War', *Welsh History Review*, 19 (1998), pp. 29–43.

11. Martyn Bennett, *The Civil Wars in Britain and Ireland 1638–1651* (Oxford: Blackwell, 1997).
12. David L. Smith, *Constitutional Royalism and the Quest for Settlement, c. 1640–1649* (Cambridge: Cambridge University Press, 1994) and *The Stuart Parliaments* (London: Arnold, 1999).
13. His most important works to historians were *Edgehill: The Campaign and the Battle* (Kineton: Roundwood, 1967) and *Marston Moor: The Campaign and the Battle* (Kineton: Roundwood, 1970).
14. R.W. Harris, *Clarendon and the English Revolution* (London: Chatto and Windus, 1983) and Richard Ollard, *Clarendon and his Friends* (London: Hamilton, 1987).
15. See, for example, Jonathan Scott, *England's Troubles* (Cambndge: Cambridge University Press, 2000); Alan Houston and Steve Pincus (eds), *A Nation Transformed: England after the Restoration* (Cambridge: Cambridge University Press, 2001); Austin Woolrych, *Britain in Revolution 1625–1660* (Oxford: Oxford University Press, 2002).
16. J.S. Morrill, *Cheshire 1630–1660: County Government and Society during the English Revolution* (Oxford: Oxford: University Press, 1974); Anthony Fletcher, *A County Community in Peace and War: Sussex 1600–1660* (London: Longman, 1975); Clive Holmes, *The Eastern Association in the English Civil War* (Cambridge: Cambridge University Press, 1975); David Underdown, *Somerset in the Civil War and Interregnum* (Newton Abbot: David and Charles, 1973). The collective import of these works and others in the form of theses and articles was presented in Polemical form by J.S. Morrill, *The Revolt of the Provinces: Conservatives and Radicals in the English Civil War 1630–1650* (Oxford: Oxford University Press, 1976).
17. For example, A.R. Bayley, *The Great Civil War in Dorset* (Taunton, 1910); Mary Coate, *Cornwall in the Great Civil War and Interregnum* (Oxford, 1933); Arthur Leonard Leach, *The History of the Civil War (1642–1649) in Pembrokeshire and on its Borders* (London, 1937); F. Stackhouse-Acton, *The Garrisons of Shropshire during the Civil War* (Shrewsbury, 1867); John and T.W. Webb, *Memorials of the Civil War ... as it Affected Herefordshire and the Adjacent Counties* (London, 1879); A.C. Wood, *Nottinghamshire in the Civil War* (London, 1937); G.N. Godwin, *The Civil War in Hampshire* (Southampton, 1904); J.W. Willis-Bund, *The Civil War in Worcestershire* (Birmingham, 1905).
18. That is, at any rate, the form in which I most commonly heard it. John Morrill recorded his own experience of a slightly different formulation in his preface to the second edition of his *The Revolt of the Provinces* (Longman, 1980), p. x.
19. Clive Holmes, 'The county community in Stuart historiography', *Journal of British Studies*, 19 (1980), pp. 54–73; Ann Hughes, 'Militancy and localism: Warwickshire politics and Westminster politics 1643–1647', *Transactions of the Royal Historical Society*, 5th series, 31, (1981), pp. 51–68.

20. Ann Hughes, *Politics, Society and Civil War in Warwickshire, 1620–1660* (Cambridge: Cambridge University Press, 1987).

21. For example, Roy Sherwood, *The Civil War in the Midlands 1642–1651* (Stroud: Alan Sutton, 1992); Brian Stone, *Derbyshire in the Civil War* (Cromford: Scarthin, 1992); Philip Tennant, *Edgehill and Beyond: The People's War in the South Midlands 1642–1645* (Stroud: Sutton, 1992); John Wroughton, *A Community at War: The Civil War in Bath and North Somerset, 1642–1660* (Bath: Lansdown, 1992) and *An Unhappy Civil War: The Experiences of Ordinary People in Gloucestershire, Somerset and Wiltshire, 1642–1646* (Bath: Lansdown, 1999).

22. Mark Stoyle, *Loyalty and Locality: Popular Allegiance in Devon during the English Civil War* (Exeter: Exeter University Press, 1996).

23. John Walter, *Understanding Popular Violence in the English Revolution: The Colchester Plunderers* (Cambridge: Cambridge University Press, 1999).

24. Hutton, *The Royalist War Effort*, p. 201.

25. Hughes, *Politics, Society and Civil War in Warwickshire*, pp. 167–8; Newman, *The Old Service*, pp. 256–8; Stoyle, *Loyalty and Locality*, pp. 231–2.

26. There have of course been exceptions, among which Carlton, *Going to the Wars*, is obvious.

27. Hutton, *Royalist War Effort*, pp. 34–5. See also George Ormerod (ed.), *Tracts Relating to Military Proceedings in Lancashire during the Great Civil War* (Chetham Society, 1844), p. 335.

28. Two in particular badly marred knowledge of the war in Wales, the Marches and the Severn valley, for over a century: John Rowland Phillips, *Memoirs of the Civil War in Wales and the Marches 1642–1649* (London, 1874), i, pp. 131–6; J.F. Rees, *Studies in Welsh History* (Cardiff, 1947), p. 66; Joyce Lee Malcolm, *Caesar's Due: Loyalty and King Charles 1642–1646* (London: Royal Historical Society, 1983), p. 108.

29. William Bourne, *The Arte of Shooting in Great Ordnance* (1643), pp. 45–8; Robert Norton, *The Gunners Dialogue* (1643), pp. 75–6; *Enchridion of Fortification* (1645), pp. 54–6.

30. Peter Young and Wilfrid Emberton, *Sieges of the Great Civil War* (London: Bell and Hyman, 1978).

31. For example, Peter Harrington, *Archaeology of the English Civil War* (Princes Risborough: Shire Publications, 1992); Tim Warner, *Newark: The Civil War Siegeworks* (Nottingham: Nottingham County Council, 1992); S. Ward, *Excavations at Chester: The Civil War Siegeworks* (Chester: Grosvenor Museum, 1987); Mark Stoyle, *Exeter City Defences Project* (Exeter: Exeter Museums Archaeological Field Unit, 1988) and *The Civil War Defences of Exeter and the Great Parliamentary Siege of 1645–46* (Exeter: Exeter Museums Archaeological Field Unit, 1990); Lawrence Butler, *Sandal Castle, Wakefield* (Wakefield Historical Publications, 1991); Malcolm Atkin and Wayne Laughlin, *Gloucester and the Civil War* (Stroud: Sutton, 1992); P. and Y. Courtney, 'A siege examined: the

Civil War archaeology of Leicester', *Post Medieval Archaeology*, 26 (1992), pp. 47–90.

32. Much of this new information is packaged neatly in Ronald Hutton and Wylie Reeves, 'Sieges and fortifications', in John Kenyon and Jane Ohlmeyer (eds), *The Civil Wars* (Oxford: Oxford University Press, 1998), pp. 195–233. I have added material here from Peter Wenham, *The Great and Close Siege of York* (Kineton: Roundwood Press, 1970), pp. 37–8, 43–4; and *A Journal, or, a True and Exact Relation of Each Dayes Passage, of that Party of the Right Honourable the Earl of Manchesters Army, under the Command of the Ever Honoured Major General Crawford* (1644).

33. Newman, *The Battle of Marston Moor*; P.R. Newman and P.R. Roberts, *Marston Moor 1644: The Battle of the Five Armies* (Pickering: Blackthorn, 2003).

34. Glenn Foard, *Naseby: The Decisive Campaign* (Guildford: Pryor, 1995).

35. Godwin, *The Civil War in Hampshire*, pp. 345–7.

36. Geoffrey Parker, *The Army of Flanders and the Spanish Road 1567–1659* (Cambridge: Cambridge University Press, 1972), p. 18 and *The Military Revolution* (Cambridge: Cambridge University Press, 1988), p. 8.

37. Quoted in David Cannadine, *In Churchill's Shadow: Confronting the Past in Modern Britain* (London: Penguin, 2002), p. 170.

38. I dealt with this story in 1982: Ronald Hutton, 'The royalist war effort', in John Morrill (ed.), *Reactions to the English Civil War* (London: Macmillan, 1982), p. 51.

39. Barbara Donagan, 'Codes and conduct in the English Civil War', *Past and Present* (1988) and 'The web of honour: Soldiers, christians and gentlemen in the English Civil War', *Historical Journal*, 44 (2001), pp. 365–90; 'The army, the state and the soldier in the English Civil War', in Michael Mendle (ed.), *The Putney Debates of 1647: The Army, The Levellers and the English State* (Cambridge: Cambridge University Press, 2001), pp. 79–102; 'Casuistry and allegiance in the English Civil War', in Derek Hirst and Richard Strier (eds), *Writing and Political Engagement in Seventeenth-Century England* (Cambridge: Cambridge University Press, 1999), pp. 89–112; 'The casualties of war: Treatment of the dead and wounded in the English Civil War', in Ian Gentles *et al.* (eds), *Soldiers, Writers and Statesmen* (Cambridge: Cambridge University Press, 1998), pp. 114–32.

40. Stephen Porter, *Destruction in the English Civil Wars* (Stroud: Sutton, 1994), pp. 124–6.

41. Porter, *Destruction in the English Civil Wars*, p. 65.

42. Stephen Porter, 'Introduction', and 'The economic and social impact of the Civil War upon London', in Stephen Porter (ed.), *London and the Civil War* (Basingstoke: Macmillan, 1996), pp. 1–30, 175–204.

43. David Underdown, *Royalist Conspiracy in England 1649–1660* (New Haven: Yale University Press, 1960) and *Pride's Purge: Politics in the Puritan Revolution* (Oxford: Oxford University Press, 1971).

44. Underdown, *Somerset in the Civil War and Interregnum*.

45. Brian Manning, *The English People and the English Revolution 1640–1649* (London: Heinemann, 1976).

46. William Hunt, *The Puritan Moment: The Coming of Revolution in an English County* (Cambridge, MA: Harvard University Press, 1983).

47. Joan Thirsk, 'Industries in the Countryside', in F.J. Fisher (ed.), *Essays in the Economic and Social History of Tudor and Stuart England* (Cambridge: Cambridge University Press, 1961), pp. 70–88; 'The Farming Regions of England', in Joan Thirsk (ed.), *The Agrarian History of England and Wales: Volume IV: 1500–1640* (Cambridge: Cambridge University Press, 1967), pp. 109–112; 'Seventeenth-century agriculture and social change', in Joan Thirsk (ed.), *Land, Church and People* (Reading: Reading University Press, 1970), pp. 148–77.

48. Alan Everitt, 'Farm labourers', in Thirsk (ed.), *Agrarian History of England and Wales*, pp. 461–5; 'Nonconformity in country parishes', in Thirsk (ed.), *Land, Church and People*, pp. 178–99.

49. Christopher Hill, *The World Turned Upside Down* (London: Temple Smith, 1972), pp. 32–45, especially 38.

50. David Underdown, 'The chalk and the cheese: Contrasts among the English Clubmen', *Past and Present*, 85 (1979), pp. 25–48; 'The problem of popular allegiance in the English Civil War', *Transactions of the Royal Historical Society*, 5th series, 31 (1981), pp. 69–94; *Revel, Riot and Rebellion: Popular Politics and Culture in England 1603–1660* (Oxford: Oxford University Press, 1985).

51. John Morrill, 'The ecology of allegiance in the English Revolution', *Journal of British Studies*, 26 (1987), pp. 451–67.

52. Martin Ingram, *Church Courts, Sex and Marriage in England 1570–1640* (Cambridge: Cambridge University Press, 1987).

53. Ann Hughes, *The Causes of the English Civil War* (Basingstoke: Macmillan, 1991), pp. 133–42.

54. Buchanan Sharp, 'Rural discontents and the English Revolution', in R.C. Richardson (ed.), *Town and Countryside in the English Revolution* (Manchester: Manchester University Press, 1992), 1992, pp. 251–72.

55. Ronald Hutton, *The Rise and Fall of Merry England: The Ritual Year 1400–1700* (Oxford: Oxford University Press, 1994), pp. 161–3.

56. Stoyle, *Loyalty and Locality*, pp. 149–61; Simon Osborne, 'Popular religion, culture and politics in the Midlands, c. 1638–1646' (unpublished Warwick University PhD thesis, 1993), pp. 341–3.

57. John Morrill, 'The Church in England, 1642–9', in John Morrill (ed.), *Reactions to the English Civil War* (Basingstoke: Macmillan, 1982), pp. 89–114; The religious context of the English Civil War', *Transactions of the Royal Historical Society*, 5th series, 34 (1984), pp. 155–78; 'Sir William Brereton and England's Wars of Religion', *Journal of British Studies*, 24 (1985), pp. 311–32; 'The attack on the Church Of England in the Long Parliament', in Derek Beales and

Geoffrey Best (eds), *History, Society and the Churches* (Cambridge: Cambridge University Press, 1985), pp. 105–24.

58. Morrill, *The Revolt of the Provinces*, p. 47.

59. Samuel Rawson Gardiner, *History of England from the Accession of James I to the Outbreak of the Civil War* (London, 1883–84, vol. x, pp. 11–13, 32.

60. I have not, in fact, been able to locate any rapid, open and direct challenge to his thesis to be published in the 1980s. Instead it was discussed extensively among specialists, with the sort of reservations that were to reach print in the 1990s.

61. Newman, *The Old Service*, pp. 1–42; Smith, *Constitutional Royalism*, pp. 11–102; Gerald Aylmer, 'Collective mentalities in mid-seventeenth-century England: II. Royalist Attitudies', *Transactions of the Royal Historical Society*, 5th series, 37 (1987), pp. 1–30.

62. Hughes, *The Causes of the English Civil War*, pp. 111–13. See also I.M. Green, ' "England's Wars of Religion"? Religious conflict and the English Civil Wars', in J. Van Den Berg and P.G. Hoftijzer (eds), *Church, Change and Revolution* (Leiden: Brill, 1991), pp. 100–21.

63. Roger Howell, *Newcastle-upon-Tyne and the English Revolution* (Oxford: Oxford University Press, 1967); A.M. Johnson, 'Politics in Chester during the Civil War and Interregnum', in Peter Clark and Paul Slack (eds), *Crisis and Order in English Towns 1500–1700* (London: 1972), pp. 204–36; John T. Evans, *Seventeenth-Century Norwich* (Oxford: Oxford University Press, 1979); Keith Lindley, 'London's citizenry in the English Revolution', in Richardson (ed.), *Town and Countryside*, pp. 19–45; David Scott, 'Politics and government in York, 1640–1662', in *Ibid.*, pp. 46–68; Ann Hughes, 'Coventry and the English Revolution', in *Ibid.*, pp. 69–99; David Harris Sacks, 'Bristol's "Wars of Religion" ', in *Ibid.*, pp. 100–29.

64. John Morrill, *The Nature of the English Revolution* (London: Longman, 1993), pp. 33–44.

65. Hughes, *The Causes of the English Civil War* (2nd edition, 1998); Norah Carlin, *The Causes of the English Civil War* (Oxford: Blackwell, 1999).

66. Hutton, *Royalist War Effort*, p. 13; Ronald Hutton, *The Rise and Fall of Merry England* (Oxford: Oxford University Press, 1994), pp. 190–4, 204–5; Eales, *Puritans and Roundheads*, chs 2–7; T.G. Barnes, *Somerset 1625–1640* (Oxford: Oxford University Press, 1961), coupled with Underdown, *Somerset*, pp. 1–59.

67. Ronald Hutton, 'The failure of the Lancashire Cavaliers', *Transactions of the Historical Society of Lancashire and Cheshire*, 129 (1980), pp. 47–57; B.G. Blackwood, 'The Lancashire Cavaliers and their tenants', *Ibid.*, 117 (1965), pp. 17–32; *The Lancashire Gentry and the Great Rebellion 1640–1660* (Chetham Society, 3rd series 25, 1978), chs 1–3; 'Parties and issues in the Civil War in Lancashire and East Anglia', *Northern History* (1993), pp. 99–125; Newman,

The Old Service, pp. 154–98; Anthony Milton, 'A qualified intolerance: The limits and ambiguities of early Stuart anti-catholicism', in Arthur F. Marotti (ed.), *Catholicism and Anti-Catholicism in Early Modern English Texts* (Basingstoke: Macmillan, 1999), pp. 85–115.

68. Andy Wood, 'Beyond post-revisionism?: The Civil War allegiances of the miners of the Derbyshire "Peak Country"', *Historical Journal*, 40 (1997), pp. 23–40.

69. R. Malcolm Smuts, *Culture and Power in England 1585–1685* (London: Macmillan, 1999), p. 103.

70. *Ibid.*, p. 106.

71. *Ibid.*, p. 108.

72. Mark Stoyle, '"Sir Richard Grenville's creatures": The new Cornish tertia, 1644–46', *Cornish Studies*, 4 (1996), pp. 26–44; 'The last refuge of a scoundrel', pp. 31–51; 'English "Nationalism", Celtic particularism and the English Civil War', *Historical Journal*, 43 (2000), pp. 1113–28; *West Britons: Rebellion, Civil War and Identity in Cornwall, 1497–1689* (Exeter: Exeter University Press, 2001).

73. Carlton, *Going to the Wars*; Richardson (ed.), *Town and Countryside*.

74. Such as its march through the streets of Nottingham to raise the King's standard in front of the castle as had been done in 1642, with the city churches ringing bells in synchronisation and a civic reception being held in honour of the society's leaders; the Tower exhibition was in town at that moment. Such re-enactments continued at every anniversary of a significant date in the war during the following four years. Perhaps the prize for enthusiasm was won by the small north Devon town of Torrington, setting for one of the last battles, in 1646. It spent two years building a replica of the parish church which was blown up at the climax of the action, so it could be destroyed in the finale to the Sealed Knot's recreation of the latter. The society provided more or less a scale replica of the fighting, with the approximate number of defenders and attackers opposing each other over the same ground, in full costume and with full equipment. It may be noted that these efforts helped to win Torrington a grant of a million pounds for redevelopment; a recognition of 'heritage' can be a powerful factor in the politics of local government finance.

75. For example, John Wardman, *The Forgotten Battle: Torrington 1646* (Torrington: Fire and Steel, 1996); Jeremy Webb, *Echoes of Cannon Fire: A Malvern Hills View of the Civil War* (privately published, 1996); Malcolm Atkin, *The Civil War in Worcestershire* (Stroud: Sutton, 1996); Philip Andrew Scaysbrook, *The Civil War in Leicestershire and Rutland* (Leicester: Melon, 1996); John Adair, *Roundhead General: The Campaigns of Sir William Waller* (Stroud: Sutton, 1997); Philipp J.C. Elliot-Wright, *Brassey's History of Uniforms: English Civil War* (London: Brassey, 1997); Alison Plowden, *Women All On Fire: The Women of the English Civil War* (Stroud: Sutton, 1998); David Disbury, *Beef, Bacon and Bag Pudding: Old Berkshire in the Civil War* (Reading: Timescape, 1999); Wroughton, *An Unhappy*

Civil War; Edward and Peter Razzell (eds), *The English Civil War: A Contemporary Account* (London: Caliban, 1999), 5 vols.; John Lynch, *For King and Parliament: Bristol and the English Civil War* (Stroud: Sutton, 1999); Roger Hudson (ed.), *The Grand Quarrel: Women's Memoirs of the English Civil War* (Stroud: Sutton, 2000); John Barratt, *Cavaliers: The Royalist Army at War 1642–1646* (Stroud: Sutton, 2001). It must be stressed that this is merely a sampling of the books on the subject, and ignores electronic publication and the series of titles produced by Stuart Peachey and his collaborators on many aspects of the war and the society in which it was set. The list also ignores the role played by radio and television: in 2002 alone, there were a full evening programme of national radio and two television series devoted to the war, and one of the series produced another book: Tristram Hunt, *The English Civil War at First Hand* (London: Weidenfeld, 2002). The influence of local patriotism on continuing interest is clear from the titles above, and one academic expert at least has shared it sufficiently to make notable contributions to the genre: Mark Stoyle, *Exeter in the Civil War* (Exeter: Devon Archaeological Society, 1995); *Plymouth in the Civil War* (Exeter: Devon Archaeological Society, 1998); *Devon and the Civil War* (Exeter: Mint Press, 2001).

3 The New Framework for Early Stuart Studies

1. For his developing use of it, and the sources on which he drew, see Conrad Russell, 'Parliament and the king's finances' in Conrad Russell (ed.), *The Origins of the English Civil War* (Basingstoke: Macmillan, 1973), ch. 3; *Parliaments and English Politics 1621–1629* (Oxford: Oxford University Press, 1979), ch. 4; *The Causes of the English Civil War* (Oxford: Oxford University Press, 1990), ch. 7.
2. See particularly Stephen G. Ellis, *Tudor Ireland* (London: Longman, 1985) and *Ireland in the Age of the Tudors* (London: Longman, 1998).
3. For recent surveys of the relevant material, see Paul Slack, *From Reformation to Improvement: Public Welfare in Early Modern England* (Oxford: Oxford University Press, 1999); Michael J. Braddick, *State Formation in Early Modern England c. 1550–1750* (Cambridge: Cambridge University Press, 2000); Steve Hindle, *The State and Social Change in Early Modern England, c. 1550–1640* (Basingstoke: Macmillan, 2000); Michael J. Braddick and John Walter (eds), *Negotiating Power in Early Modern English Society* (Cambridge: Cambridge University Press, 2001); Mark Goldie, 'The unacknowledged Republic: Officeholding in early modern England', in Tim Harris (ed.), *The Politics of the Excluded, c. 1500–1850* (Basingstoke: Palgrave, 2001), pp. 153–94.
4. Conrad Russell, 'Charles I's financial estimates for 1642', *Bulletin of the Institute of Historical Research*, 58 (1985), pp. 109–20.

5. Braddick, *State Formation in Early Modern England*, pp. 181–280; James Scott Wheeler, *The Making of a World Power: War and Military Revolution in Seventeenth-Century England* (Stroud: Sutton, 1999).

6. Wheeler, *The Making of a World Power*; Braddick, *State Formation in Early Modern England*, pp. 221–80; and 'State formation and social change in early modern England', *Social History*, 16 (1991), pp. 1–17.

7. This is a major theme of Hutton, *The Royalist War Effort*. The illusion took in James Daly: 'The implications of royalist politics 1642–6', *Historical Journal*, 27 (1984), pp. 745–55.

8. J.P. Sommerville, *Politics and Ideology in England 1603–1640* (London: Longman, 1986) and 'Ideology, property and the constitution', in Richard Cust and Ann Hughes (eds), *Conflict in Early Stuart England* (London: Longman, 1989), ch. 2.

9. Thomas Cogswell, 'Prelude to re: The Anglo-French struggle over La Rochelle 1624–1627', *History*, 71 (1986), pp. 1–21; *The Blessed Revolution: English Politics and the Coming of War 1621–1624* (Cambridge: Cambridge University Press, 1989); 'The politics of propaganda: Charles I and the people in the 1620s', *Journal of British Studies*, 29 (1990), pp. 187–215; 'A low road to extinction? Supply and redress of grievances in the parliaments of the 1620s', *Historical Journal*, 33 (1990), pp. 283–303; Richard Cust, 'News and politics in early seventeenth-century England', *Past and Present*, 112 (1986), pp. 60–90; *The Forced Loan and English Politics 1626–1628* (Oxford: Oxford University Press, 1987); 'Politics and the electorate in the 1620s', in Cust and Hughes (ed.), *Conflict in Early Stuart England*, ch. 5.

10. Kevin Sharpe, 'Ideas and politics in early Stuart England', *History Today*, 38 (1988), pp. 35–50.

11. Russell, *The Causes of the English Civil War*, ch. 6.

12. Glenn Burgess, *The Politics of the Ancient Constitution* (Basingstoke: Macmillan, 1992); *Absolute Monarchy and the Stuart Constitution* (New Haven: Yale University Press, 1996); 'The impact on political thought' in John Morrill (ed.), *The Impact of the English Civil War* (London: Collins and Brown, 1991), ch. 4.

13. Kevin Sharpe, *Remapping Early Modern England: The Culture of Seventeenth-Century Politics* (Cambridge: Cambridge University Press, 2000), chs 2, 10.

14. D. Alan Orr, 'Sovereignty, supremacy and the origins of the English Civil War', *History*, 87 (2002), pp. 474–90.

15. Jenny Wormald, 'James VI and I: Two kings or one?', *History*, 68 (1983), pp. 187–209.

16. Conrad Russell, 'The British problem and the the English Civil War', *History*, 72 (1987), pp. 395–415; 'The British background to the Irish Rebellion of 1988', *Historical Research*, 61 (1988), 166–82; *The Causes of the English Civil War* (Oxford: Oxford University Press, 1990), chs 1, 2 and 5; *The Fall of the British Monarchies 1637–1642* (Oxford: Oxford University Press, 1991).

17. For the numbers and logistics involved, see Ronald Hutton, 'The royalist war effort', in Morrill (ed.), *Reactions to the English Civil War*, pp. 57–8, and sources given there.

18. David Stevenson, *Alasdair MacColla and the Highland Problem in the Seventeenth Century* (Edinburgh: Donald, 1980); Jane Ohlmeyer, *Civil War and Restoration in the Three Stuart Kingdoms* (Cambridge: Cambridge University Press, 1993); Padraig Lenihan, *Confederate Catholics at War, 1641–1649* (Cork: Cork University Press, 2001), pp. 73–116.

19. For example, Mark Greengrass (ed.), *Conquest and Coalescence* (London: Arnold, 1991); Ronald G. Asch (ed.), *Three Nations: A Common History?* (Arbeitskreis Deutsche England-Forschung, Bochum, 1993); Brian Mac Cuarta (ed.), *Ulster 1641* (Belfast: Institute of Irish Studies, Queen's University, 1993); Brendan Bradshaw, Andrew Hadfield and Willy Malley (eds), *Representing Ireland: Literature and the Origins of Conflict 1534–1660* (Cambridge: Cambridge University Press, 1993); Jane H. Ohlmeyer (ed.), *Ireland from Independence to Occupation 1641–1660* (Cambridge: Cambridge University Press, 1995); Stephen Ellis and Sarah Barber (eds), *Conquest and Union: Fashioning a British State 1485–1725* (London: Longman, 1995); Alexander Grant and Keith J. Stringer (eds), *Uniting the Kingdom: The Making of British History* (London: Routledge, 1995); Brendan Bradshaw and John Morrill (eds), *The British Problem, c. 1534–1707* (Basingstoke: Macmillan, 1996); Brendan Bradshaw and Peter Roberts (eds), *British Consciousness and Identity* (Cambridge: Cambridge University Press, 1998); John R. Young (ed.), *Celtic Dimensions of the British Civil Wars* (Edinburgh: John Donald, 1997); Glen Burgess (ed.), *The New British History: Founding a Modern State 1603–1715* (London: Tauris, 1999).

20. See those by Hughes and Carlin, cited above.

21. Kevin Sharpe, *The Personal Rule of Charles I* (New Haven: Yale University Press, 1992), deliberately put equal emphasis on connections between England and Scotland, and the former and the Continental states. For direct questioning of the three-kingdoms, perspective by others, see Peter Lake, review of Russell, *The Causes of the English Civil War* and *The Fall of the Stuart Monarchies*, *Huntingdon Library Quarterly*, 57 (1994), pp. 167–98 and Jonathan Scott, *England's Troubles* (Cambridge: Cambridge University Press, 2000), pp. 9–16.

22. Nicholas Canny, 'The attempted anglicization of Ireland in the seventeenth century', in Asch (ed.), *Three Nations: A Common History?*, ch. 2; Keith Brown, 'British history: A sceptical comment', in *Ibid.*, ch. 4.

23. I drew attention to these problems in Ronald Hutton, 'The triple-crowned islands', in Lionel K.J. Glassey (eds), *The Reigns of Charles II and James VII and II* (Basingstoke: Macmillan, 1997), pp. 71–2, as a protest against being asked to treat Ireland and Scotland together in that volume in just such a fashion, in a chapter that was originally labelled 'The British dimension'. To my surprise, Glenn Burgess interpreted my remarks as an attack on the value of studying

the three kingdoms together at all: Glenn Burgess, 'Introduction', in Burgess (ed.), *The New British History*, p. 18. Such a response seems extraordinary given the way in which I had pioneered a three-kingdom perspective on the reign of Charles II, and re-reading the statement which provoked it, I still cannot see how it could have been understood in Burgess's sense. The fact that it could be used as an Aunt Sally in a defence of what Burgess termed 'The New British History' indicates how much the latter had become a bandwagon by the late 1990s. It was a silly moment in the work of a fine scholar, and Burgess's essay in general provides a very helpful overview of the state of that sort of history by that stage of its development. It is interesting that in the collection that it introduced, a prominent Scottish historian praised my same essay for its treatment of his nation: Keith Brown, 'Seducing the Scottish Clio', in *Ibid.*, p. 256.

24. Compare the attitudes of Brown, 'Seducing the Scottish Clio', pp. 238–65; and Nicholas Canny, 'Irish, Scottish and Welsh reponses to centralisation, c. 1530–1640' in Grant and Stringer (eds), *Uniting the Kingdom?*, pp. 147–69, with those in the works at n. 97.

25. The most celebrated exponents of these ideas by the 1960s, on respective sides of the Atlantic, were Christopher Hill and William Haller.

26. For a sampling, try Patrick Collinson, *The Religion of Protestants* (Oxford: Oxford University Press, 1982) and *The Birthpangs of Protestant England* (London: Macmillan, 1988); Diarmaid MacCulloch, *The Later Reformation in England* (London: Macmillan, 1990) and *Building a Godly Realm* (London: Historical Association, 1992); Kenneth Fincham, *Prelate as Pastor: The Episcopate of James I* (Oxford: Oxford University Press, 1990); Nicholas Tyacke, *Anti-Calvinists: The Rise of English Arminianism c. 1590–1640* (Oxford: Oxford University Press, 1987); G.W. Bernard, 'The Church of England c. 1529–c. 1642', *History*, 75 (1990), pp. 183–206; Susan Doran and Christopher Durston, *Princes, Pastors and People* (London: Routledge, 1991); Tessa Watt, *Cheap Print and Popular Piety 1560–1640* (Cambridge: Cambridge University Press, 1991); Russell, *The Causes of the English Civil War*, chs 3–4; Peter White, *Predestination, Policy and Polemic* (Cambridge: Cambridge University Press, 1992); Julian Davies, *The Caroline Captivity of the Church* (Oxford: Oxford University Press, 1992); Sharpe, *The Personal Rule of Charles I*; Kenneth Fincham (ed.), *The Early Stuart Church, 1603–1642* (Basingstoke: Macmillian, 1993); Andrew Foster, *The Church of England 1570–1640* (London: Longman, 1994); Ronald Hutton, *The Rise and Fall of Merry England* (Oxford: Oxford University Press, 1994); Christopher Durston and Jacqueline Eales (eds), *The Culture of English Puritanism, 1560–1700* (Basingstoke: Macmillan, 1996); Judith Maltby, *Prayer Book and People in Elizabethan and Early Stuart England* (Cambridge: Cambridge University Press, 1998); John Spurr, *English Puritanism 1603–1689* (Basingstoke: Macmillan, 1998); Darren Oldridge, *Religion and Society in Early Stuart England* (Aldershot: Ashgate, 1998); Christopher Marsh, *Popular Religion*

in Sixteenth-Century England (Basingstoke: Macmillan, 1998); Alexandra Walsham, *Providence in Early Modern England* (Oxford: Oxford University Press, 1999); Braddick, *State Formation in Early Modern England*; Hindle, *The State and Social Change*; Peter Lake and Michael Questier (eds), *Conformity and Orthodoxy in the English Church, c. 1560–1660* (Woodbridge: Boydell, 2000); Peter Lake, *The Boxmaker's Revenge: 'Orthodoxy', 'Heterodoxy' and the Politics of the Parish in Early Stuart London* (Manchester: Manchester University Press, 2001).

27. Lake, *The Boxmaker's Revenge*, passim.

28. Christopher Haigh, 'The troubles of Thomas Pestell: Parish squabbles and ecclesiastical politics in Caroline England', *Journal of British Studies*, 41 (2002), pp. 403–29.

29. Sharpe, *The Personal Rule of Charles I*.

30. L.J. Reeve, *Charles I and the Road to Personal Rule* (Cambridge: Cambridge University Press, 1989); G.E. Aylmer, *The Personal Rule of Charles I* (London: Historical Association, 1989); Andrew Foster, 'Church policies of the 1630s', in Cust and Hughes (eds), *Conflict in Early Stuart England*, ch. 7; Davies, *The Caroline Captivity of the Church*; Kenneth Fincham and Peter Lake, 'The ecclesiastical policies of James I and Charles I', in Fincham (ed.), *The Early Stuart Church*, ch. 1; John Fielding, 'Arminianism in the localities', in *Ibid.*, ch. 4; Andrew Foster, 'The clerical state revisited', in *Ibid.*, ch. 6; Brian Quintrell, *Charles I 1625–1640*) (London: Longman, 1993), chs 7–11; S.P. Salt, 'Sir Symonds D'Ewes and the levying of Ship Money, 1635–40', *Historical Journal*, 37 (1994), pp. 253–87; Foster, *The Church of England*, ch. 7; Anthony Milton, 'Thomas Wentworth and the political thought of the personal rule', in F. Merritt (ed.), *The Political World of Thomas Wentworth, Earl of Strafford, 1621–1641* (Cambridge: Cambridge University Press, 1996), ch. 6; Michael B. Young, *Charles I* (Basingstoke: Macmillan, 1997), chs 3–4; Maltby, *Prayer Book and People*, chs 1–3; Spurr, *English Puritanism*, ch. 6; Oldridge, *Religion and Society in Early Stuart England*, pp. 21–64, 83–120; Thomas Corns, 'Duke, prince and king', in Thomas Corns (ed.), *The Royal Image: Representations of Charles I* (Cambridge: Cambridge University Press, 1999), pp. 1–25; Christopher Durston, *Charles I* (London; Routledge, 1998), ch. 3; Anthony Milton, 'Licensing, censorship and religious orthodoxy in early Stuart England', *Historical Journal*, 41 (1998), pp. 625–51; Anthony B. Thompson, 'Licensing the press', *Historical Journal*, 41 (1998), pp. 653–78; Derek Hirst, *England in Conflict 1603–1660* (London; Arnold, 1999), pp. 130–65; Scott, *England's Troubles*, pp. 113–34; Thomas Cogswell, *Home Divisions: Aristocracy, the State and Provincial Conflict* (Manchester: Manchester University Press, 1998), pp. 188–275; Austin Woolrych, *Britain in Revolution 1625–1660* (Oxford: Oxford University Press, 2002), pp. 75–139.

31. Sharpe, *The Personal Rule of Charles I*, pp. 392–402. See also Foster, 'The clerical state revisited'.

32. Maurice Lee, 'James I and the historians', *Albion*, 16 (1984), pp. 151–63; Wormald, 'James VI and I'; Maurice Lee, *Great Britain's Solomon* (Urbana: Indiana University Press, 1990); Jenny Wormald, 'James VI and I, "Basilikon Doron" and "The Trew law of free monarchies"', in Linda Levy Peck (ed.), *The Mental World of the Jacobean Court* (Cambridge: Cambridge University Press, 1991), ch. 3; J.P. Sommerville, 'James I and the divine right of kings', in *Ibid.*, ch. 4; Fincham and Lake, 'The ecclesiastical policies of James I and Charles I'; W.B. Patterson, *King James VI and I and the Reunion of Christendom* (Cambridge: Cambridge University Press, 1997); Smith, *The Stuart Parliaments 1603–1689* (London: Arnold, 1999); Julian Goodare and Michael Lynch (eds), *The Reign of James VI* (East Linton: Tuckwell, 2000); Michael B. Young, *James VI and I and the History of Homosexuality* (Basingstoke: Macmillan, 2000); Alastair Bellamy, *The Politics of Court Scandal in Early Modern England* (Cambridge: Cambridge University Press, 2002); Judith M. Richards, 'The English accession of James VI', *English Historical Review*, 117 (2002), pp. 513–35; Woolrych, *Britain in Revolution*, pp. 24–31.
33. Russell, *The Causes of the English Civil War*, p. 211.
34. Young, *Charles I*, passim; quotation on p. 176.
35. Reeve, *Charles I and the Road to Personal Rule*, pp. 172 9.
36. Durston, *Charles I*, passim.
37. David Stevenson, *The Scottish Revolution 1637–1644* (Newton Abbot: David and Charles, 1973); Peter Donald, *An Uncounselled King: Charles I and the Scottish Troubles 1637–1641* (Cambridge: Cambridge University Press, 1990); Alan I. Macinnes, *Charles I and the Making of the Covenanting Movement 1625–1641* (Edinburgh: Donald, 1991); John Scally, 'Counsel in crisis', in John R. Young (ed.), *Celtic Dimensions of the British Civil Wars* (Edinburgh: Donald, 1997), ch. 2.
38. Woolrych, *Britain in Revolution*, pp. 49–401.
39. James Sharpe, *Instruments of Darkness: Witchcraft in England 1550–1750* (London: Hamilton, 1996), pp. 105–48, 213–35 and *The Bewitching of Anne Gunter* (London: Profile, 1999), p. 209.
40. Sharpe, *The Personal Rule of Charles I*, p. 954.
41. Kevin Sharpe, 'Private conscience and public duty in the writings of Charles I', *Historical Journal*, 40 (1997), pp. 643–66.
42. Sharpe, *The Personal Rule of Charles I*, p. 954.
43. Russell, *The Causes of the English Civil War*, p. 210.
44. The sources for the numbers are given in Ronald Hutton, *The Restoration* (Oxford: Oxford University Press, 1985), pp. 58–9.
45. This is to accept the reading of Charles's mentality made by Sharpe, 'Private conscience and public duty', which seems wholly persuasive to me and has not hitherto been challenged.

4 Oliver Cromwell

1. Timothy Lang, *The Victorians and the Stuart Heritage* (Cambridge: Cambridge University Press, 1995); Blair Worden, *Roundhead Reputations: The English Civil War and the Passions of Posterity* (London: Allen Lane, 2001), pp. 215–95. Valuable pioneering work into the subject was carried out by the colloquium reported in T.W. Mason, 'Nineteenth-century Cromwell', *Past and Present*, 40 (1968), pp. 187–91; and by J.P. Dunbabin, 'Oliver Cromwell's popular image in nineteenth-century England', in J. Bromley and E.H. Karsman (eds), *Britain and the Netherlands*, 5 (1976), pp. 140–63.

2. Alan Smith, 'The image of Cromwell in folklore and tradition', *Folklore*, 79 (1968), pp. 17–39; the Wallingford incident is on p. 17.

3. John Morrill (ed.), *Cromwell and the English Revolution* (Harlow: Longman, 1990); Barry Coward, *Oliver Cromwell* (Harlow: Longman, 1991); Peter Gaunt, *Oliver Cromwell* (Oxford: Blackwell, 1996); Derek Hirst, *England in Conflict 1603–1660* (London: Arnold, 1999), chs 11–12; Laura Lunger Knoppers, *Constructing Cromwell* (Cambridge: Cambridge University Press, 2000); J.C. Davis, *Oliver Cromwell* (London: Arnold, 2001); Austin Woolrych, *Britain in Revolution* (Oxford: Oxford University Press, 2002), pp. 363–702.

4. John Morrill, 'Textualising and contextualising Cromwell', *Historical Journal*, 33 (1990), pp. 629–39, makes an analysis of the respective editions, and editorial strategies. I have employed Abbott here for the letters, of which he has a larger collection, but Lomas's augmentation of Carlyle for the speeches, because the variant versions are more clearly represented there.

5. John Morrill, 'Cromwell and his contemporaries', in Morrill (ed.), *Oliver Cromwell*, p. 259.

6. *Ibid.*, p. 281.

7. Morrill, 'Textualising and contextualising Cromwell', pp. 629, 639.

8. Blair Worden, 'Oliver Cromwell and the sin of Achan', in Derek Beales and Geoffrey Best (eds), *History, Society and the Churches* (Cambridge: Cambridge University Press, 1985), pp. 125–46; 'Toleration and the Cromwellian protectorate', in W.J. Sheils (ed.), *Persecution and Toleration* (Studies in Church History 21, Oxford University Press, 1984), pp. 199–223; 'Providence and politics in Cromwellian England', *Past and Present*, 109 (1985), pp. 55–99.

9. Eric Porter, 'A cloak for knavery: Kingship, the army and the first protectorate parliament 1654–55', *The Seventeenth Century*, 17, 2002, pp. 187–205.

10. Carol S. Egloff, 'The search for a Cromwellian settlement: Exclusion from the second protectorate parliament', 'Part One: The process and its architects', *Parliamentary History*, 17 (1998), pp. 178–97; 'Part Two: The excluded members and the reactions to exclusion', *Parliamentary History*, 17 (1998), pp. 301–22.

11. Sean Kelsey, *Inventing a Republic: The Political Culture of the English Commonwealth 1649–1653* (Manchester: Manchester University Press, 1997).

12. Abbott, *Writings and Speeches*, i, pp. 287–8.

13. For these two qualities, see particularly J.C. Davis, 'Cromwell's religion', in Morrill (ed.), *Oliver Cromwell and the English Revolution*, ch. 7.

14. Coward, *Oliver Cromwell*, pp. 105–6; Gaunt, *Cromwell*, ch. 7; Woolrych, *Britain in Revolution*, p. 595.

15. Worden, 'Toleration and the Cromwellian protectorate'; J.C. Davis, 'Religion and the struggle for freedom in the English Revolution', Historical Journal, 25 (1992), pp. 507–30.

16. Abbott, *Writings and Speeches*, vol. i, p. 256.

17. *Ibid.*, vol. ii, pp. 258, 277–8, 287–8.

18. Glenn Burgess, 'Was the English Civil War a war of religion?', Huntington Library Quarterly, 61 (2000), pp. 173–201.

19. Abbott, *Writings and Speeches*, Vol. i, p. 360.

20. *Ibid.*, vol. iv, p. 510.

21. *Ibid.*, vol. ii, pp. 196–205, 303.

22. *Ibid.*, vol. i, pp. 541–2.

23. The logistics are worked out and the sources cited in Ronald Hutton, *Charles II* (Oxford: Oxford University Press, 1989), pp. 63–7.

24. Abbott, *Writings and Speeches*, vol. ii, p. 458.

25. *Ibid.*, vol. i, p. 365.

26. These conclusions are all drawn in the most careful study of the battle so far; Glenn Foard, *Naseby: The Decisive Campaign* (Guildford: Pryor, 1995).

27. Abbott, *Writings and Speeches*, vol. ii, p. 146.

28. *Ibid.*, vol. ii, pp. 196–205.

29. I read the original manuscript at its home of Mapperton House in 1986, because of the kindness of Victor Montagu. The transcription edited by C.H. Firth in *The Clarke Papers*, vol. iii (Camden Society, 1899), pp. 203–8, is perfectly accurate.

30. Abbott, *Writings and Speeches*, vol. iii, pp. 878–91.

31. Thomas Carlyle, *The Letters and Speeches of Oliver Cromwell*, ed. by S.C. Lomas (London, 1904), vol. ii, pp. 510–21, 534.

32. Ronald Hutton, *The Restoration: a Political and Religious History of England and Wales 1657–1667* (Oxford: Oxford University Press, 1985), p. 7 and sources cited there.

33. Carlyle, *Letters and Speeches*, vol. iii, p. 6.

34. Morrill, 'Cromwell and his contemporaries', pp. 259–81.

35. Morrill, 'Introduction', in Morrill (ed.), *Oliver Cromwell*, pp. 14, 18.

36. Carlyle, *Letter and Speeches*, vol. ii, pp. 366, 386.

37. *Ibid.*, vol. ii, pp. 511, 543, 548.

38. These incidents were highlighted in my textbook, Ronald Hutton, *The British Republic 1649–1660* (Basingstoke: Macmillan, 1990), pp. 67–9, but have not been dealt with properly in subsequent works.

39. Abbott, *Writings and Speeches*, vol. ii, p. 453.

40. Carlyle, *Letters and Speeches*, vol. ii, pp. 406, 427–8.

41. *Ibid.* vol. ii, pp. 543, 548.

42. *Ibid.*, vol. ii., p. 367.

43. *Ibid.*, vol. ii, p. 549.

44. Woolrych, *Britain in Revolution*, p. 564.

45. Carlyle, *Letters and Speeches*, vol. ii, pp. 341, 343, 413.

46. *Ibid.*, vol. ii, pp. 279–94, 341–58.

47. Davis, *Oliver Cromwell*, passim, but especially pp. 65–87.

48. Carlyle, *Letters and Speeches*, vol. ii, p. 539.

49. C.H Firth (ed.), *The Clarke Papers*, I (Camden Society, New Series 49, 1891), pp. 226–418.

50. *Ibid.*, pp. 176–214.

51. *The Hunting of the Foxes*, quoted in Abbott, *Writings and Speeches*, ii, p. 135.

52. Abbott, *Writings and Speeches*, vol. iii, p. 613.

53. *Ibid.*, vol. ii, pp. 12–62.

54. Knoppers, *Constructing Cromwell*, pp. 107–31.

55. Abbott, *Writings and Speeches*, vol. i, pp. 677–707; quotation on p. 699.

56. The two principal authorities on these events are at present Austin Woolrych, *Soldiers and Statesmen* (Oxford: Oxford University Press, 1987), pp. 106–14 and *Britain in Revolution*, pp. 350–450; and Ian Gentles, *The New Model Army in England, Scotland and Ireland 1645–1653* (Oxford: Blackwell, 1991), pp. 144–314. The best consideration of Cromwell's role in the events of December 1648 to February 1649 is in Edward Beesley, 'Aspects of the English Revolution' (unpublished Ph.D. thesis, Bristol University, 2001), ch. 1.

57. Abbott, *Writings and Speeches*, vol. i, pp. 452–5; Woolrych, *Britain in Revolution*, pp. 363–5; and *Soldiers and Statesmen*, pp. 105–13; Gentles, *New Model Army*, pp. 169–73.

58. Abbott, *Writings and Speeches*, vol. i, pp. 551–2; Woolrych, *Britain in Revolution*, pp. 394–5; and *Soliders and Statesmen*, pp. 268–9; Gentles, *New Model Army*, p. 220; Davis, *Oliver Cromwell*, pp. 149–61.

59. Accounts of the episode are printed in Abbott, *Writings and Speeches*, vol. ii, pp. 637–46. The quotations here are from that by Streater, as given in Gentles, *New Model Army*, pp. 432–7.

60. A.B. Worden, 'The bill for a new representative', *English Historical Review*, 86 (1971), pp. 473–96.

61. For example, A.B. Worden, *The Rump Parliament* (Cambridge: Cambridge University Press, 1974), pp. 334–9; Austin Woolrych, *Commonwealth to*

Protectorate (Oxford: Oxford University Press, 1982), pp. 1–99 and *Britain in Revolution*, pp. 527–35; Gentles, *New Model Army*, pp. 432–7; Hirst, *England in Conflict*, p. 278.

62. Abbott, *Writings and Speeches*, vol. iii, pp. 5–8.
63. Carlyle, *Letters and Speeches*, vol. ii, pp. 279–87.
64. *Ibid.*, vol. ii, pp. 369–70.
65. *Ibid.*, vol. iii, pp. 91–7.
66. This was suggested by Worden, 'The bill for a new representative', p. 495, and accepted by Woolrych, *Britain in Revolution*, p. 535. Significantly, both are historians normally inclined to emphasise Cromwell's nobler aspects.
67. The leading authority on these events is Woolrych, *Commonwealth to Protectorate*, pp. 145–350; and *Britain in Revolution*, pp. 542–59.
68. General accounts of these events, with the references to primary sources, are given in Antonia Fraser, *Cromwell: Our Chief of Men* (London: Weidenfeld, 1973), pp. 558–68; Cecil Roth, *A History of the Jews in England* (Oxford: Oxford University Press, 1941), pp. 149–64; David S. Katz, *Philo-Semitism and the Readmission of the Jews to England 1603–1655* (Oxford: Oxford University Press, 1982), pp. 189–241. The quotation from Cromwell's speech, the significance of which has not hitherto been associated with this issue, is taken from Carlyle, *Letters and Speeches*, vol. ii, 536.
69. This is the one favoured by Katz, in *Philo-Semitism*.
70. *Ibid.*, pp. 196, 224–5.
71. Lucien Wolf, *Essays in Jewish History*, ed. by Cecil Roth (London: Jewish Historical Society of England, 1934), pp. 93–114; Roth, *History of the Jews in England*, pp. 157–60; Fraser, *Cromwell*, p. 568.
72. For a short overview of the system, see Hutton, *British Republic*, pp. 68–72, 82–6. The detailed and comprehensive survey is from Christopher Durston, *Cromwell's Major-Generals* (Manchester: Manchester University Press, 2001).
73. *Ibid.*, pp. 206–27.
74. For example, Worden, 'Oliver Cromwell and the sin of Achan', pp. 144–5; Hirst, *England in Conflict*, pp. 308–9; Woolrych, *Britain in Revolution*, pp. 652–60; Coward, *Oliver Cromwell*, pp. 150–4.
75. Two paintings of the moment were exhibited in the 1850s alone: Thomas Musgrove Joy, 'Suspended between these fears…' (1850) and Robert Graves, 'Cromwell resolving to refuse the crown' (1858).
76. Carlyle, *Letters and Speeches*, vol. iii, pp. 77–138.
77. A point made by Austin Woolrych, normally very favourable to Cromwell: *Britain in Revolution*, p. 653.
78. Abbott, *Writings and Speeches*, vol. iv, pp. 317–18.
79. Carlyle, *Letters and Speeches*, vol. iii, pp. 27–115; quotation p. 70.
80. *Ibid.*, pp. 113–15.
81. Sources at n. 74.

82. Abbott, *Writings and Speeches*, vol. iv, pp. 531, 732.
83. Henry Reece, 'The military presence in England 1649–1660' (unpublished Oxford D.Phil. thesis, 1981), ch. 3.
84. Jeffrey R. Collins, 'The church settlement of Oliver Cromwell', *History*, 87 (2002), pp. 18–40; Davis, 'Cromwell's religion', in Morrill (ed.), *Cromwell and the English Revolution*, ch. 7.
85. The classic study of all this remains T.C. Barnard, *Cromwellian Ireland* (Oxford: Oxford University Press, 1975).
86. The best study of him is David Farr, *John Lambert* (Woodbridge: Boydell, 2003).
87. Hutton, *The Restoration*, pp. 19–21, and sources cited there.
88. In Hutton, *British Republic*, passim.

▓ 5 Charles II

1. David C. Douglas, *William the Conqueror* (London: Eyre and Spottiswoode, 1964), preface.
2. Charles Ross, *Edward IV* (1974) and *Richard III* (1981). Both published in London by Methuen.
3. John Miller, *Popery and Politics in England 1660–1688* (Cambridge: Cambridge University Press, 1973) *James II: A Study in Kingship* (Hove: Wayland, 1978).
4. Tony Claydon, *William III* (Harlow: Pearson, 2002), p. vii.
5. Andrew Browning, *Thomas Osborne, Earl of Danby* (Glasgow: Jackson, 1951); J.P. Kenyon, *Robert Spencer, Earl of Sunderland* (London: Longman, 1958); K.H.D. Haley, *The First Earl of Shaftesbury* (Oxford: Oxford University Press, 1968).
6. Robert Gittings, *The Nature of Biography* (London: Heinemann, 1978), pp. 10, 39, 58; James F. Veninga (ed), *The Biographer's Gift* (College Station, Texas: Texas A & M University Press, 1983), pp. 34, 37.
7. Thomas Babington Macaulay, *History of England* (1848: Longman repr. 1906), vol. i. p. 179.
8. George Macaulay Trevelyan, *England under the Stuarts* (London: Methuen, 1904), pp. 330, 355, 365.
9. Osmund Airy, *Charles II* (London: Goupil, 1901), pp. 276–7.
10. Keith Feiling, *British Foreign Policy 1660–1672* (London: Macmillan, 1930), pp. 22–7; David Ogg, *England in the Reign of Charles II* (Oxford: Oxford University Press, 1934), pp. 148–90, 322–50, 450–4; G.N. Clark, *The Later Stuarts 1660–1714* (Oxford: Oxford University Press, 1934), pp. 1–2.
11. Clyde L. Grose, 'Charles the Second of England', *American Historical Review*, 43 (1937–38), pp. 533–41.
12. K.H.D. Haley, *Charles II* (London: Historical Association, 1966), pp. 11, 14, 22.
13. J. Jones, 'Introduction: Main trends in Restoration England', in Jones (ed.), *The Restored Monarchy 1660–1688* (London: Macmillan, 1979), pp. 10–12; Miller,

James II, p. 39; J.P. Kenyon, *Stuart England* (Harmondsworth: Penguin, 1978), pp. 208, 237–8.

14. H.M. Imbert-Terry, *A Misjudged Monarch* (London: Heinemann, 1917).
15. E. Beresford Chancellor, *Old Rowley* (London: Allan, 1924); John Drinkwater, *Mr Charles* (London: Hodder and Stoughton, 1926); Arthur Irwin Dasent, *The Private Life of Charles II* (London: Cassell, 1927); David Loth, *Royal Charles* (London: Routledge, 1931); John Hayward, *Charles II* London (Duckworth, 1933).
16. Arthur Bryant, *King Charles II* (London: Longmans, 1931), p. 95.
17. *Ibid.*, pp. 344, 349.
18. *Ibid.*, p. 259.
19. Dennis Wheatley, *Old Rowley* (London: Hutchinson, 1933), p. 180.
20. Dennis Wheatley, *The Time Has Come: Volume III: Drink and Ink 1919–1977* (London: Hutchinson, 1979), pp. 166–7, 254–5.
21. Wheatley, *Old Rowley*, p. 11.
22. J.P. Kenyon, 'The reign of Charles II', *Historical Journal*, 13 (1957), p. 82; Haley, *Charles II*, p. 4.
23. Antonia Fraser, *King Charles II* (London: Weidenfeld, 1979), pp. 11, 463, 469.
24. Richard Ollard, *The Image of the King* (London: Hodder and Stoughton, 1979), p. 20.
25. C.D. Chandaman, *The English Public Revenue 1660–1688* (Oxford: Oxford University Press, 1975).
26. For example, Fraser, *King Charles II*, p. 276.
27. Ronald Hutton, *The Restoration* (Oxford: Oxford University Press, 1985), p. 294.
28. Ronald Hutton, 'The other Arthurian legend', *History Today*, 34 (October 1984), pp. 60–1.
29. Hutton, *The Restoration*, pp. 185–96, 239–40, 271–5.
30. *Ibid.*, pp. 275–84, 162–3; Ronald Hutton, *Charles II* (Oxford: Oxford University Press, 1989), p. 172.
31. Hutton, *The Restoration*, pp. 147, 187–90, 204–12.
32. Ronald Hutton, 'The making of the Secret Treaty of Dover', *Historical Journal*, 29 (1986), pp. 297–318.
33. Hutton, *Charles II*, pp. 413–14.
34. *Ibid.*, pp. 279–80.
35. Christopher Hill, 'The king who kept his head', *The Guardian*, 30 Nov. 1989; Jonathan Clark, 'The politics of absolute power', *The Times*, Nov. 1989 (I regret that my cutting did not include the date); J. Enoch Powell, 'God's fish! They know nothing', *The Sunday Telegraph*, 3 December 1989.
36. Antonia Fraser, 'Restoration romantic', *The Sunday Times*, 10 December 1989.
37. Richard Ollard, 'To the last syllable of recorded fact', *The Spectator*, January 1990.
38. Paul Seaward, 'Court and parliament: The making of government policy, 1661–1665' (Oxford D.Phil., 1985).

39. Hutton, *Charles II*, pp. 496–7.
40. Paul Seaward, *The Cavalier Parliament and the Reconstruction of the Old Regime* (Cambridge: Cambridge University Press, 1989).
41. John Morrill, 'The floodlit king', *History Today* (June 1990), p. 55.
42. Ronald Hutton, 'The religion of Charles II', in R. Malcolm Smuts (ed.), *The Stuart Court and Europe* (Cambridge: Cambridge University Press, 1996), pp. 228–46.
43. J. R. Jones, *Charles II: Royal Politician* (London: Allen and Unwin, 1987).
44. Ronald Hutton, 'Knocking the gilt off the Golden Days', *Historical Journal*, 31 (1988), pp. 201–6.
45. John Miller, *Charles II* (London: Weidenfeld, 1991).
46. *Ibid.*, p. 189; cf. Hutton, *Charles II*, pp. 284–5.
47. Nancy Maguire, 'The duchess of Portsmouth: English royal consort and French politician', in Smuts (ed.), *The Stuart Court and Europe*, pp. 247–73.
48. Sonya Wynne, 'The mistresses of Charles II and Restoration Court politics', in Eveline Cruickshanks (ed.), *The Stuart Courts* (Stroud: Sutton, 2000), pp. 171–90.
49. D.M. Starkey, *The Reign of Henry VIII* (London: George Philip, 1985); R.M. Warnicke, 'The fall of Anne Boleyn: A reassessment', *History*, 70 (1985), pp. 1–15; E.W. Ives, *Anne Boleyn* (Oxford: Blackwell, 1986); E.W. Ives, *Faction in Tudor England* (2nd edn, London: Historical Association, 1986); R.M. Warnicke, 'Sexual heresy at the court of Henry VIII', *Historical Journal*, 30 (1987), pp. 247–68 and *The Rise and Fall of Anne Boleyn* (Cambridge: Cambridge University Press, 1989); Peter Gwyn, *The King's Cardinal* (London: Barie and Jenkins, 1990); G.W. Bernard, 'The fall of Anne Boleyn', *'English Historical Review* 106 (1991), pp. 584–610; E.W. Ives, 'The fall of Wolsey', in S.J. Gunn and P.G. Lindley (eds), *Cardinal Wolsey* (Cambridge: Cambridge University Press, 1991), pp. 300–5; E.W. Ives, 'The fall of Anne Boleyn reconsidered', *Ibid.*, 107 (1992), pp. 651–64; G.W. Bernard, 'The fall of Anne Boleyn: A rejoinder', *Ibid.*, 97 (1992), pp. 665–74; R.M. Warnicke, 'The fall of Anne Boleyn revisited', *Ibid.*, 108 (1993), pp. 653–65; G.W. Bernard, 'Anne Boleyn's religion', *Historical Journal*, 36 (1993), pp. 1–20; J.S. Block, *Factional Politics and the English Reformation* (Woodbridge: Brewer, 1993); E.W. Ives, 'Anne Boleyn and the early reformation in England', *Historical Journal*, 37 (1994), pp. 389–400; Diarmaid MacCulloch (ed.), *The Reign of Henry VIII* (London: Macmillan, 1995) and *Thomas Cranmer* (New Haven: Yale University Press, 1996).
50. Steven Gunn, 'The structures of politics in early Tudor England', *Transactions of the Royal Historical Society* 6th ser., 5 (1995), pp. 59–90; quotation from p. 62.
51. Conrad Russell, *The Fall of the British Monarchies 1637–1642* (Oxford: Oxford University Press, 1991). For a summary of the problem see Norah Carlin, *The Causes of the English Civil War* (Oxford: Blackwell, 1999), p. 27.
52. John Guy, *Thomas More* (London: Arnold, 2000); quotations on pp. xi, 62, 223.
53. John Guy, 'General Introduction' in John Guy (ed.), *The Tudor Monarchy* (London: Arnold, 1997), pp. 1–12.

54. Stephen Alford, 'Politics and political history in the Tudor century', *Historical Journal*, 42 (1999), pp. 535–48.
55. Gunn, 'The structures of politics', pp. 59–60.
56. As examples see John Adamson (ed.), *The Princely Courts of Europe* (London: Weidenfeld, 1999) and Cruickshanks (ed.), *The Stuart Courts*.
57. Peter Burke, *The Fabrication of Louis XIV* (New Haven: Yale University Press, 1992), quotation on p. 1.
58. Ian Dunlop, *Louis XIV* (London: Chatto and Windus, 2000).
59. John Spurr, *England in the 1670s* (Oxford: Blackwell, 2000); quotation on p. xiii.
60. John Miller, *After the Civil Wars: English Politics and Government in the Reign of Charles II* (London: Longman, 2000).
61. David Starkey, *Elizabeth: Apprenticeship* (London: Chatto and Windus, 2000).
62. *Ibid.*, pp. x–xi, 225–6.
63. See the reviews by Lorna Hutson in *The Times Literary Supplement* (16 June 2000), pp. 10–11 and Patrick Collinson in *The London Review of Books* (6 July 2000), p. 17.
64. David Cressy, *Travesties and Transgressions in Tudor and Stuart England* (Oxford: Oxford University Press, 1999), p. 253.
65. R. Malcolm Smuts, *Culture and Power in England 1585–1685* (London: Macmillan, 1999), pp. 103, 106, 108.

▓ 6 The Glorious Revolution

1. For examples, see Robert Colls, 'Englishness and the political culture', in Robert Colls and Philip Dodd (eds), *Englishness: Politics and Culture* (London: Croom Helm, 1986), pp. 31–5 and Timothy Lang, *The Victorians and the Stuart Heritage* (Cambridge: Cambridge University Press, 1995), pp. 13–74.
2. Angus McInnes, 'When was the English Revolution?', *History*, 67 (1982), pp. 387–92.
3. J.R. Jones, *The Revolution of 1688 in England* (London: Weidenfeld, 1972); J.R. Western, *Monarchy and Revolution* (London: Blandford, 1972).
4. McInnes, 'When was the English Revolution?'; John Morrill, 'The sensible revolution, 1688', in John Morrill, *The Nature of the English Revolution* (London: Longman, 1993), ch. 20; Robert Beddard, 'The unexpected Whig Revolution of 1688', in Robert Beddard (ed.), *The Revolutions of 1688* (Oxford: Oxford University Press, 1991), ch. 1; John Childs, '1688', *History*, 73 (1988), pp. 398–424; W.A. Speck, *The Reluctant Revolutionaries: Englishmen and the Revolution of 1688* (Oxford: Oxford University Press, 1988); Lois Schwoerer, (ed.), *The Revolution of 1688–1689* (Cambridge: Cambridge University Press, 1992), introduction. Jonathan Israel, 'General introduction', in Jonathan I. Israel (ed.), *The Anglo-Dutch Moment* (Cambridge: Cambridge University Press, 1991), p. 10.

5. J.C.D. Clark, *Revolution and Rebellion* (Cambridge: Cambridge University Press, 1986); Daniel Szechi, 'Mythistory versus history: The fading of the Revolution of 1688', *Historical Journal*, 33 (1990), pp. 143–53; Tim Harris, 'From rage of party to age of oligarchy', *Journal of Modern History*, 64 (1992), pp. 700–20; Jeremy Black, *Eighteenth-Century Britain 1688–1783* (Basingstoke: Palgrave, 2001), p. 1; Jonathan Scott, *England's Troubles* (Cambridge: Cambridge University Press, 2000), pp. 474–96, and esp. p. 475.

6. John Miller, *Popery and Politics in England 1660–1688* (Cambridge: Cambridge University Press, 1973); *James II: A Study in Kingship* (Hove: Wayland, 1978); 'Charles II and his parliaments', *Transactions of the Royal Historical Society* 5th series, 32 (1982), pp. 1–24; 'The potential for "Absolutism" in late Stuart England', *History*, 69 (1984), pp. 187–207; *Bourbon and Stuart* (London: Philip, 1987), chs 6–8.

7. John Miller, *An English Absolutism* (London: Historical Association, 1993).

8. Jonathan Scott, 'Radicalism and Restoration: The shape of the Stuart experience', *Historical Journal*, 31 (1988), pp. 453–67; 'England's troubles: Exhuming the Popish Plot', in Tim Harris, Paul Seaward and Mark Goldie (eds), *The Politics of Religion in Restoration England* (Oxford: Blackwell, 1990), ch. 5; *Algernon Sidney and the Restoration Crisis 1677–1683* (Cambridge: Cambridge University Press, 1991); 'England's troubles 1603–1702', in R. Malcolm Smuts (ed.), *The Stuart Court and Europe* (Cambridge: Cambridge University Press, 1996), pp. 20–38; John Miller, *After the Civil Wars: English Politics and Government in the Reign of Charles II* (London: Longman, 2000), pp. 181–279.

9. Ronald Hutton, *The Restoration* (Oxford: Oxford University Press, 1985), pp. 289–90.

10. Judith L. Hurwich, 'Dissent and catholicism in English society: A study of Warwickshire, 1660–1720', *Journal of British Studies*, 16 (1976), pp. 24–58; Jonathan Barry, 'Politics and religion in seventeenth-century Bristol', in Harris *et al.* (eds), *The Politics of Religion*, ch. 7; Philip Norrey, 'The relationship between central government and local government in Dorset, Somerset and Wiltshire 1660–1688' (Bristol University PhD thesis, 1988); Henry Lancaster, 'Nonconformity and anglican dissent in Wiltshire 1660–1688' (Bristol University PhD thesis, 1995); J.D. Ramsbottom, 'Presbyterians and "Partial Conformity" in the Restoration Church of England', *Journal of Ecclesiastical History*, 43 (1992), pp. 53–65; John Spurr, *England in the 1670s* (Oxford: Blackwell, 2000), pp. 232–40; Miller, *After the Civil Wars*, pp. 141–52; John Spurr, 'Religion in Restoration England', in Lionel J. Glassey (ed.), *The Reigns of Charles II and James VII and II* (London: Macmillan, 1997), pp. 90–124.

11. J.R. Jones, *Country and Court: England 1658–1714* (London: Arnold, 1978), pp. 2–3.

12. See sources at n. 6.

13. William Beik, *Absolutism and Society in Seventeenth-Century France* (Cambridge: Cambridge University Press, 1985); James B. Collins, *Fiscal Limits of Absolutism* (Berkeley: University of California Press, 1988); David Parker, 'Sovereignty, absolutism and the function of the law in seventeenth-century France', *Past and Present*, 122 (1989), pp. 36–74; Donna Bohanan, *Old and New Nobility in Aix-en-Provence* (Baton Rouge: University of Louisiana Press, 1992); Hilton L. Root, *Peasants and king in Burgundy* (Berkeley: University of California Press, 1987); Roger Mettam, *Power and Faction in Louis XIV's France* (Oxford: Blackwell, 1988), and 'France', in John Miller (ed.), *Absolutism in Seventeenth-Century Europe* (London: Macmillan, 1990), ch. 2.

14. The essays in Miller (ed.), *Absolutism* provide the most recent survey in English. Also very relevant are Mary Fulbrook, *Piety and Politics* (Cambridge: Cambridge University Press, 1983) and A.F. Upton, *Charles XI and Swedish Absolutism* (Cambridge: Cambridge University Press, 1998).

15. Stated most clearly by John Miller, 'Britain', in Miller (ed.), *Absolutism*, ch. 8.

16. Mark Goldie, 'The political thought of the Anglican Revolution', in Beddard (ed.), *Revolutions of 1688*, ch. 2.

17. Peter Laslett (ed.), *Patriarcha and other Political Works* (1949), p. 45.

18. Tim Harris, 'Tories and the rule of law in the reign of Charles II', *The Seventeenth Century*, 8 (1993), pp. 9–27.

19. John Childs, *The Army, James II and the Glorious Revolution* (Manchester: Manchester University Press, 1980), ch. 4.

20. Western, *Monarchy and Revolution*, p. 111.

21. Norrey, thesis, chs 2–3; Andrew M. Coleby, *Central Government and the Localities: Hampshire, 1649–1689* (Cambridge: Cambridge University Press, 1987), pp. 191–5.

22. *Ibid.*, p. 222.

23. Sources to 1988 gathered and analysed in Ronald Hutton, *Charles II* (Oxford: Oxford University Press, 1989), pp. 433–5. To them can now be added Paul D. Halliday, *Dismembering the Body Politic: Partisan Politics in England's Towns, 1650–1730* (Cambridge: Cambridge University Press, 1999).

24. Hutton, *Charles II*, pp. 438–41.

25. On the details of these processes, see Michael J. Braddick, *State Formation in Early Modern England c. 1550–1750* (Cambridge: Cambridge University Press, 2000).

26. Seven out of twelve: James I, II, III and IV; Mary; Henry (Darnley); and Charles I.

27. Miller, *James II*; John Callow, *The Making of King James II* (Stroud: Sutton, 2001).

28. Hutton, *Charles II*, pp. 301–2.

29. Portrayed very effectively in Barillon's despatches, Public Record Office, PRO/31/3/160–61.

30. Miller, *Popery and Politics*, p. 206, and 'James II and toleration', in Eveline Cruickshanks (ed.), *By Force or Default?* (Edinburgh: Donald, 1989), ch. 2. It is also true that having adopted a policy of toleration, James adhered to it consistently thereafter: Eveline Cruickshanks, *The Glorious Revolution* (London: Macmillan, 2000), pp. 17–21, 56.
31. Western, *Monarchy and Revolution*, collects the examples.
32. Hutton, *Charles II*, p. 302.
33. Coleby, *Central Government*, pp. 169–78.
34. Miller, *Popery and Politics*, chs 10–12.
35. Public Record Office, PRO/31/3/161, Barillon, 16/26 July 1685.
36. Recorded, successively, in Hutton, *Charles II, passim*.
37. J.M. Sosin, *English America and the Restoration Monarchy of Charles II* (Lincoln: University of Nebraska Press, 1980) and *English America and the Revolution of 1688* (Lincoln: Nebraska University Press, 1982).
38. Charles James Fox, *A History of the Early Part of the Reign of James II* (1808), appendix, p. cxxii.
39. Miller, *Popery and Politics*, chs 10–12.
40. T.B. Howell (ed.), *A Complete Collection of State Trials* (1812), vol. 12, pp. 183–522; Bodleian Library, Rawlinson Letters 9a, ff. 107–8.
41. Robin Clifton, *The Last Popular Rebellion* (London: Temple Smith, 1984), pp. 231–9.
42. Childs, *The Army*, ch. 4.
43. Anthony Fletcher, *Reform in the Provinces* (New Haven: Yale UP, 1986), p. 25.
44. Norrey, thesis, ch. III.ii.
45. Eveline Cruickshanks, 'The Revolution and the localities: Examples of loyalty to James II', in Cruickshanks (ed.), *By Force or Default?*, ch. 3; Mark Goldie, 'John Locke's circle and James II', *Historical Journal*, 35 (1992), pp. 557–86 and 'James II and the dissenters' revenge', *Bulletin of the Institute of Historical Research*, 66 (1993), pp. 53–88; Norrey, thesis, ch. III.ii.
46. Western, *Monarchy and Revolution*, pp. 86, 131–3.
47. Jones, *Revolution of 1688*, p. 165; Miller, *James II*, p. 197; Speck, *Reluctant Revolutionaries*, pp. 131–2; M.J. Short, 'The corporation of Hull and the government of James II', *Bulletin of the Institute of Historical Research*, 71 (1998), pp. 172–95.
48. What follows is based on an analysis of the sources listed in footnotes 16, 18 and 19 of Chapter 3 of this book, plus Steven G. Ellis, *Reform and Revival: English Government in Ireland 1470–1534* (Woodbridge: Boydell, 1986); and *Tudor Ireland* (London: Longman, 1985); Michelle O Riordan, *The Gaelic Mind and the Collapse of the Gaelic World* (Cork: Studies in Irish History, 1990); George Boyce, Robert Eccleshall and Vincent Geoghan (eds), *Political Thought in Ireland Since the Seventeenth Century* (London: Routledge, 1993); Steven G. Ellis, 'The collapse of the Gaelic world, 1540–1650', *Irish Historical Studies*, 31 (1999),

pp. 449–69; Julian Goodare and Michael Lynch (eds), *The Reign of James VI* (East Linton: Tuckwell, 2000); Allen I. MacInnes, *Clanship, Commerce and the House of Stuart, 1603–1788* (East Linton: Tuckwell, 1996).

49. N. Japikse (ed.), *Correspondentie van Willem III en van Hans Willem Bentinck* (1928), vol. i, pt ii, no. 8.

50. Jeremy Black, 'The Revolution and the development of British foreign policy', in Cruickshanks (ed.), *By Force or Default?*, ch. 8; James Jones, 'French intervention in English and Dutch politics 1677–88', in Jeremy Black (ed.), *Knights Errant and True Englishmen* (Edinburgh: Donald, 1989), ch. 1; John Stoye, 'Europe and the Revolution of 1688' and Simon Groenveld, 'The Dutch side of the Glorious Revolution', in Beddard (ed.), *Revolutions of 1688*, chs 5 and 6; K.H.D. Haley, 'The Dutch, the invasion of England, and the alliance of 1689' and John C. Rule, 'France caught between two balances', in Schwoerer (ed.), *Revolution of 1688–9*, chs 1 and 2.

51. Dale Hoak, 'The Anglo-Dutch Revolution of 1688–89', in Dale Hoak and Mordechai Feingold (ed.), *The World of William and Mary* (Stanford, CA: Stanford University Press, 1996), p. 24.

52. Japikse, *Correspondentie*, vol. i, pt. ii, pp. 249–50; Jones, *Revolution of 1688*, pp. 198–9.

53. Beddard, *Revolutions of 1688*, ch. 1.

54. Speck, *Reluctant Revolutionaries*, ch. 6.

55. F.W. Maitland, *The Constitutional History of England* (1908), p. 343.

56. Speck, *Reluctant Revolutionaries*, chs 7 and 11; Schwoerer, introduction to *The Revolution of 1688–9*.

57. Morrill, 'The sensible revolution', *passim*.

58. Clark, *Revolution and Rebellion*, pp. 1–7, 97–106.

59. A point made by Szechi, 'Mythistory', pp. 144–53.

60. A point made by Harris, 'Rage of party', pp. 700–02.

61. Herbert Butterfield, *The Whig Interpretation of History* (London: Bell, 1931), v.

62. *Ibid.*, pp. 39–40.

63. The entry on him by Maurice Cowling in *Who Was Who* for the 1970s makes these points with convenient concision, and a bibliography to support them.

64. Hilaire Belloc, *James II* (London: Faber, 1928).

65. For such a determined recent attempt, see Eveline Cruickshanks, *The Glorious Revolution* (London: Macmillan, 2000).

66. Jonathan I. Israel, 'Introduction' and 'The Dutch role in the Glorious Revolution', in Jonathan I. Israel (ed.), *The Anglo-Dutch Moment* (Cambridge: Cambridge University Press, 1991), pp. 1–43, 105–62; Jonathan Scott, *England's Troubles* (Cambridge: Cambridge University Press, 2000), pp. 454–73; Tony Claydon, *William III* (Harlow: Longman, 2002), passim.

Index

Abbott, Wilbur C. 97
absolutism 172, 173, 175–6, 179, 189
academic culture 2, 3, 8–10, 71,
    194–7
   see also research
Adamites 168
Adamson, John 29, 35
Adolphus, Gustavus 64
Airy, Osmund 136
Alford, Stephen 166
Anabaptists 103
Anglicanism, conservative 49, 50, 52
anthropology 155, 197
archaeology 44–5
aristocracy 26, 94
Arminianism 77, 78, 80–2, 84, 90
army
   Charles I's military reforms 64
   and Cromwell 98–9, 114–17, 118,
      120, 122–3, 124–6, 127
   development of English military
      power 63
   logistics 42–3
   professionalisation of 176
   Putney Debates 113
   see also New Model Army
Ashton, Robert 35
Aylmer, Gerald 35, 51

Baldwin, Stanley 46
Baschet transcripts 150
Beddard, Robert 172, 186
Belloc, Hilaire 190
Bennett, Martyn 36–7, 95
biography genre 132–3, 134–5, 170
Black Death 32
Black, Jeremy 172–3
Bodleian Library, Oxford University
   148
Bonnie Prince Charlie 33
Booth, George 91
Bowker, Margaret 22–3

Bradshaw, Brendan 182
Bristol, siege of 44
British Library 148, 149, 154
'the British problem' 72–3, 181–3, ·
   184–5
   see also three-kingdoms perspective
Bryant, Arthur 37, 138–40, 143–4
Burgess, Glenn 19, 66, 103
Burke, Peter 166
Butterfield, Herbert 28, 172, 188–9

Callow, John 178
Cannadine, David 8
cannon 43–4
Canny, Nicholas 182
Canterbury, Archbishop of 180
Carlin, Norah 53–4
Carlyle, Thomas 97, 100
Catherine of Braganza 145
Catholicism 21–5, 74, 77, 79
   Charles II 136, 161
   Civil War 33, 54
   Counter-Reformation 67, 174–5
   Cromwell's foreign policy 107–8
   under Elizabeth I 75, 76, 77, 78
   Ireland 36, 51, 54, 105–6,
      184, 190
   James II 178, 179, 180,
      189–90, 191
   parliamentarian conspiracy
      theories 90
   persecution of Catholics under
      Cromwell 102, 105–6, 107–8
   see also Arminianism; Christianity;
      Church
The Causes of the English Civil War
   (Hughes) 49–50
cavalry tactics 64
Cecil, William 60
Celtic cultures 182
central government 62, 64
Chandaman, C.D. 142

Charles I, King of England 86–92, 94, 164
  Burgess on 66
  Church of England 80, 81–2, 84
  common support for 48
  Elton on 13
  escape from army's custody 116
  execution of 175
  failure to conform to kingly ideal 177
  finance 61–2
  Hirst on 16
  Hutton family members 5
  and Ireland 69–70
  military reforms 64
  Parliament role 65
  Personal Rule 19, 62–3, 68, 80–1, 82–3, 84, 86–8
  Scottish uprising against 51, 68–9, 83, 88, 184
  seizure by the army 115–16
  Ship Money 5, 63, 180
  trial of 115
  see also royalists
Charles II, King of England 91, 132–70
  dismissal of Clarendon 144–5
  failure to conform to kingly ideal 177
  gossip 159, 162–3
  personality traits 136, 137–8, 140, 141, 156, 157
  popular biographies of 138–42, 143–4, 160
  popularity of 137, 138, 139, 144
  Privy Council's Committee for Foreign Affairs 163
  public image 170
  and the Quakers 145–6
  scholarly accounts 135–8, 142, 160, 162–3, 166–7
  and Scotland 184
  Secret Treaty of Dover 153, 154
  shifts in local power 176
  see also Restoration
Charles VIII, King of France 46
Childs, John 172, 176
Christianity 4–5, 74–85
  Butterfield 189
  conservative Anglicanism 49, 50, 52
  Counter-Reformation 67, 174–5

English Reformation 19, 21–5, 30, 78, 79, 84, 182
  Quakers 145–6
  Scottish Reformation 181, 182
  see also Catholicism; Church; Protestantism; religion
Christianson, Paul 14, 15, 16, 29
Church 16, 74–85
  Arminianism 77, 78, 80–2, 84, 90
  Charles II 139
  Civil War effect on 33
  Clark's emphasis on 26
  conservative/royalist loyalty towards 37
  Cromwell 94, 101, 102, 103, 119, 127
  freedom of worship 7
  intolerance 191
  and James II 186
  pre-Reformation 23, 24
  revisionism 29, 30
  royal authority 176
  Russell on 19
  weakened 191
  see also Catholicism; Christianity; Protestantism; Reformation; religion
Churchill, Winston 37
civil law 66
Civil War 32–58, 59, 164, 172
  350th anniversary 57, 193
  and the Church of England 74–85
  Clarendon's account of 11
  county studies 38–9, 40, 41, 42–3, 47, 48
  creation of military machinery 63
  Elton on 13
  end of 91, 173
  military technicalities 43–6
  revisionist accounts of 14–21, 30
  Second 32, 59, 91, 92, 115
  Severn valley 10
  Smuts on 169
  Third 32, 59
  three-kingdoms perspective 68–70, 72–3
  see also Charles I; Cromwell; parliamentarians; royalists
Clarendon, Edward, earl of 11, 37, 44, 144–5

Clark, George   136
Clark, Jonathan C.D.   25–7, 28, 29, 158, 172, 187
class   2, 7, 38, 48, 56
   see also middle class
Claydon, Tony   3, 133–4, 191
Cliffords of Chudleigh   153–4
Clubman associations   38, 40
Cogswell, Thomas   17, 65
Coleby, Andrew   176
Collins, Jeffrey   127
Collinson, Patrick   23, 168
common law   66, 67, 180
community   56
conservatism   12, 13, 37, 139, 140
Conservative Party   37
Convention Parliament   187
Cornish separatist identity   56–7, 70
Council of State   98, 120, 121, 127
Counter-Reformation   67, 174–5
country houses   152–4
county records offices   9, 150–1
county studies   38–9, 40
   armies and their logistics   42–3
   partisanship   41, 47, 48
   Reformation   22
   see also local evidence
'Court and Country' dichotomy   14, 16, 66
court studies   166
Coward, Barry   95
Cressy, David   168–9
Cromwell, Henry   128
Cromwell, Oliver   93–131, 170
   and the army   98–9, 114–17, 118, 120, 122–3, 124–6, 127
   biographies   97–8, 130–1
   dismissal of Parliament   117–19
   foreign policy   106–8
   his officers   126, 127–8
   Jews allowed in England   120–2
   and the law   109–11
   letters of   99–101, 102
   liberty of conscience   101–2, 103, 106, 112, 124, 130
   and the Major-Generals   122–3, 125
   military successes   45, 93, 104–5
   policy-making documents   153
   Putney Debates   113
   refusal of kingship   124–6
   reputation of   94–5, 97, 113–14
   self-justification   104, 117
   succession   128–9
Cromwell, Richard   114, 125, 127, 129
Cruickshanks, Eveline   181
Cuddy, Neil   177
cultural studies   20, 25, 56, 155
Cust, Richard   17, 18, 65
customs dues   61, 110

Darwin, Charles   148
Davis, J.C.   27, 95, 102, 112, 127
democracy
   Bryant   139
   Cromwell   130
   parliamentary   7, 64, 139, 193
   Putney Debates   113
   representative   8, 29, 113
   Wheatley   140
   see also Parliament; politics
Denison, Stephen   81
Derby, earl of   54
Derbyshire mining communities   55
devolution   71–2, 190, 197
Devon   32, 40, 50
Dickens, Geoffrey   21, 23, 24, 28
discourse theory   66
Dissenting Churches   95
Donagan, Barbara   46
Douglas, David   132–3
Dover, Secret Treaty of   153, 154
Duffy, Eamon   24
Dunlop, Ian   166
Durston, Christopher   86, 123, 130

ecological determinism   49, 50
economic determinism   17, 19–20, 49, 52, 55
Edgehill, battle of (1642)   46
Edward II, King of England   178
Edward VI, King of England   21
Elizabeth I, Queen of England   7, 86, 183
   Church of England   21, 22, 76–7, 78, 79, 80
   executions   87
   financial legacy   60, 61, 64
   mass forbidden in Ireland   106
   Starkey biography   167–8
Ellis, Steven   181, 182

Elton, Geoffrey R.   3, 194
   critique of Marxism   12
   and revisionism   13–14, 18, 21, 27, 28
   support for Clark   26, 28
Emberton, Wilfrid   44
English Civil War Society   57
The English Reformation Revised
   (Haigh)   23
English Revolution (1688)   57, 135,
   158, 171–3, 185–93
Essex   48, 49
ethnicity   56, 75
European context   191–2
European Union   72, 192
Everitt, Alan   13, 38, 49
Exclusion Crisis   186

famine   4
Farjeon, Eleanor   178
Feiling, Keith   136
Filmer, Robert   37, 176
films   34
finance   60–1, 62, 63–4, 122–3
Fleetwood, Charles   127–8
Fletcher, Anthony   15, 35, 38, 180
Foard, Glenn   45
fortifications   43–4, 64
France
   Charles II   136, 138, 153
   Cromwell alliance with   107, 108,
      127
   French Revolution   135
   influence on British culture   71, 72
   rise in power   174, 175, 182
   William of Orange opposition to
      191, 192
Fraser, Antonia   141, 142, 144, 158–9

Gardiner, Samuel Rawson   3, 15, 21
   on Cromwell   95–6
   Glorious Revolution   171–2
   on importance of religion   51
   parliamentarians   33
   Personal Rule   82, 83
   traditional historiography   6–7, 28,
      29, 86
Gaunt, Peter   95
gender   56
   see also women
Gentles, Ian   35

Gittings, Robert   134
globalisation   72
Glorious Revolution (1688)   57, 135,
   158, 171–3, 185–93
Gloucester, siege of   44
Gloucestershire   49
Goldie, Mark   176, 181
Grose, Clyde L.   136, 140
Gunn, Steven   164, 166
guns   43–4, 45–6
Guy, John   23, 165, 166

Haigh, Christopher   22–3, 24, 28,
   29, 81
Haley, Kenneth   136–7, 140
Hammond, Robert   116
Hampshire   45–6
Harris, Ronald   37
Harris, Tim   3, 172, 176
Henry I, King of England   5
Henry VIII, King of England   164, 165,
   168
Herefordshire   54, 79
'heritage' industry   58, 196
Herodotus   11
Hexter, J.H.   15, 16, 26, 28
higher education, expansion of   2, 9,
   195
Hill, Christopher   35, 49, 158
   Clark critique   26, 27
   revisionism   12, 15
   socialist modernisation of
      historiography   7
Hirst, Derek   15–16, 18, 28–9, 95
historian characteristics   12, 197
historiography   1, 3, 6, 10, 169
   'British problem'   72–3, 181–3,
      184–5
   Butterfield critique of   188, 189
   Clark   26, 27
   county studies   39
   Glorious Revolution   171
   ideology   52
   individuals   85, 86
   Personal Rule   82
   postmodern   188
   the Reformation   23, 24–5
   socio-economic vs. political
      interpretations   7
   traditional   8, 13, 15, 23, 26, 86

historiography – *continued*
  Victorian 7, 29, 30, 101, 171
  see also revisionism
History of the Rebellion (Clarendon) 11
Hobbes, Thomas 37
Holmes, Clive 35, 38, 40
Hoton, Edmund de 5
House of Commons
  Cromwell 94, 95, 96, 103, 117
  Gardiner/Notestein historiography 7
  James I 61
  purging of 91, 125
  revisionism 20
  social background of members 13
  see also Parliament
House of Lords
  abolition of 91, 111, 127
  Cromwell 94, 113
  Hirst on 16
  published journals of 10
  revisionism 16, 20
  see also Parliament
Hughes, Ann
  critique of Underdown thesis 49–50
  local issues 17, 40, 41
  parliamentarians 35
  social causes of Civil War 18, 51,
    53, 54, 55
Hunt, William 48
Hutton, Richard 5

identity
  American 19, 56, 193, 198
  Cornish and Welsh separatist
    identity 56–7, 70
  religious 75, 79
ideology 16, 18, 40, 52
Imbert-Terry, Henry 137–8, 139, 142
imperialism 35, 177
individualism 8, 74
Ingram, Martin 49
Interregnum 138, 174
Ireland, Republic of
  Catholic Confederacy 36, 51
  Celtic culture 182
  Charles II 157, 158, 184
  Counter-Reformation Catholicism 67
  creation of triple kingdom 177
  Cromwell 104, 105–6, 128
  and the English Civil War 68–71

Fleetwood governance 127–8
fragmented society 181
Glorious Revolution 187, 190–1
government of 182–3
independence of 7, 190
influence on English Crown revenues
    60–1
Irish historians' critique of
    three-kingdoms approach 73
James II's use of Irish regiments
    180–1
nationalism 192
Protestant elites 184, 192
revisionist history of 6
rising of 1641 54, 90
support for restored monarchy 174,
    183, 184
see also Northern Ireland;
    three-kingdoms perspective
Ireton, Henry 129
Israel, Jonathan 172, 191

Jacobites 36, 80, 81, 82
James I, King of England (James VI of
    Scotland)
  Church of England under 79–80
  failure to conform to kingly ideal
    177
  political thought during his reign
    65, 66
  reputation of 85–6
  rule in Scotland 183
  Scottish historians view of 67–8
  state finances 61–2
  succession to the throne 177
James II, King of England (James VII of
    Scotland)
  attempt to manipulate elections
    176
  authoritarianism 179–80
  Catholicism 178, 179, 180, 189–90,
    191
  Exclusion Crisis 186
  failure to conform to kingly ideal
    177
  and the Glorious Revolution 185–6
  Ireland 184
  Miller biography 133, 134
  poor reputation of 177–81
  religious objectives 179–80, 184–5

James II, King of England (James VII of
    Scotland) – *continued*
  Scotland   184
  see also Glorious Revolution
Jews   120–2
Johnston, Archibald   145
Jones, James R.   137, 162, 172, 175,
    176, 181
The Journal of Modern History   14
Joyce, Cornet   115–16
judiciary   180

Kelsey, Sean   98–9, 130
Kent   84
Kenyon, John   137, 140
Keroualle, Louise de   156–7
Kishlansky, Mark   18, 26, 28–9, 35
Knoppers, Laura L.   95

Lake, Peter   8, 81
Lake-Prescott, Anne   168
Lambert, John   91, 107, 129
Lamont, Willie   35
Lancashire   22, 79
land use   48–50
Lang, Timothy   35, 94, 97
Laud, Archbishop   86
Lawrence, Henry   127
lay elites   84
Levellers   37, 112, 113
Liberal Party   95, 192
liberalism   12, 137
  Clark critique   26
  prejudice against royalists   36
  Victorian   74, 188
liberty of conscience   91, 101–2, 103,
    106, 112, 124, 130
local evidence   38–9
  Charles II   144
  country houses   152–4
  county records offices   9, 150–1
  London   46–7
  partisanship   48, 53, 55
  shifts in local power during late
    Stuart era   176–7
  see also county studies; research;
    source material
local government   62, 87, 176–7, 179
localism
  county studies   38, 39, 40, 42

Morrill   51
  partisanship   40–1
  see also provincialism
Lockyer, Roger   15
Lomas, S.C.   97
London   46–7
Long Parliament
  and the Church   80, 83, 84
  and Cromwell   112, 114
  negotiations with Charles I   86, 87,
    164
  and the New Model Army   115
  Scots invasion   68
looting   47
Louis XIV, King of France   153, 156,
    166, 176, 186

Macaulay, Thomas Babington   3,
    29–30, 177
  Charles II   135
  Glorious Revolution   171, 187
  James II   178
  Whiggish interpretation of history
    172, 188, 189
MacCulloch, Diarmaid   23, 24
Macfarlane, Alan   27
McGrath, Patrick   23
McInnes, Angus   172
Maguire, Nancy   163–4
Maitland, F.W.   187
Major-Generals   122–3, 125
Manchester, earl of   44
Manning, Brian   48
Marston Moor, battle of (1644)   45,
    46, 99
Marx, Karl   7, 12, 51, 148
Marxism
  Carlin   53
  class struggle   38
  collapse of   19, 74
  critiques of   27
  economic determinism   19, 49, 55
  former colonies   10
  historical processes   172
  Hughes   53
  Liberal myth   74
  Manning   48
  revisionism   12, 13, 16, 17, 20, 28
  see also socialism
Mary I, Queen of England   21, 22, 76

Mary, daughter of James II (wife of
    William of Orange) 185–6, 187,
    192
Mary, Queen of Scots 89
Mazarin, Cardinal 108
Menasseh ben Israel 120, 121
Mercurius Aulicus 42
middle class 29, 35, 53
militarism 94
military technicalities 43–6
Miller, John
    Charles II 137, 147–8, 162–4, 166,
        167
    James II 133, 134, 178, 179, 180,
        181
    post-1660 politics 173, 175
modernity 8, 74
monarchy 36, 158, 191
    absolute 173, 175, 176, 179, 189
    Clark's arguments 25, 26
    contemporary advocates of 65
    Cromwell opposition to 93–4
    defenders of 5, 176
    multiple monarchies 67, 192
    see also Restoration; royalists
Monmouth, duke of 180, 186
Montrose, marquis of 70, 184
More, Thomas 165
Morrill, John 3
    Charles II's faith 161
    Cromwell 95, 97–8, 109
    Glorious Revolution 187
    Ireland 182
    Jones-Western thesis 172
    parliamentarian emphasis 35
    partisan loyalties 47, 49, 50–2
    provincialism 13, 14, 38
    revisionism 16, 18
    The Revolt of the Provinces 42
    Ugbrooke Park 153
multiculturalism 19, 56, 193, 198
myths 46, 169

Naseby, battle of 45, 103, 105
nationalism
    American 74
    Irish 192
Neale, John 7, 14, 18, 28
neutralism
    county studies 38, 39, 40–1, 47

Morrill 51
Underdown 47, 48, 50
New Model Army 63, 69, 70, 86, 90
    Cromwell 105, 115
    historians' parliamentarian bias 96
    Naseby 45
    siege train 43–4
    see also army
Newman, Peter 36–7, 41, 45, 51
Norrey, Philip 181
Northamptonshire 151
Northern Ireland 39, 72, 75, 192
nostalgia 46
Notestein, Wallace 7, 14, 15, 16, 28

Oates, Stephen B. 134
Ogg, David 136
Ollard, Richard 37, 141, 143, 144–5,
    158, 159–60
Ormond, duke of 184
Orr, Alan 66–7
Osborne, Simon 50
Oxford University 12–13, 148

Parliament
    Cavalier 160–1, 162
    and Charles I 63, 65
    and Charles II 138, 139
    Clark on 25
    control of religious affairs 67
    Convention Parliament 187
    Cromwell 98, 103, 106–7, 109–12,
        116–19, 123–4, 125–6
    Elton on 13–14, 18
    and finance 60, 61, 63
    First Protectorate 98, 110–12
    Gardiner on 7
    and James II 180, 186
    purges 91, 98, 99, 110, 111, 115
    religious intolerance 102
    revisionist historiographies 13, 16,
        25
    Scottish support for 69
    see also democracy; House of
        Commons; House of Lords; Long
        Parliament
parliamentarians
    checks on Crown power 65
    contribution to English military
        machinery 63

parliamentarians – *continued*
  county studies   42
  criticisms of   90
  Derbyshire mining communities   55
  early Stuart politics   65, 66
  Essex   48
  evangelical Protestantism   50, 51
  historians' support/prejudice for   33,
    35–6, 37, 96
  land use relationship   49
  local partisanship   41, 49, 50, 51, 52
  Marxist interpretation   48
  popular view of   34, 35
  social background similar to
    royalists   13
  twentieth-century radicals' support
    for   34
  see also Cromwell; New Model Army;
    puritanism
partisanship   40–1, 52–3, 54–6
  Hughes–Carlin model   53–4
  Morrill   50–2
  Underdown   47–50
Pennington, Donald   35
periodisation   82, 83
pessimism   55–6
Pestell, Thomas   81
Pilgrim Fathers   74
plague   4, 32
Plumb, John H.   3, 26, 28
politics
  centrality of   30
  Civil War   33
  contemporary loss of faith in
    institutions   197–8
  court studies   166
  during the 1650s   91–2
  early Stuart history   65–7
  Glorious Revolution   171–2, 173
  historians' perspectives   166
  historiography   7
  Hughes–Carlin model   53
  post-1660   174–5
  see also democracy; Parliament
poor relief   4
populism
  charismatic leaders   139
  Cromwell   111, 119
Porter, Stephen   46–7
positivism   134

post-revisionism   18, 20
  Clark   26–7
  English Reformation   23, 24
Powell, Enoch   158
prehistorians   6
Presbyterianism   28, 190, 192
Preston, battle of (1648)   104–5
Pride, Colonel   125
Privy Council   163, 177
Protectorate   98, 108, 110–12, 128
Protestantism   21–5, 29, 74–80, 181
  Civil War   33
  Cromwell   94, 102, 106, 107, 112,
    119, 124
  Elizabeth I   168
  evangelical   41, 50, 51, 78–9, 90, 94
  James I   183
  local culture of   41
  nonconformity   174
  patriotism   65
  radical   48, 69, 91
  Scotland   67, 80, 184, 190, 192
  William of Orange   192
  see also Christianity; Church;
    puritanism; Reformation
provincialism   13, 17, 38
  see also localism
public opinion   83, 89, 167
Public Record Office   148, 149
puritanism   51, 52, 91, 169
  Charles I's leniency towards   87
  and the Church of England   74,
    76–7, 78–81, 82
  Cromwell   101, 102, 109, 119,
    125, 127
  Essex parliamentarians   48
  and Jews   122
  local land use relationship   49
  public opinion   83
  Victorians   35, 140
  see also Protestantism
Putney Debates (1647)   113

Quakers   145–6

Ranters   27, 168
Redworth, Glyn   23
Reece, Henry   127
Reeve, L.J.   17, 86
reflexivity   1, 198

Reformation
  English   19, 21–5, 30, 78, 79, 84, 182
  Scottish   181, 182
  see also Counter-Reformation;
    Protestantism
religion   74–85, 92
  Charles I   87
  Charles II   138, 139, 145–6, 161–2
  Clark's emphasis on   25, 26–7
  Cromwell   101, 102–4, 105–6,
    108–9, 119, 121–2
  ecclesiastical government   67
  Elizabeth I   167, 168
  fundamentalism   75, 94
  James II   178, 179
  Morrill on   50–2
  revisionism   8
  Russell on   67
  wood-and-pasture communities   49
  see also Christianity; Church;
    puritanism; Reformation
research
  collaborative   196
  competition   39–40, 195
  funding   2, 9, 195, 196
  practice   148–55, 194, 195–7
  revisionism effect on   30
  see also academic culture; county
    studies; local evidence; source
    material
resistance to Civil war   38, 39
Restoration   36, 63, 85, 135, 138
  end of Cromwell's regime   97
  financial settlement   142
  Irish/Scottish support for   183
  Protestant nonconformity   174
  see also monarchy
Revel, Riot and Rebellion (Underdown)
  49, 50, 52, 151
revisionism   6, 8–10, 12, 13–21, 27–31,
  195
  Charles II   137–8, 140
  Clark   25–7
  Cromwell   96
  early Stuart history   59, 60, 62,
    64–6, 67, 172
  English Reformation   22, 23, 24
  puritanism   74
  reputation of monarchs   85, 86
  three-kingdoms perspective   72

'Whigs'   28–9
  see also post-revisionism
The Revolt of the Provinces (Morrill)   42
Revolution, Glorious (1688)   57, 135,
  158, 171–3, 185–93
Roberts, P.R.   45
Roberts, Stephen   17, 35
Rogers, John   113
Roman Catholicism *see* Catholicism
romanticisation of court life   157
Roots, Ivan   35
Rosebery, Lord   95
Ross, Charles   133
Royal Historical Society   14
royalists
  Catholic reinforcements   54
  conservative Anglicanism   49, 50, 52
  contribution to English military
    machinery   63, 64
  county studies   42
  Cromwell's trial of   110
  defeated by the Scots   69
  Derbyshire mining communities   55
  early Stuart politics   65, 66
  Irish support for   69
  land use relationship   49
  local partisanship   41, 49, 50, 51, 52
  Marston Moor   45
  Marxist interpretation   48
  Naseby   45
  popular support for   33, 34–5
  prejudice against   33, 35–7, 70
  the Restoration   36
  sieges of Bristol and Gloucester   44
  social background similar to
    parliamentarians   13
  tax on   122, 123
  Wales   32, 41, 70
  see also Charles I; Charles II;
    monarchy
Rupert, Prince   45, 64, 69
Russell, Bertrand   17
Russell, Conrad
  on Charles I   86, 89
  origins of Civil War   164
  political polarisation   66
  revisionism   14–15, 16, 18–19
  state finance   60, 63
  three-kingdoms perspective   67–9,
    70, 73, 177, 181

Samuel, Raphael 35
Sancroft, Archbishop 176, 191
Scarisbrick, Jack 23, 24
Schwoerer, Lois 172, 187
Scotland
    Celtic culture 182
    Charles II 157, 158
    Covenanters 51, 104
    creation of triple kingdom 177
    devolution 71–2, 190
    and the English Civil War 67–8,
        69–71
    Glorious Revolution 187, 190–1
    Highlands 184, 190
    Jacobites 36
    James II's use of Scottish regiments
        180–1
    Presbyterianism 28, 190, 192
    Protestantism 67, 80, 184, 190, 192
    Reformation 181, 182
    Scottish historians' critique of
        three-kingdoms approach 73
    support for restored monarchy 174,
        183
    uprising against Charles I 51, 68–9,
        83, 88, 184
    see also three-kingdoms perspective
Scott, David 52
Scott, Jonathan 173, 174, 191
the Sealed Knot 34, 37, 57
Seaward, Paul 160–1, 162
Second Civil War 32, 59, 91, 92, 115
Second World War 96
Secret Treaty of Dover 153, 154
secularism 10, 94
Selden, John 16
Self-Denying Ordinance 64
Sellar, W.C. 35
Shagan, Ethan 24, 25
Sharp, Buchanan 50
Sharpe, Kevin 3
    on Charles I 87, 88, 89
    Personal Rule 82, 83, 84, 87, 88
    political polarisation 66
    revisionism 14, 16, 18, 19
Shaw, George Bernard 140, 153
Shaw, W.A. 142
Ship Money 5, 63, 180
Short, M.J. 181
siege artillery 43–4, 45–6

Smith, David 37, 51
Smuts, Malcolm 55–6, 169
social changes
    Hughes–Carlin model 53
    puritans 76–7
social class see class
socialism 137, 193
    Clark critique 26
    prejudice against royalists 36
    and revisionism 12, 13, 17
    Welfare State 7
    see also Marxism
socio-economic factors 7, 174
    land use 48–50
    revisionism 13, 17, 18, 20
    Underdown 48, 49
Somerset 48, 49, 50, 54, 84
Sommerville, Johann P. 8, 17, 19,
    64–5
source material 1–2, 93, 139, 165, 194
    inadequacies of 21
    public opinion 83
    the Reformation 25
    reluctance to question 11
    see also county studies; local
        evidence; research
Spain
    Cromwell's war against 106–8, 121,
        123, 127
    Jews 121, 122
Speck, Bill 172, 181, 186, 187
Spurr, John 166–7
Stamford, earl of 10
Starkey, David 167–8
Stone, Lawrence 7, 13, 14, 15, 27
Stour valley riots (1642) 41
Stoyle, Mark 40–1, 50, 56, 70
Strafford, earl of 33, 86
Strouse, Jean 134
Sussex 78
Szechi, Daniel 172

Talbot, Richard 184
Tanner, J.R. 142
taxation 60–1, 63–4, 122–3, 176
    see also customs dues
Taylor, A.J.P. 3
technology 196, 198
Thatcher, Margaret 192
Thatcherism 8, 12, 26, 37

theology   66, 75
Third Civil War   32, 59
Thirsk, Joan   48–9
three-kingdoms perspective   67–73,
     177, 181, 182
   see also 'the British problem'
Thurloe, John   125
Tories   37, 137, 176, 177, 181, 186, 191
Trevelyan, George Macaulay   3, 135–6,
     171, 188
Trevor-Roper, H.R.   3
Tyrconnel, Richard Talbot, duke of   184

Ugbrooke Park   153–4
Underdown, David   17, 38, 47–50, 51,
     52, 55, 151
United States
   Americanisation   72
   Confederate States of America   36
   decline of interest in English history
     19–20
   multicultural identity   19, 56, 193,
     198
   nationalism   74

Vane, Henry   145
Victoria, Queen of England   33, 34, 95
Victorians
   Cromwell   97, 101, 126, 130
   Glorious Revolution   171, 192
   historians   2
   importance given to 17th century
     history by   4
   puritanism   35, 140
Vietnam War   39
violence
   of Civil War   41, 42
   redemptive   94
   sectarian   39, 75

Wales
   assimilation of   182
   devolution   71–2

royalism   32, 41, 70
ruling elites   182
separatist identity   56–7, 70
Walsham, Alexandra   25
Walter, John   41
Wedgwood, Veronica   34
Welfare State   7, 8
West Country   49, 152
Western, J.R.   172, 176
Whalley, Edward   116
Wharton, Lord   111
Wheatley, Dennis   140, 143
Whigs   37, 137, 181
   Glorious Revolution   171, 172,
     188–9, 190, 191, 192
   revisionist debates   28–9
Whiting, Robert   23, 24
William of Orange (William III)
     133–4, 172, 179, 181, 185–7,
     189–90, 191–2
Wiltshire   45–6, 49, 180
Winnington Bridge, battle of (1659)
     91
Winstanley, Gerrard   34, 37
Wolsey, Cardinal   28
women   141, 163–4
Wood, Andy   55
wood-and-pasture communities
     48–9
Woolrych, Austin   35, 86, 95
Worcester, battle of (1651)   91, 105
Worden, Blair   35, 94, 97, 98, 102, 117
The World Turned Upside Down (Hill)
     49
Wormald, Jenny   68, 177
Wrightson, Keith   48
Wynne, Sonya   164

Yeatman, R.J.   35
York   52
Yorkshire   78–9
Young, Michael   86
Young, Peter   37, 43, 44